```
TL
215
.E78    Chilton's repair &
C48      tune-up guide,
1981     Escort, Lynx, 1981-
         82
```

DATE			

Business/Science/Technology
Division

© THE BAKER & TAYLOR CO.

CHILTON'S
REPAIR & TUNE-UP GUIDE
ESCORT LYNX 1981-82

Ford Escort and EXP • Mercury Lynx and LN-7

Managing Editor **KERRY A. FREEMAN, S.A.E.**
Senior Editor **RICHARD J. RIVELE, S.A.E.**
Editor **RON WEBB**

President **WILLIAM A. BARBOUR**
Executive Vice President **JAMES A. MIADES**
Vice President and General Manager **JOHN P. KUSHNERICK**

CHILTON BOOK COMPANY
Radnor, Pennsylvania
19089

TL
215
.E78
C48
1981

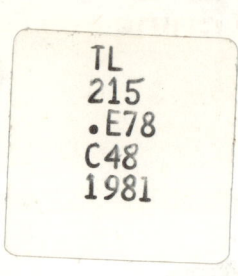

SAFETY NOTICE
Proper service and repair procedures are vital to the safe, reliable operation of all motor vehicles, as well as the personal safety of those performing repairs. This book outlines procedures for servicing and repairing vehicles using safe, effective methods. The procedures contain many NOTES, CAUTIONS and WARNINGS which should be followed along with standard safety procedures to eliminate the possibility of personal injury or improper service which could damage the vehicle or compromise its safety.

It is important to note that repair procedures and techniques, tools and parts for servicing motor vehicles, as well as the skill and experience of the individual performing the work vary widely. It is not possible to anticipate all of the conceivable ways or conditions under which vehicles may be serviced, or to provide cautions as to all of the possible hazards that may result. Standard and accepted safety precautions and equipment should be used when handling toxic or flammable fluids, and safety goggles or other protection should be used during cutting, grinding, chiseling, prying, or any other process that can cause material removal or projectiles.

Some procedures require the use of tools specially designed for a specific purpose. Before substituting another tool or procedure, you must be completely satisfied that neither your personal safety, nor the performance of the vehicle will be endangered.

Although information in this guide is based on industry sources and is as complete as possible at the time of publication, the possibility exists that the manufacturer made later changes which could not be included here. While striving for total accuracy, Chilton Book Company cannot assume responsibility for any errors, changes, or omissions that may occur in the compilation of this data.

PART NUMBERS
Part numbers listed in this reference are not recommendations by Chilton for any product by brand name. They are references that can be used with interchange manuals and aftermarket supplier catalogs to locate each brand supplier's discrete part number.

ACKNOWLEDGMENTS
The Chilton Book Company expresses its appreciation to The Ford Motor Company for their generous assistance.

Copyright © 1981 by Chilton Book Company
All Rights Reserved
Published in Radnor, Pa., by Chilton Book Company
and simultaneously in Ontario, Canada
by Nelson Canada, Limited

Manufactured in the United States of America
   234567890   098765432

Chilton's Repair & Tune-Up Guide: Escort and Lynx 1981–82
ISBN 0-8019-7055-5 pbk.
Library of Congress Catalog Card No. 80-70332

CONTENTS

 **General Information and Maintenance**
- **1** How to Use this Book
- **2** Tools and Equipment
- **8** Routine Maintenance and Lubrication
- **30** How to Buy A Used Car

 **Tune-Up**
- **33** Tune-Up Procedures
- **34** Tune-Up Specifications

 **Engine and Engine Rebuilding**
- **49** Engine Electrical System
- **58** Engine Service and Specifications
- **76** Engine Rebuilding

 **Emission Controls and Fuel System**
- **95** Emission Control System and Service
- **102** Fuel System Service

 **Chassis Electrical**
- **108** Accessory Service
- **115** Instrument Panel Service
- **116** Lights, Fuses and Flashers

100 Chilton's Fuel Economy and Tune-Up Tips

 **Clutch and Transaxle**
- **124** Manual Transaxle
- **127** Clutch
- **131** Automatic Transaxle

 **Suspension and Steering**
- **137** Front Suspension
- **142** Rear Suspension
- **147** Steering

 **Brakes**
- **162** Front Brakes
- **168** Rear Brakes
- **168** Brake Specifications

 **Body**
- **182** Repairing Scratches and Small Dents
- **186** Repairing Rust
- **192** Body Care

Troubleshooting
- **195** Problem Diagnosis

229 Appendix
233 Index

Quick Reference Specifications For Your Vehicle

Fill in this chart with the most commonly used specifications for your vehicle. Specifications can be found in Chapters 1 through 3 or on the tune-up decal under the hood of the vehicle.

Tune-Up

Firing Order _____

Spark Plugs:

    Type _____

    Gap (in.) _____

Point Gap (in.) _____

Dwell Angle (°) _____

Ignition Timing (°) _____

    Vacuum (Connected/Disconnected) _____

Valve Clearance (in.)

    Intake _____   **Exhaust** _____

Capacities

Engine Oil (qts)

    With Filter Change _____

    Without Filter Change _____

Cooling System (qts) _____

Manual Transmission (pts) _____

    Type _____

Automatic Transmission (pts) _____

    Type _____

Front Differential (pts) _____

    Type _____

Rear Differential (pts) _____

    Type _____

Transfer Case (pts) _____

    Type _____

FREQUENTLY REPLACED PARTS

Use these spaces to record the part numbers of frequently replaced parts.

PCV VALVE	**OIL FILTER**	**AIR FILTER**
Manufacturer_____	Manufacturer_____	Manufacturer_____
Part No._____	Part No._____	Part No._____

General Information and Maintenance

HOW TO USE THIS BOOK

Chilton's Repair & Tune-Up Guide for the Escort/Lynx, EXP and LN7 is intended to teach you more about the inner workings of your car and save you money on its upkeep. The first two chapters will be used the most, since they contain maintenance and tune-up information and procedures. The following chapters concern themselves with the more complex systems. Operating systems from engine through brakes are covered to the extent that we feel the average do-it-yourselfer should get involved. This book will not explain such things as rebuilding the differential for the simple reason that the expertise required and the investment in special tools make this task uneconomical. We will tell you how to change your own brake pads and shoes, replace spark plugs, perform routine maintenance, and many more jobs that will save you money, give you personal satisfaction, and help you avoid problems.

A secondary purpose of this book is as a reference for owners who want to understand their car and/or their mechanics better. In this case, no tools at all are required.

Before removing any parts, read through the entire procedure. This will give you the overall view of what tools and supplies will be required.

The sections begin with a brief discussion of the system and what it involves, followed by adjustments, maintenance, removal and installation procedures, and repair or overhaul procedures. When repair is not considered feasible, we tell you how to remove the part and then how to install the new or rebuilt replacement. In this way, you at least save the labor costs. Backyard repair of such components as the alternator is just not practical.

Two basic mechanic's rules should be mentioned here. One, whenever the left side of your car or engine is referred to, it is meant to specify the driver's side. Conversely, the right side means the passenger's side. Secondly, most screws and bolts are removed by turning counterclockwise, and tightened by turning clockwise. Safety is always the most important rule. Constantly be aware of the dangers involved in working on an automobile and take the proper precautions. Use jackstands when working under a raised vehicle. Don't smoke or allow an exposed flame to come near the battery or any part of the fuel system. Always use the proper tool and use it correctly; bruised knuckles and skinned fingers aren't a mechanic's standard equipment. Always take your time and have patience; once you have some experience, working on your Escort/Lynx, EXP and LN7 will become an enjoyable hobby.

GENERAL INFORMATION AND MAINTENANCE

TOOLS AND EQUIPMENT

It would be impossible to catalog each and every tool that you may need to perform all the operations included in this book. It would also not be wise for the amateur to rush out and buy an expensive set of tools on the theory that he may need one of them at some time. The best approach is to proceed slowly, gathering together a good quality set of those tools that are used most frequently. Don't be misled by the low cost of bargain tools. It is far better to spend a little more for quality, name brand tools. Forged wrenches, 10 or 12 point sockets and finetooth ratchets are by far preferable to their less expensive counterparts. As any good mechanic can tell you, there are few worse experiences than trying to work with bad tools. Your monetary savings will be far outweighed by frustration and mangled knuckles.

Begin accumulating those tools that are used most frequently; those associated with routine maintenance and tune-up. In addition to the normal assortment of screwdrivers and pliers, you should have the following tools for routine maintenance jobs:
1. SAE and metric wrenches, sockets and combination open end/box end wrenches;
2. Jackstands—for support;
3. Oil filter wrench;
4. Oil filler spout or funnel;
5. Grease gun—for chassis lubrication;
6. Hydrometer—for checking the battery;
7. A low flat pan for draining oil;
8. Lots of rags for wiping up the inevitable mess.

In addition to the above items, there are several others that are not absolutely necessary, but are handy to have around. These include oil drying compound, a transmission funnel, and the usual supply of lubricants, antifreeze and fluids, although these can be purchased as needed. This is a basic list for routine maintenance, but only your personal needs can accurately determine your list of tools.

The second list of tools is for tune-ups. While the tools involved here are slightly more sophisticated, they need not be outrageously expensive. There are several inexpensive tach/dwell meters on the market that are every bit as good for the average mechanic as a $100.00 professional model. Just be sure that it goes to at least 1200–1500 rpm on the tach scale, and that it works on 4, 6, and 8 cylinder engines. A basic list of tune-up equipment could include:
1. Tach/dwell meter;
2. Spark plug wrench;
3. Timing light (preferably a DC light that works from the car's battery);
4. A set of flat feeler gauges;
5. A set of round wire spark plug gauges.

In addition to these basic tools, there are several other tools and gauges you may find useful. These include:
1. A compression gauge. The screw-in type is slower to use, but eliminates the possibility of a faulty reading due to escaping pressure;
2. A manifold vacuum gauge;
3. A test light;
4. An induction meter. This is used for determining whether or not there is current in a wire. These are handy for use if a wire is broken somewhere in a wiring harness. As a final note, you will probably find a torque wrench necessary for all but the most basic work. The beam type models are perfectly adequate, although the newer click type are more precise.

Special Tools

Normally, the use of special factory tools is avoided for repair procedures, since these are not readily available for the do-it-yourself mechanic. When it is possible to perform the job with more commonly available tools, it will be pointed out, but occasionally, a special tool was designed to perform a specific function and should be used. Before substituting another tool, you should be convinced that neither your safety nor the performance of the vehicle will be compromised.

Some special tools are available commercially from major tool manufacturers. Others for your Escort/Lynx can be purchased from your dealer or from Owatonna Tool Co., Owatonna, Minnesota 55060.

SERVICING YOUR CAR SAFELY

It is virtually impossible to anticipate all of the hazards involved with automotive maintenance and service but care and common sense will prevent most accidents.

The rules of safety for mechanics range from "don't smoke around gasoline," to "use the proper tool for the job." The trick to avoid

GENERAL INFORMATION AND MAINTENANCE 3

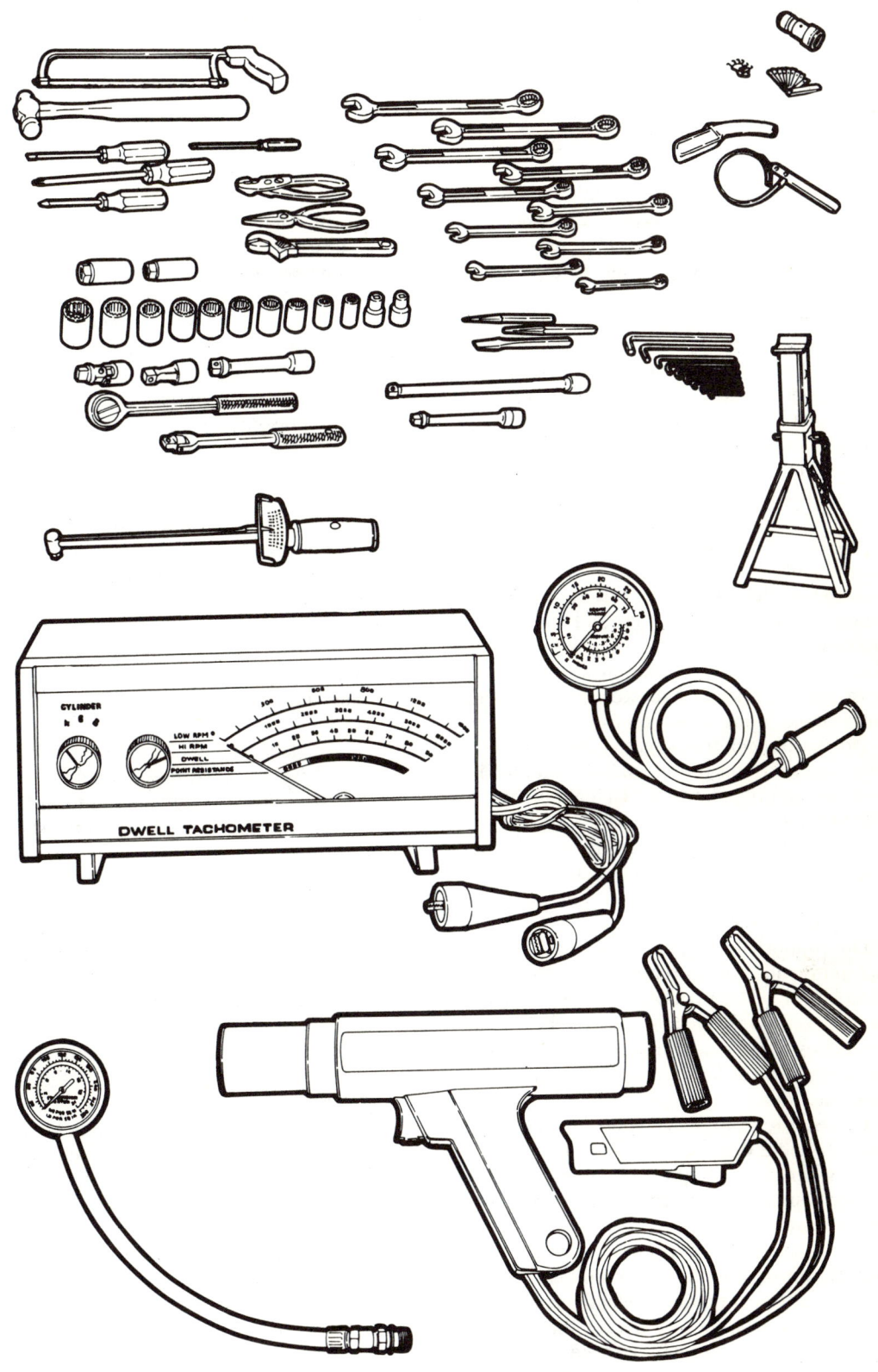

You need only a basic assortment of hand tools for most maintenance and repair jobs

4 GENERAL INFORMATION AND MAINTENANCE

injuries is to develop safe work habits and take every possible precaution.

Do's

- Do keep a fire extinguisher and first aid kit within easy reach.
- Do wear safety glasses or goggles when cutting, drilling, grinding or prying. If you wear glasses for the sake of vision, then they should be made of hardened glass that can serve also as safety glasses, or wear safety goggles over your regular glasses.
- Do shield your eyes whenever you work around the battery. Batteries contain sulphuric acid; in case of contact with the eyes or skin, flush the area with water or a mixture of water and baking soda and get medical attention immediately.
- Do use safety stands for any under-car service. Jacks are for raising vehicles; safety stands are for making sure the vehicle stays raised until you want it to come down. Whenever the vehicle is raised, block the wheels remaining on the ground and set the parking brake.
- Do use adequate ventilation when working with any chemicals. Asbestos dust resulting from brake lining wear can cause cancer.
- Do disconnect the negative battery cable when working on the electrical system. The primary ignition system can contain up to 40,000 volts.
- Do follow manufacturer's directions whenever working with potentially hazardous materials. Both brake fluid and antifreeze are poisonous if taken internally.
- Do properly maintain your tools. Loose hammerheads, mushroomed punches and chisels, frayed or poorly grounded electrical cords, excessively worn screwdrivers, spread wrenches (open end), cracked sockets, slipping ratchets, or faulty droplight sockets can cause accidents.
- Do use the proper size and type of tool for the job being done.
- Do when possible, pull on a wrench handle rather than push on it, and adjust your stance to prevent a fall.
- Do be sure that adjustable wrenches are tightly adjusted on the nut or bolt and pulled so that the face is on the side of the fixed jaw.
- Do select a wrench or socket that fits the nut or bolt. The wrench or socket should sit straight, not cocked.
- Do strike squarely with a hammer to avoid glancing blows.
- Do set the parking brake and block the drive wheels if the work requires that the engine be running.

Dont's

- Don't run an engine in a garage or anywhere else without proper ventilation—EVER! Carbon monoxide is poisonous; it is absorbed by the body 400 times faster than oxygen; it takes a long time to leave the human body and you can build up a deadly supply of it in your system by simply breathing in a little every day. You may not realize you are slowly poisoning yourself. Always use power vents, windows, fans or open the garage doors.
- Don't work around moving parts while wearing a necktie or other loose clothing. Short sleeves are much safer than long, loose sleeves. Hard-toed shoes with neoprene soles protect your toes and give a better grip on slippery surfaces. Jewelry such as watches, fancy belt buckles, beads or body adornment of any kind is not safe working around a car. Long hair should be hidden under a hat or cap.
- Don't use pockets for toolboxes. A fall or bump can drive a screwdriver deep into your body. Even a wiping cloth hanging from the back pocket can wrap around a spinning shaft or fan.
- Don't smoke when working around gasoline, cleaning solvent or other flammable material.
- Don't smoke when working around the battery. When the battery is being charged, it gives off explosive hydrogen gas.
- Don't use gasoline to wash your hands; there are excellent soaps available. Gasoline may contain lead, and lead can enter the body through a cut, accumulating in the body until you are very ill. Gasoline also removes all the natural oils from the skin so that bone dry hands will suck up oil and grease.
- Don't service the air conditioning system unless you are equipped with the necessary tools and training. The refrigerant, R-12, is extremely cold and when exposed to the air, will instantly freeze any surface it comes in contact with, including your eyes. Although the refrigerant is normally non-toxic, R-12 becomes a deadly poisonous gas in the presence of an open flame. One good whiff of the vapors from buring refrigerant can be fatal.

GENERAL INFORMATION AND MAINTENANCE 5

Escort

LN 7

6 GENERAL INFORMATION AND MAINTENANCE

HISTORY

The Escort/Lynx and the sporty EXP and LN7 are Ford's first domestically produced front-wheel-drive cars. The production of the Escort/Lynx combined the talents of Ford's best engineers, designers and technicians worldwide making it indeed a "World Car".

These small, fuel and space efficient front wheel-drive cars are built primarily by Americans and designed for the way Americans will drive in the "80s", combining the fuel economy required in today's market with the ride and handling that buyers have come to expect in a precision-built automobile.

The Escort/Lynx's engine, transaxle, suspension and body all were designed specifically for the car. There were no major carryover parts or components to compromise fuel economy, space efficiency or aerodynamic styling. A great deal of engineering expertise was devoted to meeting several key objectives—not the least of which was fuel economy.

The fully unitized body structure has no separate frame and all structural loading is contained within. Unitized construction provides significant advantages for interior size and reduced vehicle weight. The two most important engineering features—front-wheel-drive and four-wheel independent suspension—also aid interior size. The advantages of front wheel drive are evident in the small car. The hump in the middle of the car which houses the driveshaft and transmission in a rear wheel drive car have all but been eliminated allowing a flatter floor. As a result, there is more seating space and leg room in the passenger compartment. Because there is no solid axle with independent rear suspension, a deeper rear floor is allowed. Seats can be positioned closer to the rear for more leg room and for the ease of entry and exit, not to mention the greater cargo hauling area. There are also significant ride and handling advantages gained with the independent rear suspension.

The body styling of the Escort/Lynx was

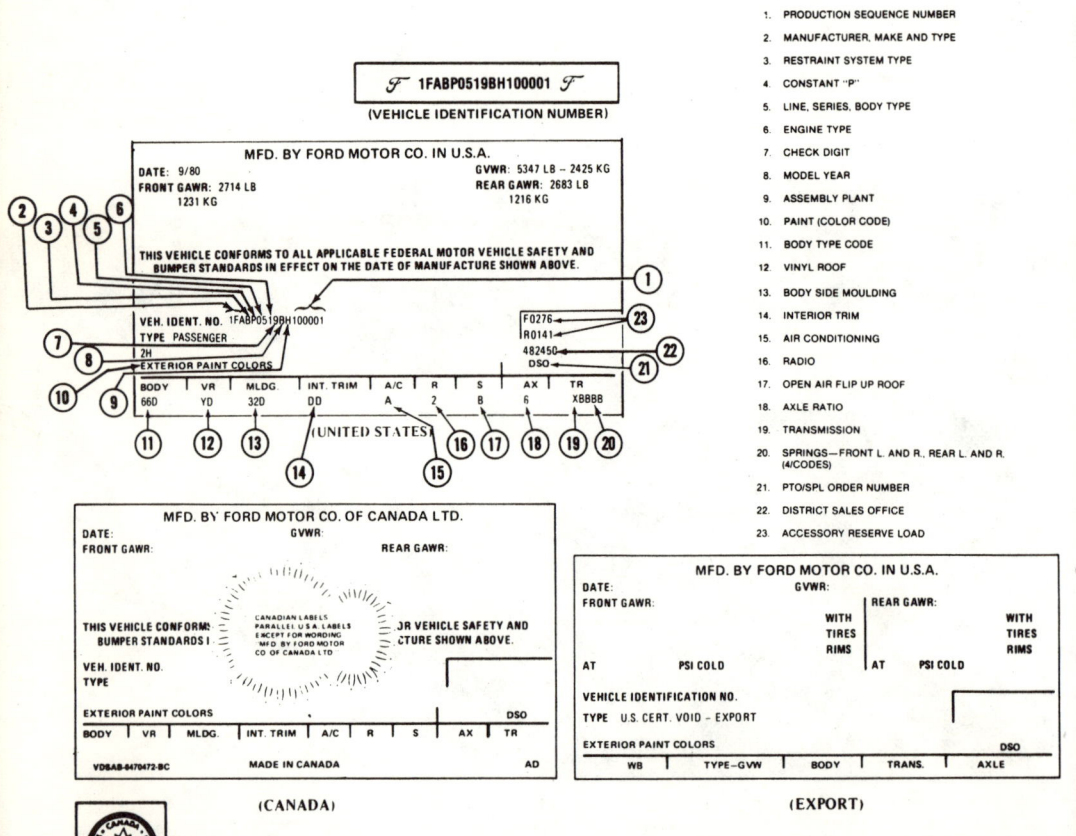

Vehicle Identification and Certification Plates

GENERAL INFORMATION AND MAINTENANCE

developed with extensive wind-tunnel testing to reduce aerodynamic drag. The design allows for an estimated one-mile-per-gallon improvement in fuel economy. A low beltline, thin "C" pillars and substantial glass area also aid aerodynamics and greatly improve driver and passenger visibility.

As you read through this book, or refer to the various chapters while servicing your Escort/Lynx, EXP or LN7, other features of these "World Cars" will be pointed out to you.

The history of the Escort/Lynx is short at this time, however, later pages of history will record their role in Ford's massive program to redesign all of its product lines for the cost and energy conscious consumers of the "world."

VEHICLE IDENTIFICATION NUMBER (VIN)

The official vehicle identification (serial) number (used for title and registration purposes) is stamped on a metal tab fastened to the instrument panel and visible through the driver's side of the windshield from the outside. The vehicle identification (serial) number contains a 17 character number. The number is used for warranty identification of the vehicle and indicates: manufacturer, type of restraint system, line, series, body type, engine, model year, and consecutive unit number.

VEHICLE CERTIFICATION LABEL

The vehicle Certification Label is found on the left door lock face panel or door pillar. The upper half of the label contains the name of the manufacturer, month and year of manufacture, gross weight rating, gross axle weight, and the certification statements pertinent. The certification also repeats the VIN number and gives the color code and the accessories found on the car.

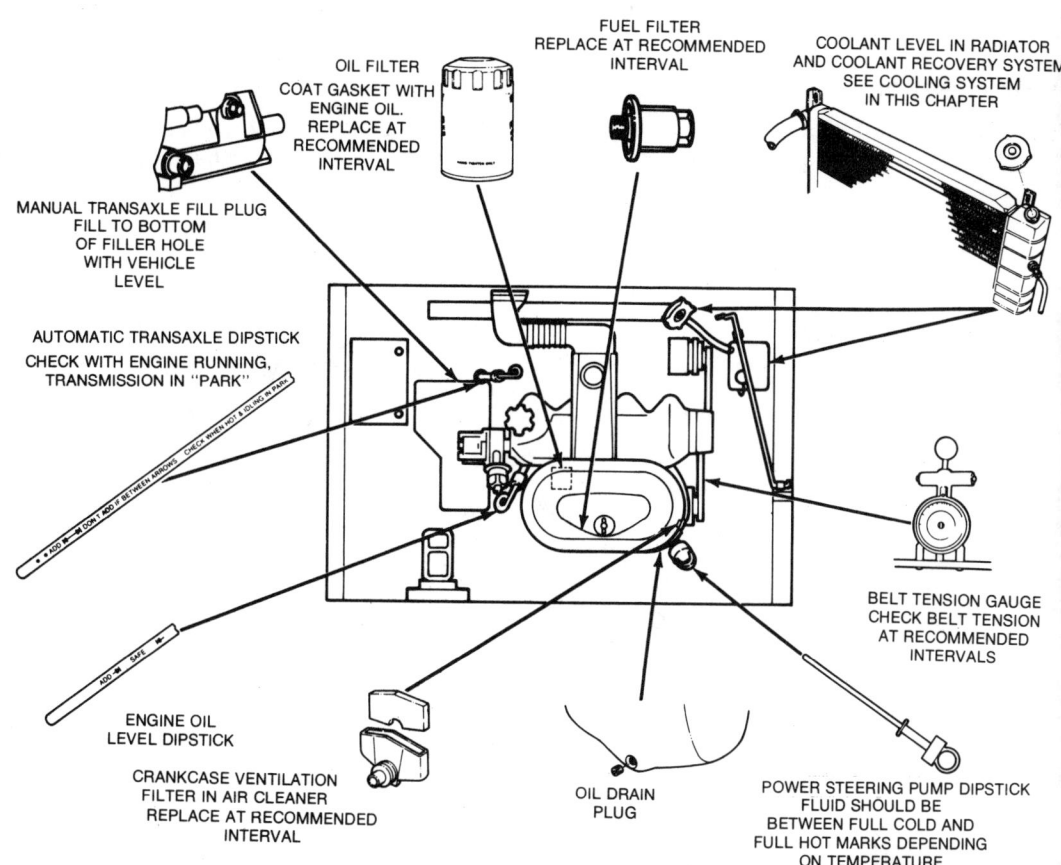

Lubrication and service points

8 GENERAL INFORMATION AND MAINTENANCE

Engine Codes

	Displacement	
VIN Code	Liter	CID
2	1.6	98

The engine code number is the eighth character on the VIN plate.

TRANSAXLE CODES

The transmission code is located on the bottom edge of the Vehicle Certification Label. The number 4 or 9 indicates a 4-speed manual transaxle; while the letter B, indicates an automatic transaxle.

ROUTINE MAINTENANCE

Major efforts have been undertaken by Ford to improve serviceability and provide reduced scheduled maintenance for the Escort/Lynx. This is a built-in savings to you, the owner, in man hours and dollars.

Air Cleaner

The air cleaner element should be replaced every 30 months or 30,000 miles. More frequent changes are necessary if the car is operated in dusty conditions.

Air Cleaner Element and Crankcase Emission Filter

REMOVAL AND INSTALLATION

NOTE: *The crankcase emission filter should be changed each time you replace the air cleaner element.*

1. Remove the wing nut that retains the air cleaner assembly to the carburetor. Remove any support bracket bolts (engine to air cleaner). Disconnect the air duct tubing, vacuum lines and heat tubes connected to the air cleaner.
2. Remove the air cleaner assembly from the car.

NOTE: *Removing the air cleaner as an assembly helps prevent dirt from falling into the carburetor.*

3. Remove the spring clips that hold the top of the air cleaner to the body. Remove the cover.
4. Remove the air cleaner element. Disconnect the spring clip that retains the emission filter to the air cleaner body, and remove the filter.
5. Clean the inside of the air cleaner body by wiping with a rag. Check the mounting gasket (gaskets, if the car is equipped with a spacer), replace any gasket(s) that show wear.

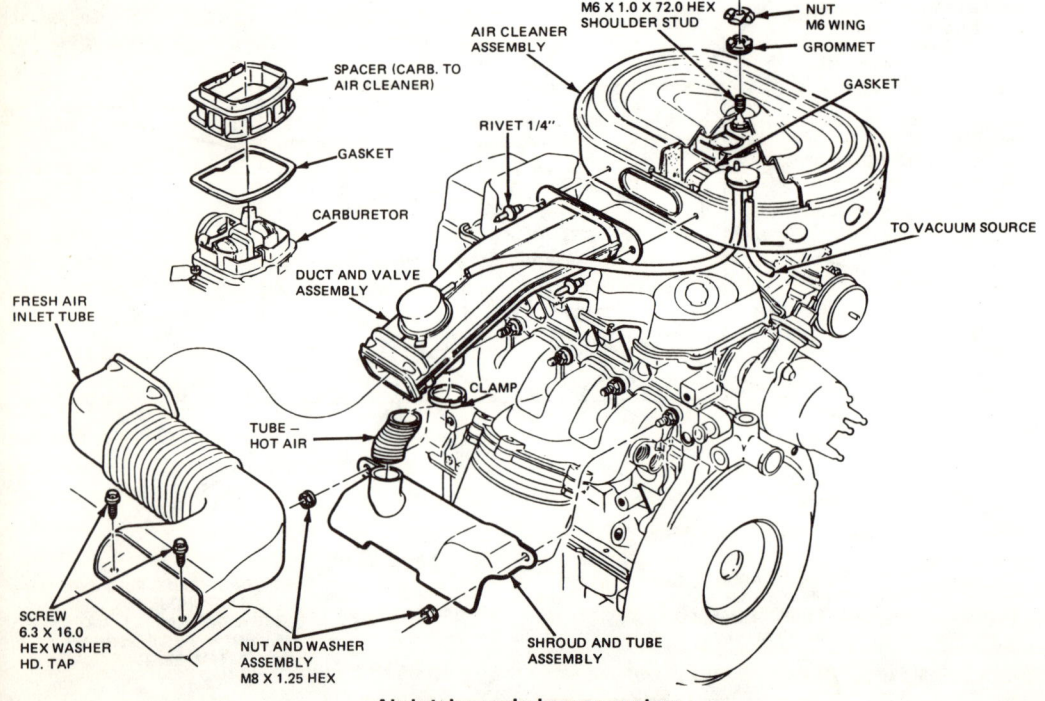

Air intake and cleaner system

GENERAL INFORMATION AND MAINTENANCE

6. Install a new emission filter and a new air cleaner element. Reverse the removal procedure to reinstall the air cleaner assembly.

NOTE: *Do not over tighten the mounting wing nut.*

PCV Valve

No PCV (positive crankcase ventilation) valve is used on the Escort/Lynx engine. Instead, an internal baffle and an orfice control the flow of crankcase gases. (See Chapter 4 for more details on emission controls).

Evaporative Emission Canister

To prevent gasoline vapors from being vented into the atmosphere, an evaporative emission system captures the vapors and stores them in a charcoal-filled canister. The canister is located ahead of the left front wheel arch in the engine compartment.

SERVICING THE EMISSION CANISTER

Since the canister is purged of fumes when the engine is operating, no real maintenance is required. However, the canister should be visually inspected for cracks, loose connections, etc. Replacement is simply a matter of disconnecting the hoses, loosening the mount and replacing the canister.

Battery

Your car is equipped with a maintenance free battery which eliminates the need for periodic checking and adding fluid.

NOTE: *If you replace your battery with a non-maintenance free battery see the following section.*

FLUID LEVEL (EXCEPT "MAINTENANCE FREE" BATTERIES)

Check the battery electrolyte level at least once a month, or more often in hot weather or during periods of extended car operation. The level can be checked through the case on translucent polypropylene batteries; the cell caps must be removed on other models. The electrolyte level in each cell should be kept filled to the split ring inside, or the line marked on the outside of the case.

If the level is low, add only distilled water, or colorless, odorless drinking water, through the opening until the level is correct. Each cell is completely separate from the others,

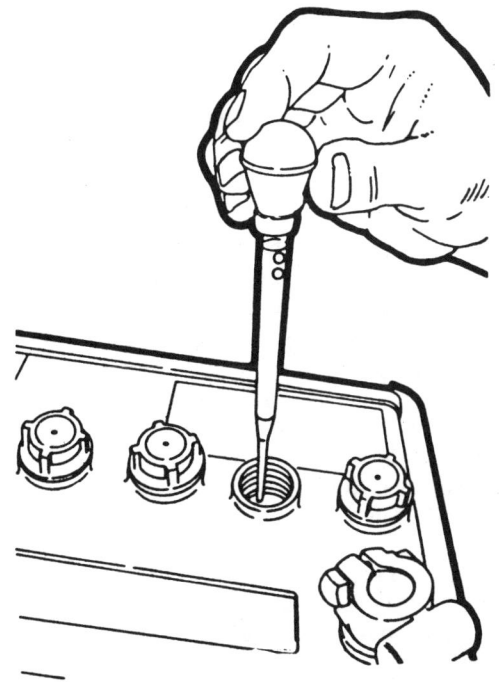

Checking the battery with a battery hydrometer

so each must be checked and filled individually.

If water is added in freezing weather, the car should be driven several miles to allow the water to mix with the electrolyte. Otherwise, the battery could freeze.

SPECIFIC GRAVITY (EXCEPT "MAINTENANCE FREE" BATTERIES)

At least once a year, check the specific gravity of the battery. It should be between 1.20 and 1.26 at room temperature.

The specific gravity can be checked with the use of an hydrometer, an inexpensive instrument available from many sources, including auto parts stores. The hydrometer has a squeeze bulb at one end and a nozzle at the other. Battery electrolyte is sucked into the hydrometer until the float is lifted from its seat. The specific gravity is then read by noting the position of the float. Generally, if after charging, the specific gravity between any two cells varies more than 50 points (.050), the battery is bad and should be replaced.

It is not possible to check the specific gravity in this manner on sealed ("maintenance free") batteries. Instead, the indicator built into the top of the case must be relied on to display any signs of battery deterioration. If the indicator is dark, the battery can be assumed to be OK. If the indicator is light, the

GENERAL INFORMATION AND MAINTENANCE

specific gravity is low, and the battery should be charged or replaced.

Cables and Clamps

Once a year, the battery terminals and the cable clamps should be cleaned. Loosen the clamps and remove the cables, negative cable first. On batteries with posts on top, the use of a puller specially made for the purpose is recommended. These are inexpensive, and available in auto parts stores. Side terminal battery cables are secured with a bolt.

Clean the cable clamps and the battery terminal with a wire brush, until all corrosion, grease, etc. is removed and the metal is shiny. It is especially important to clean the inside of the clamp thoroughly, since a small deposit of foreign material or oxidation there will prevent a sound electrical connection and inhibit either starting or charging. Special tools are available for cleaning these parts, one type for conventional batteries and another type for side terminal batteries.

Before installing the cables, loosen the battery hold-down clamp or strap, remove the battery and check the battery tray. Clear it of any debris, and check it for soundness. Rust should be wire brushed away, and the metal given a coat of anti-rust paint. Replace the battery and tighten the hold-down clamp or strap securely, but be careful not to overtighten, which will crack the battery case.

After the clamps and terminals are clean, reinstall the cables, negative cable last; do not hammer on the clamps to install. Tighten the clamps securely, but do not distort them.

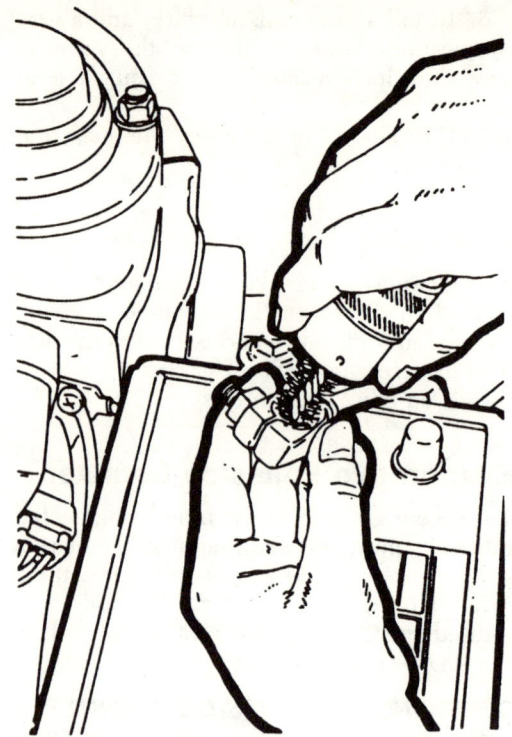

Clean battery cable clamps with a wire brush

Give the clamps and terminals a thin external coat of grease after installation, to retard corrosion.

Check the cables at the same time that the terminals are cleaned. If the cable insulation is cracked or broken, or if the ends are frayed, the cable should be replaced with a new cable of the same length and gauge.

NOTE: *Keep flame or sparks away from the battery; it gives off explosive hydrogen gas. Battery electrolyte contains sulphuric acid. If you should splash any on your skin or in your eyes, flush the affected area with plenty of clear water; if it lands in your eyes, get medical help immediately.*

REPLACEMENT

When it becomes necessary to replace the battery, select a battery with a rating equal to or greater than the battery originally installed. Deterioration, embrittlement and just plain aging of the battery cables, starter motor, and associated wires makes the battery's job harder in successive years. The slow increase in electrical resistance over time makes it prudent to install a new battery with a greater capacity than the old. Details on battery removal and installation are covered in Chapter 3.

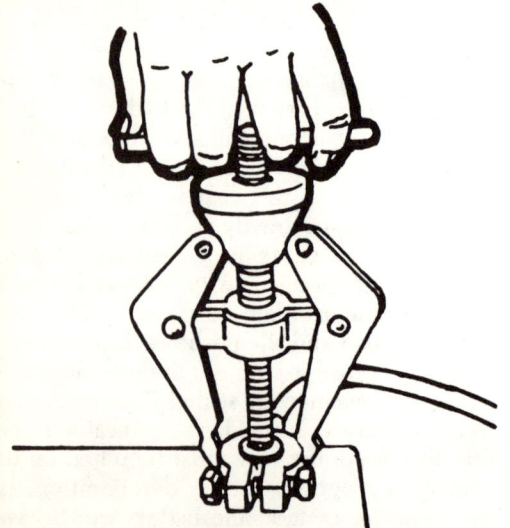

Use a puller to remove the battery cable

GENERAL INFORMATION AND MAINTENANCE

Belts

NOTE: *Due to the compactness of the engine compartment, it may be necessary to disconnect some spark plug leads when adjusting or replacing drive belts. If a spark plug lead is disconnected it is necessary to coat the terminal of the lead with silicone grease (Part number D7AZ19A331A or the equivalent).*

Escort/Lynx may be equipped with 4 rib, 5 rib, or a conventional ¼ inch V-belt depending on accessories.

CAUTION: *On models equipped with power steering, the air pump belt tension cannot be adjusted until the power steering belt has been replaced and adjusted (or just adjusted if an old belt).*

INSPECTION

Inspect all drive belts for excessive wear, cracks, glazed condition and frayed or broken cords. Replace any drive belt showing the above condition(s).

NOTE: *If a drive belt continually gets cut, the crankshaft pulley might have a sharp projection on it. Have the pulley replaced if this condition exists.*

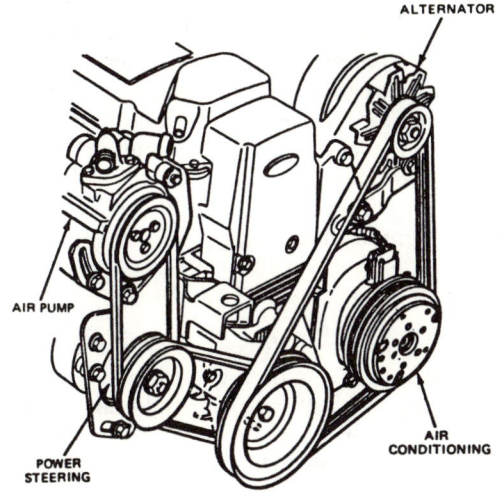

Drive belts, engine with air conditioning

REPLACEMENT

1. Loosen the pivot bolt and/or the adjustment bolt.
2. Move the driven unit (power steering pump, air pump, etc.) toward or away from the engine to loosen the belt. Remove the belt.
3. Install the new belt on the driven unit and either move toward or away from the engine to put tension on the belt.
4. Snug up the mounting and/or adjusting bolt to hold the driven unit—but do not completely tighten.
5. See the following procedure for the deflection method of belt adjustment.

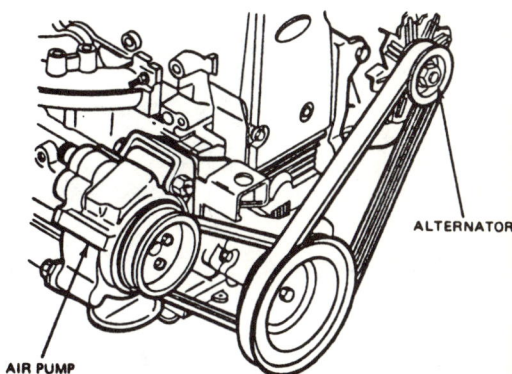

Drive belts, engine without air conditioning

ADJUSTMENT

NOTE: *Proper adjustment requires the use of a tension gauge—since the consumer may not have the necessary gauge, a deflection method of adjustment is given.*

1. Locate a point on the belt about midway between the two pulleys driven.
2. The deflection of the belt should be:
   • For all belts with a distance of 12 inches between pulleys; ⅛ inch to ¼ inch.
   • For all belts with a distance greater than 12 inches between pulleys; ⅛ inch to ⅜ inch.
3. Correctly adjust the belt deflection and tighten all mounting bolts. Start the engine and allow it to reach the normal operating temperature. Shut the engine OFF and recheck belt deflection—readjust if necessary.

ALTERNATOR BELT ADJUSTMENT

Modified Bracket

Some later models are equipped with a modified alternator bracket (high mount alternator). The bracket incorporates a slot that will accommodate a tapered pry bar, such as a lug wrench, to give a place to apply leverage.

Insert the tire lug wrench into the slot opening. Pry on the alternator until the correct belt tension is reached.

While maintaining belt tension, first tighten the ⅜ adjusting bolt (24–30 ft. lbs.), then tighten the pivot bolt (45–65 ft. lbs.).

12 GENERAL INFORMATION AND MAINTENANCE

HOW TO SPOT WORN V-BELTS

V-Belts are vital to efficient engine operation—they drive the fan, water pump and other accessories. They require little maintenance (occasional tightening) but they will not last forever. Slipping or failure of the V-belt will lead to overheating. If your V-belt looks like any of these, it should be replaced.

This belt has deep cracks, which cause it to flex. Too much flexing leads to heat build-up and premature failure. These cracks can be caused by using the belt on a pulley that is too small. Notched belts are available for small diameter pulleys.

Cracking or weathering

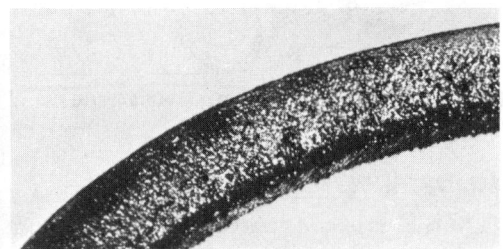

Oil and grease on a belt can cause the belt's rubber compounds to soften and separate from the reinforcing cords that hold the belt together. The belt will first slip, then finally fail altogether.

Softening (grease and oil)

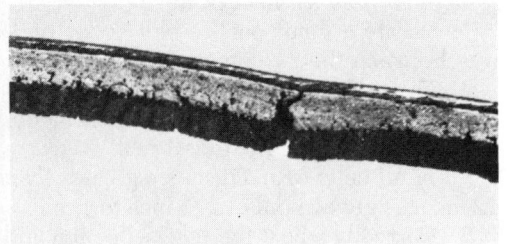

Glazing is caused by a belt that is slipping. A slipping belt can cause a run-down battery, erratic power steering, overheating or poor accessory performance. The more the belt slips, the more glazing will be built up on the surface of the belt. The more the belt is glazed, the more it will slip. If the glazing is light, tighten the belt.

Glazing

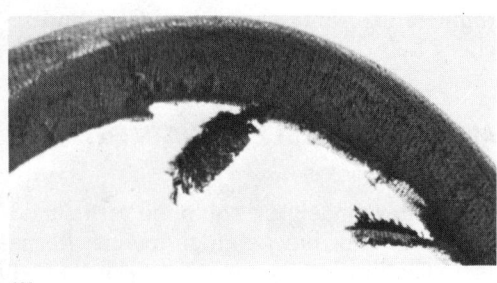

The cover of this belt is worn off and is peeling away. The reinforcing cords will begin to wear and the belt will shortly break. When the belt cover wears in spots or has a rough jagged appearance, check the pulley grooves for roughness.

Worn cover

This belt is on the verge of breaking and leaving you stranded. The layers of the belt are separating and the reinforcing cords are exposed. It's just a matter of time before it breaks completely.

Separation

GENERAL INFORMATION AND MAINTENANCE

HOW TO SPOT BAD HOSES

Both the upper and lower radiator hoses are called upon to perform difficult jobs in an inhospitable environment. They are subject to nearly 18 psi at under hood temperatures often over 280°F., and must circulate nearly 7500 gallons of coolant an hour—3 good reasons to have good hoses.

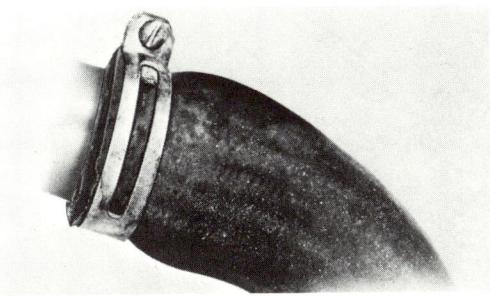

Swollen hose

A good test for any hose is to feel it for soft or spongy spots. Frequently these will appear as swollen areas of the hose. The most likely cause is oil soaking. This hose could burst at any time, when hot or under pressure.

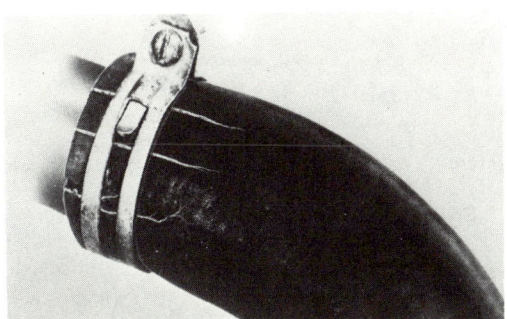

Cracked hose

Cracked hoses can usually be seen but feel the hoses to be sure they have not hardened; a prime cause of cracking. This hose has cracked down to the reinforcing cords and could split at any of the cracks.

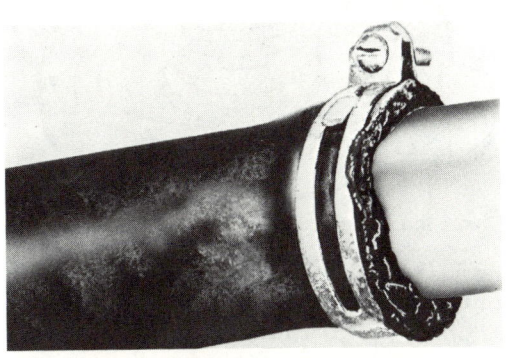

Frayed hose end (due to weak clamp)

Weakened clamps frequently are the cause of hose and cooling system failure. The connection between the pipe and hose has deteriorated enough to allow coolant to escape when the engine is hot.

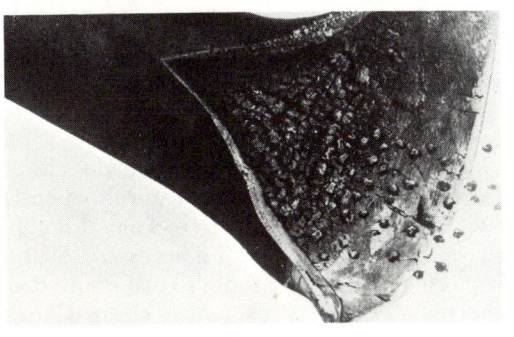

Debris in cooling system

Debris, rust and scale in the cooling system can cause the inside of a hose to weaken. This can usually be felt on the outside of the hose as soft or thinner areas.

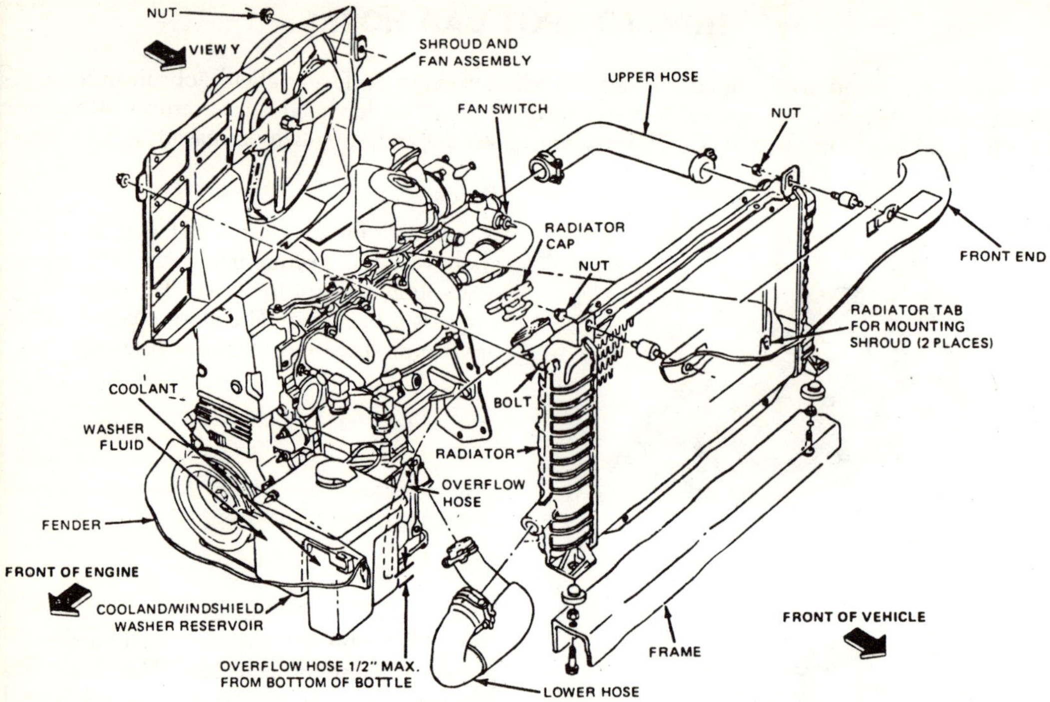

GENERAL INFORMATION AND MAINTENANCE

Cooling system

Cooling System

CAUTION: *The cooling fan motor is controlled by a temperature switch. The fan may come on and run when the engine is off. It will continue to run until the correct temperature is reached. Take care not to get your fingers, etc. caught in the fan blades.*

CAUTION: *Never remove the radiator cap under any circumstances when the engine is operating. Before removing the cap, switch off the engine and wait until it has cooled. Even then, use extreme care when removing the cap from a hot radiator. Wrap a thick cloth around the cap and turn it slowly to the first stop. Step back while the pressure is released from the cooling system. When you are sure all the pressure has been released, press down on the cap—still with a cloth—turn and remove it.*

CHECKING COOLANT

Check the freezing protection rating of the coolant at least once a year, just before winter. Maintain a protection rating of at least 20 degrees F (−29 degrees C) to prevent engine damage as a result of freezing and to assure proper engine operating temperature. Rust and corrosion inhibitors tend to deteriorate with time, changing the coolant every 3 years

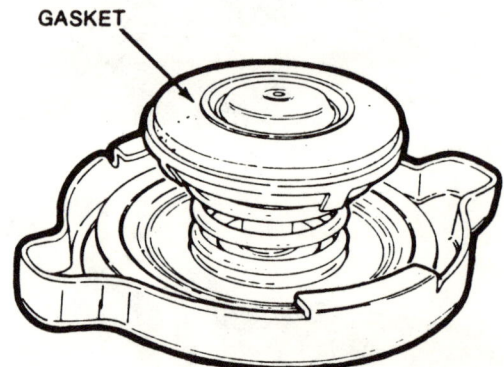

Check the radiator cap gasket for cuts or cracks

or 30,000 miles is recommended for proper protection of the cooling system.

Check the coolant level in the radiator at least once a month, only when the engine is cool. If the level is more than 2 inches below the radiator filler neck, fill to the neck with a 50/50 mixture of specified coolant and water.

NOTE: *On a full system, it is normal to have coolant in the reservoir when the engine is hot.*

Whenever coolant checks are made, check the condition of the radiator cap rubber seal. Make sure it is clean and free of any dirt particles. Rinse off with water if necessary. When replacing cap on radiator, also make sure that the radiator filler neck seat is clean. Check that over-flow hose in the reservoir is not

GENERAL INFORMATION AND MAINTENANCE

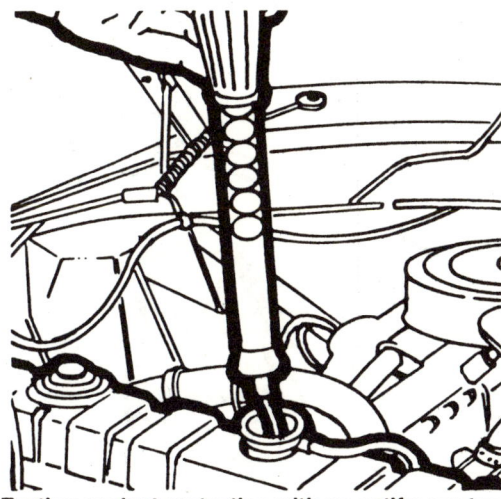

Testing coolant protection with an antifreeze tester

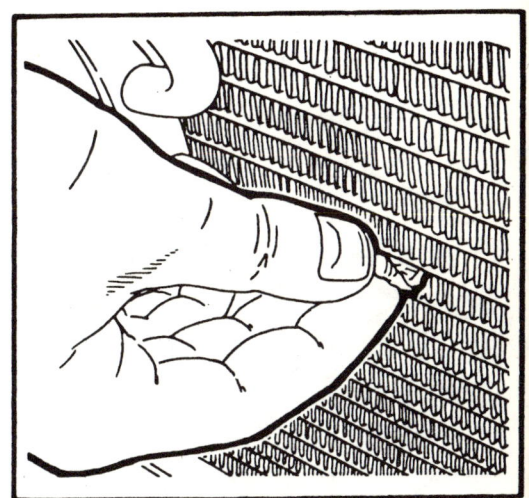

Clean the radiator fins of debris

kinked and is inserted to within ½ inch of bottom of the bottle.

ADDING COOLANT

Anytime you add coolant to the radiator, use a 50/50 mixture of coolant and water. If you have to add coolant more than once a month, or if you have to add more than one quart at a time, have the cooling system checked for leaks.

COOLANT SPECIFICATION

CAUTION: *This engine has an aluminum cylinder head and requires a special unique corrosion inhibited coolant formulation to avoid radiator damage. Use only a permanent type coolant that meets Ford Specification ESE-M97B43-A, such as Ford Cooling System Fluid (E1FZ-19549-A) or Prestone II. As of this printing date, Prestone II is an approved retail equivalent. Contact your Ford Motor Company dealer who will be notified when additional coolants are approved as equivalent. DO NOT USE previous Ford Specification ESE-M97B18-C or alcohol or methanol antifreeze, or mix them with the specified coolant.*

DRAINING COOLANT

To drain the coolant, connect an 18 inch long, ⅜ inch inside diameter hose to the nipple on the drain valve located on the bottom of the radiator. With the engine cool, remove the radiator cap and open the drain valve allowing the coolant to drain into a container. When all of the coolant has drained, remove the ⅜ inch hose and close the drain valve.

REPLACING COOLANT

If there is any evidence of rust or scaling in the cooling system, the system should be flushed thoroughly before refilling. With the engine OFF and COOL:

1. Add 4 Liters (4.2 quarts) of specified coolant to the radiator. Then add water until the radiator is full.
2. Re-install the radiator cap to the pressure relief position by installing the cap to the fully installed position and then backing off to the first stop.
3. Start and idle the engine until the upper radiator hose is warm.
4. Immediately shut off engine. Cautiously remove radiator cap and add water until the radiator is full. Re-install radiator cap securely.
5. Remove the hose from the coolant recover reservoir and add ½ Liter (1.1 pint) of water to the reservoir through the hose opening.
6. Replace the hose into the reservoir to a fully inserted position, then raise to ½ inch from the bottom as indicated from the white paint mark. (NOTE: be sure that the hose attachment at the radiator is secure.)
7. Upon subsequent engine operation to normal operating temperatures, some coolant will normally be in the recovery reservoir and will later transfer to the radiator after the engine has cooled.

HOSE REPLACEMENT

1. Open the hood and cover the fenders to protect them from scratches.
2. Disconnect the negative (ground) battery cable at the battery.

16 GENERAL INFORMATION AND MAINTENANCE

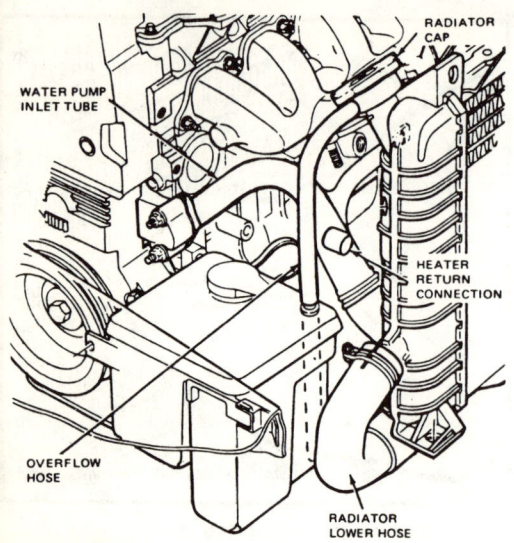

Hose locations

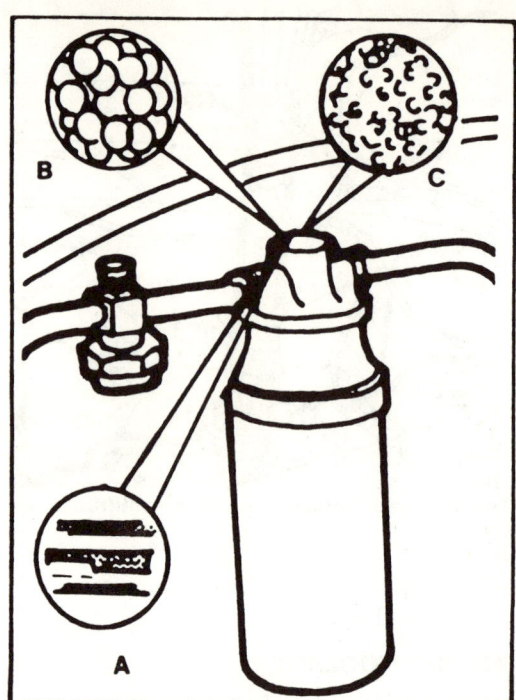

Oil streaks (A), constant bubbles (B) or foam (C) indicate there is not enough refrigerant in the system. Occasional bubbles during initial operation is normal. A clear sight glass indicates a proper charge of refrigerant or no refrigerant at all, which can be determined by the presence of cold air at the outlets in the car. If the glass is clouded with a milky white substance, have the receiver/drier checked professionally

3. Place a suitable drain pan under the radiator and drain the cooling system.
NOTE: *Place a small hose on the end of the radiator petcock, this will direct the coolant into the drain pan.*
4. After the radiator has drained, position the drain pan under the lower hose. Loosen the lower hose clamps, disconnect the hose from the water pump inlet pipe and allow to drain. Disconnect the other end of the hose from the radiator and remove the hose.
5. Loosen the clamps retaining the upper hose, disconnect and remove the hose.
NOTE: *If only the upper hose is to be replaced, drain off enough coolant so the level is below the hose.*
6. If heater hoses need replacement, drain the coolant, loosen the clamps and remove the hose(s).
7. Installation of new hose(s) is in the reverse order of removal.
8. Be sure the petcock is closed. Fill the cooling system with the required protection mixture of water and permanent coolant/antifreeze. Connect the negative battery cable.
9. Run the engine until normal operating temperature is reached. Shut off the engine and check for coolant leaks. When the engine cools, recheck the coolant level in the radiator.

Air Conditioning
SAFETY PRECAUTIONS
There are two particular hazards associated with air conditioning systems and they both relate to the refrigerant gas.

First, the refrigerant gas is an extremely cold substance. When exposed to air, it will instantly freeze any surface it comes in contact with, including your eyes. The other hazard relates to fire. Although normally nontoxic, refrigerant gas becomes highly poisonous in the presence of an open flame. One good whiff of the vapor formed by burning refrigerant can be fatal. Keep all forms of fire (including cigarettes) well clear of the air-conditioning system.

Any repair work to an air conditioning system should be left to a professional. Do not, under any circumstances, attempt to loosen or tighten any fittings or perform any work other than that outlined here.

CHECKING FOR OIL LEAKS
Refrigerant leaks show up as oily areas on the various components because the compressor oil is transported around the entire system

GENERAL INFORMATION AND MAINTENANCE

along with the refrigerant. Look for only spots on all the hoses and lines, and especially on the hose and tubing connections. If there are oily deposits, the system may have a leak, and you should have it checked by a qualified repairman.

NOTE: *A small area of oil on the front of the compressor is normal and no cause for alarm.*

KEEP THE CONDENSER CLEAR

Periodically inspect the front of the condenser for bent fins or foreign material (dirt, bugs, leaves, etc.) If any cooling fins are bent, straighten them carefully with needle-nosed pliers. You can remove any debris with a stiff bristle brush or hose.

OPERATE THE A/C SYSTEM PERIODICALLY

A lot of A/C problems can be avoided by simply running the air conditioner at least once a week, regardless of the season. Let the system run for at least 5 minutes a week (even in the winter), and you'll keep the internal parts lubricated as well as preventing the hoses from hardening.

REFRIGERANT LEVEL CHECK

There are two ways to check refrigerant level, depending on how your model is equipped.

With Sight Glass

The first order of business when checking the sight glass is to find the sight glass. It will either be in the head of the receiver/drier, or in one of the metal lines leading from the top of the receiver/drier. Once you've found it, wipe it clean and proceed as follows:

1. With the engine and the air conditioning system running, look for the flow of refrigerant through the sight glass. If the air conditioner is working properly, you'll be able to see a continuous flow of clear refrigerant through the sight glass, with perhaps an occasional bubble at very high temperatures.

2. Cycle the air conditioner on and off to make sure what you are seeing is clear refrigerant. Since the refrigerant is clear, it is possible to mistake a completely discharged system for one that is fully charged. Turn the system off and watch the sight glass. If there is refrigerant in the system, you'll see bubbles during the off cycle. If you observe no bubbles when the system is running, and the air flow from the unit in the car is delivering cold air, everything is OK.

3. If you observe bubbles in the sight glass while the system is operating, the system is low on refrigerant. Have it checked by a professional.

4. Oil streaks in the sight glass are an indication of trouble. Most of the time, if you see oil in the sight glass, it will appear as a series of streaks, although occasionally it may be a solid stream of oil. In either case, it means that part of the charge has been lost.

Without Sight Glass

On vehicles that are not equipped with sight glasses, it is necessary to feel the temperature difference in the inlet and outlet lines at the receiver/drier to gauge the refrigerant level. Use the following procedure:

1. Locate the receiver/drier. It will generally be up front near the condenser. It is shaped like a small fire extinguisher and will always have two lines connected to it. One line goes to the expansion valve and the other goes to the condenser.

2. With the engine and the air ctnditioner running, hold a line in each hand and gauge their relative temperatures. If they are both the same approximate temperature, the system is correctly charged.

3. If the line from the expansion valve to the receiver/drier is a lot colder than the line from the receiver/drier to the condenser, then the system is overcharged. It should be noted that this is an extremely rare condition.

4. If the line that leads from the receiver/drier to the condenser is a lot colder than the other line, the system is undercharged.

5. If the system is undercharged or overcharged, have it checked by a professional air conditioning mechanic.

Windshield Wipers

BLADE AND ARM REPLACEMENT

1. Cycle the wiper arm and blade assembly and stop at a position on the windshield where removal can be accomplished without difficulty.

2. To remove the blade: Pull the wiper arm out and away from the windshield. Grasp the wiper blade assembly and pull away from the mounting pin of the wiper arm (Trico type). Or; pull back on the spring lock, where the arm is connected to the blade, and pull the wiper blade assembly from the wiper arm (Tridon type).

3. To remove the wiper arm: Pull the blade

18 GENERAL INFORMATION AND MAINTENANCE

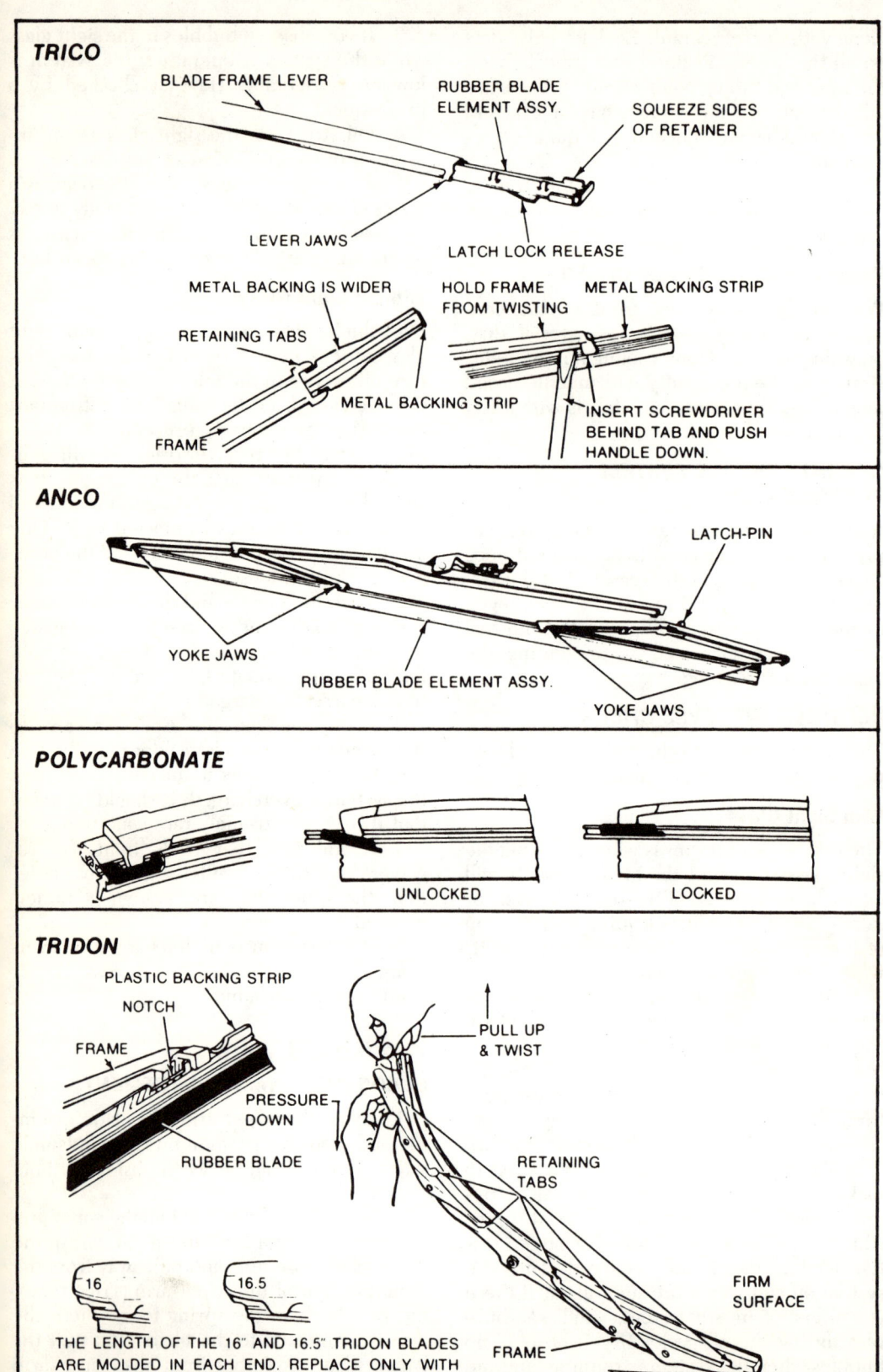

Wiper insert replacement

GENERAL INFORMATION AND MAINTENANCE

and arm assembly away from the windshield. Move the slide latch (located at base of wiper arm) away from the arm mounting pivot shaft. The arm is now unlocked. Lift the arm up and away from the pivot shaft.

4. Installation is in the reverse order of removal.

Fluid Level Checks

ENGINE OIL

It is a good idea to check the engine oil each time or at least every other time you fill your gas tank.

1. Be sure your car is on level ground. Shut off the engine and wait for a few minutes to allow the oil to drain back into the oil pan.

2. Remove the engine oil dipstick and wipe clean with a rag.

3. Reinsert the dipstick and push it down until it is fully seated in the tube.

4. Remove the stick and check the oil level shown. If the oil level is below the lower mark, add one quart.

5. If you wish, you may carefully fill the oil pan to the upper mark on the dipstick with less than a full quart. Do not, however, add a full quart when it would overfill the crankcase (level above the upper mark on the dipstick). The excess oil will generally be consumed at an excessive rate even if no damage to the engine seals occurs.

COOLING SYSTEM

The cooling system of your car contains, among other items, a radiator and an expansion tank. When the engine is running heat is generated. The rise in temperature causes the coolant, in the radiator, to expand and builds up internal pressure. When a certain pressure is reached, a pressure relief valve in the radiator filler cap (pressure cap) is lifted from its seat and allows coolant to flow through the radiator filler neck, down a hose, and into the expansion reservoir.

When the system temperature and pressure are reduced in the radiator, the water in the expansion reservoir is syphoned back into the radiator.

NOTE: *The coolant in the expansion reservoir does not indicate the coolant level in the cooling system. It is important to check the coolant level in the radiator by removing the radiator cap* WHEN THE ENGINE IS COLD.

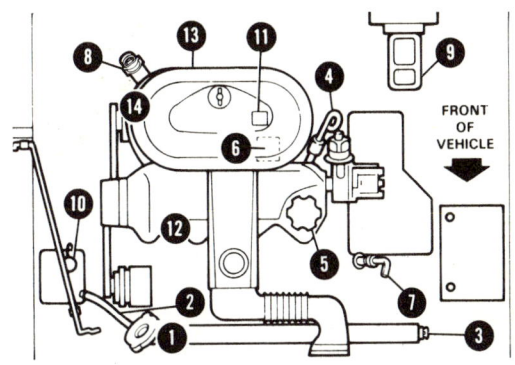

1. Radiator cap
2. Expansion tank
3. Drain cock for radiator
4. Engine oil dipstick
5. Oil filler cap
6. Oil filter
7. Automatic transaxle dipstick
8. Power steering dipstick
9. Brake fluid level check (master cylinder)
10. Washer fluid (windshield wipers)
11. Fuel filter
12. Spark plugs (see Chapter 2)
13. Air cleaner
14. Crankcase emissions filter

Maintenance check points

With a cold engine, the level of coolant should be within 2 inches of the internal flange of the filler neck below the filler cap (pressure cap).

BRAKE MASTER CYLINDER

The brake master cylinder is located under the hood, on the left side firewall. Before removing the master cylinder reservoir cap, make sure the vehicle is resting on level ground and clean all the dirt away from the top of the master cylinder. Pry the retaining clip off to the side. Remove the master cylinder cover.

If the level of the brake fluid is within ¼ inch of the top it is OK. If the level is less than half the volume of the reservoir, check the brake system for leaks. Leaks in the brake system most commonly occur at the rear wheel cylinders or at the front calipers. Leaks at brake lines or the master cylinder can also be the cause of the loss of brake fluid.

There is a rubber diaphragm at the top of the master cylinder cap. As the fluid level lowers due to normal brake shoe wear or leakage, the diaphragm takes up the space. This is to prevent the loss of brake fluid out the vented cap and to help stop contamination by dirt. After filling the master cylinder to the proper level with brake fluid (Type

GENERAL INFORMATION AND MAINTENANCE

DOT 3), but before replacing the cap, fold the rubber diaphragm up into the cap, then replace the cap on the reservoir and snap the retaining clip back in place.

TRANSAXLE (TRANSMISSION AND DIFFERENTIAL)

Manual Transaxle

Each time the engine oil is changed, the fluid level of the transaxle should be checked. The car must be resting on level ground or supported on jackstands (front and back) evenly. To check the fluid; remove the filler plug, located on the upper front (driver's side) of the transaxle with a $^9/$ inch wrench.

CAUTION: *The filler plug has a hex-head, do not mistake any other bolts for the filler.*

Damage to the transaxle could occur if the wrong "plug" is removed.

The oil level should be even with the edge of the filler hole or within ¼ inch of the hole. If the oil is low, add Type F automatic fluid. Manual transmission type GL is NOT to be used.

NOTE: *A rubber bulb syringe will be helpful in adding the Type "F" fluid to the manual transaxle.*

Automatic Transaxle

A dipstick is provided in the engine compartment to check the level of the automatic transaxle. Be sure the car is on level ground and that the car's engine and transmission have reached normal operating temperatures. Start the engine, put the parking brake on and the transmission selector lever in the PARK position. Move the selector lever through all the positions and return to the PARK position. DO NOT TURN OFF THE ENGINE DURING THE FLUID LEVEL CHECK. Clean all dirt from the dipstick cap before removing the dipstick. Remove the dipstick and wipe clean. Reinsert the dipstick making sure it is fully seated. Pull the dipstick out of the tube and check the fluid level. The fluid level should be between the FULL and ADD marks.

If necessary, add enough fluid through the dipstick tube/filler to bring the level to the FULL mark on the dipstick. Use only Dexron-II® fluid.

CAUTION: *Do not overfill. Make sure the dipstick is fully seated.*

MANUAL STEERING

No periodic lubrication is required unless the system is disassembled for service.

POWER STEERING PUMP RESERVOIR

Run the engine until it reaches normal operating temperature. While the engine is idling, turn the steering wheel all the way to the right and then left several times. Shut OFF the engine. Open the hood and remove the power steering pump dipstick. Wipe the dipstick clean and reinstall into the pump reservoir. Withdraw the dipstick and note the fluid level shown. The level must show between the cold full mark and the hot full mark. Add fluid if necessary, but do not overfill. Remove any excess fluid with a suction bulb or "gun."

BATTERY

Check the battery fluid level at least once a month; more often in hot weather. Some batteries do not require a fluid level check; these are known as sealed batteries.

Water may be added to a battery when the level drops below the bottom of the filler neck (under the cover cap). Add water until the level contacts the bottom of the neck. Some batteries use a filler cap with a glass rod attached, which will appear to glow when the fluid level in that cell is low. Another brand has a small "eye" in the top of the case which glows when the electrolyte is low and still other brands of batteries may have a translucent case which will show the water level through the outside case.

When filling the battery, clean tap water may be used if the water in your area is not unusually hard. Distilled water is better, if you can get it, and must be used if only hard tap water is available. Too "hard" water will cause formation of deposits on the battery plates and will finally cause the cell to short out. Add water slowly to avoid splashing the water/acid (electrolyte) out of the cells. Make sure the caps/covers are replaced tightly. If, for any reason the water/acid is spilled on the car finish; flush with cold water or a baking soda and water mixture.

In winter time, or cold weather, run the engine for a few minutes after adding water to the battery. The charging rate of the alternator will mix the fresh water with the acid and help prevent freezing.

GENERAL INFORMATION AND MAINTENANCE

Capacities

Year	Engine No. Cyl. Displacement (cc)	Engine Crankcase Capacity Including Filter (qts.)	Transmission Pts To Refill After Draining - Manual 4-Speed	Transmission Pts To Refill After Draining - Automatic	Drive Axle (pts)	Gasoline Tank (gals)	Cooling System ③ (qts) With Heater	Cooling System ③ (qts) With A/C
1981–82	4-1597	4.0	5.0	19.6	①	10②	8.0	8.0

① Included in transmission capacity
② Optional tank: 11.3, became standard for 1982
③ Capacity may be less on some EXP/LN7 models

If the battery requires frequent refilling, have the battery and charging system checked for mechanical and electrical problems.

WINDSHIELD WASHER RESERVOIR

The windshield washer tank is located on the left/front corner of the engine compartment and shares a divided but common case with the radiator expansion tank. You can fill the washer tank with plain water in the summer time, but the pre-mixed solvents available help dissolve grime and dirt better and provide protection against freezing in the winter. Add fluid through the filler cover when the level drops below the line on the side of the reservoir case.

Tires

INFLATION PRESSURE

Tire inflation is the most ignored item of auto maintenance. Gasoline mileage can drop as much as .8% for every 1 pound per square inch (psi) of under inflation.

Two items should be a permanent fixture in every glove compartment; a tire pressure gauge and a tread depth gauge. Check the tire air pressure (including the spare) regularly with a pocket type gauge. Kicking the tires won't tell you a thing, and the gauge on the service station air hose is notoriously inaccurate.

The tire pressures recommended for your car are usually found on a label attached to the door pillar or on the glove box inner cover or in the owner's manual. Ideally, inflation pressure should be checked when the tires are cool. When the air becomes heated it expands and the pressure increases. Every 10° rise (or drop) in temperature means a differ-

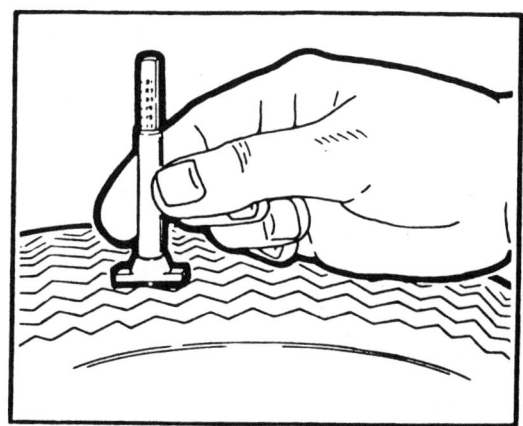

Tire tread depth gauge

ence of 1 psi, which also explains why the tire appears to lose air on a very cold night. When it is impossible to check the tires "cold," allow for pressure build-up due to heat. If the "hot" pressure exceeds the "cold" pressure by more than 15 psi, reduce your speed, load or both. Otherwise internal heat is created in the tire. When the heat approaches the temperature at which the tire was cured, during manufacture, the tread can separate from the body.

CAUTION: *Never counteract excessive pressure build-up by bleeding off air pressure (letting some air out). This will only further raise the tire operating temperature.*

Before starting a long trip with lots of luggage, you can add about 2–4 psi to the tires to make them run cooler, but never exceed the maximum inflation pressure on the side of the tire.

TREAD DEPTH

All tires made since 1968 have 8 built-in tread wear indicator bars that show up as ½" wide

GENERAL INFORMATION AND MAINTENANCE

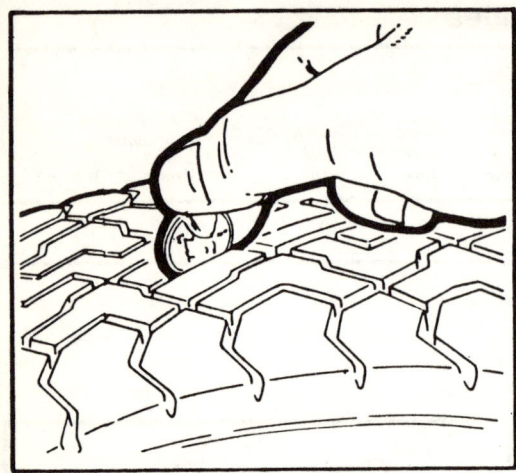

A penny used to determine tread depth

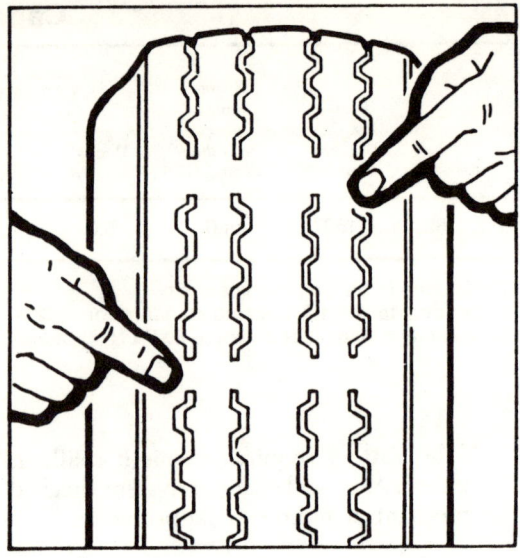

Replace a tire that shows the built-in "bump strip"

smooth bands across the tire when $1/16''$ of tread remains. The appearance of tread wear indicators means that the tires should be replaced. In fact, many states have laws prohibiting the use of tires with less than $1/16''$ tread.

You can check your own tread depth with an inexpensive gauge or by using a Lincoln head penny. Slip the Lincoln penny into several tread grooves. If you can see the top of Lincoln's head in 2 adjacent grooves, the tires have less than $1/16''$ tread left and should be replaced. You can measure snow tires in the same manner by using the "tails" side of the Lincoln penny. If you can see the top of the Lincoln memorial, it's time to replace the snow tires.

TIRE ROTATION

Tire wear can be equalized by switching the position of the tires about every 6000 miles. Including a conventional spare in the rotation pattern can give up to 20% more tire life.

CAUTION: *Do not include the new "Space-Saver® or temporary spare tires in the rotation pattern.*

There are certain exceptions to tire rotation, however. Studded snow tires should not be rotated, and radials should be kept on the same side of the car (maintain the same direc-

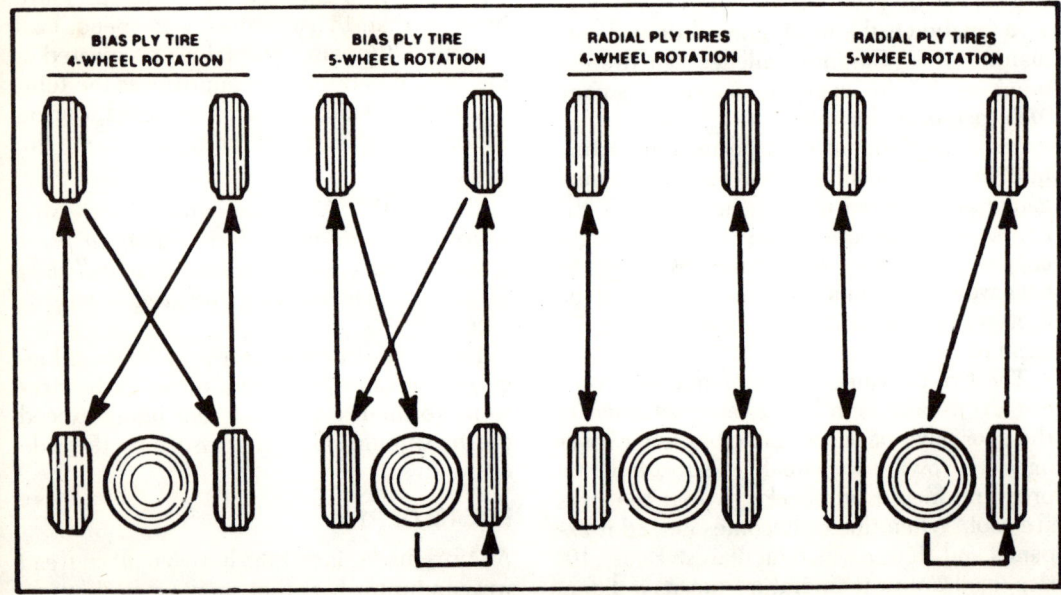

Tire rotation patterns

GENERAL INFORMATION AND MAINTENANCE

tion of rotation). The belts on radial tires get set in a pattern. If the direction of rotation is reversed, it can cause rough ride and vibration.

NOTE: *When radials or studded snows are taken off the car, mark them, so you can maintain the same direction of rotation.*

TIRE STORAGE

Store the tires at proper inflation pressures if they are mounted on wheels. All tires should be kept in a cool, dry place. If they are stored in the garage or basement, do not let them stand on a concrete floor; set them on strips of wood.

Fuel Filter

The fuel filter should be replaced, immediately, upon evidence of dirt in the fuel system. Regular replacement of the fuel filter should be every 30,000 miles. If the engine seems to be suffering from fuel starvation, remove the filter and blow through it to see if it is clogged. If air won't pass through the filter easily, or if dirt is visible in the inlet passage, replace the filter.

FILTER REPLACEMENT

1. Make sure the engine is cold. *Spilled fuel on a hot engine could ignite and cause serious injury and/or damage!* Open the hood. If you have fender covers, install them. Otherwise, be careful not to spill fuel on the painted surface of your car.
2. Remove the air cleaner assembly (see air cleaner element replacement in this chapter). Place a rag under the fuel filter and its connections.
3. Use an 11/16 inch open end wrench to hold the fuel filter while disconnecting the fuel line with a ½ inch wrench.
4. After disconnecting the fuel line, unscrew the fuel filter after loosening it with the 11/16 inch wrench.
5. Hand start the new fuel filter into carburetor and tighten with the open-end wrench.

NOTE: *It might be easier to start the fuel line into the filter before completely tightening the fuel filter on the carburetor.*

6. Tighten the fuel line into the fuel filter.
7. Remove the rag under the filter and connections. Start the engine and check for fuel leaks. Shut off the engine and re-install the air cleaner assembly.

LUBRICATION

Fuel Recommendations

Unleaded gasoline having a Research Octane Number (RON) of 91, or an Antiknock Index of 87 is recommended for your car. Leaded gasoline will quickly interfere with the operation of the catalytic converter and just a few tankfuls of leaded gasoline will render the converter useless. This will cause the emission of much greater amounts of hydrocarbons and carbon monoxide from the exhaust system, void your warranty and cost a considerable amount of money for converter replacement.

Oil Recommendations

Oil meeting API classification SF or at least SE is recommended for use in your Escort/Lynx. Viscosity grades 10W-30 or 10W-40 are recommended, but you may also use 5W-20 in very cold weather, or 20W-50 in very hot weather. See the viscosity to temperature chart in this section.

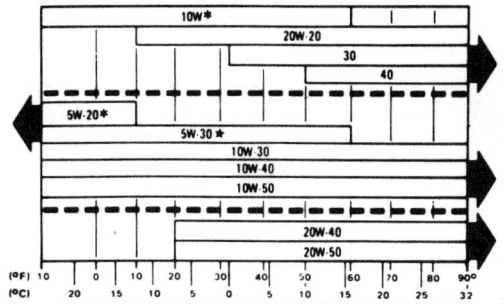

* NOT RECOMMENDED FOR SUSTAINED HIGH SPEED DRIVING.
★ 5W-30 RECOMMENDED WHEN TEMPERATURES ARE +10°F. (−12.2°C.) OR BELOW TO FACILITATE COLD CRANKING.

Oil viscosity recommendations

Fluid Changes

ENGINE OIL AND OIL FILTER

Change the engine oil and oil filter every 10 months or 10,000 miles. If the car is used in severe service or dusty conditions; change the engine oil and oil filter every 3 months or 3,000 miles. Following these recommended intervals will help keep your car engine in good condition.

CHANGING THE ENGINE OIL AND FILTER

1. Make sure the engine is at normal operating temperature (this promotes complete draining of the old oil).

24 GENERAL INFORMATION AND MAINTENANCE

Maintenance Intervals 1981

All items with either a "B" or "(B)" code are required to be performed in all states except California.

For vehicles sold in California, all "B" items are at the maintenance intervals in accordance with California regulations. All "(B)" items are recommended by Ford Motor Company for best vehicle operation.

MAINTENANCE SCHEDULE "B"

MAINTENANCE OPERATION

SERVICE INTERVAL—Time in Months or Miles (or Kilometers) in thousands, whichever occurs first, unless otherwise specified.

MONTHS	10	20	30	40	50	60
MILES (000)	10	20	30	40	50	60
KILOMETERS (000)	16	32	48	64	80	96
EMISSION CONTROL DEVICES AND SYSTEMS						
Change Engine Oil ①	B	B	B	B	B	B
Replace Engine Oil Filter ①	B	B	B	B	B	B
Replace Spark Plugs ① ②			B			B
Check** Coolant Protection and Condition ③			ANNUALLY			
Check*** Cooling System, Hoses and Clamps; replace coolant ③			B			B
Check** Accessory Drive Belt Condition and Tension	(B)		B			B
Replace Carburetor Air Cleaner Element ④			B			B
Check Idle Speeds ②	B		(B)			B
Replace Crankcase Emissions Filter ④ ⑤			(B)			B
Choke System Linkage. Clean and verify freedom of movement.			B			B
OTHER SYSTEMS						
Replace Engine Timing Belt ★						B★
Inspect Exhaust System Heat Shields ⑥ *			B			B
Drain and Refill Automatic Transaxle Fluid—Severe or Continuous Service Only ①			B		B	B
Check Automatic Transaxle T.V. Linkage	B	B				

CAUTION:

★ Replacement of the engine timing belt is required at 60,000 miles (96,000 kilometers). Failure to replace the engine timing belt may result in serious damage to the engine. Each time the timing belt tension is released or the belt is removed, a new belt must be installed.

*Inspect means a visual observation of a system. (Footnotes continued on page 25).

GENERAL INFORMATION AND MAINTENANCE

**Check means a functional measurement of a system's operation (performance, leaks or condition of parts)—correct as required.
***Coolant should be replaced every 36 months or scheduled miles (kilometers), whichever occurs first.
NOTES:
① Severe service operation: when operating your vehicle under any of the following conditions, change engine oil every three (3) months or 3,000 miles (4,800 km), whichever occurs first, and replace oil filter at alternate oil changes. Check, clean and regap spark plugs every 6,000 miles (9,600 km).
- Extended periods of idling or low speed operation such as police, taxi or door-to-door delivery.
- Towing trailers (refer to special situations section in owners guide for specifics).
- Operation when outside temperature remains below +10°F. (−12°C.) For sixty (60) days or more and when most trips are less than ten (10) MILES (16 KM).
- Operation in severe dust conditions (does not apply to spark plug maintenance).

② Refer to the Vehicle Emissions Control Information decal for specification.
③ Coolant protection checks should be made annually just prior to the onset of freezing weather; where applicable. If coolant is dirty or rusty in appearance, the system should be drained, flushed and refilled with the prescribed solution of cooling system fluid and water. Use only a permanent type coolant that meets Ford specification ESE-M97B43-A.
④ More often if operated in severe dust conditions.
⑤ In replacing crankcase emission filter also replace vent adaptor tube connector (P/N-6758).
⑥ • If so equipped.
- Remove accumulated debris and inspect shield and attachment, or replace shield as required. Perform each 10,000 miles (16,000 kilometers) for severe service usage over unpaved roadways or off road applications.

Maintenance Intervals—1982

The following services are required to be performed at scheduled intervals because they are considered essential to the life and performance of your vehicle. All items with either a "B" or a "(B)" code are *required* to be performed in all states except California. For vehicles sold in California, only "B" are *required* to be performed. However, Ford recommends that you also perform maintenance on items designated by a "(B)" in order to achieve best vehicle operation.

SERVICE INTERVALS—Perform at the months or distances shown, whichever comes first.	Miles	7,500	15,000	22,500	30,000	37,500	45,000	52,500	60,000
	Kilometers	12 000	24 000	36 000	48 000	60 000	72 000	84 000	96 000
EMISSION CONTROL SYSTEMS									
Change engine oil — Every 12 months or**		B	B	B	B	B	B	B	B
Change engine oil filter — Every 12 months or**		B		B		B		B	
Replace engine coolant and check hoses and clamps — Every 36 months or 30,000 miles (48 000 km) (2)					B				B
Check engine coolant condition and protection		ANNUALLY							
Replace spark plugs at**					B				B
Check drive belt tension and condition at		(B)			B				B
Check idle speeds at		B							
Replace carburetor air cleaner filter at					B(1)				B(1)
Replace crankcase emission filter at					B(1)				B(1)
Clean choke linkage at					B				B
* REPLACE ENGINE TIMING BELT									B*
GENERAL MAINTENANCE									
Inspect exhaust system heat shields at					B				B
Check automatic transaxle throttle valve linkage		B			B				
Automatic Transaxle Fluid Change**									

** SEVERE SERVICE—Such as extensive idling, frequent short trips of 10 miles (16 km) or less, driving when the temperature remains below +10F (−12C) for 60 days or more, sustained high speed driving during hot weather (+90F, +32C), towing a trailer for long distances, driving in severe dust conditions — the following maintenance intervals apply:

  Engine oil — Change every 3 months or 3,000 miles (4 800 km), whichever occurs first
  Engine oil filter — Replace at alternate oil changes
  Spark plugs — Check, clean and regap every 6,000 miles (9 600 km)
  Automatic transaxle fluid — Change every 22,500 miles (36 000 km)

  In addition to the above, the automatic transaxle is also considered operating under severe conditions and the transaxle fluid must be changed every 22,500 miles (36 000 km) on vehicles not equipped with auxiliary transaxle oil coolers if operated in fleet usage or accumulating 2,000 miles (3 200 km) or more per month.

(1) Replace air cleaner and emission air filters more often if operating in severe dust conditions. Ask your dealer for the proper replacement intervals for your driving conditions.
(2) Use only a permanent type coolant that meets Ford Specification ESE-M97B44-A.

* **CAUTION—REPLACEMENT OF THE ENGINE TIMING BELT IS REQUIRED AT 60,000 MILES (96 000 km). FAILURE TO REPLACE THE ENGINE TIMING BELT MAY RESULT IN SERIOUS DAMAGE TO THE ENGINE.**

GENERAL INFORMATION AND MAINTENANCE

2. Apply the parking brake and block the wheels; or raise and support the car evenly on jackstands.

3. Place a drain pan of about a gallon and a half capacity under the engine oil pan drain plug. Use the proper size wrench, loosen and remove the plug. Allow all the old oil to drain. Wipe the pan and the drain plug with a clean rag. Inspect the drain plug gasket, replace if necessary.

4. Reinstall and tighten the drain plug. DO NOT OVERTIGHTEN.

5. Move the drain pan under the engine oil filter. Use a strap wrench and loosen the oil filter (do not remove), allow the oil to drain. Unscrew the filter the rest of the way by hand. Use a rag, if necessary, to keep from burning your fingers. When the filter comes loose from the engine, turn the mounting base upward to avoid spilling the remaining oil.

6. Wipe the engine filter mount clean with a rag. Coat the rubber gasket on the new oil

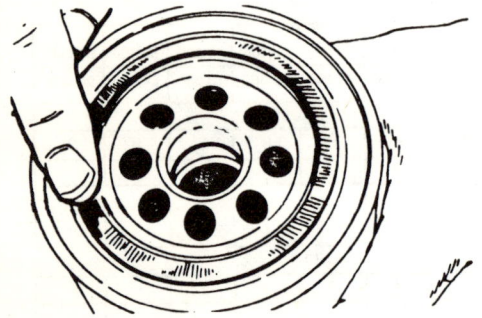

Lubricate the gasket on the new filter with clean engine oil. A dry gasket may not make a good seal and will allow the filter to leak

filter with clean engine oil, applying it with a finger. Carefully start the filter onto the threaded engine mount. Turn the filter until it touches the engine mounting surface. Tighten the filter, *by hand*, ½ turn more.

7. Refill the crankcase with four quarts of engine oil. Replace the filler cap and start the engine. Allow the engine to idle and check for oil leaks. Shut off the engine, wait for several minutes, then check the oil level with the dipstick. Add oil if necessary. Lower car if supported on jackstands.

TRANSMISSION FLUIDS

Changing the fluid in either the automatic or manual transaxle is not necessary under normal operating conditions. However, the fluid levels should be checked at normal intervals as described previously in this chapter.

If your Escort/Lynx is equipped with an automatic transaxle and the region in which you live has severe cold weather, a multi-viscosity automatic transaxle fluid should be used. Ask your dealer about the use of the MV Automatic Transaxle Fluid.

Automatic Transaxle—Severe Service

If you operate your car in very dusty conditions, tow a trailer, have extended idling or low speed operation, it may be necessary to change the ATX fluid at regular intervals (20 months or 20,000 miles). Ask your dealer for his recommendations. A description of the fluid change procedure may be found in Chapter 6.

Drive Axle (Differential)

The "differential" is incorporated with the transmission, hence transaxle. The transmis-

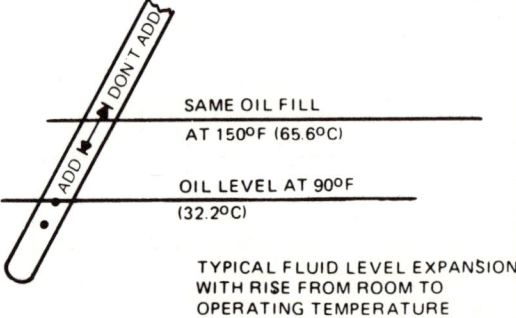

Dipstick markings showing typical fluid expansion from "room" to normal operating temperatures

sion fluid lubricates the "differential" so any checks or fluid changes can be done by following the procedures described in Chapter 6 or in the beginning of this Chapter.

COOLANT

Refer to the cooling system section of this Chapter for the procedure of draining and refilling the cooling system.

Body and Chassis

Refer to the illustration in this Chapter for body and chassis lubrication points.

The preceding chart gives the recommended lubricants.

GENERAL INFORMATION AND MAINTENANCE

Lubrication Recommendations

Item	Part Name
Hinges, Hinge Checks and Pivots*	Polyethylene Grease
Hood Latch and Auxiliary Catch	Polyethylene Grease
Lock Cylinders	Lock Lubricant
Steering Gear Housing (Manual)	Steering Gear Grease
Steering Gear (Rack and Pinion)	Hypoid Gear Lube
Steering-Power (Pump Reservoir)	Motorcraft Auto. Trans. Fluid—Type F
Transmission (Automatic)	Motorcraft Auto. Trans. Fluid Dexron® II
Transmission (Manual)	Manual Trans. Lube
Engine Oil Filter	Long Life Oil Filter
Engine Oil	Motorcraft 10W40 Super Premium
	10W30 Premium
	20W40 Premium
	SAE 30 Single Weight
Speedometer Cable	Speedometer Cable Lube
Engine Coolant	Cooling System Fluid
Front Wheel Bearings and Hubs Front Wheel Bearing Seals	Long Life Lubricant
Brake Master Cylinder	H.D. Brake Fluid
Brake Master Cylinder Push Rod and Bushing	Motorcraft SAE 10W-30 Engine Oil
Drum Brake Shoe Ledges	High Temp. Grease
Parking Brake Cable	Polyethylene Grease
Brake Pedal Pivot Bushing	Motorcraft SAE 10W-30 Engine Oil
Tire Mounting Bead (of Tire)	Tire Mounting Lube
Clutch Pedal Pivot Bushing	Motorcraft SAE 10W-30 Engine Oil

28 GENERAL INFORMATION AND MAINTENANCE

Lubrication Recommendations (cont.)

Item	Part Name
Clutch Pedal Quadrant and Pawl Pivot Holes	
Clutch Cable Connection Transmission End	
Clutch Release Level—At Fingers (Both Sides and Fulcrum)	Long Life Lubricant
Clutch Release Bearing Retainer	

*For Escort/Lynx door hinges use Disc Brake Caliper slide grease.

Wheel Bearings

Refer to Chapter 8 for instructions on servicing the wheel bearings.

PUSHING

Pushing a manual transaxle model to start it is feasible, but must be done with great care, as damage to the bumpers, etc. frequently occurs. Make sure the bumpers of your car and the push car align exactly before attempting a push start. Turn the ignition on in the car to be started. Accelerate steadily with the push car in order to maintain bumper contact—avoid shifting gears. At about 15 miles per hour, depress the clutch pedal, car being pushed, and place the transmission into second gear. Depress the gas pedal slightly (if the engine is cold, press the gas pedal to the floor and release so the choke will engage) and then slowly release the clutch until it becomes fully engaged. As the engine starts, signal to the driver of the push car to back off.

TOWING

Whenever you are towing another vehicle, or being towed, make sure the chain or strap is sufficiently long and strong. Attach the chain securely at a point on the frame, shipping tie-down slots are provided on the front and rear of your car and should be used. Never attach a chain or strap to any steering or suspension part. Never try to start the vehicle when being towed, it might run into the back of the tow car. Do not allow too much slack in the tow line, the towed car could run over the line and damage to both cars could occur. If your car is being towed by a tow truck, the towing speed should be limited to 50 mph with the driving wheels off the ground. If it is necessary to tow the car with the drive wheels on the ground, speed should be limited to no more than 35 mph and the towing distance should not be greater than 50 miles. If towing distance is more than 50 miles the front of the car should be put on dollies.

NOTE: *If the car is being towed with the front (drive) wheels on the ground, never allow the steering lock to keep the wheels straight, damage to the steering could occur.*

JACKING

Contact points for jacking with either the jack supplied with the car, or with a floor jack are located on the side rocker flanges. When using a floor jack, the front of the car may be raised by positioning the jack under the front body rail behind the suspension arm-to-body bracket. The rear of the car may be raised by positioning the jack forward of the rear suspension rod on the bracket.

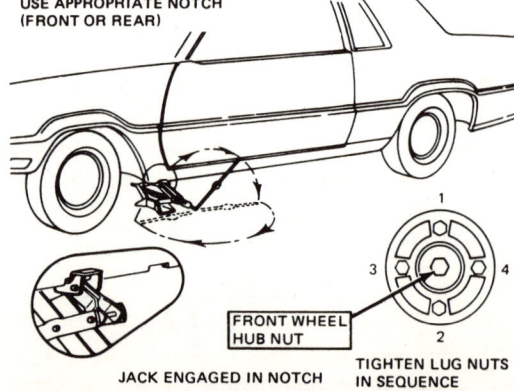

Jack locations, using the jack equipped with your car

GENERAL INFORMATION AND MAINTENANCE

JUMP STARTING A DEAD BATTERY

The chemical reaction in a battery produces explosive hydrogen gas. This is the safe way to jump start a dead battery, reducing the chances of an accidental spark that could cause an explosion.

Jump Starting Precautions

1. Be sure both batteries are of the same voltage.
2. Be sure both batteries are of the same polarity (have the same grounded terminal).
3. Be sure the vehicles are not touching.
4. Be sure the vent cap holes are not obstructed.
5. Do not smoke or allow sparks around the battery.
6. In cold weather, check for frozen electrolyte in the battery.
7. Do not allow electrolyte on your skin or clothing.
8. Be sure the electrolyte is not frozen.

Jump Starting Procedure

1. Determine voltages of the two batteries; they must be the same.
2. Bring the starting vehicle close (they must not touch) so that the batteries can be reached easily.
3. Turn off all accessories and both engines. Put both cars in Neutral or Park and set the handbrake.
4. Cover the cell caps with a rag—do not cover terminals.
5. If the terminals on the run-down battery are heavily corroded, clean them.
6. Identify the positive and negative posts on both batteries and connect the cables in the order shown.
7. Start the engine of the starting vehicle and run it at fast idle. Try to start the car with the dead battery. Crank it for no more than 10 seconds at a time and let it cool off for 20 seconds in between tries.
8. If it doesn't start in 3 tries, there is something else wrong.
9. Disconnect the cables in the reverse order.
10. Replace the cell covers and dispose of the rags.

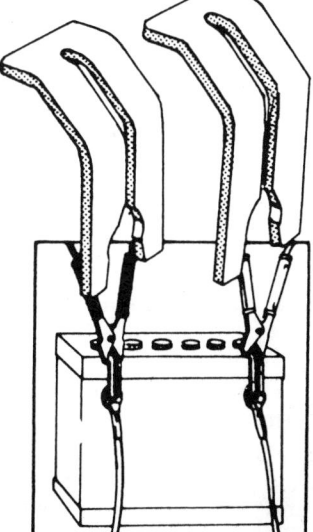

Side terminal batteries occasionally pose a problem when connecting jumper cables. There frequently isn't enough room to clamp the cables without touching sheet metal. Side terminal adaptors are available to alleviate this problem and should be removed after use.

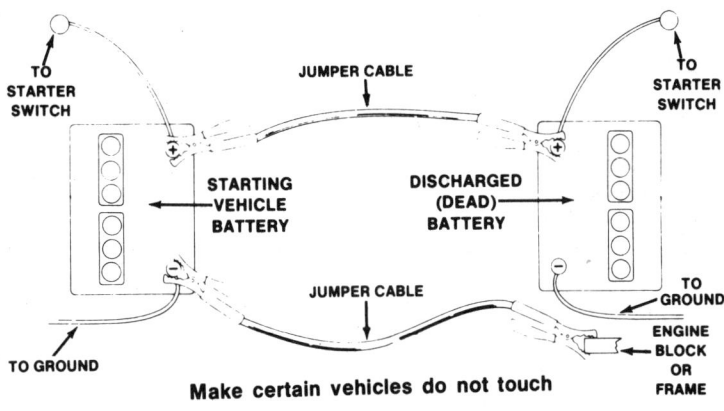

Make certain vehicles do not touch

This hook-up for negative ground cars only

HOW TO BUY A USED CAR

Many people believe that a two or three year old used car is a better buy than a new car. This may be true; the new car suffers the heaviest depreciation in the first two years, but is not old enough to present a lot of costly repair problems. Whatever the age of the used car you might want to buy, this section and a little patience will help you select one that should be safe and dependable.

TIPS

1. First decide what model you want, and how much you want to spend.
2. Check the used car lots and your local newspaper ads. Privately owned cars are usually less expensive, however you will not get a warranty that, in most cases, comes with a used car purchased from a lot.
3. Never shop at night. The glare of the lights make it easy to miss faults on the body caused by accident or rust repair.
4. Try to get the name and phone number of the previous owner. Contact him/her and ask about the car. If the owner of the lot refuses this information, look for a car somewhere else.

A private seller can tell you about the car and maintenance. Remember, however, there's no law requiring honesty from private citizens selling used cars. There is a law that forbids the tampering with or turning back the odometer mileage. This includes both the private citizen and the lot owner. The law also requires that the seller or anyone transferring ownership of the car must provide the buyer with a signed statement indicating the mileage on the odometer at the time of transfer.

5. Write down the year, model and serial number before you buy any used car. Then dial 1-800-424-9393, the toll free number of the National Highway Traffic Safety Administration, and ask if the car has ever been included on any manufacturer's recall list. If so, make sure the needed repairs were made.
6. Use the "Used Car Checklist" in this section and check all the items on the used car you are considering. Some items are more important than others. You know how much money you can afford for repairs, and, depending on the price of the car, may consider doing any needed work yourself. Beware, however, of trouble in areas that will affect operation, safety or emission. Problems in the "Used Car Checklist" break down as follows:

1-8: Two or more problems in these areas indicate a lack of maintenance. You should beware.

9-13: Indicates a lack of proper care, however, these can usually be corrected with a tune-up or relatively simple parts replacement.

14-17: Problems in the engine or transmission can be very expensive. Walk away from any car with problems in both of these areas.

7. If you are satisfied with the apparent condition of the car, take it to an independent diagnostic center or mechanic for a complete check. If you have a state inspection program, have it inspected immediately before purchase, or specify on the bill of sale that the sale is conditional on passing state inspection.
8. Road test the car—refer to the "Road Test Checklist" in this section. If your original evaluation and the road test agree—the rest is up to you.

USED CAR CHECKLIST

NOTE: *The numbers on the illustrations refer to the numbers on this checklist.*

1. *Mileage:* Average mileage is about 12,000 miles per year. More than average mileage may indicate hard usage. 1975 and later catalytic converter equipped models may need converter service at 50,000 miles.
2. *Paint:* Check around the tailpipe, molding and windows for overspray indicating that the car has been repainted.
3. *Rust:* Check fenders, doors, rocker panels, window moldings, wheelwells, floorboards, under floormats, and in the trunk for signs of rust. Any rust at all will be a problem. There is no way to check the spread of rust, except to replace the part or panel.
4. *Body appearance:* Check the moldings, bumpers, grille, vinyl roof, glass, doors, trunk lid and body panels for general overall condition. Check for misalignment, loose holdown clips, ripples, scratches in glass, rips or patches in the top. Mismatched paint, welding in the trunk, severe misalignment of body panels or ripples may indicate crash work.
5. *Leaks:* Get down and look under the car. There are no normal "leaks", other than water from the air conditioning condenser.
6. *Tires;* Check the tire air pressure. A common trick is to pump the tire pressure up

GENERAL INFORMATION AND MAINTENANCE

to make the car roll easier. Check the tread wear, open the trunk and check the spare too. Uneven wear is a clue that the front end needs alignment. See the troubleshooting chapter for clues to the causes of tire wear.

7. *Shock absorbers:* Check the shock absorbers by forcing downward sharply on each corner of the car. Good shocks will not allow the car to bounce more than twice after you let go.

8. *Interior:* Check the entire interior. You're looking for an interior condition that agrees with the overall condition of the car. Reasonable wear is expected, but be suspicious of new seatcovers on sagging seats, new pedal pads, and worn armrests. These indicate an attempt to cover up hard use. Pull back the carpets and look for evidence of water leaks or flooding. Look for missing hardware, door handles, control knobs etc. Check lights and signal operations. Make sure all accessories (air conditioner, heater, radio etc.) work. Check windshield wiper operation.

9. *Belts and Hoses:* Open the hood and check all belts and hoses for wear, cracks or weak spots.

10. *Battery:* Low electrolyte level, corroded terminals and/or cracked case indicate a lack of maintenance.

11. *Radiator:* Look for corrosion or rust in the coolant indicating a lack of maintenance.

12. *Air filter:* A dirty air filter usually means a lack of maintenance.

13. *Ignition Wires:* Check the ignition wires for cracks, burned spots, or wear. Worn wires will have to be replaced.

14. *Oil level:* If the oil level is low, chances are the engine uses oil or leaks. Beware of water in the oil (cracked block), excessively thick oil (used to quiet a noisy engine), or thin, dirty oil with a distinct gasoline smell (internal engine problems).

15. *Automatic Transmission:* Pull the transmission dipstick out when the engine is running. The level should read "Full", and the fluid should be clear or bright red. Dark brown or black fluid that has distinct burnt odor, signals a transmission in need of repair or overhaul.

16. *Exhaust:* Check the color of the exhaust smoke. Blue smoke indicates, among other problems, worn rings; black smoke can indicate burnt valves or carburetor problems. Check the exhaust system for leaks; it can be expensive to replace.

17. *Spark Plugs:* Remove one of the spark plugs (the most accessible will do). An engine in good condition will show plugs with a light tan or gray deposit on the firing tip. See the color Tune-Up tips section for spark plug conditions.

ROAD TEST CHECK LIST

1. *Engine Performance:* The car should be peppy whether cold or warm, with adequate power and good pickup. It should respond smoothly through the gears.

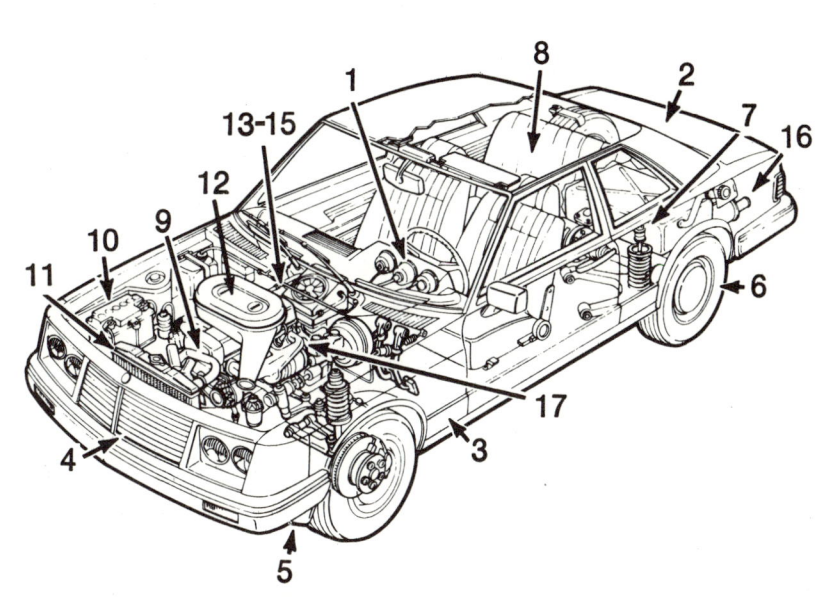

You should check these points when buying a used car. The "Used Car Checklist" gives an explanation of the numbered items

2. *Brakes:* They should provide quick, firm stops with no noise, pulling or brake fade.

3. *Steering:* Sure control with no binding, harshness, or looseness and no shimmy in the wheel should be expected. Noise or vibration from the steering wheel when turning the car means trouble.

4. *Clutch (Manual Transmission):* Clutch action should give quick, smooth response with easy shifting. The clutch pedal should have about 1–1½ inches of free-play before it disengages the clutch. Start the engine, set the parking brake, put the transmission in first gear and slowly release the clutch pedal. The engine should begin to stall when the pedal is one-half to three-quarters of the way up.

5. *Automatic Transmission:* The transmission should shift rapidly and smoothly, with no noise, hesitation, or slipping.

6. *Differential:* No noise or thumps should be present. Differentials have no "normal" leaks.

7. *Driveshaft, Universal Joints:* Vibration and noise could mean driveshaft problems. Clicking at low speed or coast conditions means worn U-joints.

8. *Suspension:* Try hitting bumps at different speeds. A car that bounces has weak shock absorbers. Clunks mean worn bushings or ball joints.

9. *Frame:* Wet the tires and drive in a straight line. Tracks should show two straight lines, not four. Four tire tracks indicate a frame bent by collision damage. If the tires can't be wet for this purpose, have a friend drive along behind you and see if the car appears to be traveling in a straight line.

Tune-Up

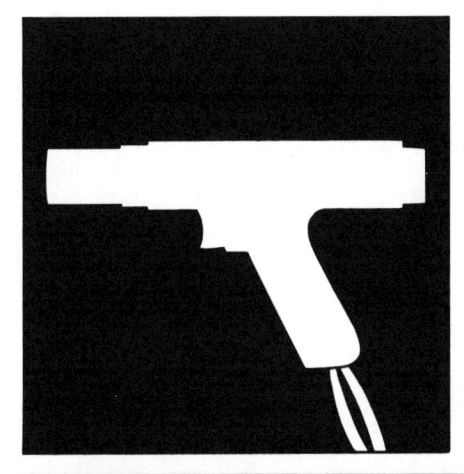

TUNE-UP PROCEDURES

Spark Plugs

Spark plugs ignite the air and fuel mixture in the cylinder as the piston reaches the top of the compression stroke. The controlled explosion that results forces the piston down, turning the crankshaft and the rest of the drive train.

Ford recommends that spark plugs be changed every 30,000 miles (60,000 Calif.). Under severe driving conditions, those intervals should be halved. Severe driving conditions are:

1. Extended periods of idling or low speed operation, such as off-road or door-to-door delivery.
2. Driving short distances (less than 10 miles) when the average temperature is below 10°F for 60 days or more.
3. Excessive dust or blowing dirt conditions.

When you remove the spark plugs, check their condition. They are a good indicator of the condition of the engine. It is a good idea to remove the spark plugs at regular intervals, such as every 6,000 or so miles, just so you can keep an eye on the mechanical state of the engine.

A small deposit of light tan or gray material on a spark plug that has been used for any period of time is considered normal. Any other color, or abnormal amounts of deposit, indicate that there is something amiss in the engine.

The gap between the center electrode and the side or ground electrode can be expected to increase not more than 0.001 in. every 1,000 miles under normal conditions. When, and if, a plug fouls and begins to misfire, you will have to investigate, correct the cause of the fouling and either clean or replace the plug.

There are several reasons why a spark plug will foul and you can learn which reason is at fault by just looking at the plug. A few of the most common reasons for plug fouling and a description of fouled plug appearance are shown in the "Four-Color" section.

SPARK PLUG HEAT RANGE

Spark plug heat range is the ability of the plug to dissipate heat. The longer the insulator (or the farther it extends into the engine), the hotter the plug will operate; the shorter the insulator the cooler it will operate. A plug that absorbs little heat and remains too cool will quickly accumulate deposits of oil and carbon since it is not hot enough to burn them off. This leads to plug fouling and consequently to misfiring. A plug that absorbs too much

TUNE-UP

Tune-Up Specifications by Calibration Level [1]

Calibration Number	Engine	Spark Plug Gap	Ignition Timing (°BTDC)	Timing (RPM)	Fast Idle RPM Kick Down	Curb Idle RPM A/C On	Curb Idle RPM A/C Off	Curb Idle RPM Non A/C	Dashpot Clearance (mm)	VOTM Off (RPM)	VOTM On (RPM)
1-3A-R1	1.6L	.042–.046	10 N	800 N	2400 N / 2200 [1] N	—	900 N / 750 [1] N	900 N / 750 [1] N	3.25–3.75	—	—
1-3C-R1	1.6L	.042–.046	10 N	800 N	2400 N / 2200 [1] N	1700 N	900 N / 750 [1] N	—	3.25–3.75	—	—
1-3D-R10	1.6L	.042–.046	10 N	800 N	2200 N	—	—	—	3.75–4.25	700 N	1150 N
1-3N-R0	1.6L	.042–.046	6 N	800 N	2400 N / 2200 [1] N	1700 N	900 N / 750 [1] N	900 N / 750 [1] N	3.25–3.75	—	—
1-3W-R0	1.6L	.042–.046	10 N	800 N	2400 N / 2200 [1] N	—	900 N / 750 [1] N	900 N / 750 [1] N	3.25–3.75	—	—
1-3X-R0	1.6L	.042–.046	10 N	800 N	2400 N / 2200 [1] N	1700 N	900 N / 750 [1] N	—	3.25–3.75	—	—
1-4A-R0	1.6L	.042–.046	10 N	800 N	2400 N	—	—	—	3.75–4.25	750 D	1300 N
1-4A-R11	1.6L	.042–.046	10 N	800 N	2400 N	—	—	—	3.75–4.25	750 D	1300 N

TUNE-UP

1-4A-R12	1.6L	.042–.046	10 N	800 N	2400 N	—	—	3.75–4.25	750 D	1300 N
1-4C-R0	1.6L	.042–.046	10 N	800 N	2400 N	1850 N	750 D	3.75–4.25	—	—
1-4C-R10	1.6L	.042–.046	10 N	800 N	2400 N	1850 N	750 D	3.75–4.25	—	—
1-4C-R12	1.6L	.042–.046	12 N	800 N	2400 N	1850 N	800 D	3.75–4.25	800 D	1300 N
1-4C-R13	1.6L	.042–.046	10 N	800 N	2400 N	1700 N	750 D	3.75–4.25	750 D	1700 N
1-4Q-R1	1.6L	.042–.046	6 N	800 N	2400 N	1850 N	750 D	3.50–4.50	750 D	1300 N
1-4Q-R11	1.6L	.042–.046	6 N	800 N	2400 N	1700 N	750 D	3.50–4.50	750 D	1700 N
1-4W-R0	1.6L	.042–.046	10 N	800 N	2400 N	—	—	3.75–4.25	750 D	1300 N
1-4W-R10	1.6L	.042–.046	10 N	800 N	2400 N	—	—	3.75–4.25	750 D	1300 N
1-4X-R0	1.6L	.042–.046	10 N	800 N	2400 N	1850 N	750 D	3.75–4.25	—	—
1-4X-R10	1.6L	.042–.046	10 N	800 N	2400 N	1850 N	750 D	3.75–4.25	—	—
1-4X-R13	1.6L	.042–.046	10 N	800 N	2400 N	1700 N	750 D	3.75–4.25	750 D	1700 N

① The calibration number is identified by a decal located on the engine timing belt cover. The next to bottom line gives the level number. If your calibration number is note shown on this chart, refer to the emissions label on the engine for tune-up specifications.

36 TUNE-UP

heat will have no deposits, but, due to the excessive heat, the electrodes will burn away quickly and in some instances, preignition may result. Preignition takes place when plug tips get so hot that they glow sufficiently to ignite the fuel/air mixture before the actual spark occurs. This early ignition will usually cause a pinging during low speeds and heavy loads.

The general rule of thumb for choosing the correct heat range when picking a spark plug is: if most of your driving is long distance, high speed travel, use a cooler plug; if most of your driving is stop and go; use a hotter plug. Original equipment plugs are compromise plugs, but most people never have occasion to change their plugs from the factory-recommended heat range.

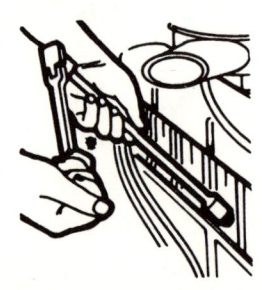

Remove the spark plugs with a ratchet and long extension

REPLACING SPARK PLUGS

CAUTION: *The cylinder head on your Escort/Lynx is made out of aluminum. Do not over tighten the spark plugs (correct torque is 17–22 ft. lbs.). Excessive tightening can result in stripped cylinder head threads.*

A set of spark plugs usually requires replacement every 30,000 miles, depending on your style of driving. In normal operation, plug gap increases about .001 in. for every 1,000–2,500 miles. As the gap increases, the plug's voltage requirement also increases. It requires greater voltage to jump the wider gap and about two to three times as much voltage to fire a plug at higher speeds than at idle.

The spark plugs used in your car require a ⅝ in. deep spark plug socket for removal and installation. A special designed pair of plug wire removal pliers is also a good tool to have. The special pliers have cupped jaws that grip the plug wire boot and make the job of twisting and pulling the wire from the plug easier.

The original spark plugs, in your car, have a captive, reusable gasket mounted on them.

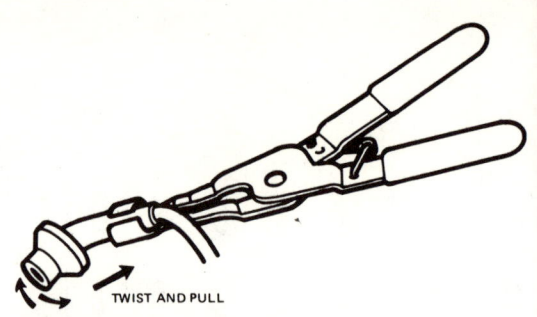

Special pliers used to remove the boots and wire from the spark plug

Replacement plugs will have a gasket supplied loose in the package. Thread the gasket onto the spark plug before installing in the engine.

REMOVAL

NOTE: *The original spark plug wires are marked for cylinder location. If replacement wires have been installed, be sure to tag them for proper location. It is a good idea to remove the wires one at a time, service the spark plug, reinstall the wire and move onto the next cylinder.*

NOTE: *For easy access for servicing the spark plugs, remove the air cleaner assembly and air intake tube.*

1. Twist the spark plug boot and gently pull it and the wire from the spark plug. This is where the special plug wire pliers come in handy.

CAUTION: *Never pull on the wire itself, damage to the inside conductor could occur.*

2. The plug wire boot has a cover which shields the plug cavity (in the head) against dirt. After removing the wire, blow out the cavity with air or clean it out with a small brush so dirt will not fall into the engine when the spark plug is removed.

3. Remove the spark plug with a ⅝ inch plug socket. Turn the socket counterclockwise to remove the plug. Be sure to hold the socket straight on the plug to avoid breaking the insulator (a deep socket designed for spark plugs has a rubber cushion built-in to help prevent plug breakage).

4. Once the plug is out, compare it with the spark plug illustrations to determine the engine condition. This is crucial since spark plug readings are vital signs of engine condition and pending problems.

5. If the old plugs are to be reused, clean and regap them. If new spark plugs are to be installed, always check the gap. Use a round

Check the spark plug gap with a wire feeler gauge

wire feeler gauge to check plug gap. The correct size gauge should pass through the electrode gap with a slight drag. If you're in doubt, try the next smaller and one size larger. The smaller gauge should go through easily and the larger should not go through at all. If adjustment is necessary use the bending tool on the end of the gauge. When adjusting the gap, always bend the side electrode. The center electrode is non-adjustable.

6. Squirt a drop of penetrating oil on the threads of the spark plug and install it. Don't oil the threads heavily. Turn the plug in clockwise by hand until it is snug.

7. When the plug is finger tight, tighten it to the proper torque 17–22 ft. lbs. DO NOT OVER-TIGHTEN. Note that under-tightening the plug will not allow the gasket to seat. This could cause the plug to loosen up and cause engine damage through overheating and preignition.

8. Install the plug wire and boot firmly over the spark plug after coating the inside of the boot and terminal with a thin coat of dielectric compound (Motorcraft D7AZ19A331A or the equivalent).

9. Proceed to the next spark plug.

CHECKING AND REPLACING SPARK PLUG CABLES

Your car is equipped with a Dura Spark II ignition system which utilizes 8mm wires to conduct the hotter spark produced. The boots on these wires are designed to cover the spark plug cavities on the cylinder head.

Inspect the wires without removing them from the spark plugs, distributor cap or coil. Look for visible damage such as cuts, pinches, cracks or torn boots. Replace any wires that show damage. If the boot is damaged, it may be replaced by itself. It is not necessary to replace the complete wire just for the boot.

To replace the wire, grasp and twist the boot back and forth while pulling away from the spark plug. Use the special pliers if available.

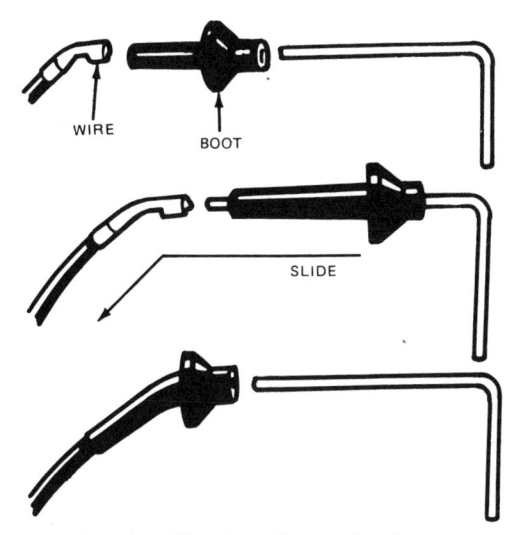

Use a bent "tool" to install new plug boots

NOTE: *Always coat the terminals of any wire removed or replaced with a thin layer of di-electric compound.*

When installing a wire be sure it is firmly mounted over or on the plug, distributor cap connector or coil terminal.

FIRING ORDER

If new wires have been installed (original wires are marked for cylinder location) and are not identified, or the wires have been removed from the distributor cap; the firing order is 1-3-4-2 counterclockwise around the distributor cap. Number 1 position is marked on the cap.

Ignition System

NOTE: *Some 1982 models are equipped with TFI ignition. The "Thick Film Integrated" (TFI) ignition module is contained in moulded thermo-plastic and is mounted on the distributor base. A new "E" core ignition coil is incorporated in the system. The TFI ignition system should be serviced by an authorized mechanic.*

Your Escort/Lynx uses a solid-state ignition system known as Dura Spark II. The purpose of using a solid state system are: To eliminate the deterioration of spark quality which occur in the breaker point ignition system as the breaker points wore. To extend maintenance intervals. To provide a more intense and reliable spark at every firing impulse in order to ignite the leaner gas mixtures necessary to control emissions.

The breaker points, point actuating cam

38 TUNE-UP

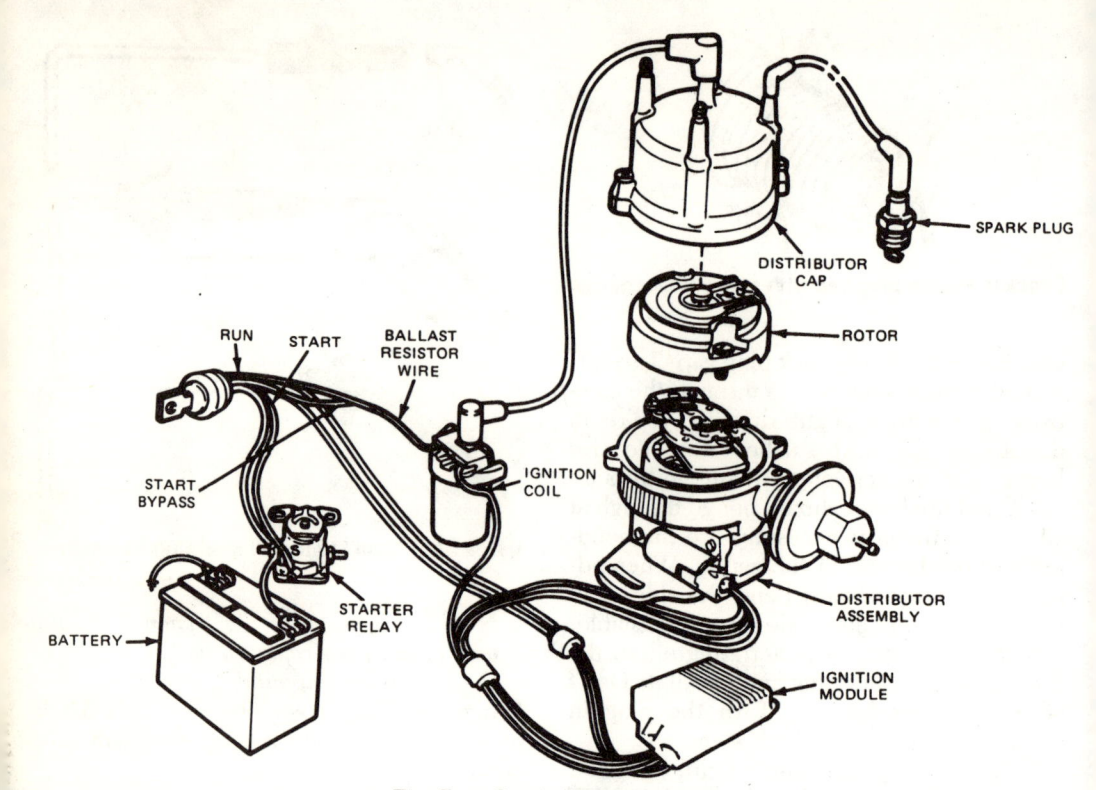

The Dura Spark ignition system

and the condenser have been eliminated in the solid state distributor. They are replaced by an ignition module and a magnetic pulse-signal generator (pick-up).

The Dura Spark II is a pulse-triggered, transistor controlled breakerless ignition system. With the ignition switch "on," the primary circuit is on and the ignition coil is en-

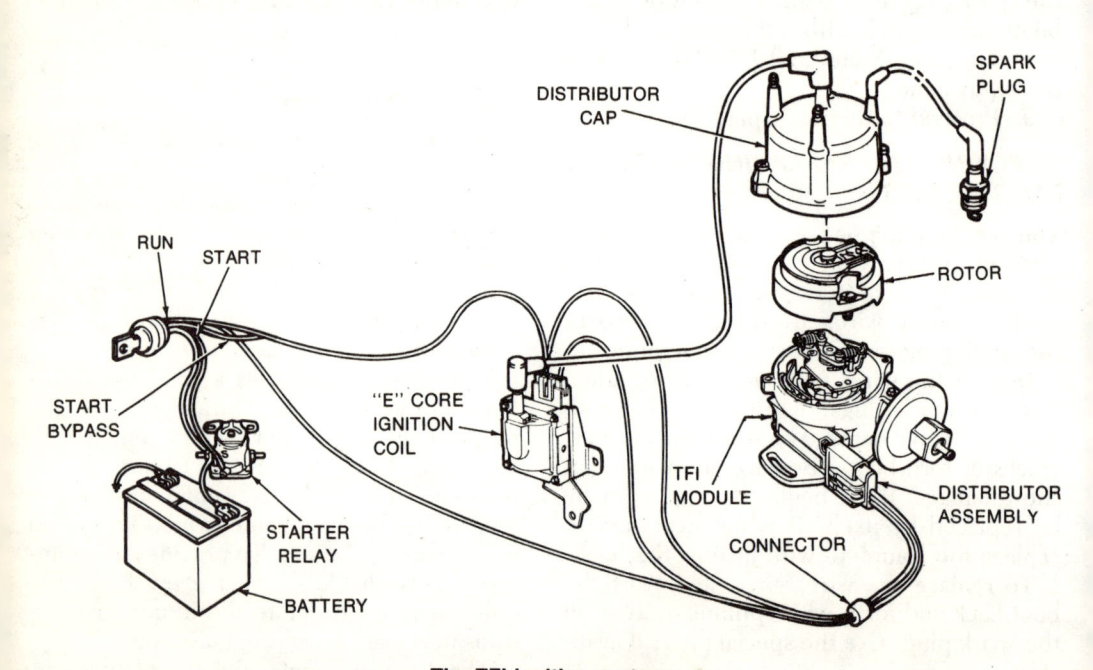

The TFI ignition system

energized. When the armature spokes approach the magnetic pick-up coil assembly, they induce a voltage which tells the amplifier to turn the coil primary current off. A timing circuit in the amplifier module will turn the current on again after the coil field has collapsed. When the current is on, it flows from the battery through the ignition switch, the primary windings of the ignition coil, and through the amplifier module circuits to ground. When the current is off, the magnetic field built up in the ignition coil is allowed to collapse, inducing a high voltage into the secondary windings of the coil. High voltage is produced each time the field is thus built up and collapsed.

Dwell Angle

Dwell is controlled by the solid state ignition system and no adjustment is necessary.

Ignition Timing

Ignition timing is the measurement, in degrees of crankshaft rotation, of the point at which the spark plugs fire in each of the cylinders. It is measured in degrees before or after Top Dead Center (TDC) of the compression stroke. Ignition timing is controlled by turning the distributor body in the engine.

Ideally, the air/fuel mixture in the cylinder will be ignited by the spark plug just as the piston passes TDC of the compression stroke. If this happens, the piston will be beginning the power stroke just as the compressed and ignited air/fuel mixture starts to expand. The expansion of the air/fuel mixture then forces the piston down on the power stroke and turns the crankshaft.

Because it takes a fraction of a second for the spark plug to ignite the mixture in the cylinder, the spark plug must fire a little before the piston reaches TDC. Otherwise, the mixture will not be completely ignited as the piston passes TDC and the full power of the explosion will not be used by the engine.

The timing measurement is given in degrees of crankshaft rotation before the piston reaches TDC (BTDC). If the setting for the ignition timing is 5° BTDC, the spark plug must fire 5° before each piston reaches TDC. This only holds true, however, when the engine is at idle speed.

As the engine speed increases, the pistons go faster. The spark plugs have to ignite the fuel even sooner if it is to be completely ignited when the piston reaches TDC. To do this, the distributor has a means to advance the timing of the spark as the engine speed increases. This is accomplished by centrifugal weights within the distributor and a vacuum diaphragm mounted on the side of the distributor. It is necessary to disconnect the vacuum line from the diaphragm when the ignition timing is being set.

If the ignition is set too far advanced (BTDC), the ignition and expansion of the fuel in the cylinder will occur too soon and tend to force the piston down while it is still traveling up. This causes engine ping. If the ignition spark is set too far retarded after TDC (ATDC), the piston will have already passed TDC and started on its way down when the fuel is ignited. This will cause the piston to be forced down for only a portion of its travel. This will result in poor engine performance and lack of power.

The timing is best checked with a timing light. This device is connected in series with the No. 1 spark plug. The current that fires the spark plug also causes the timing light to flash.

There is a notch on the crankshaft pulley. A scale of degrees of crankshaft rotation is attached to the engine timing belt cover in such a position that the notch will pass close by the scale.

IGNITION TIMING ADJUSTMENT

1. Refer to the decal mounted on the rocker arm cover. The decal shows the degree value of each mark. Locate the timing marks on the crankshaft pulley and the front of the engine.

2. Clean off the timing marks on the front cover.

3. Mark the timing marks with a piece of chalk or with paint. Color the mark on the scale that will indicate the correct timing when it is aligned with the mark on the pulley or the pointer. It is also helpful to mark the notch in the pulley or the tip of the pointer with a small dab of color.

4. Attach a tachometer to the engine. See tachometer hook-up section.

5. Attach a timing light according to the manufacturer's instructions.

6. Disconnect the distributor vacuum line(s) at the distributor and plug the vacuum line(s). A small bolt, center punch or similar object is satisfactory for a plug.

CAUTION: *While the engine is running the*

TUNE-UP

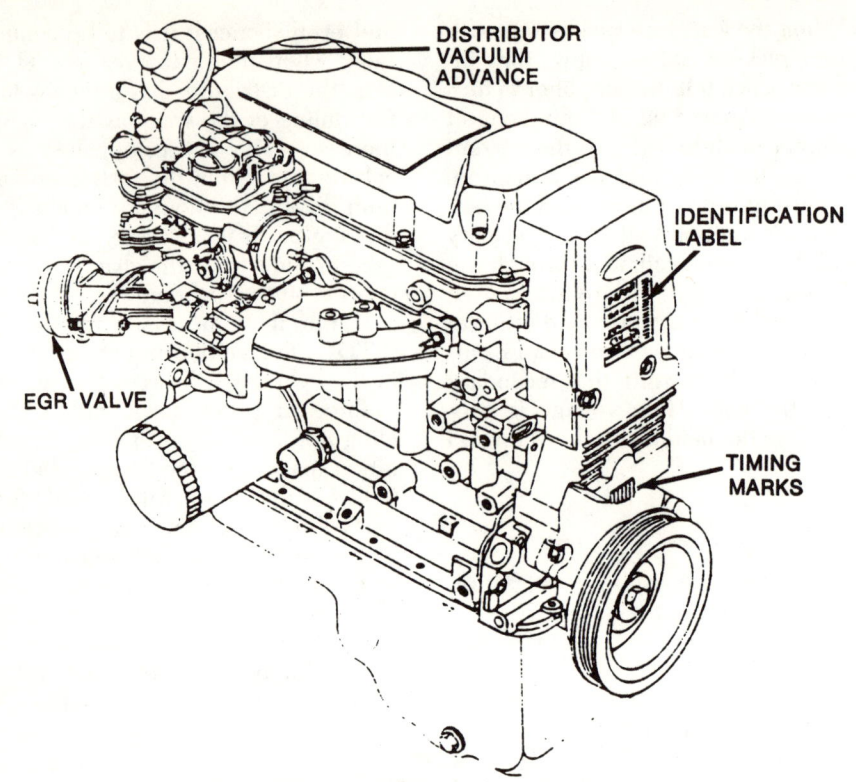

Timing marks are located on the "front" cover

electric cooling fan may operate. Be careful not to get the timing light wires or your fingers caught in the fan. Also note that the fan will operate after the engine has been shut off.

7. Check to make sure that all of the wires are clear of various pulleys and the electric fan; then start the engine.

8. Adjust the idle to the correct setting. (See idle adjustment section that follows).

9. Aim the timing light at the timing marks. If the marks that you put on the pulley and the engine are aligned when the light flashes, the timing is correct. Turn off the engine and remove the tachometer and the timing light. If the marks are not in alignment, proceed with the following steps.

10. Loosen the distributor lockbolts just enough so that the distributor can be turned with a little effort.

11. With the timing light aimed at the pulley and the marks on the engine, turn the distributor in the direction of rotor rotation to retard the spark, and in the opposite direction of rotor rotation to advance the spark. Align the marks on the pulley and the engine with the flashes of the timing light.

12. When the marks are aligned, tighten the distributor lockbolts and recheck the timing with the timing light to make sure that the distributor did not move when you tightened the lockbolt.

13. Turn off the engine and remove the timing light. Reconnect the vacuum hose(s).

Distributor Cap and Rotor

1. The distributor cap is held on by two cap screws. Release them with a screwdriver and lift the cap straight up and off, with the wires attached. Inspect the cap for cracks, carbon tracks, or a worn center contact. Replace it if necessary, transferring the wires one at a time from the old cap to the new.

2. Remove the screw retaining the ignition rotor and remove the rotor. Replace it if its contacts are worn, burned, or pitted. Do not file the contact.

NOTE: *Always coat the cap and rotor contacts with dielectric compound.*

Dura Spark II Troubleshooting

The following procedures can be used to determine whether the ignition system is working or not. If these procedures fail to correct the problem, a full troubleshooting proce-

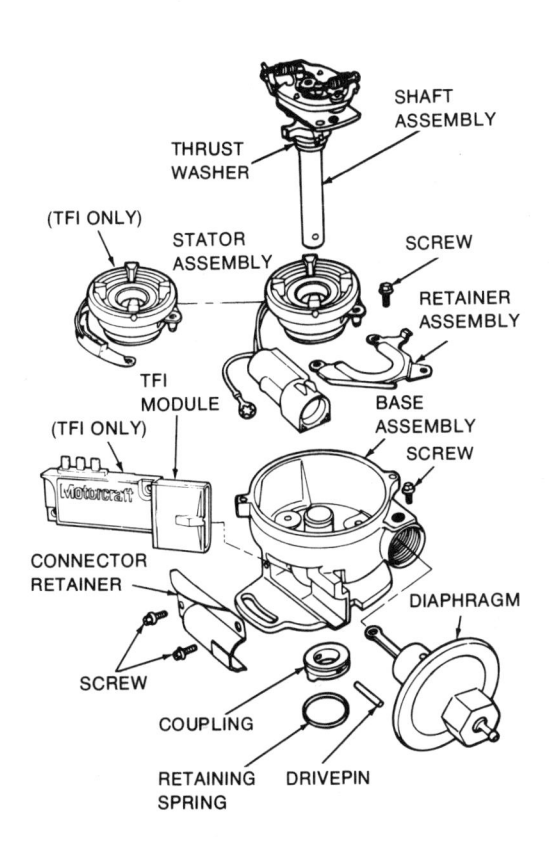

TUNE-UP

Semi-exploded view of the distributor

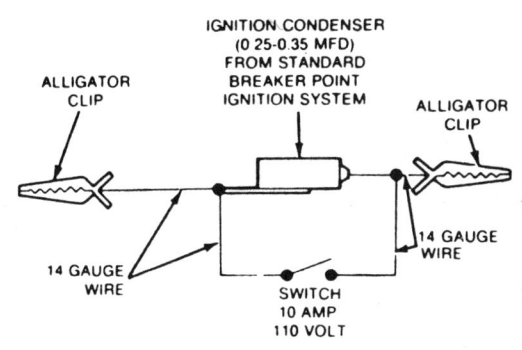

Test jumper switch used for troubleshooting the Ford electronic ignition system

dure should be performed by a qualified service department.

PRELIMINARY CHECKS

1. Check the battery's state of charge and connections.
2. Inspect all wires and connections for breaks, cuts, abrasions, or burn spots. Repair as necessary.
3. Unplug all connectors one at a time and inspect for corroded or burned contacts. Repair and plug connectors back together. DO NOT remove the di-electric compound in the connectors.
4. Check for loose or damaged spark plug or coil wires. Check for excessive resistance. If the boots or nipples are removed on 8mm ignition wires, reline the inside of each with silicone di-electric compound (Motorcraft WA 10).

Special Tools

To perform the following tests, two special tools are needed; the ignition test jumper shown in the illustration and a modified spark plug. Use the illustration to assemble the ignition test jumper. The test jumper must be used when performing the following tests. The modified spark plug is basically a spark plug with the side electrode removed. Ford makes a special tool called a Spark Tester for this purpose, which besides not having a side electrode is equipped with a spring clip so that it can be grounded to engine metal. It is recommended that the Spark Tester be used as there is less chance of being shocked.

Run Mode Spark Test

NOTE: *The wire colors given here are the main color of the wires, not the dots or stripe marks.*

STEP 1

1. Remove the distributor cap and rotor from the distributor.
2. With the ignition off, turn the engine over by hand until one of the teeth on the distributor armature aligns with the magnet in the pick-up coil.
3. Remove the coil wire from the distributor cap. Install the modified spark plug (see Special Tools) in the coil wire terminal and using insulated pliers, hold the spark plug base against the engine block.
4. Turn the ignition to RUN (not START) and tap the distributor body with a screwdriver handle. There should be a spark at the modified spark plug or at the coil wire terminal.
5. If a good spark is evident, the primary circuit is OK; perform Start Mode Spark Test. If there is no spark, proceed to Step 2.

STEP 2

1. Unplug the module connector(s) which contain(s) the green and black module leads.
2. In the harness side of the connector(s), connect the special test jumper (see special

42 TUNE-UP

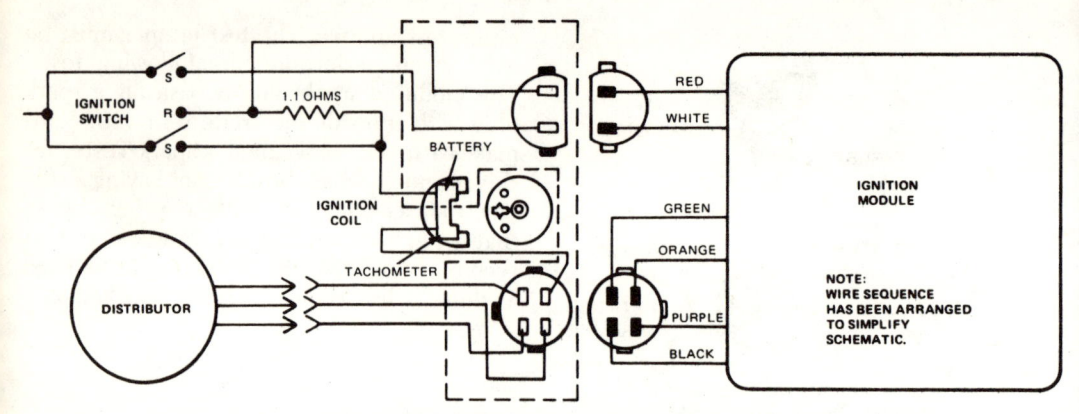

Module and distributor harness color codes

tools) between the leads which connect to the green and black leads of the module pig tails. Use paper clips on connector socket holes to make contact. Do not allow clips to ground.

3. Turn the ignition switch to RUN (not START) and close the test jumper switch. Leave closed for about one second, then open. Repeat several times. There should be a spark each time the switch is opened.

4. If there is NO spark, the problem is probably in the primary circuit through the ignition switch, the coil, the green lead or the black lead, or the ground connection in the distributor. Perform Step 3. If there IS a spark, the primary circuit wiring and coil are probably OK. The problem is probably in the distributor pick-up, the module red wire, or the module. Perform Step 6.

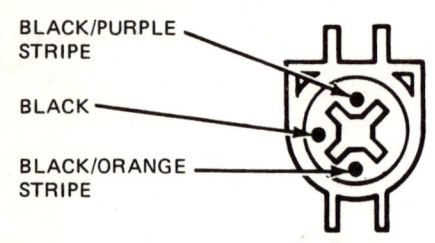

Distributor connector showing the color codes

STEP 3

1. Disconnect the test jumper lead from the black lead and connect it to a good ground. Turn the test jumper switch on and off several times as in Step 2.

2. If there is NO spark, the problem is probably in the green lead, the coil, or the coil feed circuit. Perform Step 5.

3. If there IS spark, the problem is probably in the black lead or the distributor ground connection. Perform Step 4.

STEP 4

1. Connect an ohmmeter between the black lead and ground. With the meter on its lowest scale, there should be NO measurable resistance in the circuit. If there is resistance, check the distributor ground connection and the black lead from the module. Repair as necessary, remove the ohmmeter, plug in all connections and repeat Step 1.

If there is NO resistance, the primary ground wiring is OK. Perform Step 6.

STEP 5

1. Disconnect the test jumper from the green lead and ground and connect it between the TACH-TEST terminal of the coil and a good ground on the engine.

2. With the ignition switch in the RUN position, turn the jumper switch on. Hold it on for about one second then turn it off as in Step 2. Repeat several times. There should be a spark each time the switch is turned off. If there is NO spark, the problem is probably in the primary circuit running through the ignition switch to the coil BAT terminal, or in the coil itself. Check coil resistance (test given later in this section), and check the coil for internal shorts or opens. Check the coil feed circuit for opens, shorts or high resistance. Repair as necessary, reconnect all connectors and repeat Step 1. If there IS spark, the coil and its feed circuit are OK. The problem could be in the green lead between the coil and the module. Check for open or short, repair as necessary, reconnect all connectors and repeat Step 1.

STEP 6

To perform this step, a voltmeter which is not combined with a dwellmeter is needed. The slight needle oscillations (½ V) you'll be looking for may not be detectable on the combined voltmeter/dwellmeter unit.

1. Connect a voltmeter between the orange and purple leads on the harness side of the module connectors.

CAUTION: *On catalytic converter equipped cars, disconnect the air supply line between the Thermactor by-pass valve and the manifold before cranking the engine with the ignition off. This will prevent damage to the catalytic converter. After testing, run the engine for at least 3 minutes before reconnecting the by-pass valve, to clear excess fuel from the exhaust system.*

2. Set the voltmeter on its lowest scale and crank the engine. The meter needle should oscillate slightly (about ½ volt). If the meter does not oscillate, check the circuit through the magnetic pick-up in the distributor for open, shorts, shorts to ground and resistance. Resistance between the orange and purple leads should be 400–1000 ohms, and between each lead and ground should be more than 70,000 ohms. Repair as necessary, reconnect all connectors and repeat Step 1.

If the meter oscillates, the problem is probably in the power feed to the module (red wire) or in the module itself. Proceed to Step 7.

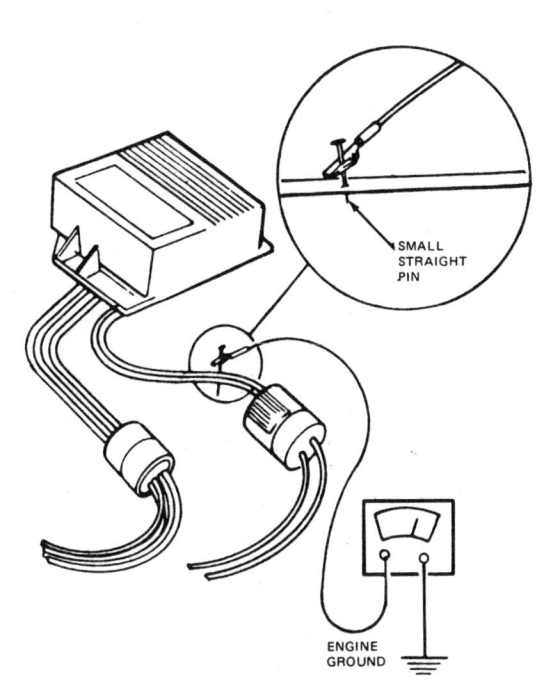

Inserting straight pin to test a circuit

STEP 7

1. Remove all meters and jumpers and plug in all connectors.
2. Turn the ignition switch to the RUN position and measure voltage between the battery positive terminal and engine ground. It should be 12 volts.
3. Next, measure voltage between the red lead of the module and engine ground. To make this measurement, it will be necessary to pierce the red wire with a straight pin and connect the voltmeter to the straight pin and to ground. DO NOT ALLOW THE STRAIGHT PIN TO GROUND ITSELF.
4. The two readings should be within one volt of each other. If not within one volt, the problem is in the power feed to the red lead. Check for shorts, open, or high resistance and correct as necessary. After repairs, repeat Step 1.

If the readings are within one volt, the problem is probably in the module. Replace with a good module and repeat Step 1. If this corrects the problem, reconnect the old module and repeat Step 1. If the problem returns, replace the module.

Start Mode Spark Test

NOTE: *The wire colors given here are the main color of the wires, not the dots or stripe marks.*

1. Remove the coil wire from the distributor cap. Install the modified spark plug mentioned under "Special Tools", above, in the coil wire and ground it to engine metal either by its spring clip (Spark Tester) or by holding the spark plug shell against the engine block with insulated pliers.

CAUTION: *See "CAUTION" under Step 6 of "Run Mode Spark Test".*

2. Have an assistant crank the engine using the ignition switch and check for spark. If there IS good spark, the problem is most probably in the distributor cap, rotor, ignition cables or spark plugs. If there is NO spark, proceed to Step 3.
3. Measure the battery voltage. Next, measure the voltage at the white wire of the module while cranking the engine. To make this measurement, it will be necessary to pierce the white wire with a straight pin and connect the voltmeter to the straight pin and to ground. DO NOT ALLOW THE STRAIGHT PIN TO GROUND ITSELF. The battery voltage and the voltage at the white wire should be within one volt of each other. If the readings are not within one volt of each

TUNE-UP

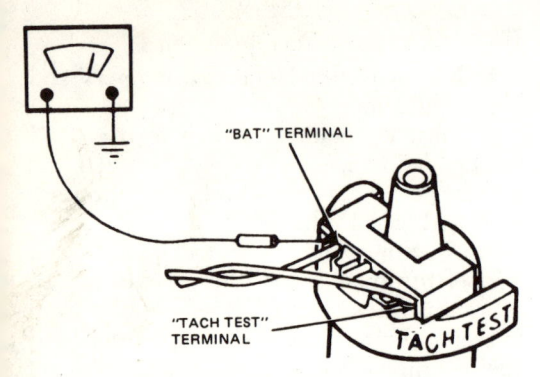

Hook up to test on coil "Bat" terminal

other, check and repair the feed through the ignition switch to the white wire. Recheck for spark (Step 1). If the readings are within one volt of each other, or if there is still NO spark after power feed to white wire is repaired, proceed to Step 4.

4. Measure the coil "BAT" terminal voltage while cranking the engine. The reading should be within one volt of battery voltage. If the readings are not within one volt of each other, check and repair the feed through the ignition switch to the coil. If the readings are within one volt of each other, the problem is probably in the ignition module. Substitute another module and repeat test for spark (Step 1).

Using an Engine Tachometer

There are several inexpensive engine tachometers on the market that will do the job nicely for you. Just be sure the "tach" that you buy has a 4 cylinder scale on it.

TACHOMETER-TO-COIL CONNECTION—ELECTRONIC IGNITION

The new solid state ignition coil connector allows a tachometer test lead with an alligator-type clip to be connected to the DEC (Distributor Electronic Control) terminal without removing the connector.

When engine rpm must be checked, install the tachometer alligator clip into the "TACH TEST" cavity as shown. If the coil connector must be removed, grasp the wires and pull horizontally until it disconnects from the terminals.

Ignition Coil
PRIMARY RESISTANCE CHECK

To check the coil primary resistance, refer to Chapter 10; test 3.6. The procedure for breaker point ignition systems and electronic ignition systems is the same except that the resistance of the electronic ignition should be between 1.13 and 1.23 ohms. Before performing this check on the electronic ignition you must also remove the horseshoe shaped coil connector on the top surface of the coil.

SECONDARY RESISTANCE CHECK

To check the coil secondary resistance, refer to Chapter 11; test 4.4. The procedure for breaker point ignition systems and electronic ignition systems is the same except that the resistance of the electronic ignition should be between 7,700 and 9,300 ohms. Before performing this check on the electronic ignition you must also remove the horseshoe shaped coil connector on the top surface of the coil.

BALLAST RESISTOR

The ballast resistor wire is usually red with light green stripes. To check it you must disconnect it at the coil "BAT" connection and at the connector at the end of the wiring harness. The connector at the end of the wiring harness is a rectangular connector with eight terminals. Connect an ohmmeter to each end of the wire and set it to the "High" scale. The resistance of the wire should be between 1.05 and 1.15 ohms. Any other reading merits replacement of the resistor wire with one of the correct service resistor wires.

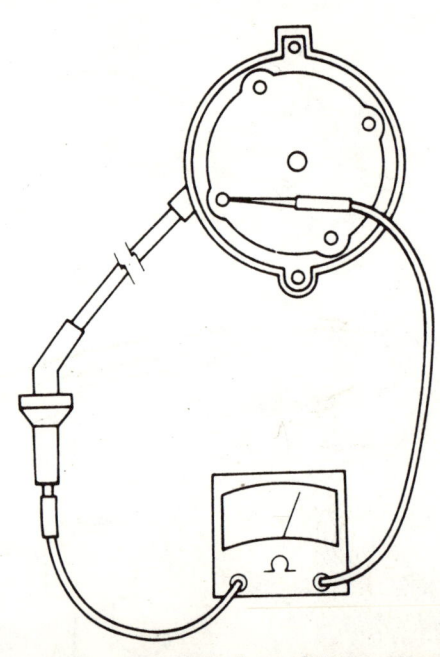

To check the spark plug wire resistance, measure from the cap terminal to the plug end of the wire with an ohmmeter. Resistance should be less than 5000 ohms per inch of plug wire length

TUNE-UP

Valve Lash

Valve adjustment determines how far the valves enter the cylinder and how long they stay open and closed.

If the valve clearance is too large, part of the lift of the camshaft will be used in removing the excessive clearance. Consequently, the valve will not be opening as far as it should. This condition has two effects: the valve train components will emit a tapping sound as they take up the excessive clearance and the engine will perform poorly because the valves don't open fully and allow the proper amount of gases to flow into and out of the engine.

If the valve clearance is too small, the intake valve and the exhaust valves will open too far and they will not fully seat on the cylinder head when they close. When a valve seats itself on the cylinder head, it does two things: it seals the combustion chamber so that none of the gases in the cylinder escape and it cools itself by transferring some of the heat it absorbs from the combustion in the cylinder to the cylinder head and to the engine's cooling system. If the valve clearance is too small, the engine will run poorly because of the gases escaping from the combustion chamber. The valves will also become overheated and will warp, since they cannot transfer heat unless they are touching the valve seat in the cylinder head.

VALVE LASH ADJUSTMENT

The intake and exhaust valves are driven by the camshaft, working through hydraulic lash adjusters and stamped steel rocker arms. The lash adjusters eliminate the need for periodic valve lash adjustments.

Idle Speed Adjustments

Most carburetor adjustments are factory set and are designed to reduce engine emissions. The following adjustments should be made only if absolutely necessary and should be checked on a machine as soon as possible to see if the emission level is OK.

NOTE: *A tachometer must be used while making any idle rpm adjustments. Refer to the proceeding section for "tach" hook up instructions.*

CURB IDLE RPM

NOTE: *Refer to emissions decal for idle speed.*

1. Place the transmission in Neutral (manual) or Park (automatic) and apply the parking brake.
2. Start the engine and allow it to reach normal operating temperature.
3. Locate the vacuum source to the air bypass section of the air supply control valve. If the vacuum hose is connected to the carburetor, disconnect the hose, plug the hose at the air supply control valve. Install a piece of vacuum hose (slave hose) between the intake manifold and the air bypass connection on the air supply valve.
4. Place the fast idle adjustment on the second step of the fast idle cam. Run the engine until the cooling fan comes on.
5. Slowly depress the throttle to allow the fast idle cam to swing. Place the transmission in the specified gear (automatic transaxle; refer to the underhood emissions decal) and check or adjust the curb idle rpm to specification.

NOTE: *The engine electric cooling fan must be running when checking or adjusting the curb idle.*

6. After adjusting the idle, place the transmission in Neutral or Park, rev the engine several times and recheck the curb idle speed. Readjust if necessary.
7. If the car is equipped with a dashpot, check and adjust clearance if necessary. See following section for details.
8. Remove the "slave hose" if installed. Reinstall the intake manifold air supply hose to its original position. Remove the plug from the carburetor vacuum hose and reconnect the hose to the air bypass valve.

NOTE: *If the car is equipped with an automatic transaxle and the curb idle is increased by 100 rpm or more or is decreased by any amount, refer to Chapter 6 for the proper adjustment of the transmission linkage.*

Dashpot Clearance Adjustment

NOTE: *If the carburetor is equipped with a dashpot, it must be adjusted if the curb idle speed is adjusted.*

1. With the engine OFF, push the dashpot plunger in as far as possible and check the clearance between the plunger and the throttle lever pad.

NOTE: *Refer to the emissions decal for proper dashpot clearance.*

2. Adjust the dashpot clearance by loosening the mounting locknut and rotating the dashpot.

CAUTION: *If the locknut is very tight, re-*

46 TUNE-UP

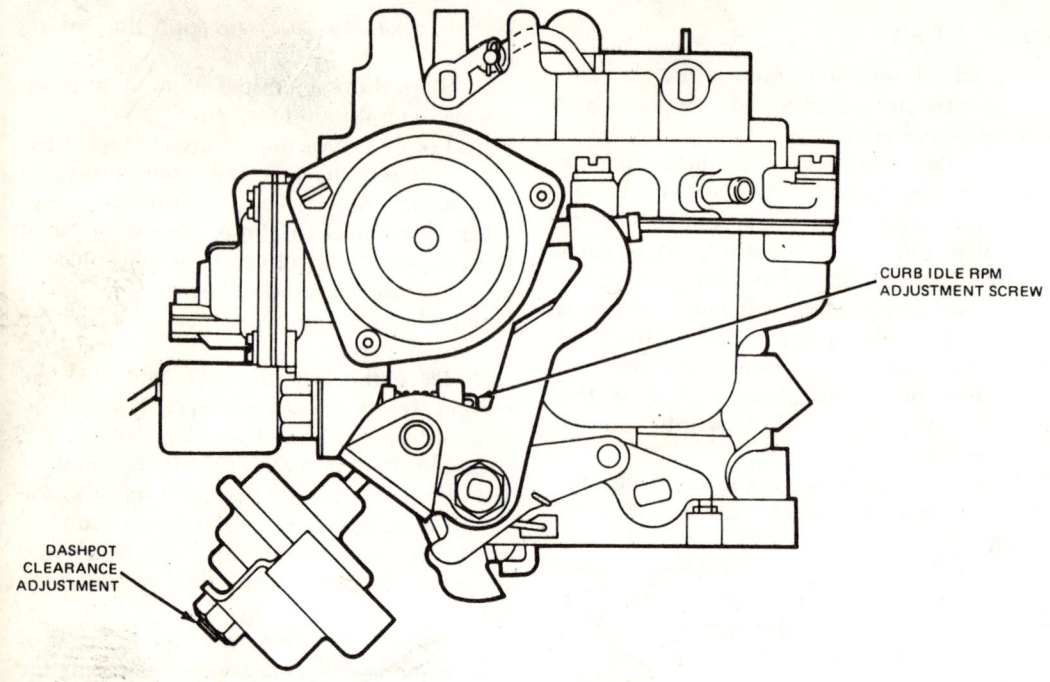

Location of curb idle adjusting screw

move the mounting bracket, hold it in a suitable device, so that it will not bend, and loosen the locknut. Reinstall bracket and dashpot.

3. After gaining the required clearance, tighten the locknut and recheck adjustment.

Fast Idle RPM

NOTE: *Refer to the emissions decal for the required fast idle speed.*

1. Place the transmission in Neutral (manual) or Park (automatic) and apply the parking brake.
2. Start the engine and allow it to reach normal operating temperature.
3. Disconnect and plug the vacuum lines to the EGR valve and purge valve.
4. Locate the vacuum source to the air bypass section of the air supply control valve. If the vacuum hose is connected to the carburetor, disconnect the hose, plug the hose at the air supply control valve. Install a piece of vacuum hose (slave hose) between the intake manifold and the air bypass connection on the air supply valve.
5. Place the fast idle adjustment screw on the second step of the fast idle cam. Run the engine until the electric cooling fan comes on.
6. Check the fast idle rpm and adjust to specifications if necessary. If adjustment is necessary, loosen the locknut on the adjusting screw, set to correct rpm and retighten the locknut.

NOTE: *The electric cooling fan must be operating while checking the fast idle rpm.*

Remove the plugs from the EGR and purge valve hoses and reconnect the hoses.

7. Remove the "slave hose" if installed. Reinstall the intake manifold air supply hose to its original position. Remove the plug from the carburetor vacuum hose and reconnect the hose to the air bypass valve.

Air Conditioning/Throttle Kicker Adjustment

1. Place the transmission in Neutral or Park.
2. Bring engine to normal operating temperature.
3. Identify vacuum source to air bypass section of air supply control valve. If vacuum hose is connected to carburetor, disconnect and plug hose at air supply control valve. Install slave vacuum hose between intake manifold and air bypass connection on air supply control valve.
4. To check/adjust A/C or throttle kicker rpm:
• If vehicle is equipped with A/C, place selector to maximum cooling, blower switch on High. Disconnect A/C compressor clutch wire.

TUNE-UP 47

**EMISSION CONTROL DECAL

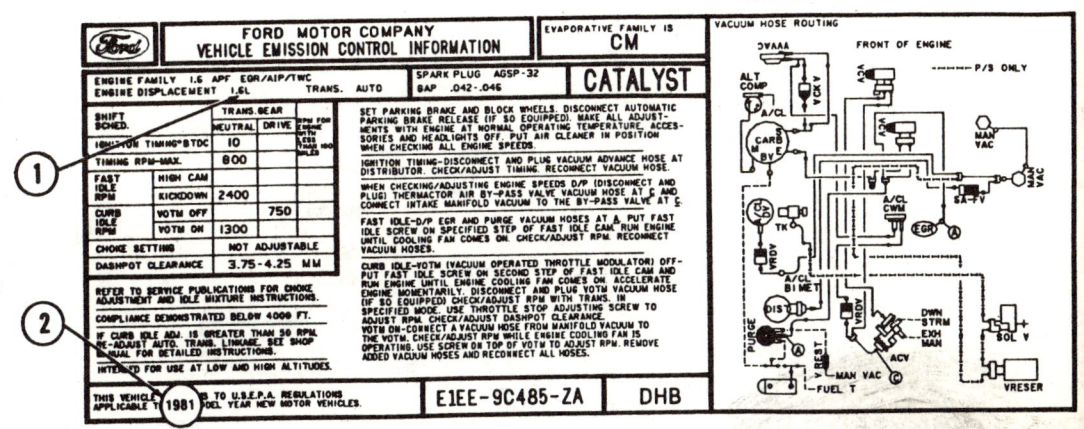

① DETERMINE ENGINE DISPLACEMENT FROM EMISSION CONTROL DECAL** — ENTER IN BLANK "A" OF EXAMPLE SHOWN BELOW.

② DETERMINE VEHICLE MODEL YEAR FROM EMISSION CONTROL DECAL** — ENTER LAST DIGIT IN BLANK "B". SEE NOTE BELOW.

③ DETERMINE CALIBRATION BASE NUMBER FROM ENGINE CODE LABEL* — ENTER NUMBERS & LETTERS IN BLANK "C".

④ DETERMINE REVISION LEVEL FROM ENGINE CODE LABEL* — ENTER IN BLANK "D"

*** ENGINE CODE LABEL 1.6L ENGINE ONLY

CODE LABEL ALL OTHER ENGINES

EXAMPLE: ENGINE: <u>3.3L (200 CID)</u> CALIBRATION <u>0</u> – <u>93J</u> – <u>R0</u>
                          (A)   (B)   (C)   (D)

*Located on engine valve cover (Yellow or White)
**Located on engine valve cover, radiator support bracket, underside of hood or fresh air inlet tube (Gold or Silver), or windshield washer bottle.
***Located on Timing Chain Cover

> NOTE: Some calibrations are carried over from prior model years. If you cannot locate calibration number using "1" prefix, check "0", "9", "8", "7" or "5" prefixes.

How to determine the calibration of your engine

48 TUNE-UP

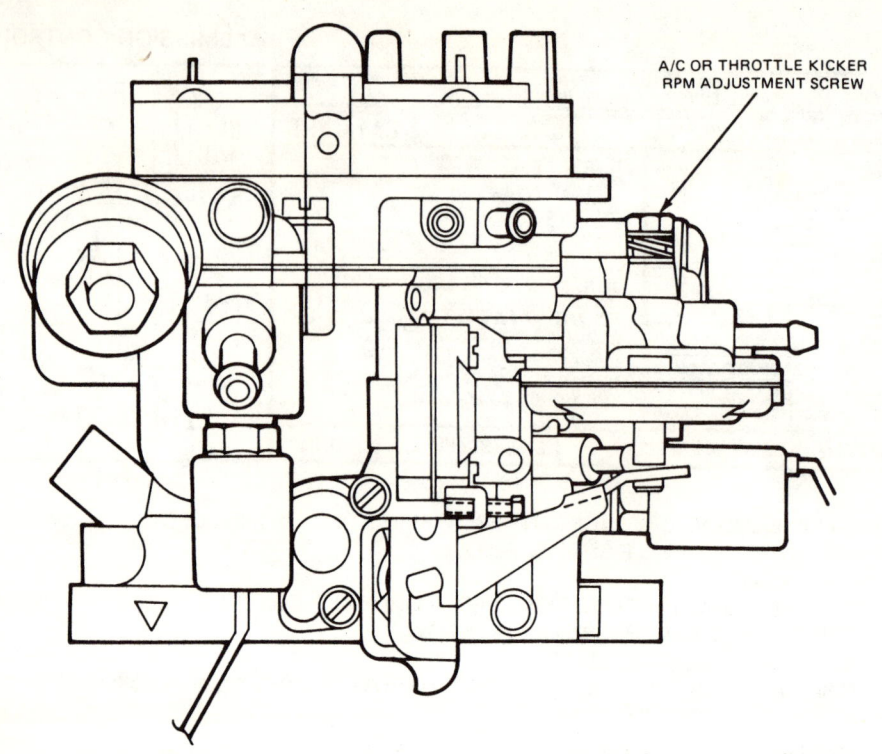

An adjustment is necessary, at times, if your car is equipped with air conditioning

- If vehicle is equipped with kicker and no A/C, disconnect vacuum hose from kicker and plug, install slave vacuum hose from intake manifold vacuum to kicker.

5. Run engine until engine cooling fan comes on.

6. Place transmission in specified gear and check/adjust A/C or throttle kicker rpm to specification.

NOTE: *Engine cooling fan must be running when checking A/C or throttle kicker rpm. Adjust rpm by turning screw on kicker.*

7. If slave vacuum hose was installed to check/adjust kicker rpm, remove slave vacuum hose. Remove plug from kicker vacuum hose and reconnect hose to kicker.

8. Remove slave vacuum hose. Return intake manifold supply source to original condition. Remove plug from carburetor vacuum hose and reconnect to air bypass valve.

Engine and Engine Rebuilding

ENGINE ELECTRICAL

Understanding the Engine Electrical System

The engine electrical system can be broken down into three separate and distinct systems: (1) the starting system, (2) the charging system, and (3) the ignition system.

BATTERY AND STARTING SYSTEM

Basic Operating Principles

The battery is the first link in the chain of mechanisms which work together to provide cranking of the automobile engine. In most modern cars, the battery is a lead-acid electrochemical device consisting of six two-volt (2 V) subsections connected in series so the unit is capable of producing approximately 12 V of electrical pressure. Each subsection, or cell, consists of a series of positive and negative plates held a short distance apart in a solution of sulfuric acid and water. The two types of plates are of dissimilar metals. This causes a chemical reaction to be set up, and it is this reaction which produces current flow from the battery when its positive and negative terminals are connected to an electrical appliance such as a lamp or motor. The continued transfer of electrons would eventually convert the sulfuric acid in the electrolyte to water, and make the two plates identical in chemical composition. As electrical energy is removed from the battery, its voltage output tends to drop. Thus, measuring battery voltage and battery electrolyte composition are two ways of checking the ability of the unit to supply power. During the starting of the engine, electrical energy is removed from the battery. However, if the charging circuit is in good condition and the operating conditions are normal, the power removed from the battery will be replaced by the generator (or alternator) which will force electrons back through the battery, reversing the normal flow, and restoring the battery to its original chemical state.

The battery and starting motor are linked by very heavy electrical cables designed to minimize resistance to the flow of current. Generally, the major power supply cable that leaves the battery goes directly to the starter, while other electrical system needs are supplied by a smaller cable. During starter operation, power flows from the battery to the starter and is grounded through the car's frame and the battery's negative ground strap.

The starting motor is a specially designed, direct current electric motor capable of producing a very great amount of power for its size. One thing that allows the motor to produce a great deal of power is its tremendous rotating speed. It drives the engine through a tiny pinion gear (attached to the starter's armature), which drives the very large flywheel ring gear at a greatly reduced speed. Another factor allowing it to produce so much power is that only intermittent operation is required of it. Thus, little allowance for air circulation is required, and the windings can be built into a very small space.

The starter solenoid is a magnetic device which employs the small current supplied by the starting switch circuit of the ignition switch. This magnetic action moves a plunger which mechanically engages the starter and electrically closes the heavy switch which connects it to the battery. The starting switch circuit consists of the starting switch contained within the ignition switch, a transmission neutral safety switch or clutch pedal switch, and the wiring necessary to connect these in series with the starter solenoid or relay.

A pinion, which is a small gear, is mounted to a one-way drive clutch. This clutch is splined to the starter armature shaft. When the ignition switch is moved to the "start" position, the solenoid plunger slides the pinion toward the flywheel ring gear via a collar and spring. If the teeth on the pinion and flywheel match properly, the pinion will engage the flywheel immediately. If the gear teeth butt one another, the spring will be compressed and will force the gears to mesh as soon as the starter turns far enough to allow them to do so. As the solenoid plunger reaches the end of its travel, it closes the contacts that connect the battery and starter and then the engine is cranked.

As soon as the engine starts, the flywheel ring gear begins turning fast enough to drive the pinion at an extremely high rate of speed. At this point, the one-way clutch begins allowing the pinion to spin faster than the starter shaft so that the starter will not operate at excessive speed. When the ignition switch is released from the starter position, the solenoid is de-energized, and a spring contained within the solenoid assembly pulls the gear out of mesh and interrupts the current flow to the starter.

Some starters employ a separate relay, mounted away from the starter, to switch the motor and solenoid current on and off. The relay thus replaces the solenoid electrical switch, but does not eliminate the need for a solenoid mounted on the starter used to mechanically engage the starter drive gears. The relay is used to reduce the amount of current the starting switch must carry.

THE CHARGING SYSTEM
Basic Operating Principles

The automobile charging system provides electrical power for operation of the vehicle's ignition and starting systems and all the electrical accessories. The battery serves as an electrical surge or storage tank, storing (in chemical form) the energy originally produced by the engine-driven generator. The system also provides a means of regulating generator output to protect the battery from being overcharged and to avoid excessive voltage to the accessories.

The storage battery is a chemical device incorporating parallel lead plates in a tank containing a sulfuric acid-water solution. Adjacent plates are slightly dissimilar, and the chemical reaction of the two dissimilar plates produces electrical energy when the battery is connected to a load such as the starter motor. The chemical reaction is reversible, so that when the generator is producing a voltage (electrical pressure) greater than that produced by the battery, electricity is forced into the battery, and the battery is returned to its fully charged state.

The vehicle's generator is driven mechanically, through V belts, by the engine crankshaft. It consists of two coils of fine wire, one stationary (the "stator"), and one movable (the "rotor"). The rotor may also be known as the "armature," and consists of fine wire wrapped around an iron core which is mounted on a shaft. The electricity which flows through the two coils of wire (provided initially by the battery in some cases) creates an intense magnetic field around both rotor and stator, and the interaction between the two fields creates voltage, allowing the generator to power the accessories and charge the battery.

There are two types of generators; the earlier is the direct current (DC) type. The current produced by the DC generator is generated in the armature and carried off the spinning armature by stationary brushes contacting the commutator. The commutator is a series of smooth metal contact plates on the end of the armature. The commutator plates, which are separated from one another by a very short gap, are connected to the armature circuits so that current will flow in one direction only in the wires carrying the generator output. The generator stator consists of two stationary coils of wire which draw some of the output current of the generator to form a powerful magnetic field and create the interaction of fields which generates the voltage. The generator field is wired in series with the regulator.

Newer automobiles use alternating current generators or "alternators," because they are more efficient, can be rotated at higher speeds, and have fewer brush problems. In an alternator, the field rotates while all the current produced passes only through the stator windings. The brushes bear against continuous slip rings rather than a commutator. This causes the current produced to periodically reverse the direction of its flow. Diodes (electrical one-way switches) block the flow of current from traveling in the wrong direction. A series of diodes is wired together to permit the alternating flow of the stator to be converted to a pulsating, but unidirectional flow at the alternator output. The alternator's field is wired in series with the voltage regulator.

The regulator consists of several circuits. Each circuit has a core, or magnetic coil of wire, which operates a switch. Each switch is connected to ground through one or more resistors. The coil of wire responds directly to system voltage. When the voltage reaches the required level, the magnetic field created by the winding of wire closes the switch and inserts a resistance into the generator field circuit, thus reducing the output. The contacts of the switch cycle open and close many times each second to precisely control voltage.

While alternators are self-limiting as far as maximum current is concerned, DC generators employ a current regulating circuit which responds directly to the total amount of current flowing through the generator circuit rather than to the output voltage. The current regulator is similar to the voltage regulator except that all system current must flow through the energizing coil on its way to the various accessories.

SAFETY PRECAUTIONS

Observing these precautions will ensure safe handling of the electrical system components, and will avoid damage to the vehicle's electrical system:

A. Be *absolutely* sure of the polarity of a booster battery before making connections. Connect the cables positive to positive, and negative to negative. Connect positive cables first and then make the last connection to a ground on the body of the booster vehicle so that arcing cannot ignite hydrogen gas that may have accumulated near the battery. Even momentary connection of a booster battery with the polarity reversed will damage alternator diodes.

B. Disconnect both vehicle battery cables before attempting to charge a battery.

C. Never ground the alternator or generator output or battery terminal. Be cautious when using metal tools around a battery to avoid creating a short circuit between the terminals.

D. Never ground the field circuit between the alternator and regulator.

E. Never run an alternator or generator without load unless the field circuit is disconnected.

F. Never attempt to polarize an alternator.

G. Keep the regulator cover in place when taking voltage and current limiter readings.

H. Use insulated tools when adjusting the regulator.

I. Whenever DC generator-to-regulator wires have been disconnected, the generator *must* be polarized. To do this with an externally grounded, light duty generator, momentarily place a jumper wire between the battery terminal and the generator terminal of the regulator. With an internally grounded heavy duty unit, disconnect the wire to the regulator field terminal and touch the regulator battery terminal with it.

Distributor

All models are equipped with a dual advance distributor. The centrifugal advance unit governs ignition timing according to engine rpm, the vacuum advance unit controls the timing according to engine load. Centrifugal advance is controlled by spring-mounted weights contained in the distributor. As engine speed increases, centrifugal force moves the weights outward from the distributor shaft advancing the position of the armature, thereby advancing the ignition timing. Vacuum advance is controlled by a vacuum diaphragm which is mounted on the side of the distributor and attached to the magnetic pickup coil assembly via the vacuum advance

ENGINE AND ENGINE REBUILDING

link. Under light acceleration, the engine is operating under a low-load condition, causing the carburetor vacuum to act on the distributor vacuum diaphragm, moving the pickup coil assembly opposite the direction of distributor shaft rotation, thereby advancing the ignition timing.

The distributors on some models also incorporate a vacuum retard mechanism. The retard mechanism is contained in the rear part of the vacuum diaphragm chamber. When the engine is operating under high-vacuum conditions (deceleration or idle), intake manifold vacuum is applied to the retard mechanism. The retard mechanism moves the breaker point mounting plate (conventional) or pickup coil assembly (breakerless) in the direction of distributor rotation, thereby retarding the ignition timing. Ignition retard, under these conditions, reduces exhaust emissions of hydrocarbons, although it does reduce engine efficiency somewhat.

REMOVAL AND INSTALLATION

The camshaft-driven distributor is located at the top left end of the cylinder head. It is retained by double clamp bolts at the base of the distributor shaft housing.

NOTE: *Security type distributor hold-down bolts are used on some models. Ford tool number T82L12270A is required for removal and installation of these bolts.*

1. Disconnect the vacuum hose from the advance unit. Disconnect the primary wire at the coil.
2. Remove the capscrews and remove the distributor cap.
3. Scribe a mark on the distributor body, showing the position of the ignition rotor. Scribe another mark on the distributor body and cylinder head, showing the position of the body in relation to the head. These marks can be used for reference when installing the distributor, as long as the engine remains undisturbed.
4. Remove the distributor clamp bolts. Pull the distributor from the head.
5. To install the distributor with the engine undisturbed, align the rotor with the mark, made with the distributor removed. Install the distributor into the head. Align the mark on the distributor body with the mark on the cylinder head. Install the clamp bolts and tighten until the distributor body can be moved with a little effort. Install the coil primary wire and the distributor cap. Plug the vacuum advance hose, set the ignition timing, tighten the clamp bolt, and install the vacuum hose.
6. If the crankshaft was rotated while the distributor was removed, the engine must be brought to TDC (Top Dead Center) on the compression stroke of the No. 1 cylinder. Remove the No. 1 spark plug. Place your finger over the hole and rotate the crankshaft slowly (use a wrench on the crankshaft pulley bolt)

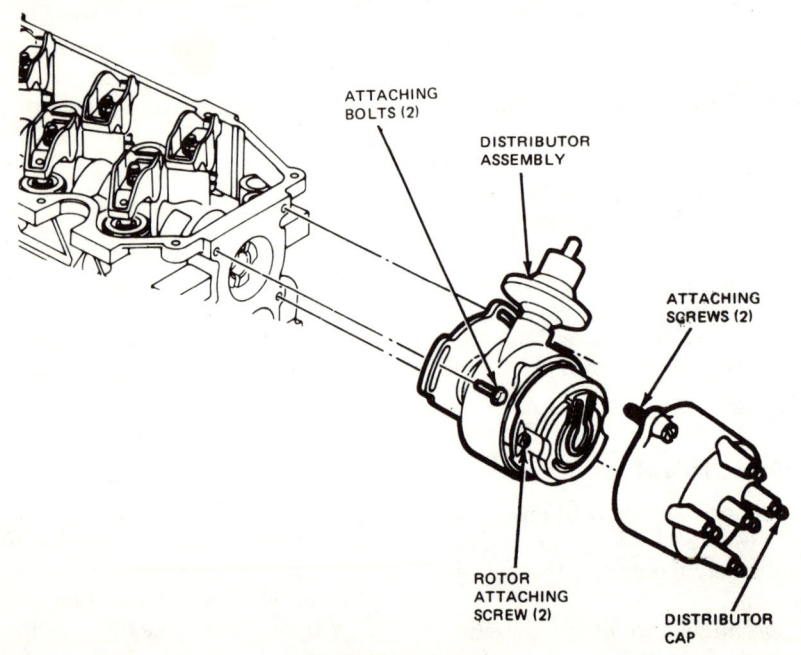

Distributor mounting

ENGINE AND ENGINE REBUILDING

in the direction of normal engine rotation, until engine compression is felt.

CAUTION: *Turn the engine only in the direction of normal rotation. Backward rotation will cause the cam belt to slip or lose teeth, altering engine timing.*

When engine compression is felt at the spark plug hole, indicating that the piston is approaching TDC, continue to turn the crankshaft until the timing mark on the pulley is aligned with the "O" mark (timing mark) on the engine front cover. Turn the distributor shaft until the ignition rotor is at the No. 1 firing position. Install the distributor into the cylinder head, as outlined in Step 5 of this procedure.

Firing Order

Original spark plug wires are numbered as to location. If installing non-numbered wires, replace the wires one at a time to avoid confusion.

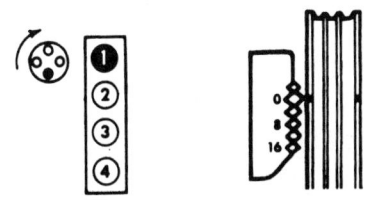

The firing order is 1-4-3-2: #1 cylinder location is high-lighted

Alternator

ALTERNATOR PRECAUTIONS

To prevent damage to the alternator and regulator, the following precautionary measures must be taken when working with the electrical system.

1. Never reverse battery connections. Always check the battery polarity visually. This is to be done before any connections are made to ensure that all of the connections correspond to the battery ground polarity of the car.
2. Booster batteries must be connected properly. Make sure the positive cable of the booster battery is connected to the positive terminal of the battery which is getting the boost.
3. Disconnect the battery cables before using a fast charger; the charger has a tendency to force current through the diodes in the opposite direction for which they were designed.
4. Never use a fast charger as a booster for starting the car.
5. Never disconnect the voltage regulator while the engine is running, unless as noted for testing purposes.
6. Do not ground the alternator output terminal.
7. Do not operate the alternator on an open circuit with the field energized.
8. Do not attempt to polarize the alternator.
9. Disconnect the battery cables and remove the alternator before using an electric arc welder on the car.
10. Protect the alternator from excessive moisture. If the engine is to be steam cleaned, cover or remove the alternator.

REMOVAL

While internal alternator repairs are possible, they require specialized tools and train-

Alternator Specifications

Supplier	Stamp Color	Rating Amperes @ 15V	Rating Watts @ 15V	Field Current Amps @ 12V ①	Slip-Ring Turning mm (Inches) Min. Dia.	Slip-Ring Turning mm (Inches) Max Runabout	Brush Length mm (Inches) New	Brush Length mm (Inches) Wear-Limit	Pulley Nut Torque N-m (lb.-ft.)
Ford	Orange	40	600	4.0	31 (1.22)	.0127 (0.0005)	12.19 (.480)	6.35 (1/4)	82–135 (60–100)
Ford	Black	65	975	4.0	31 (1.22)	.0127 (0.0005)	12.19	6.35 (1/4)	82–135 (60–100)
Ford	Green	60	900	4.0	31 (1.22)	.0127 (0.0005)	12.19 (.480)	6.35 (1/4)	82–135 (60–100)

① A Field Current of 4 amps is used with solid-state regulation.

54 ENGINE AND ENGINE REBUILDING

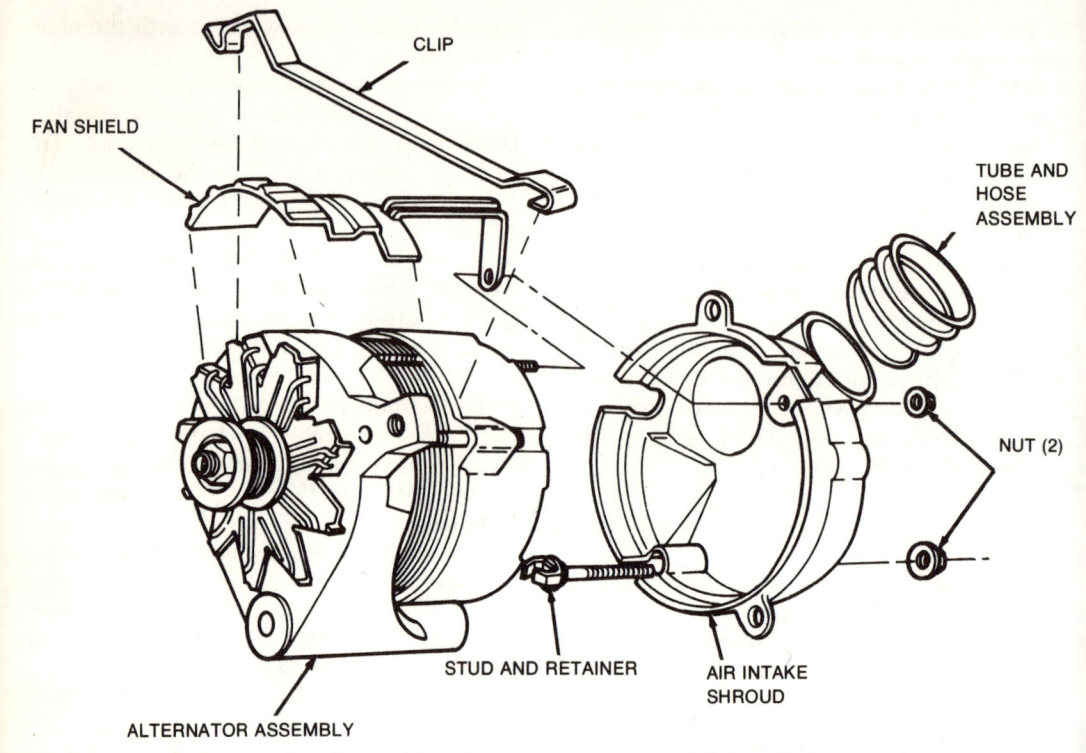

On air-conditioned cars, cool air shrouding is added

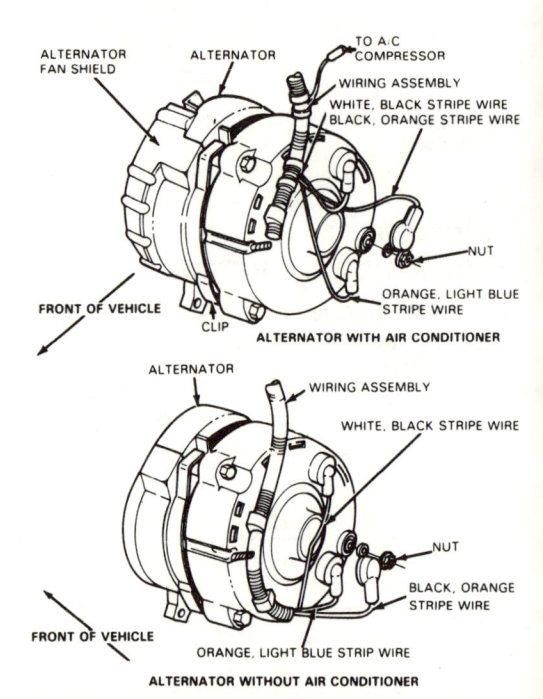

Harness connections for alternators

ing. Therefore, it is advisable to replace a defective alternator, or have it repaired by a qualified shop.

1. Disconnect the negative battery cable from the battery.
2. Disconnect the wires from the rear of the alternator. Remove clip-on shield and cooling shroud (if equipped).
3. Loosen the alternator mounting bolts.
4. Remove the belt.
5. Remove the alternator mounting bolts and remove the alternator.

INSTALLATION

1. Position the alternator on the engine and install the attaching bolts.
2. Connect the wires on the rear of the alternator. Install the cooling shroud and clip-on shield (if equipped).
3. Position the belt on the alternator.
4. Adjust the alternator belt tension as described in Chapter 1.
5. Connect the negative battery cable.

Regulator

The regulator is a device which controls the output of the alternator. If the regulator did not limit the voltage output of the alternator, the excessive output could burn out components of the electrical system.

The voltage regulator is 100 percent solid state and is not adjustable.

ENGINE AND ENGINE REBUILDING 55

Alternator wiring; dash mounted light

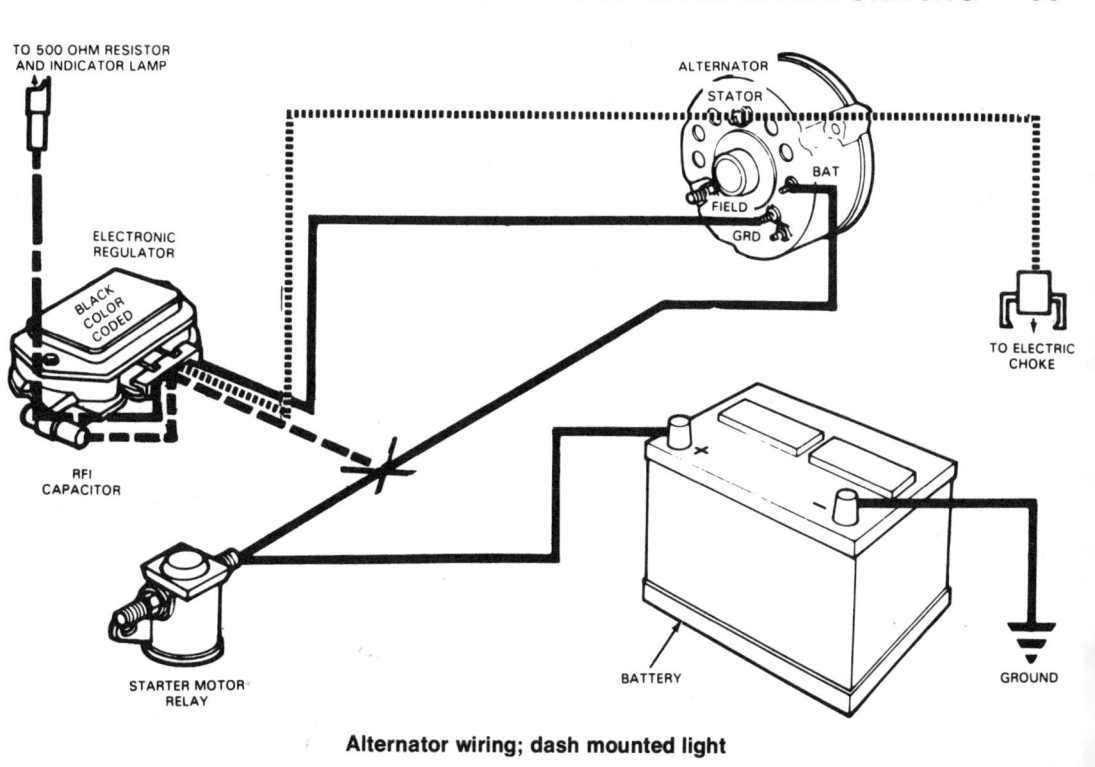

REMOVAL

1. Disconnect the negative battery cable from the battery.
2. Disconnect the wiring harness from the regulator.
3. Remove the regulator attaching screws and remove the regulator.

INSTALLATION

1. Position the regulator on the car and install the attaching screws.

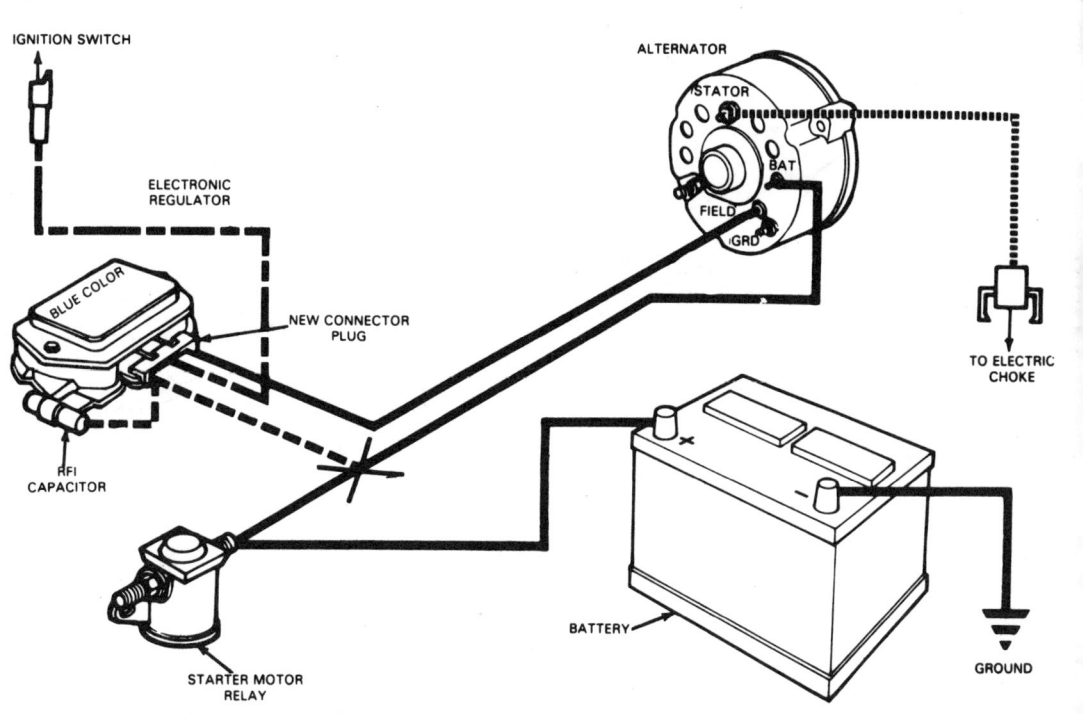

Alternator wiring; dash mounted meter

ENGINE AND ENGINE REBUILDING

2. Attach the wiring to the regulator.
3. Connect the negative battery cable.

Fuse Link

The fuse link is a short length of insulated wire contained in the alternator wiring harness, between the alternator and the starter relay. The fuse link is several wire gauge sizes smaller than the other wires in the harness. If a booster battery is connected incorrectly to the car battery or if some component of the charging system is shorted to ground, the fuse link melts and protects the alternator. The fuse link is attached to the starter relay. The insulation on the wire reads: Fuse Link. A melted fuse link can usually be identified by cracked or bubbled insulation. If it is difficult to determine if the fuse link is melted, connect a test light to both ends of the wire. If the fuse link is not melted, the test light will light showing that an open circuit does not exist in the wire.

REPLACEMENT

1. Disconnect the negative battery cable.
2. Disconnect the eyelet end of the link from the starter relay.
3. Cut the other end of the link from the wiring harness at the splice.
4. Connect the eyelet end of the new fuse link to the starter relay.

NOTE: *Use only an original equipment type fuse link. Do not replace with standard wire.*

5. Splice the open end of the new fuse link into the wiring harness.
6. Solder the splice with rosin core solder and wrap the splice in electrical tape. This splice *must* be soldered.
7. Connect the negative battery cable.

Starter

REMOVAL AND INSTALLATION

1. Disconnect the negative battery cable from the battery.
2. Jack up the front of the car and safely support it on jackstands.
3. Disconnect the starter cable from the starter motor terminal.
4. If your car is equipped with a manual transmission, remove the three nuts that attach the roll restrictor brace to the starter motor studs at the transmission. Remove the brace.

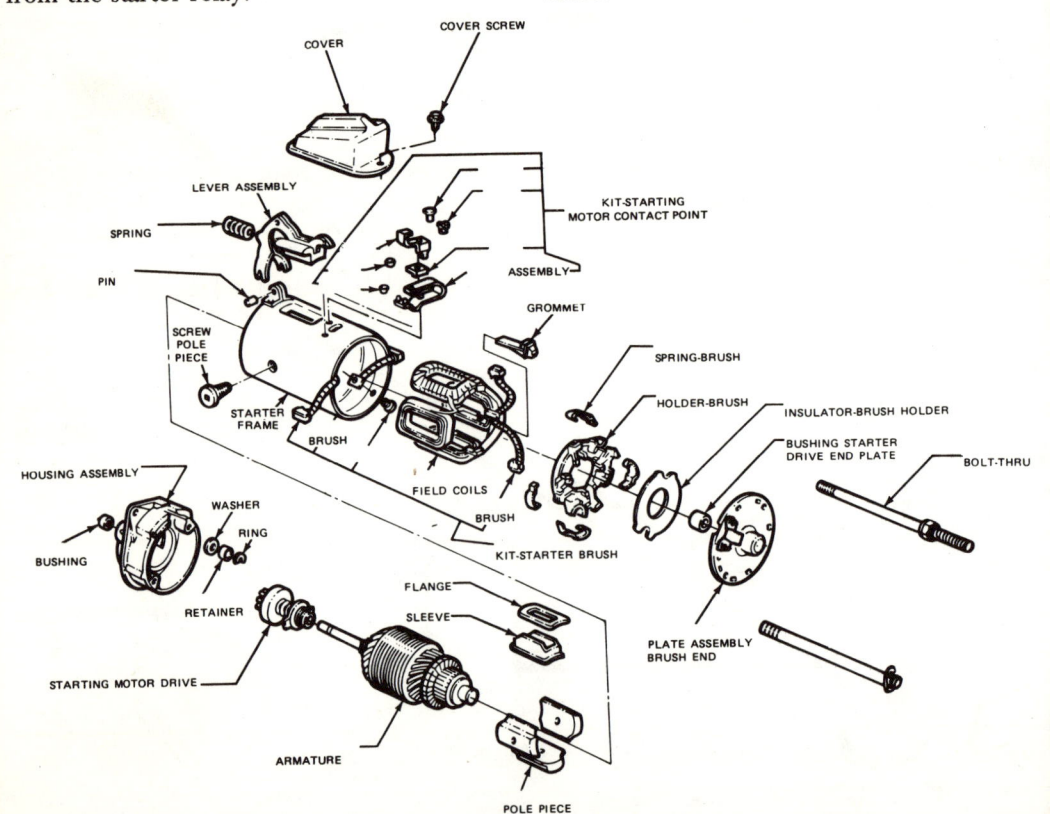

Exploded view of a starter motor

ENGINE AND ENGINE REBUILDING

5. Remove the two bolts attaching the starter rear support bracket, remove the retaining nut from the rear of the starter stud thru bolt. Remove the bracket.

6. On cars equipped with a manual transmission, remove the three starter mounting studs. Remove the starter motor. If your car has an automatic transmission, remove the three mounting bolts. Remove the starter motor.

7. Installation is in the reverse order of removal.

OVERHAUL

Brush Replacement

1. Remove the top cover by taking out the retaining screw. Loosen and remove the two through bolts. Remove the starter drive end housing and the starter drive plunger lever return spring.

2. Remove the starter drive plunger lever pivot pin and lever, and remove the armature.

3. Remove the brush end plate.

4. Remove the ground brush retaining screws from the frame and remove the brushes.

5. Cut the insulated brush leads from the field coils, as close to the field connection point as possible.

6. Clean and inspect the starter motor.

7. Replace the brush end plate if the insulator between the field brush holder and the end plate is cracked or broken.

8. Position the new insulated field brushes lead on the field coil connection. Position and crimp the clip provided with the brushes to hold the brush lead to the connection. Solder the lead, clip, and connection together using rosin core solder. Use a 300-watt soldering iron.

9. Install the ground brush leads to the frame with the retaining screws.

10. Clean the commutator with 00 or 000 sandpaper.

11. Position the brush end plate to the starter frame, with the end plate boss in the frame slot.

12. Install the armature in the starter frame.

13. Install the starter drive gear plunger lever to the frame and starter drive assembly, and install the pivot pin.

14. Partially fill the drive end housing bearing bore with grease (approximately ¼ full). Position the return spring on the plunger lever, and the drive end housing to the starter frame. Install the through-bolts and tighten to specified torque (55 to 75 in. lbs.). Be sure that the stop ring retainer is seated properly in the drive end housing.

15. Install the commutator brushes in the brush holders. Center the brush springs on the brushes.

16. Position the plunger lever cover and brush cover band, with its gasket, on the starter. Tighten the band retaining screw.

17. Connect the starter to a battery to check its operation.

STARTER DRIVE REPLACEMENT

1. Remove the starter from the engine.
2. Remove the starter drive plunger lever cover.
3. Loosen the thru-bolts just enough to allow removal of the drive end housing and the starter drive plunger lever return spring.
4. Remove the pivot pin which attaches the starter drive plunger lever to the starter frame and remove the lever.
5. Remove the stop ring retainer and stop-ring from the armature shaft.
6. Remove the starter drive from the armature shaft.
7. Inspect the teeth on the starter drive. If they are excessively worn, inspect the teeth on the ring gear of the flywheel. If the teeth

Starter Specifications

Positive Engagement Starter Motor

Current Draw Under Normal Load (Amps)	Normal Engine Cranking Speed (rpm)	Min. Stall Torque @ 5 Volts N·m	Min. Stall Torque @ 5 Volts Ft.-Lbs.	Max. Load (Amps)	No. Load (Amps)	Starter Brushes Mfg. Length mm	Starter Brushes Mfg. Length in.	Spring Tension N	Spring Tension oz.
150–250	190–260	12.9	9.5	500	80	11.4	.45	22	80

Maximum Commutator runout is 0.005 inch. Maximum starting circuit voltage drop (battery positive terminal to starter terminal).

58 ENGINE AND ENGINE REBUILDING

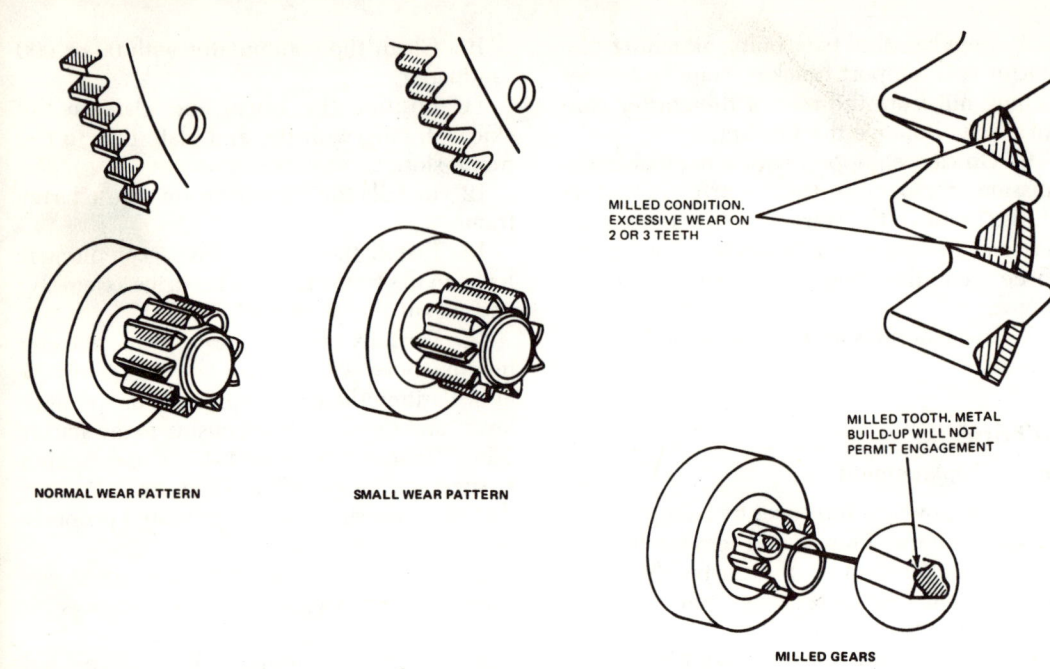

Starter drive gear wear patterns

on the flywheel are excessively worn, the flywheel ring gear should be replaced.

8. Apply a thin coat of white grease to the armature shaft, in the area in which the starter drive operates.
9. Install the starter drive on the armature shaft and install a new stop-ring.
10. Position the starter drive plunger lever on the starter frame and install the pivot pin. *Make sure the plunger lever is properly engaged with the starter drive.*
11. Install a new stop ring retainer on the armature shaft.
12. Fill the drive end housing bearing fore ¼ full with grease.
13. Position the starter drive plunger lever return spring and the drive end housing to the starter frame.
14. Tighten the starter thru-bolts to 55–75 in. lbs.
15. Install the starter drive plunger lever cover and the brush cover band on the starter.
16. Install the starter.

Battery

REMOVAL AND INSTALLATION

1. Loosen the battery cable bolts and spread the ends of the battery cable terminals.
2. Disconnect the negative battery cable first.
3. Disconnect the positive battery cable.
4. Remove the battery hold-down.
5. Wearing heavy gloves, remove the battery from under the hood. *Be careful not to tip the battery and spill acid on yourself or the car during removal.*
6. To install, wearing heavy gloves, place the battery in its holder under the hood. *Use care not to spill the acid.*
7. Install the battery hold-down.
8. Install the positive battery cable first.
9. Install the negative battery cable.
10. Apply a *light* coating of grease to the cable ends.

Battery Specifications
BATTERY DISCHARGE RATE TABLE

Battery Capacity (Ampere—Hours)	Discharge Rate (Amperes)
36 Maintenance Free	155
45 Maintenance Free	190
48 Maintenance Free	205

ENGINE MECHANICAL

Design

The Escort, Lynx, EXP and LN7 are equipped with an entirely new engine jointly

ENGINE AND ENGINE REBUILDING 59

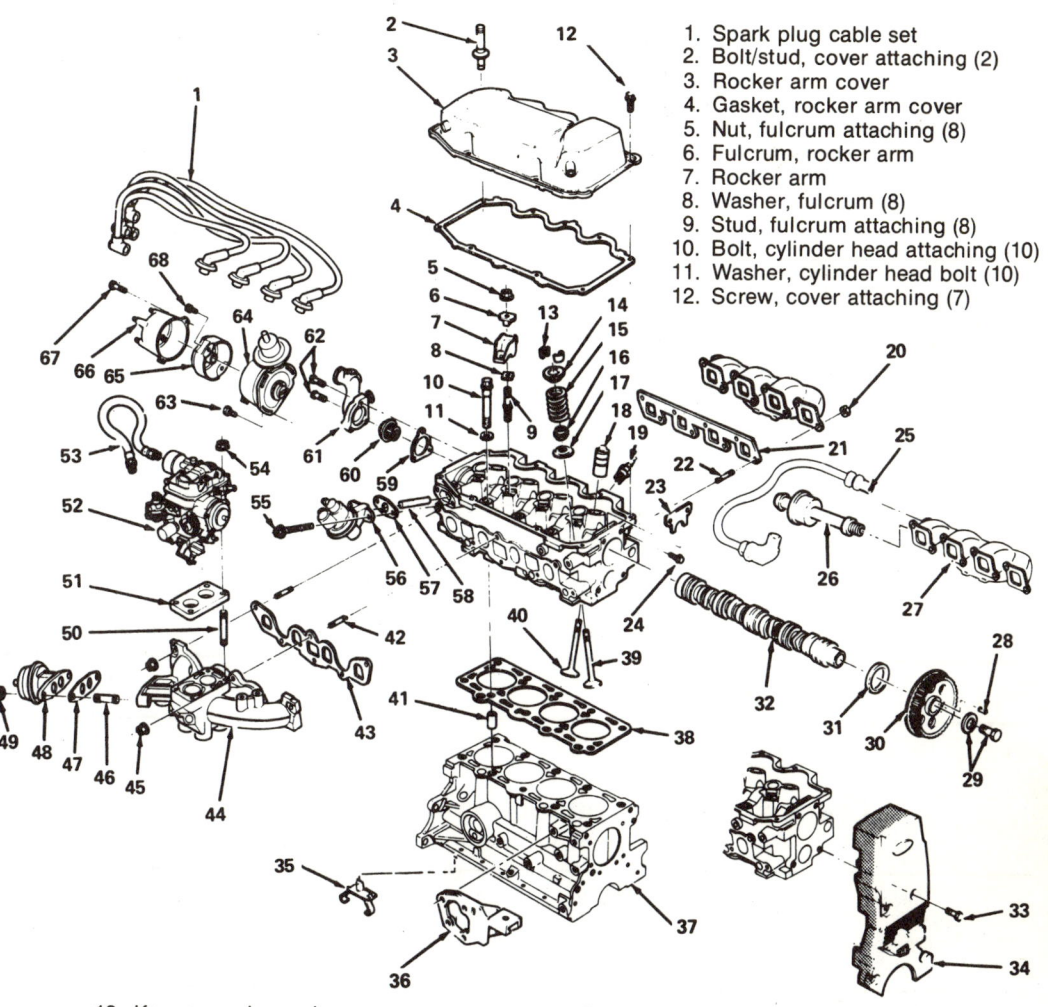

1. Spark plug cable set
2. Bolt/stud, cover attaching (2)
3. Rocker arm cover
4. Gasket, rocker arm cover
5. Nut, fulcrum attaching (8)
6. Fulcrum, rocker arm
7. Rocker arm
8. Washer, fulcrum (8)
9. Stud, fulcrum attaching (8)
10. Bolt, cylinder head attaching (10)
11. Washer, cylinder head bolt (10)
12. Screw, cover attaching (7)
13. Keepers, valve springs
14. Retainer, valve spring
15. Valve spring
16. Seal, valve stem
17. Washer, valve spring
18. Valve lifter
19. Spark plug
20. Nut, manifold attaching (8)
21. Gasket, exhaust manifold
22. Stud, manifold attaching (8)
23. Plate, camshaft thrust
24. Bolt, thrust plate attaching (2)
25. EGR tube
26. Check valve, air injection
27. Exhaust manifold
28. Shaft key, cam sprocket
29. Bolt/washer sprocket attaching (1)
30. Camshaft sprocket
31. Seal, camshaft
32. Camshaft
33. Bolts (2) & nuts (2), cover attaching (2)
34. Timing belt cover
35. Crankcase ventilation baffle
36. Engine mount
37. Cylinder block
38. Gasket, cylinder head
39. Exhaust valve
40. Intake valve
41. Dowel, cylinder head alignment (2)
42. Stud, manifold attaching (6)
43. Gasket, intake manifold
44. Intake manifold
45. Nut, manifold attaching (6)
46. Stud, valve attaching (2)
47. Gasket, EGR valve
48. EGR valve
49. Nut, valve attaching (2)
50. Stud, carburetor attaching (4)
51. Gasket, carburetor mounting
52. Carburetor
53. Fuel line
54. Nut, carburetor attaching (4)
55. Bolt, pump attaching (2)
56. Fuel pump
57. Gasket, fuel pump
58. Push rod, fuel pump
59. Gasket, housing
60. Thermostat
61. Thermostat housing
62. Bolt, housing attaching (2)
63. Bolt, distributor attaching (3)
64. Distributor
65. Rotor
66. Distributor cap
67. Screwn cap attaching (2).
68. Screw, rotor attaching (2)

Exploded view of the upper part of the engine

ENGINE AND ENGINE REBUILDING

designed by Ford of Europe and Ford of North America.

Dubbed the Compound Valve Hemispherical (CVH) engine by its designers, the belt-driven in-head camshaft engine contains a large number of unique features. Most striking is the design of the aluminum alloy cross-flow cylinder head. After extensive research, which included building prototypes of three different cylinder head configurations, it was determined that a hemispherical combustion chamber provided the highest power, lowest

General Engine Specifications

Year	Engine No. Cyl. Displacement (cc)	Carburetor Type	Horsepower @ rpm	Torque @ rpm (ft. lbs.)	Bore x Stroke (mm)	Compression Ratio	Oil Pressure @ 2000 rpm
1981–82	4-1597	2 bbl	69 @ 5000	86 @ 3200	80.0 x 79.5	8.8 : 1 ①	40

① Performance option; EXP/LN7: 9.0:1

Valve Specifications

Year	Engine No. Cyl. Displacement (cc)	Seat Angle (deg)	Face Angle (deg)	Spring Test Pressure (lbs. @ in.)	Spring Installed Height (in.)	Stem to Guide Clearance (in.) Intake	Stem to Guide Clearance (in.) Exhaust	Stem Diameter (in.) Intake	Stem Diameter (in.) Exhaust
1981–82	4-1597	45	91°25′	①	1.460	.0008–.0027	.0018–.0037	.3160	.3160

① Intake: 180 @ 1.090   Exhaust: 75 @ 1.461

Crankshaft and Connecting Rod Specifications
All measurements are given in inches

Year	Engine No. Cyl. Displacement (cc)	Main Brg. Journal Dia	Main Brg. Oil Clearance	Shaft End-Play	Thrust on No.	Journal Diameter	Oil Clearance	Side Clearance
1981–82	4-1597	2.2826–2.2834	.002–.004	.004–.012	5	1.885–1.886	.0002–.0003	.004–.011

Torque Specifications
All readings in ft. lbs.

Year	Engine No. Cyl. Displacement (cc)	Cylinder Head Bolts	Rod Bearing Bolts	Main Bearing Bolts	Crankshaft Bolt	Flywheel to Crankshaft Bolts	Manifold Intake	Manifold Exhaust
1981–82	4-1597	44	19–25	67–80	74–90	59–69	12–15	15–20

Camshaft Specifications
All measurements are given in inches

Year	Engine No. Cyl. Displacement (cc)	Lobe Lift	Valve Lift @ Zero Lash Intake	Valve Lift @ Zero Lash Exhaust	Camshaft End Play	Journal-to-Bearing Clearance	Journal Diameter	Journal Out-of-Round Limit
1981–82	4-1597	.5806	.3760	.3750	.0019–.0059	.0009–.0027	①	.008

① No. 1: 1.761–1.762   No. 4: 1.791–1.792
  No. 2: 1.771–1.772   No. 5: 1.801–1.802
  No. 3: 1.781–1.782

ENGINE AND ENGINE REBUILDING

Ring Gap
All measurements are given in inches

Year	Engine	Top Compression	Bottom Compression	Oil Control
1981–82	All	.012–.020	.012–.020	.034–.037

Ring Side Clearance
All measurements are given in inches

Year	Engine	Top Compression	Bottom Compression	Oil Control
1981–82	All	.002–.004 ①	.002–.004 ①	Snug

① 0.006 in. maximum

fuel consumption, and lowest level of engine emissions of all existing engine designs. Additionally, the basic shape and design was quite simple, especially in comparison to that of a stratified charge (three valve) engine. However, a true hemispherical chamber seemed to require the use of double overhead cams, so that the intake and exhaust valves could be displaced at 45° angles, be operated by individual cam lobes, and allow room for a centrally-located spark plug. But double overhead cams were prohibitively expensive. Ford engineers discovered a way around the problem. By rotating the valve axis around the chamber, and by canting the valves, it was possible to operate the valves by a single camshaft working though hydraulic lash adjusters and stamped steel rocker arms. Angling the valves allowed their size to be maximized, resulting in greater air flow. The plane of each valve train is canted in such a way that each valve and port are offset from the longitudinal and transverse center lines of each cylinder bore.

A contoured piston crown is used to promote "squish" during the compression stroke. This leads to high turbulence and forces the charge towards the center of the chamber, improving combustion.

In other respects, the engine is more conventional. The belt-driven camshaft rides in replaceable bearings in the cylinder head. Distributor and fuel pump drives are taken from the cam. Aluminum is also used for the intake manifold and water pump. The cylinder block is made from cast iron; the exhaust manifold is made of nodular iron. The nodular iron crankshaft runs in five main bearings. Connecting rods are forged steel: the pistons are die-cast light alloy.

REMOVAL AND INSTALLATION

NOTE: *A special engine support bar is necessary. The bar is used to support the engine/transaxle while disconnect the various engine mounts Ford Part #T81P6000A. A suitable support can be made using angle iron, a heavy "J" hook and some strong chain.*

CAUTION: *If your car is equipped with air-conditioning, take it to a qualified repair shop and have the system discharged. Any work or discharging of the air conditioning system should be left to a professional because of the hazards associated with refrigerant gas. Disconnecting the air compressor is required when removing the engine and transaxle.*

1. Drain the cooling system, then position the car in the work area where the engine hoist is available.

2. Disconnect the negative battery cable from the battery. Disconnect the positive battery cable, remove the battery hold-down and the battery. Remove the battery tray.

3. Disconnect the electric fan wiring harness. Remove the fan motor and shroud. Disconnect the upper and lower radiator hoses and the oil cooler lines (if equipped with an automatic transaxle) from the radiator. Remove the radiator.

4. Disconnect the coil wire at the distributor, remove the coil and mounting bracket. Disconnect the air conditioner suction hose at the hose coupler located above the compressor. THE SYSTEM MUST BE DISCHARGED FIRST. SEE CAUTION AT THE BEGINNING OF THIS SECTION.

5. Disconnect the heater hoses. Remove the alternator fresh air tube. Remove the power steering pump filler tube. Disconnect the following:
   - Engine main wiring harness
   - Neutral safety switch
   - Choke cap wire
   - Starter cable
   - Alternator wiring
   - Fuel lines; supply and return at the metal connector on the engine
   - Vacuum lines to the carburetor; label them first for identification
   - Vacuum tree from the dash panel
   - Vacuum hose from the power brake booster

62 ENGINE AND ENGINE REBUILDING

1. Dowell, pressure plate alignment
2. Flywheel
3. Seal, crankshaft rear
4. Bolt, retainer attaching (6)
5. Seal retainer
6. Gasket, retainer
7. Cylinder block
8. Engine lifting eye
9. Plug and gasket, monolithic timing
10. Plug, coolant drain
11. Gasket, pump (oil)
12. Oil pump
13. Gasket, pump (water)
14. Water pump
15. Bolt, pump (water) attaching (4)
16. Timing belt—installed view
17. Spring, tensioner
18. Bracket and idler, tensioner
19. Bolt, tensioner attaching (2)
20. Timing belt cover
21. Crankshaft pulley
22. Washer, pulley bolt (1)
23. Bolt, Pulley attaching (1)
24. Bolt, cover attaching (4)
25. Oil pump
26. Gasket, pick up tube
27. Pick up and tube assembly
28. Bolt, pick up attaching (2)
29. Gear, crankshaft
30. Guide, timing belt
31. Seal, crankshaft front
32. Bolt, pump (oil) attaching (6)
33. Bolt, brace attaching (1)
34. Seal, pan front
35. Gasket, pan side
36. Oil pan
37. Seal, drain plug
38. Plug, oil pan drain
39. Bolt, Pan attaching (18)
40. Gasket, Pan side
41. Seal, pan rear
42. Bolt, cap attaching (10)
43. Main bearing caps
44. Main bearing inserts, lower
45. Crankshaft
46. Main bearing inserts, upper
47. Oil pressure sending unit
48. Dowel, transmission alignment
49. Adapter, oil filter
50. Oil filter
51. Piston
52. Piston pin
53. Connecting rod
54. Connecting rod bearings
55. Connecting rod cap
56. Nut, cap attaching
57. Bolt, cap attaching

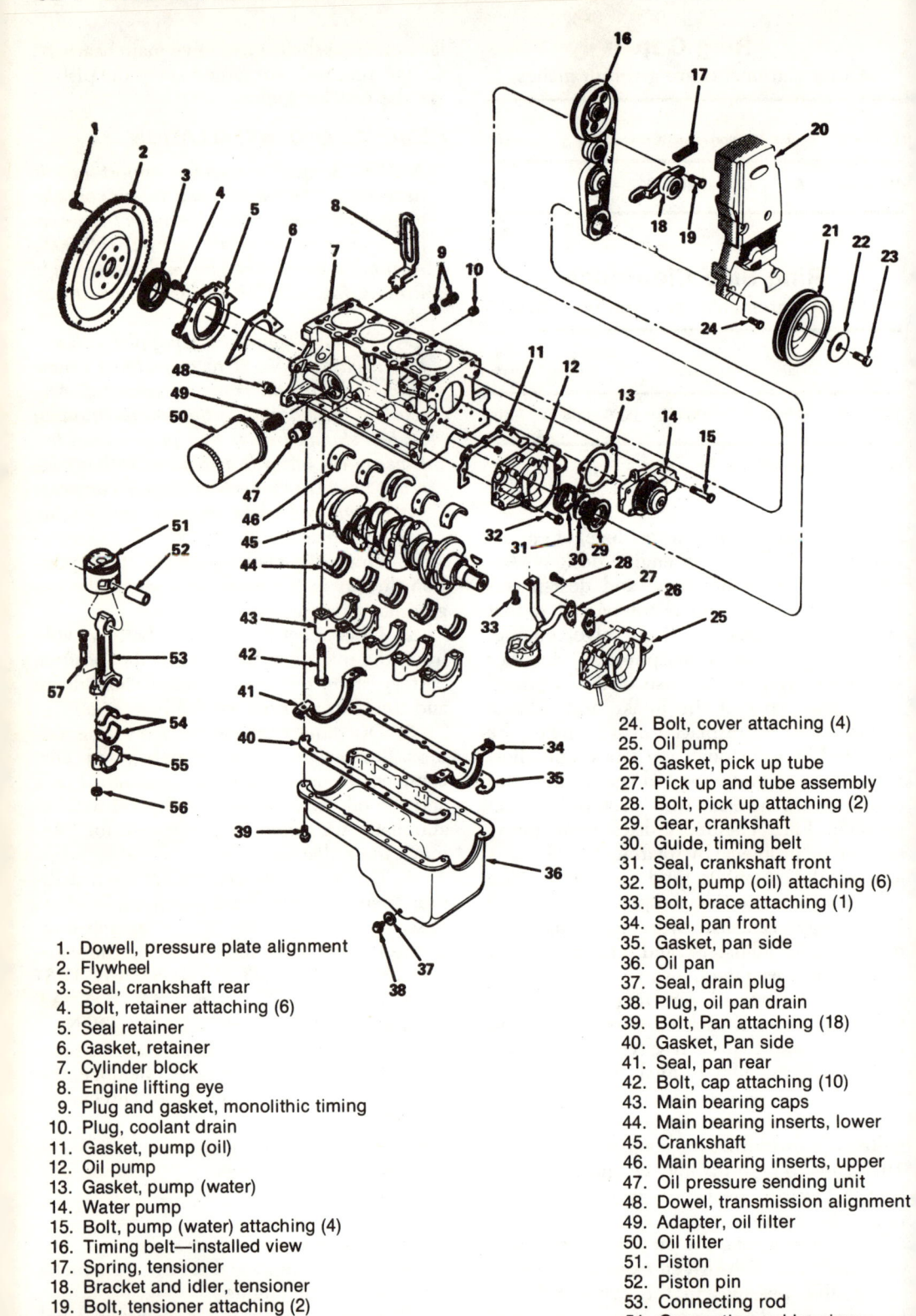

Exploded view of the lower part of the engine

ENGINE AND ENGINE REBUILDING

- Speed control servo; remove attaching screws and move the servo to the side
- Accelerator cable at the carburetor
- Fuel EVAP hose from the metal tube at the left front fender apron. Position the air conditioner liquid line over the metal EVAP tube
- Clutch cable from the transaxle

6. Remove the throttle cable, speed control bracket and the thermactor pump bracket bolt.

7. Connect a short piece of chain to the bolt hole at the transaxle end (using a 10mm bolt) and to the thermactor bracket bolt hole at the other end. Install the special engine support bar and connect the "J" hook to the chain. Tighten the "J" hook until the chain is taunt.

8. Take a look around and disconnect any wires, hoses, lines or cables that are still connected to the engine.

9. Jack up the front of the car and safely support it on jackstands.

10. Drain the engine oil and transaxle lubricant.

11. Remove the front splash shields.

12. If your car is equipped with a manual transaxle, remove the roll restrictor from the engine and body. Remove the stabilizer bar. Remove the lower control arm the inner body mounting bolts.

13. Disconnect the left side tie rod end from the steering knuckle. Disconnect the secondary air tube (converter) at the check valve. Disconnect the exhaust pipe from the manifold and at the tailpipe.

14. Remove the halfshafts from the transaxle, refer to Chapter 6 for instructions.

15. Disconnect the speedometer cable from the transaxle.

16. Disconnect the transmission controls from the transaxles. Disconnect the power steering lines, if equipped.

17. Remove the left front mount insulator attaching bracket and the insulator with the through bolts.

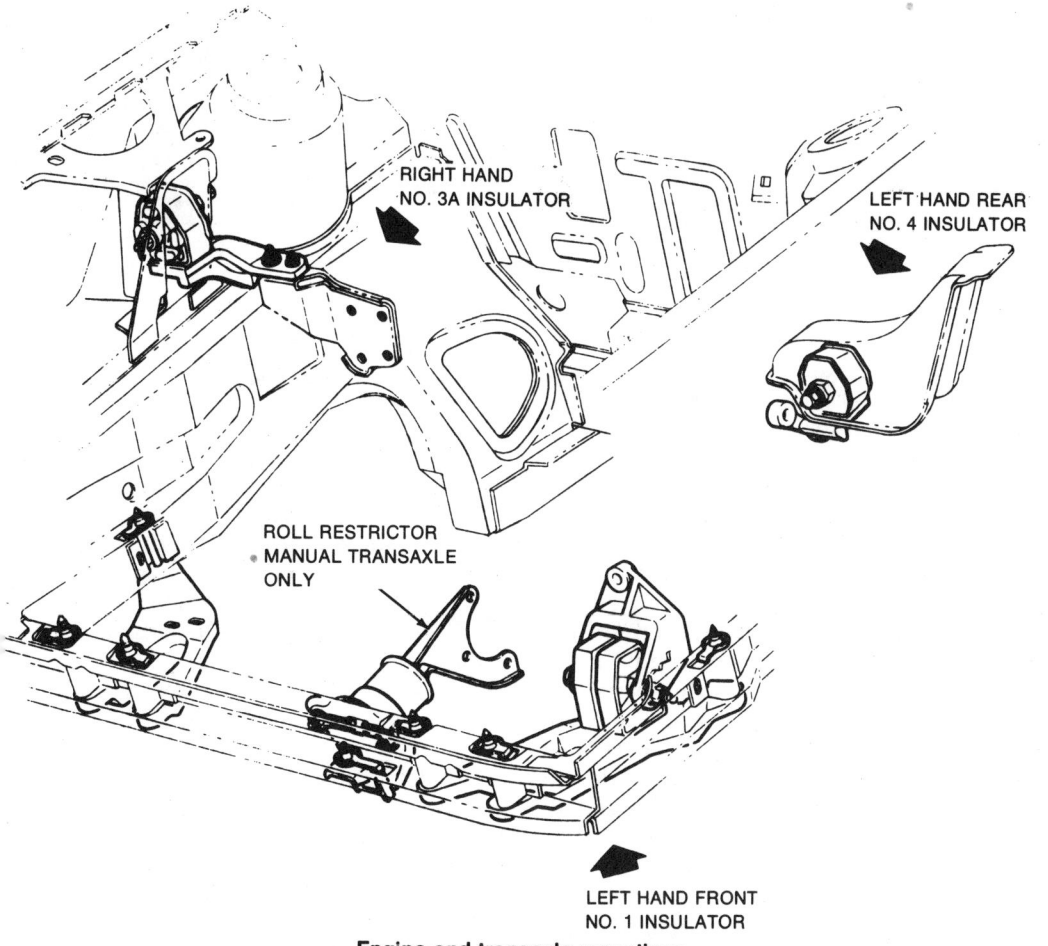

Engine and transaxle mountings

64 ENGINE AND ENGINE REBUILDING

18. Remove the left rear mount stud nut. Release tension on the engine support "J" bolt until the engine is low enough to clear the mount stud. Remove the left rear mount and bracket.

19. Lower the car from the jackstands.

20. Tighten the engine support "J" bolt until the engine is back to its normal installed position.

21. Attach the engine hoist, disconnect the remaining engine mount and remove the engine and transaxle.

22. Installation is in the reverse order of removal.

Cylinder Head

REMOVAL AND INSTALLATION

NOTE: *The engine must be "overnight" cold before removing the cylinder head, to reduce the possibility of warpage or distortion.*

1. Disconnect the negative battery cable.
2. Drain the cooling system. Remove the air cleaner and ducts. Disconnect and label all wires connected to or crossing the valve cover.
3. Using a wrench on the crankshaft pulley, rotate the engine, in the direction of normal rotation, until No. 1 piston is at TDC of the compression stroke. See the "Distributor Removal and Installation" procedure for details.
4. Remove the camshaft belt cover.
5. Remove the valve cover.
6. Loosen the cam belt tensioner. Slip the cam belt off of the camshaft sprocket. Do not remove the belt or allow it to change its position on the crankshaft sprocket.
7. Disconnect the coolant hoses from the head. Disconnect and label the thermosensor wiring, and all other hoses and wires connected to the head.
8. The cylinder head can be removed with the distributor, intake manifold and carburetor, and exhaust manifold attached, or the parts can be removed prior to cylinder head removal. For removal with the parts attached, disconnect the exhaust manifold flange-to-pipe connection. Disconnect the Thermactor (air pump) hose at the exhaust manifold. Disconnect the throttle linkage at the carburetor, the fuel line at the fuel pump, and all hoses and wires from the carburetor and intake manifold. Disconnect the coil-to-distributor wiring.
9. For cylinder head removal with the manifolds removed, refer to the appropriate sections for manifold removal procedures.

10. Loosen the cylinder head bolts a little at a time, working from the ends to the center, to prevent warpage. Remove the bolts.

11. Remove the cylinder head.

12. To install, first clean the head and block mating surfaces. Check the block and head for warpage and correct as necessary.

13. Install a new head gasket onto the block.

14. Before installing the head, make sure the camshaft is in the firing position for No. 1 cylinder (both No. 1 valves closed, distributor rotor under the No. 1 spark plug tower). This is done to preclude valve and piston interference. As long as the camshaft and crankshaft are both set at TDC of the

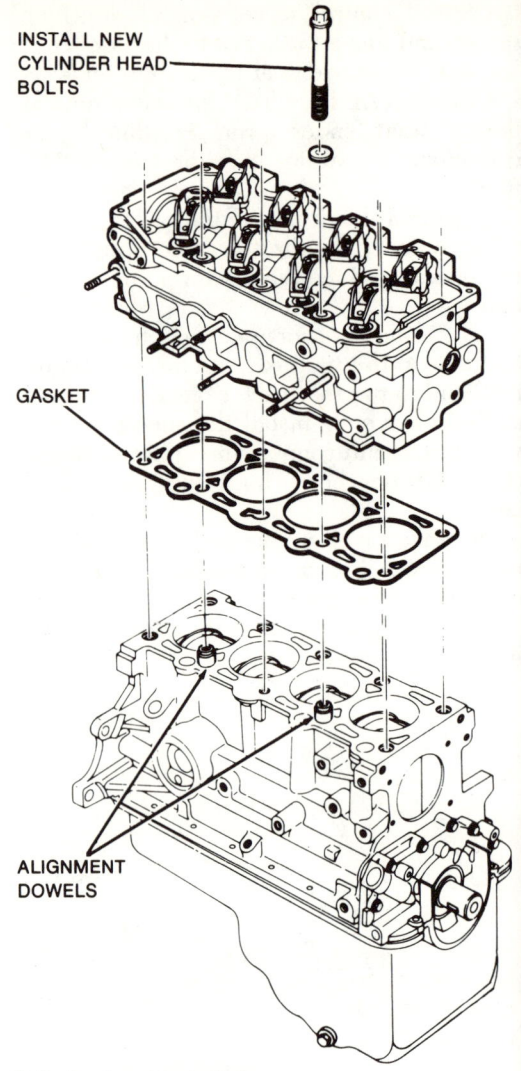

Cylinder head installation

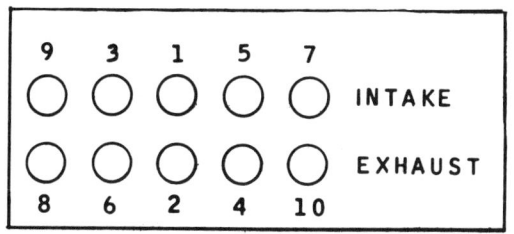

Tighten the cylinder head in this sequence

compression stroke for No. 1 cylinder, the valves will not contact the pistons.

15. Lower the head into position onto the block, being careful not to damage the gasket.

16. Install the cylinder head bolts. Tighten them in a circular pattern, working from the center to the ends, in three progressive steps.

NOTE: *It is advisable to use new cylinder head bolts whenever the head is removed. These should be obtained from a Ford dealer, since they are a special design.*

17. Slip the camshaft belt over the sprocket. Release the tensioner. Rotate the crankshaft two complete turns in the direction of normal rotation, stopping at TDC of the compression stroke for No. 1 cylinder.

18. Check the engine timing. No. 1 piston should be at TDC, the camshaft sprocket mark should be aligned with the mark on the cylinder head, and the distributor rotor should be under the No. 1 cylinder spark plug tower. If these conditions are not met, the engine has slipped time. Remove the belt from the cam sprocket and repeat the engine timing procedure.

19. Connect the coolant hoses. Install the cam belt cover and the valve cover. Install the manifolds, if removed; use new gaskets. Install the throttle linkage. Connect all wires and hoses. Fill the cooling system. Check the oil level. Install the air cleaner. Start the engine and check for leaks. Check and reset the ignition timing as necessary.

Valve System

The intake and exhaust valves are driven by the camshaft, working through hydraulic lash adjusters and stamped steel rocker arms. The hydraulic lash adjusters eliminate the need for periodic valve adjustment.

Rocker Arm

REMOVAL AND INSTALLATION

1. Disconnect the negative battery cable. Remove the air cleaner and air inlet duct.

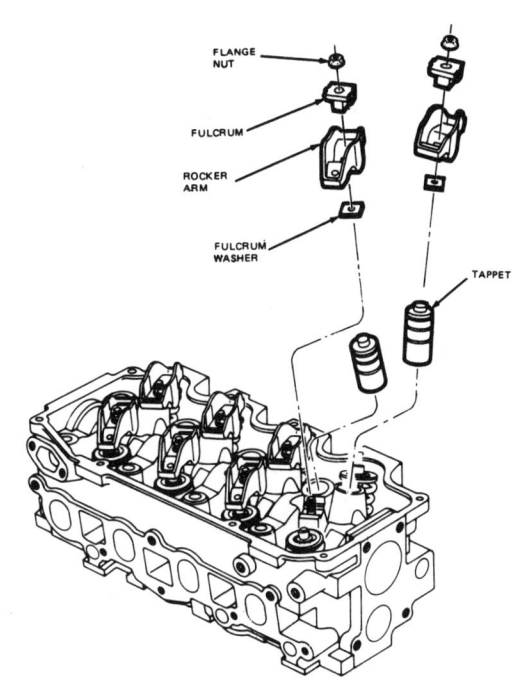

Exploded view of the upper valve train

Disconnect and label all hoses and wires connected to or crossing the valve cover. Remove the cover.

2. Remove the rocker arm retaining nuts and remove the rocker arms and fulcrums. Keep all parts in order; they must be returned to their original positions.

3. Before installation, coat the valve tips and the rocker arm contact areas with Lubriplate® or the equivalent.

4. Rotate the engine until the lifter is on the base circle of the cam (valve closed).

CAUTION: *Turn the engine only in the direction of normal rotation. Backward rotation will cause the camshaft belt to slip or lose teeth, altering valve timing and causing serious engine damage.*

5. Install the rocker arm, fulcrum and retaining nut. Torque to 15–19 ft. lbs. Be sure the lifter is on the base circle of the cam for each rocker arm as it is installed.

6. Clean the valve cover mating surfaces. Apply a bead of sealer to the cover flange and install the cover. Install all disconnected hoses and wires.

Intake Manifold

REMOVAL AND INSTALLATION

The manifold and carburetor can be removed as an assembly.

1. Disconnect the negative battery cable.

66 ENGINE AND ENGINE REBUILDING

TIGHTEN THE ATTACHING NUTS TO 16-17 N·m (12-13 LB-FT)

INTAKE MANIFOLD

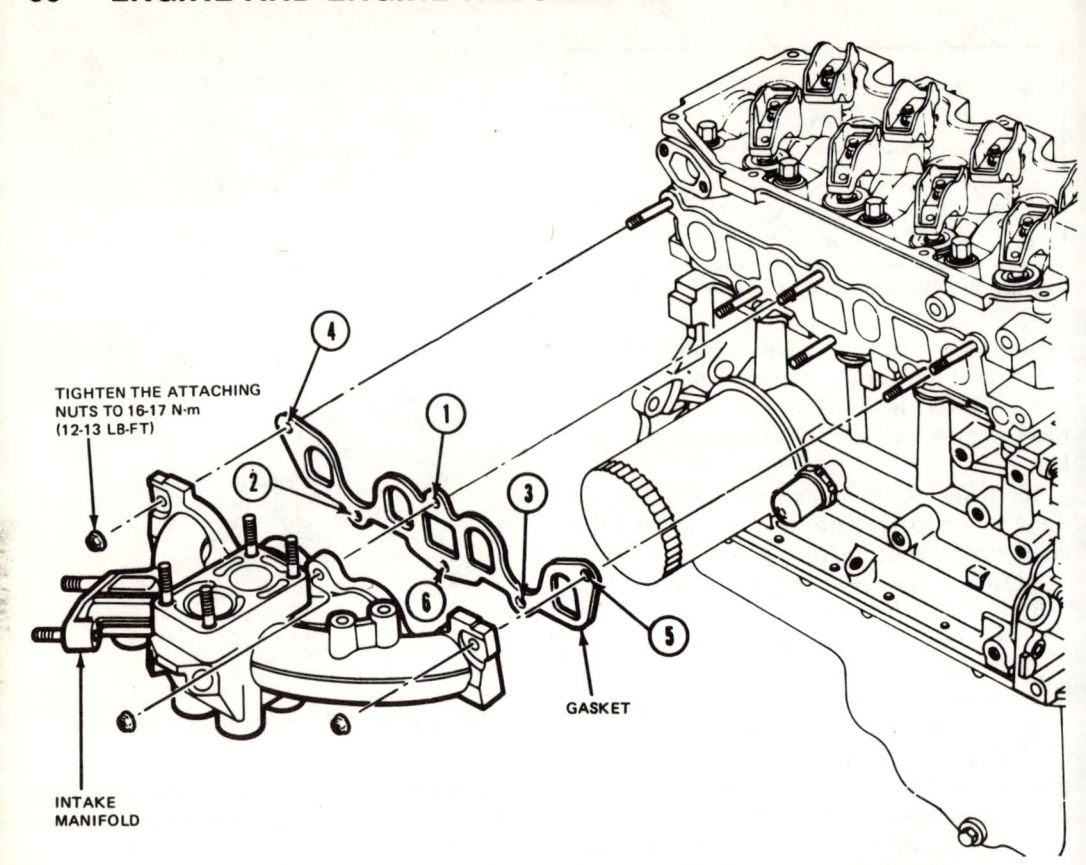

Install the intake manifold and tighten the retaining bolts in the sequence shown

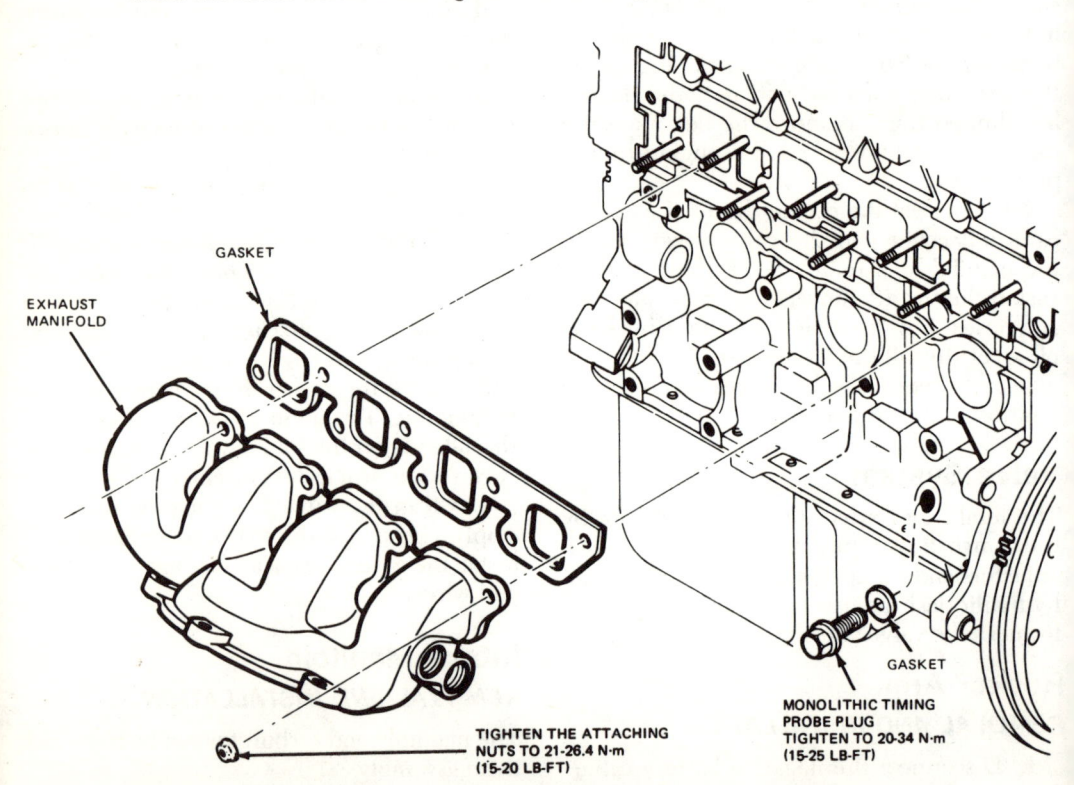

EXHAUST MANIFOLD

GASKET

TIGHTEN THE ATTACHING NUTS TO 21-26.4 N·m (15-20 LB-FT)

GASKET

MONOLITHIC TIMING PROBE PLUG TIGHTEN TO 20-34 N·m (15-25 LB-FT)

Install the exhaust manifold and tighten the retaining bolts in the sequence shown

ENGINE AND ENGINE REBUILDING

2. Remove the air cleaner housing. Disconnect the fuel line and throttle linkage from the carburetor. Disconnect and label all vacuum and electrical connections to the manifold and carburetor. Disconnect the EGR vacuum hose and tube.

3. Unbolt and remove the manifold.

4. Clean the mating surfaces on the gasket and head. Install a new gasket. Install the manifold. Tighten the mounting bolts in a circular pattern, working from the center to the ends, in three progressive steps.

5. Install the throttle linkage, fuel line, vacuum hoses, EGR vacuum line and tube, and the electrical connectors. Install the air cleaner and connect the battery cable.

Exhaust Manifold
REMOVAL AND INSTALLATION

1. Disconnect the negative battery cable.
2. Remove the air cleaner duct for access to the manifold.
3. Disconnect the Thermactor (air pump) line from the manifold. Disconnect the EGR tube. Unbolt the exhaust pipe from the manifold flange.
4. Unbolt and remove the exhaust manifold.
5. Clean the manifold mating surfaces. Place a new gasket on the exhaust pipe-to-manifold flange.
6. Install the manifold. Tighten the bolts in a circular pattern, working from the center to the ends, in three progressive steps.

Timing Belt
CHECKING ENGINE TIMING

Should the camshaft drive belt jump timing by a tooth or two, the engine could still run, although very poorly. To visually check for correct timing, remove the No. 1 spark plug and place your thumb over the hole. Use a wrench on the crankshaft pulley bolt to rotate

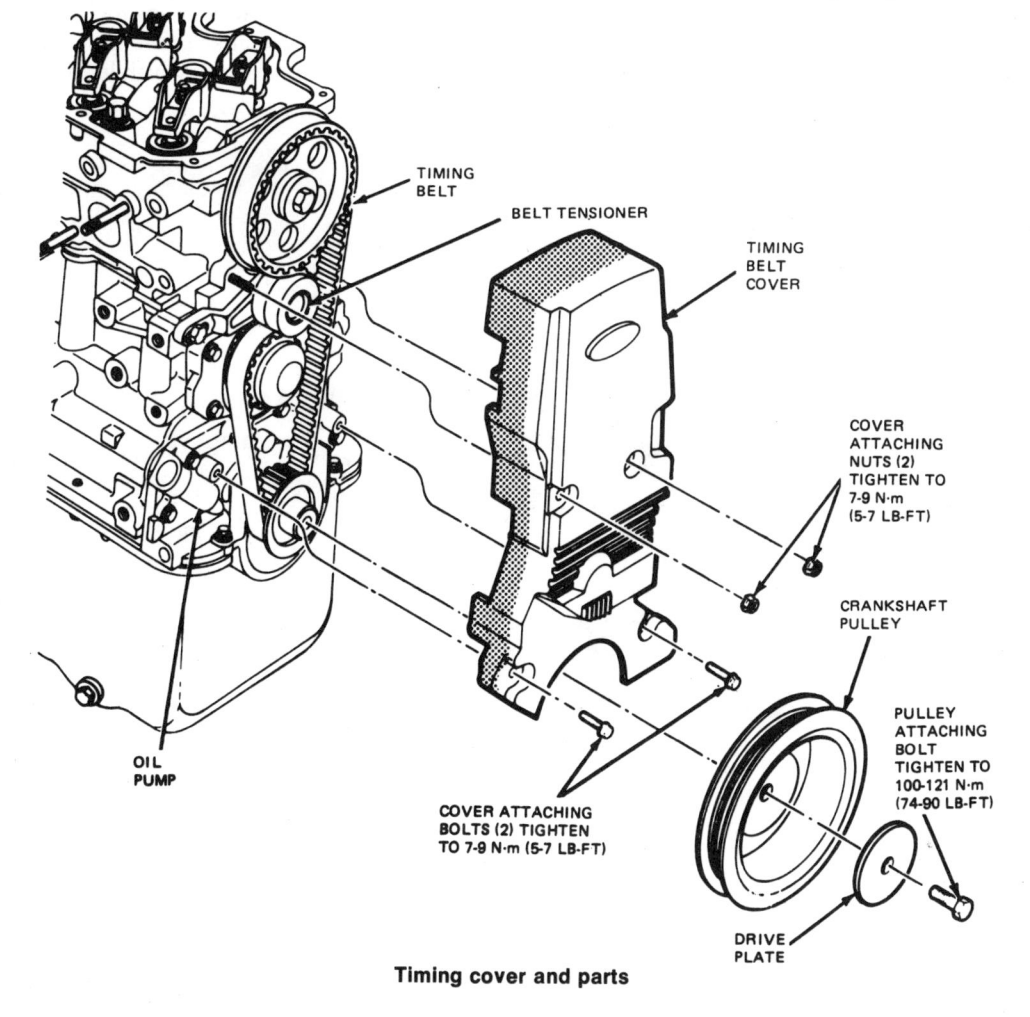

Timing cover and parts

the engine to TDC of the compression stroke for No. 1 cylinder.

CAUTION: *Turn the crankshaft only in the direction of normal rotation. Backward rotation will cause the belt to slip or lose teeth, altering engine timing.*

As the No. 1 piston rises on the compression stroke, your thumb will be pushed out by compression pressure. At the same time, the timing notch on the crankshaft pulley will be approaching the "O", or TDC, mark on the timing degree scale molded into the camshaft belt cover. Continue to turn the crankshaft until the pulley mark and "O" mark are aligned, indicating that No. 1 cylinder is at TDC.

Remove the alternator drive belt, and the power steering pump and air conditioning compressor drive belts, if so equipped. Remove the camshaft belt cover.

The camshaft sprocket has a mark next to one of the holes. The cylinder head is similarly marked. These marks should be aligned, dot-to-dot, indicating that camshaft timing is correct.

NOTE: *As a further check, the distributor cap can be removed: the ignition rotor should be pointing toward the No. 1 spark plug tower in the cap.*

If the marks are aligned, the engine timing is correct. If not, the belt must be removed from the cam sprocket and the camshaft turned until its marks are aligned (crankshaft still at TDC).

CAUTION: *Never attempt to rotate the engine by means of the camshaft sprocket. The 2:1 ratio between the camshaft and crankshaft sprockets will place a severe strain on the belt, stretching or tearing it.*

REMOVAL AND INSTALLATION

1. Set the engine to TDC as outlined in the "Checking Timing" procedure.
2. Check the engine timing. If correct, the belt can simply be removed and replaced. If incorrect, the camshaft position will have to be altered once the belt is removed.
3. Loosen the belt tensioner.
4. Remove the crankshaft pulley bolt and washer. You will have to lock up the engine to do this, to prevent crankshaft rotation. The best way is with a special tool which locks onto

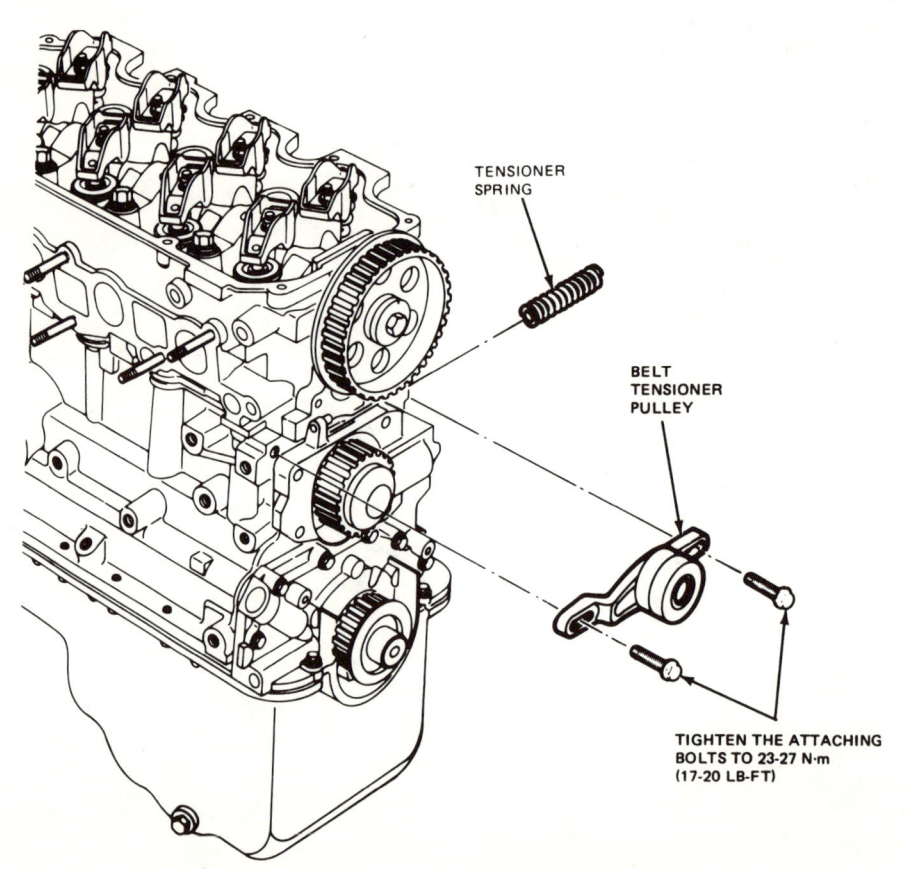

Tensioner and spring installation

ENGINE AND ENGINE REBUILDING 69

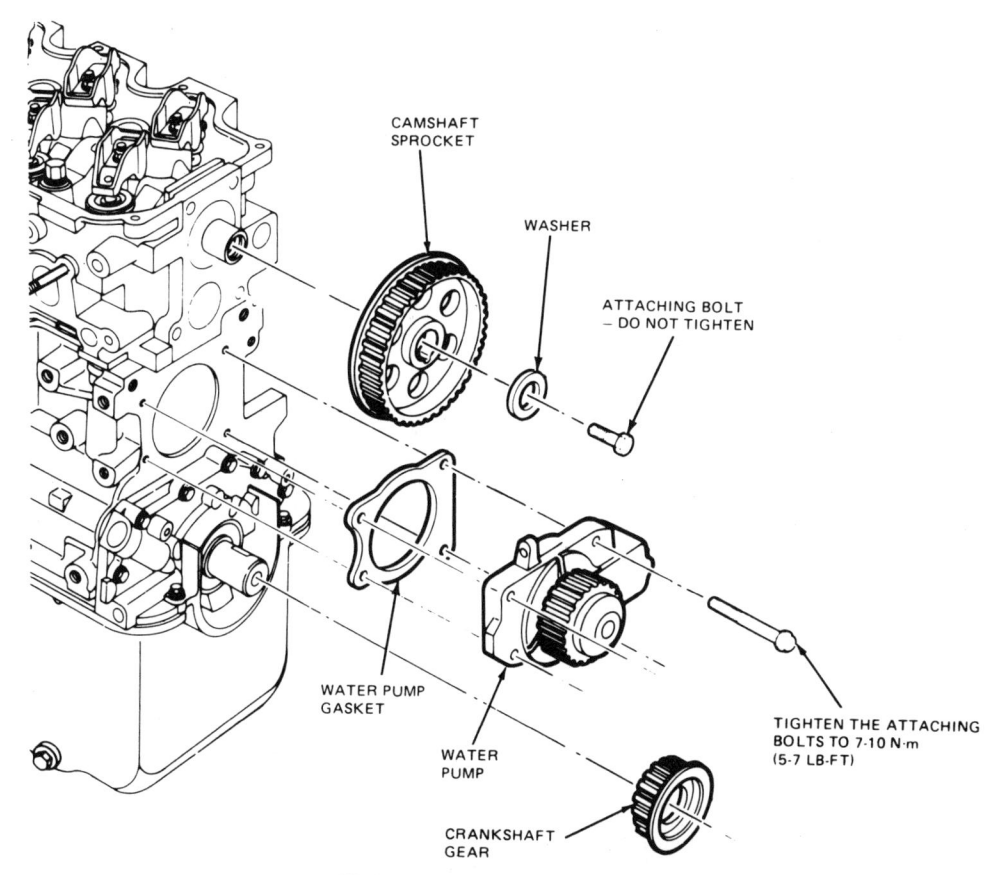

Timing components installation

the flywheel teeth. An alternative on manual transmission cars is to shift into fourth gear, set the parking brake, and block the wheels.

5. Remove the crankshaft pulley with a puller.

6. Pull the belt from the sprockets.

7. Install the new belt over the crankshaft pulley first, then counterclockwise over the camshaft sprocket, and around the water pump sprocket. Adjust the belt so that it is centered fore and aft on the sprockets.

8. Loosen the tensioner adjustment bolt, allowing it to spring back against the belt.

9. Rotate the crankshaft two complete turns in the direction of normal rotation to remove any belt slack. Turn the crankshaft until the timing marks are aligned. If timing is incorrect, or if the belt slips, remove the belt and repeat the procedure.

10. Install the crankshaft pulley, bolt, and washer.

11. Install the timing belt cover. Install the alternator and accessory drive belts. Adjust the drive belt tension.

12. Start the engine; check and adjust the ignition timing as necessary.

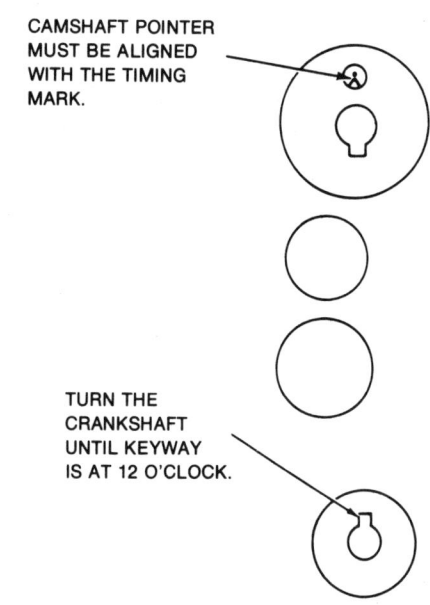

Line up the crankshaft and cam as shown when installing the timing belt

ENGINE AND ENGINE REBUILDING

Camshaft
REMOVAL AND INSTALLATION

The camshaft can be removed with the engine in the car.

1. Set the engine to TDC on the compression stroke of No. 1 cylinder. See the "Checking Timing" procedure.
2. Remove the alternator drive belt. Remove the power steering and air conditioning compressor drive belts, if equipped.
3. Remove the camshaft belt cover.
4. Remove the distributor. Refer to the procedure earlier in this section.
5. Remove the rocker arms. Refer to the procedure earlier in this section.
6. Remove the hydraulic lash adjusters. Keep the parts in order; they must be returned to their original positions.
7. Loosen the belt tensioner. Slip the camshaft belt from the cam sprocket. Do not remove or alter the position of the belt on the crankshaft sprocket.
8. Remove the cam sprocket retaining bolt.
9. Remove the cam sprocket with a puller.
10. Slide the cam out of the left side (distributor side) of the cylinder head.
11. Before installing the camshaft, coat it with 40W SF engine oil. Slide it into the head, being careful not to nick the lobes or bearing surfaces.
12. Install new camshaft seals.
13. Install the cam sprocket and retaining bolt. Rotate the cam until the timing marks on the sprocket and head align. Push the belt onto the sprocket.
14. Install the lash adjusters.
15. Install the rocker arms. Be sure the lash adjusters are on the base circle of the cam before tightening the rocker arm pivot bolts, as outlined in the "Rocker Arm Removal and Installation" procedure.
16. Loosen the tensioner, allowing it to spring back against the belt. Follow Step 9 of the "Timing Belt Removal and Installation" procedure.
17. Install the distributor.
18. Install the belt cover and accessory drive belts. Start the engine; check and adjust the ignition timing as necessary.

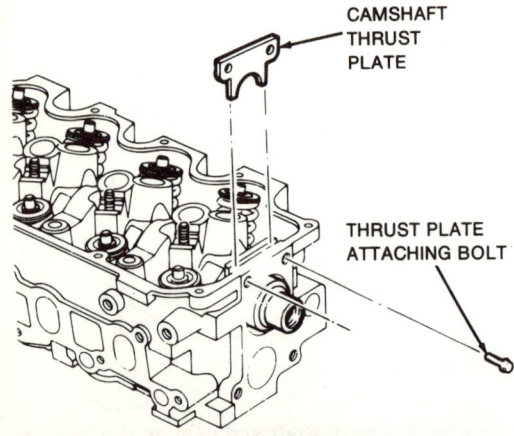

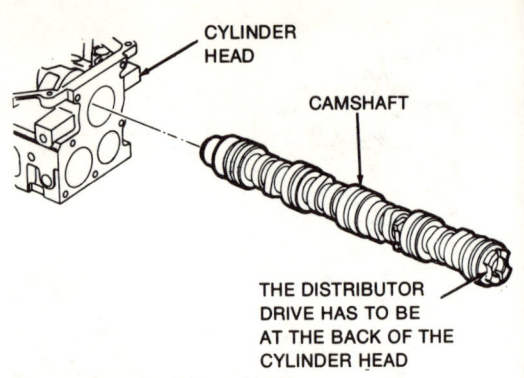

Correct camshaft installation

Remove the camshaft thrust plate

Pistons and Connecting Rods
REMOVAL

NOTE: *The pistons and connecting rods may be serviced either with the engine mounted in or removed from the car.*

1. Remove the timing cover, timing belt and crankshaft pulley.
2. Remove the cylinder head and oil pan.
3. Remove the bolt that holds the oil pick up tube to the engine block. Remove the six bolts that mount the oil pump. Remove the oil pump and pick up tube.
4. Check the connecting rods to make sure they are numbered. If not, mark the cap and rod with corresponding numbers.
5. Remove the ridge at the top of each bore with a ridge reamer (see the engine rebuilding section).
6. Partially remove the bearing cap nuts and tap each bolt with a wooden hammer handle to release the caps. Remove the nuts and cap. Put a piece of rubber hose on each rod bolt to protect the crankshaft journal. Push the piston and rod upward and remove from the cylinder.

FITTING PISTONS

Pistons are available for service in standard and standard oversizes. The standard size

ENGINE AND ENGINE REBUILDING

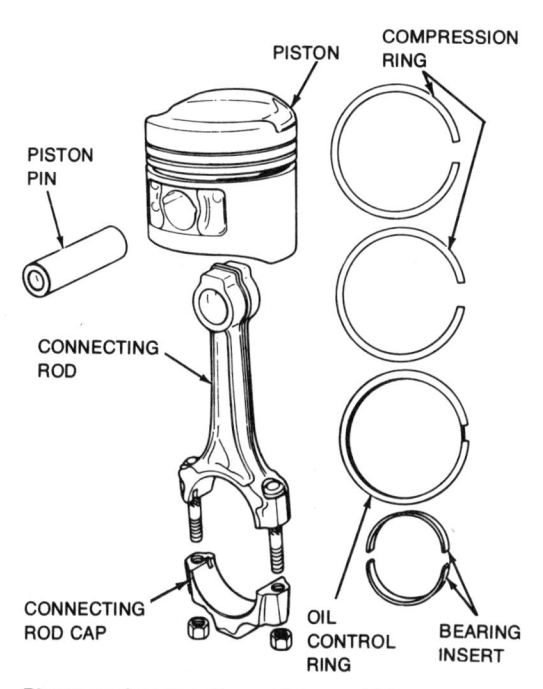

Piston and connecting rod assembly

pistons are colored coded red or blue or have 0.003 OS stamped on the dome. The piston and rod assembly must be reinstalled in the same cylinder it was removed from unless the cylinder bore is worn and must be honed or bored. An oversize piston will then be required.

INSTALLATION

1. Position the bearing inserts in the connecting rods and end caps. Turn the crankshaft as necessary to fit each connecting rod big end to the crankpin.
2. Measure the bearing clearances with Plastigage® as described in the Engine Rebuilding Section.
3. After the proper bearing inserts have been fitted, remove all Plastigage material, and install connecting rod caps, torquing rod bolts to specifications.
4. Reverse disassembly procedures for the remaining disassembled items, referring to the proper procedures for oil pan, cylinder head, and engine installation.

PISTON AND CONNECTING ROD POSITIONING

1. The "Front" markings on the connecting rod must align with the arrow on the piston crown.
2. "Front" and arrow markings must face the "front" of the engine when rods and pistons are reinstalled.
3. Position the oil ring gap to the rear of the piston and the top and second compression ring gaps at 180 degree and 90 degree angles.

NOTE: *Dip the piston assembly into an oil filled container before compressing the rings. Make sure the cylinder walls and connecting rod journals are clean and oiled before installation of the piston/rod assembly.*

LUBRICATION

Oil Pan

REMOVAL AND INSTALLATION

The oil pan can be removed with the engine in the car. No suspension or chassis components need be removed.

1. Drain the engine oil.
2. Remove the oil pan-to-engine block bolts.
3. Remove the pan. If it sticks, rap it gently with a rubber mallet. Be careful during removal not to contact the oil intake tube and screen.
4. Clean the mating surfaces thoroughly.
5. Apply a thin film of sealer to the side, front, and rear gaskets. Stick the side gaskets to the pan, not the block.
6. Install the pan and retaining bolts. Tighten the bolts in a circular pattern, working from the center to the ends, in three progressive steps to 6–8 ft. lbs.

Oil Pump

REMOVAL AND INSTALLATION

1. Remove the crankshaft pulley bolt and washer, the crankshaft pulley, and the camshaft timing belt. See the "Timing Belt Removal and Installation" procedure. Remove the crankshaft timing belt sprocket.
2. Remove the starter.
3. Remove the transaxle inspection plate and rear section of the knee brace.
4. Remove the oil pan.
5. Remove the oil pump pickup tube brace bolt.
6. Remove the oil pump-to-block mounting bolts. Remove the pump.
7. To install, first clean the pump and block mating surfaces.
8. Lubricate the oil pump seal with clean

72 ENGINE AND ENGINE REBUILDING

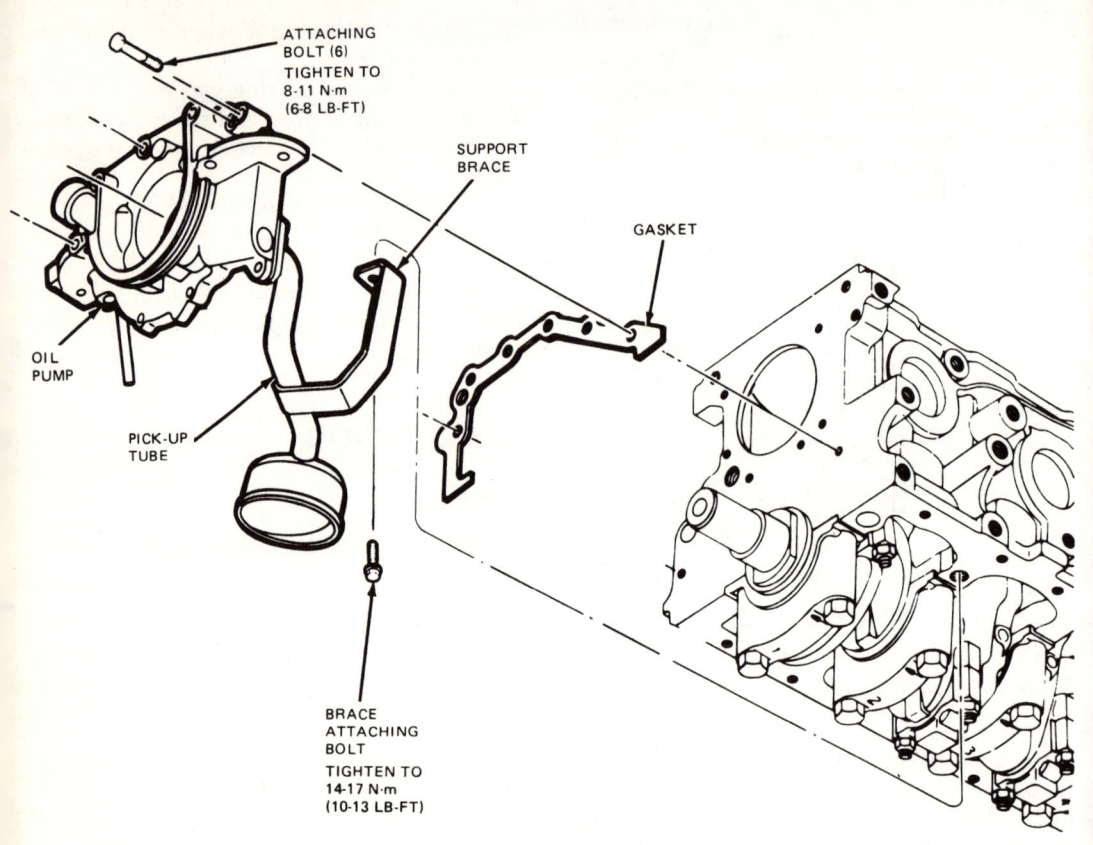

Oil pump installation

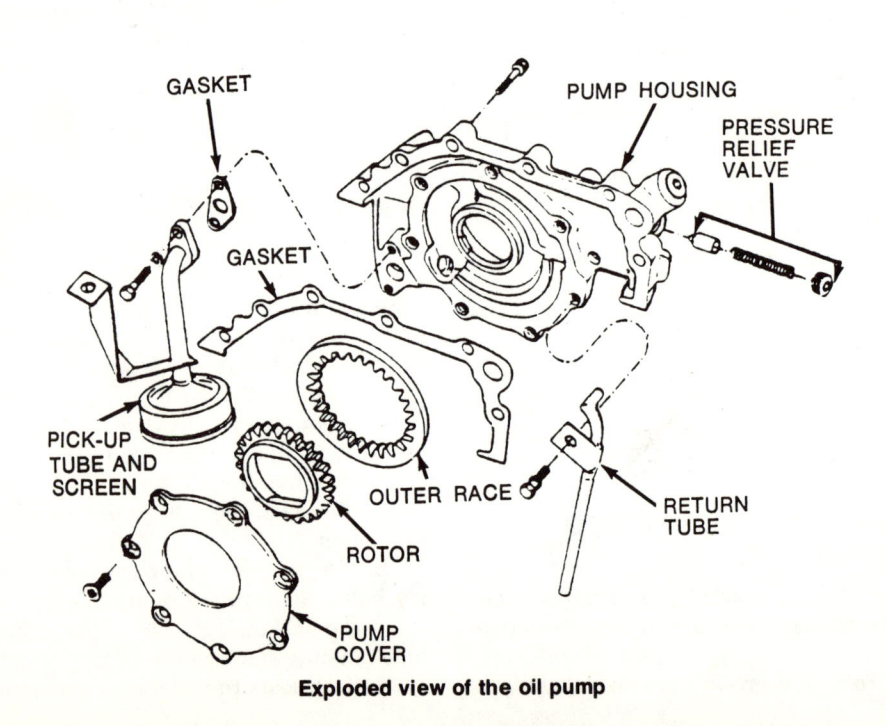

Exploded view of the oil pump

ENGINE AND ENGINE REBUILDING

SF engine oil. Install the seal with Ford seal installer T81P-6700-A For the equivalent.

9. Install a new oil pump gasket over the dowels.
10. Install the oil pump on the block. Tighten the mounting bolts to 6–8 ft. lbs.
11. Install the pickup tube brace bolt.
12. Install the oil pan.
13. Install the transaxle inspection plate and the rear section of the knee brace.
14. Install the starter, crankshaft sprocket, timing belt, crankshaft pulley, timing cover, and accessory drive belts.

Rear Main Oil Seal

REMOVAL AND INSTALLATION

A one-piece ring-type rear main oil seal is used.

1. Remove the transaxle and flywheel or flexplate.
2. Remove the rear main seal with a screwdriver. Be extremely careful not to scratch the crankshaft or seal mating surface.
3. Coat the lips of a new seal with clean engine oil. Install the new seal by hand onto the crankshaft flange.
4. Install the flywheel or flexplate and the transaxle.

COOLING SYSTEM

CAUTION: *The electric fan may still operate after the engine has been shut off.*

The sealed cooling system consists of a crossflow radiator with nylon end tanks, a thermostatically-controlled electric cooling fan, a sealed water pump, and the coolant recovery tank, connected to the radiator by a length of hose. The water pump is mounted on the front of the engine, driven by the camshaft belt.

Radiator

REMOVAL AND INSTALLATION

1. Drain the cooling system.
2. Disconnect the upper and lower radiator hoses. Disconnect the hose to the coolant recovery tank. If the car has an automatic transmission, disconnect and plug the transmission fluid cooler lines.
3. Remove the fan shroud-to-radiator support bolts. Remove the radiator mounting bolts and remove the radiator.
4. Installation is the reverse.

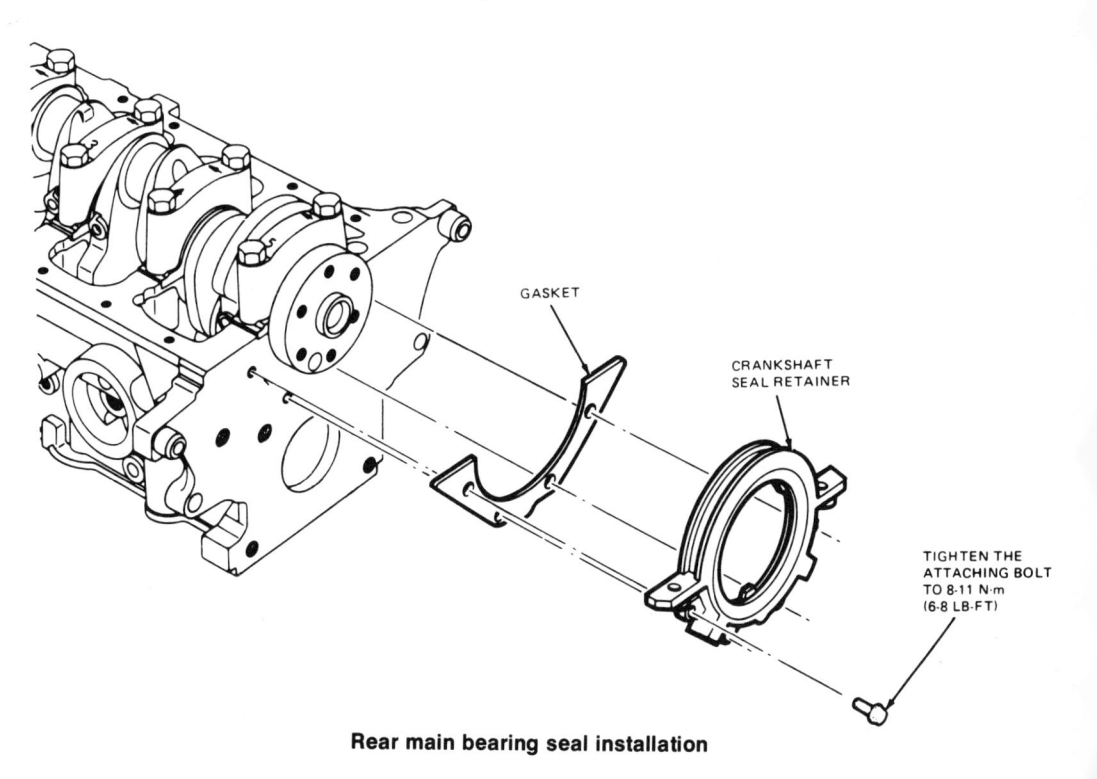

Rear main bearing seal installation

74 ENGINE AND ENGINE REBUILDING

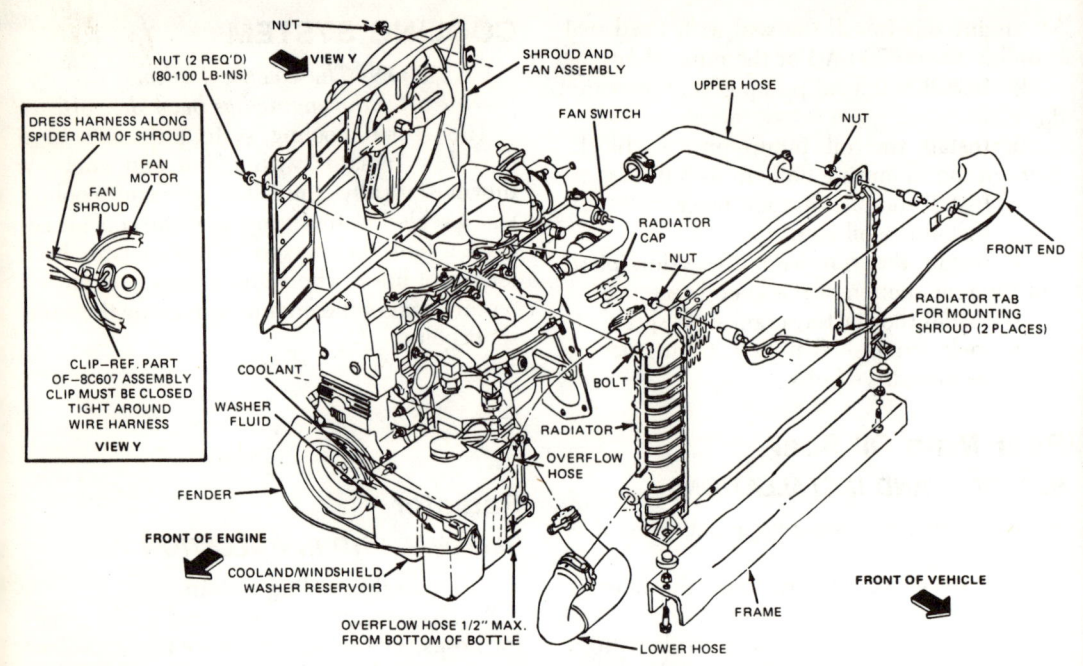

Cooling system components

Water Pump

REMOVAL AND INSTALLATION

1. Disconnect the negative battery cable. Drain the cooling system.
2. Remove the alternator drive belt. If equipped with air conditioning or power steering, remove the drive belts.
3. Use a wrench on the crankshaft pulley to rotate the engine to TDC of the compression stroke.

CAUTION: *Turn the engine only in the di-*

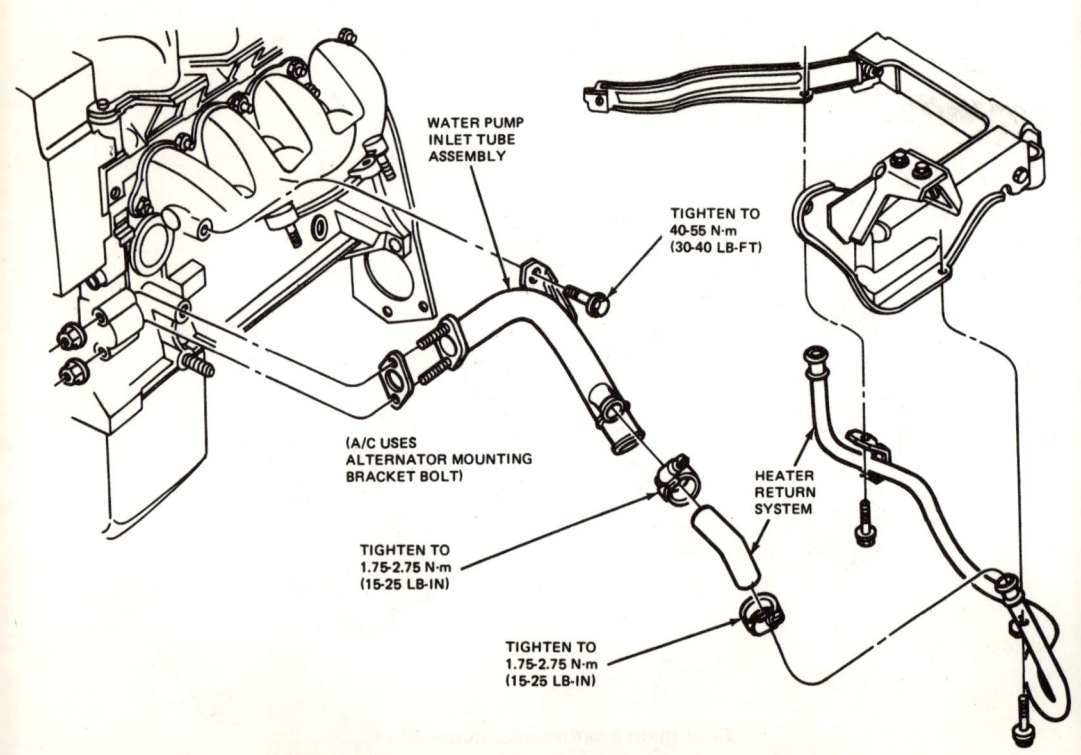

Typical water inlet system, car shown non air conditioned

ENGINE AND ENGINE REBUILDING

rection of normal rotation. Backward rotation will cause the camshaft belt to slip or lose teeth.

4. Remove the cam belt cover.
5. Loosen the belt tensioner.
6. Pull the belt from the camshaft, tensioner, and water pump sprockets. Do not remove it from, or allow it to change its position on, the crankshaft sprocket.

NOTE: *Do not rotate the engine with the camshaft belt removed.*

7. Remove the water pump bolts and remove the pump.
8. Clean the water pump and engine mating surfaces. Apply a thin bead of sealer to the pump surface and install the pump. Tighten the mounting bolts in rotation in three progressive steps.
9. Push the cam belt onto the water pump, tensioner, and camshaft sprockets. Align the belt fore and aft on the sprockets.
10. Release the tensioner. Rotate the crankshaft two complete turns in the direction of normal rotation, returning it to TDC of the compression stroke for No. 1 cylinder. Tighten the tensioner.
11. Check the engine timing. With the crankshaft pulley and the No. 1 piston at TDC of the compression stroke, the camshaft mark should be aligned with the mark on the head, and the distributor rotor should be below the No. 1 spark plug tower.
12. Install the cam belt cover. Install and tension the alternator, power steering, and air conditioner compressor drive belts. Fill the cooling system. Connect the battery cable, start the engine, and check for leaks.

Thermostat

REMOVAL AND INSTALLATION

1. Disconnect the two battery cables, and the electrical connector at the thermostat housing.
2. Remove the radiator cap. Put a drain pan under the radiator, open the radiator drain cock or loosen the lower hose clamp at the radiator, and pull off the hose to drain about half the coolant from the system.
3. Loosen the upper hose clamp at the radiator. Remove the two thermostat housing mounting bolts, pull the housing clear and remove the thermostat by twisting it counterclockwise.
4. To install, reverse the removal procedure, be sure to clean the mounting surfaces and install a new gasket. Torque housing bolts to 12–15 ft. lbs.

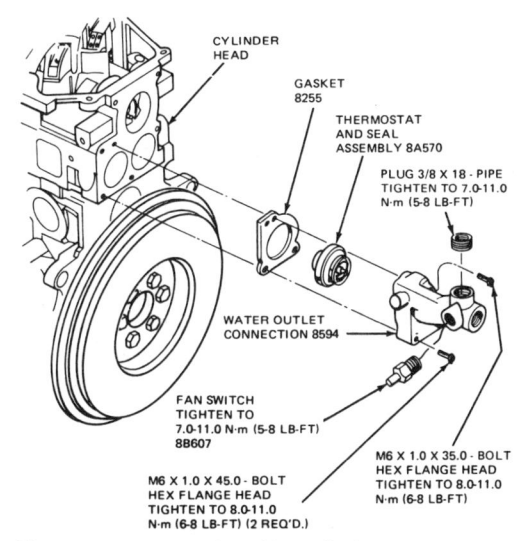

Thermostat removal and installation

Electric Fan

OPERATION

The electric cooling fan is mounted in the shroud behind the radiator.

A thermal switch mounted in the thermostat housing activates the fan when the coolant reaches a specified temperature. When the temperature is approximately 221 degrees F the thermal switch closes thus starting the fan.

The electric fan also operates when the air conditioner (if equipped) is turned on. When the temperature drops to between 185–193 degrees F the thermal switch opens and the fan shuts off.

CAUTION: *Since the fan is governed by temperature the engine does not have to be "on" for the fan to operate. If any underhood operations must be performed on a "warm" engine, disconnect the wiring harness to the fan.*

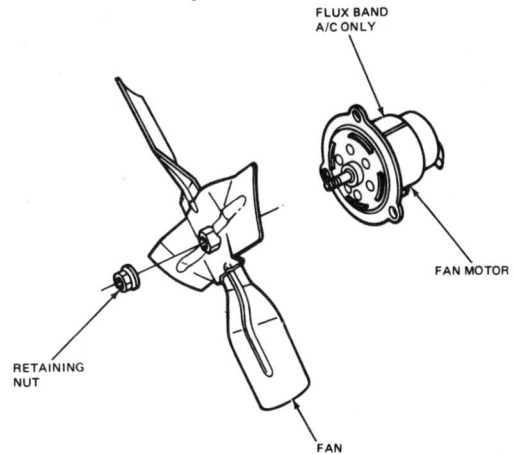

Cooling fan and electric motor

ENGINE REBUILDING

Most procedures involved in rebuilding an engine are fairly standard, regardless of the type of engine involved. This section is a guide to accepted rebuilding procedures. Examples of standard rebuilding practices are illustrated and should be used along with specific details concerning your particular engine, found earlier in this chapter.

The procedures given here are those used by any competent rebuilder. Obviously some of the procedures cannot be performed by the do-it-yourself mechanic, but are provided so that you will be familiar with the services that should be offered by rebuilding or machine shops. As an example, in most instances, it is more profitable for the home mechanic to remove the cylinder heads, buy the necessary parts (new valves, seals, keepers, keys, etc.) and deliver these to a machine shop for the necessary work. In this way you will save the money to remove and install the cylinder head and the mark-up on parts.

On the other hand, most of the work involved in rebuilding the lower end is well within the scope of the do-it-yourself mechanic. Only work such as hot-tanking, actually boring the block or Magnafluxing (invisible crack detection) need be sent to a machine shop.

Tools

The tools required for basic engine rebuilding should, with a few exceptions, be those included in a mechanic's tool kit. An accurate torque wrench, and a dial indicator (reading in thousandths) mounted on a universal base should be available. Special tools, where required, are available from the major tool suppliers. The services of a competent automotive machine shop must also be readily available.

Precautions

Aluminum has become increasingly popular for use in engines, due to its low weight and excellent heat transfer characteristics. The following precautions must be observed when handling aluminum (or any other) engine parts:

—Never hot-tank aluminum parts.

—Remove all aluminum parts (identification tags, etc.) from engine parts before hot-tanking (otherwise they will be removed during the process).

—Always coat threads lightly with engine oil or anti-seize compounds before installation, to prevent seizure.

—Never over-torque bolts or spark plugs in aluminum threads. Should stripping occur, threads can be restored using any of a number of thread repair kits available (see next section).

Inspection Techniques

Magnaflux and Zyglo are inspection techniques used to locate material flaws, such as stress cracks. Magnaflux is a magnetic process, applicable only to ferrous materials. The Zyglo process coats the material with a fluorescent dye penetrant, and any material may be tested using Zyglo. Specific checks of suspected surface cracks may be made at lower cost and more readily using spot check dye. The dye is sprayed onto the suspected area, wiped off, and the area is then sprayed with a developer. Cracks then will show up brightly.

Overhaul

The section is divided into two parts. The first, Cylinder Head Reconditioning, assumes that the cylinder head is removed from the engine, all manifolds are removed, and the cylinder head is on a workbench. The camshaft should be removed from overhead cam cylinder heads. The second section, Cylinder Block Reconditioning, covers the block, pistons, connecting rods and crankshaft. It is assumed that the engine is mounted on a work stand, and the cylinder head and all accessories are removed.

Procedures are identified as follows:

Unmarked—Basic procedures that must be performed in order to successfully complete the rebuilding process.

Starred (*)—Procedures that should be performed to ensure maximum performance and engine life.

Double starred (**)—Procedures that may be performed to increase engine performance and reliability.

When assembling the engine, any parts that will be in frictional contact must be pre-lubricated, to provide protection on initial start-up. Any product specifically formulated for this purpose may be used. NOTE: *Do not use engine oil.* Where semi-permanent (locked but removable) installation of bolts or nuts is desired, threads should be cleaned and located with Loctite® or a similar product (non-hardening).

ENGINE AND ENGINE REBUILDING

Repairing Damaged Threads

Several methods of repairing damaged threads are available. Heli-Coil® (shown here), Keenserts® and Microdot® are among the most widely used. All involve basically the same principle—drilling out stripped threads, tapping the hole and installing a prewound insert—making welding, plugging and oversize fasteners unnecessary.

Two types of thread repair inserts are usually supplied—a standard type for most Inch Coarse, Inch Fine, Metric Coarse and Metric Fine thread sizes and a spark plug type to fit most spark plug port sizes. Consult the individual manufacturer's catalog to determine exact applications. Typical thread repair kits will contain a selection of prewound threaded inserts, a tap (corresponding to the outside diameter threads of the insert) and an installation tool. Spark plug inserts usually differ because they require a tap equipped with pilot threads and a combined reamer/tap section. Most manufacturers also supply blister-packed thread repair inserts separately in addition to a master kit containing a variety of taps and inserts plus installation tools.

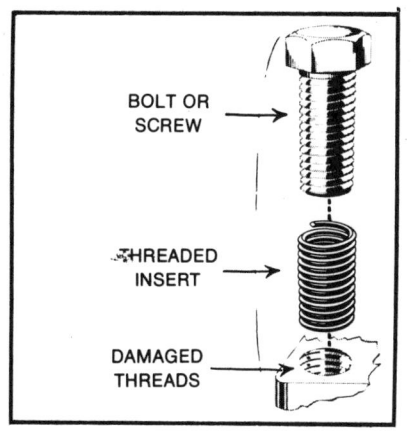

Before effecting a repair to a threaded hole, remove any snapped, broken or damaged bolts or studs. Penetrating oil can be used to free frozen threads; the offending item can be removed with locking pliers or with a screw or stud extractor. After the hole is clear, the thread can be repaired, as follows:

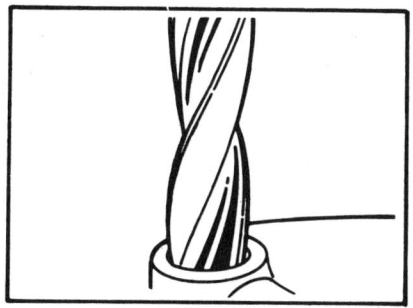

Drill out the damaged threads with specified drill. Drill completely through the hole or to the bottom of a blind hole

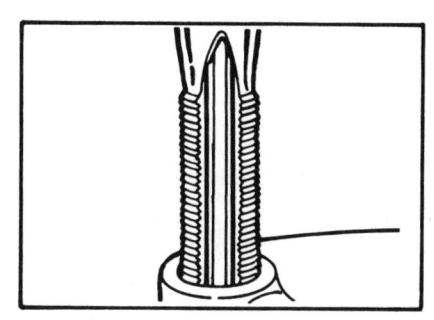

With the tap supplied, tap the hole to receive the thread insert. Keep the tap well oiled and back it out frequently to avoid clogging the threads

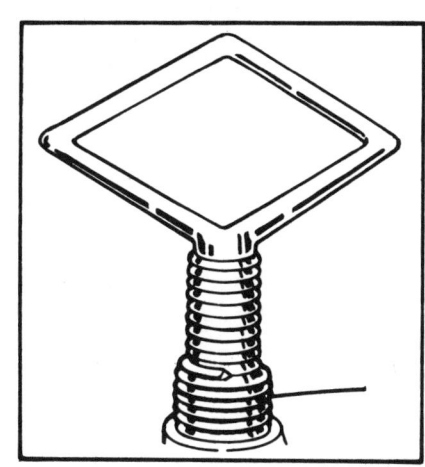

Damaged bolt holes can be repaired with thread repair inserts

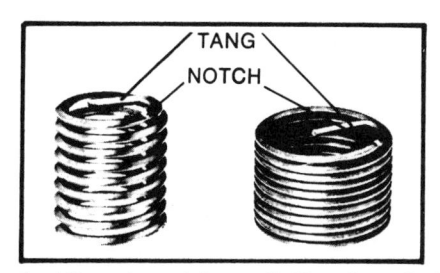

Standard thread repair insert (left) and spark plug thread insert (right)

Screw the threaded insert onto the installation tool until the tang engages the slot. Screw the insert into the tapped hole until it is ¼–½ turn below the top surface. After installation break off the tang with a hammer and punch

ENGINE AND ENGINE REBUILDING

Standard Torque Specifications and Fastener Markings

The Newton-metre has been designated the world standard for measuring torque and will gradually replace the foot-pound and kilogram-meter. In the absence of specific torques, the following chart can be used as a guide to the maximum safe torque of a particular size/grade of fastener.

- There is no torque difference for fine or coarse threads.
- Torque values are based on clean, dry threads. Reduce the value by 10% if threads are oiled prior to assembly.
- The torque required for aluminum components or fasteners is considerably less.

U. S. BOLTS

SAE Grade Number	1 or 2			5			6 or 7		
Bolt Markings Manufacturer's marks may vary—number of lines always 2 less than the grade number.									
Usage	Frequent			Frequent			Infrequent		
Bolt Size (inches)—(Thread)	Maximum Torque			Maximum Torque			Maximum Torque		
	Ft-Lb	kgm	Nm	Ft-Lb	kgm	Nm	Ft-Lb	kgm	Nm
¼—20	5	0.7	6.8	8	1.1	10.8	10	1.4	13.5
—28	6	0.8	8.1	10	1.4	13.6			
5/16—18	11	1.5	14.9	17	2.3	23.0	19	2.6	25.8
—24	13	1.8	17.6	19	2.6	25.7			
3/8—16	18	2.5	24.4	31	4.3	42.0	34	4.7	46.0
—24	20	2.75	27.1	35	4.8	47.5			
7/16—14	28	3.8	37.0	49	6.8	66.4	55	7.6	74.5
—20	30	4.2	40.7	55	7.6	74.5			
½—13	39	5.4	52.8	75	10.4	101.7	85	11.75	115.2
—20	41	5.7	55.6	85	11.7	115.2			
9/16—12	51	7.0	69.2	110	15.2	149.1	120	16.6	162.7
—18	55	7.6	74.5	120	16.6	162.7			
5/8—11	83	11.5	112.5	150	20.7	203.3	167	23.0	226.5
—18	95	13.1	128.8	170	23.5	230.5			
¾—10	105	14.5	142.3	270	37.3	366.0	280	38.7	379.6
—16	115	15.9	155.9	295	40.8	400.0			
7/8— 9	160	22.1	216.9	395	54.6	535.5	440	60.9	596.5
—14	175	24.2	237.2	435	60.1	589.7			
1— 8	236	32.5	318.6	590	81.6	799.9	660	91.3	894.8
—14	250	34.6	338.9	660	91.3	849.8			

ENGINE AND ENGINE REBUILDING

METRIC BOLTS

NOTE: *Metric bolts are marked with a number indicating the relative strength of the bolt. These numbers have nothing to do with size.*

Description	Torque ft-lbs (Nm)	
Thread size x pitch (mm)	Head mark—4	Head mark—7
6 x 1.0	2.2–2.9 (3.0–3.9)	3.6–5.8 (4.9–7.8)
8 x 1.25	5.8–8.7 (7.9–12)	9.4–14 (13–19)
10 x 1.25	12–17 (16–23)	20–29 (27–39)
12 x 1.25	21–32 (29–43)	35–53 (47–72)
14 x 1.5	35–52 (48–70)	57–85 (77–110)
16 x 1.5	51–77 (67–100)	90–120 (130–160)
18 x 1.5	74–110 (100–150)	130–170 (180–230)
20 x 1.5	110–140 (150–190)	190–240 (160–320)
22 x 1.5	150–190 (200–260)	250–320 (340–430)
24 x 1.5	190–240 (260–320)	310–410 (420–550)

NOTE: *This engine rebuilding section is a guide to accepted rebuilding procedures. Typical examples of standard rebuilding procedures are illustrated. Use these procedures along with the detailed instructions earlier in this chapter, concerning your particular engine.*

Cylinder Head Reconditioning

Procedure	Method
Remove the cylinder head:	See the engine service procedures earlier in this chapter for details concerning specific engines.
Identify the valves:	Invert the cylinder head, and number the valve faces front to rear, using a permanent felt-tip marker.
Remove the camshaft:	See the engine service procedures earlier in this chapter for details concerning specific engines.
Remove the valves and springs:	Using an appropriate valve spring compressor (depending on the configuration of the cylinder head), compress the valve springs. Lift out the keepers with needlenose pliers, release the compressor, and remove the valve, spring, and spring retainer. See the engine service procedures earlier in this chapter for details concerning specific engines.
Check the valve stem-to-guide clearance:	Clean the valve stem with lacquer thinner or a similar solvent to remove all gum and varnish. Clean the valve guides using solvent and an expanding wire-type valve guide cleaner. Mount a dial indicator so that the stem is at 90° to the valve stem, as close to the valve guide as possible. Move the valve off its seat, and measure the valve guide-to-stem clearance by rocking the stem back and forth to actuate the dial indicator. Measure the valve stems using a micrometer, and compare to specifications, to determine whether stem or guide wear is responsible for excessive clearance. NOTE: *Consult the Specifications tables earlier in this chapter.*

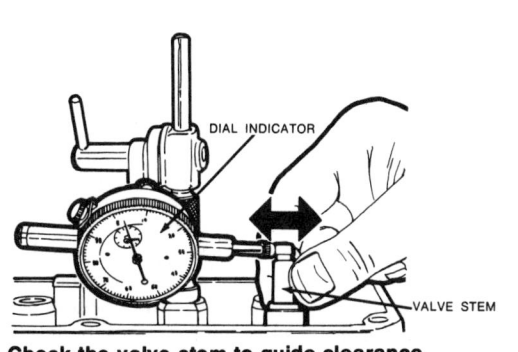

Check the valve stem-to-guide clearance

80 ENGINE AND ENGINE REBUILDING

Cylinder Head Reconditioning

Procedure	Method
De-carbon the cylinder head and valves: Remove the carbon from the cylinder head with a wire brush and electric drill	Chip carbon away from the valve heads, combustion chambers, and ports, using a chisel made of hardwood. Remove the remaining deposits with a stiff wire brush. **NOTE:** *Be sure that the deposits are actually removed, rather than burnished.*
Hot-tank the cylinder head (cast iron heads only): **CAUTION:** *Do not hot-tank aluminum parts.*	Have the cylinder head hot-tanked to remove grease, corrosion, and scale from the water passages. **NOTE:** *In the case of overhead cam cylinder heads, consult the operator to determine whether the camshaft bearings will be damaged by the caustic solution.*
Degrease the remaining cylinder head parts:	Clean the remaining cylinder head parts in an engine cleaning solvent. Do not remove the protective coating from the springs.
Check the cylinder head for warpage: Check the cylinder head for warpage	Place a straight-edge across the gasket surface of the cylinder head. Using feeler gauges, determine the clearance at the center of the straight-edge. If warpage exceeds .003″ in a 6″ span, or .006″ over the total length, the cylinder head must be resurfaced. **NOTE:** *If warpage exceeds the manufacturer's maximum tolerance for material removal, the cylinder head must be replaced.* When milling the cylinder heads of V-type engines, the intake manifold mounting position is altered, and must be corrected by milling the manifold flange a proportionate amount.
***Knurl the valve guides:** Cut-away view of a knurled valve guide	*Valve guides which are not excessively worn or distorted may, in some cases, be knurled rather than replaced. Knurling is a process in which metal is displaced and raised, thereby reducing clearance. Knurling also provides excellent oil control. The possibility of knurling rather than replacing valve guides should be discussed with a machinist.
Replace the valve guides: **NOTE:** *Valve guides should only be replaced if damaged or if an oversize valve stem is not available.*	See the engine service procedures earlier in this chapter for details concerning specific engines. Depending on the type of cylinder head, valve guides may be pressed, hammered, or shrunk in. In cases where the guides are shrunk into the head, replacement should be left to an equipped machine shop. In other

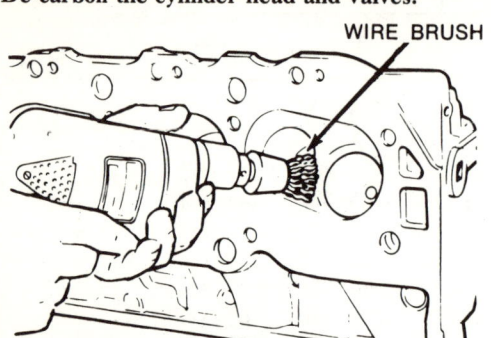

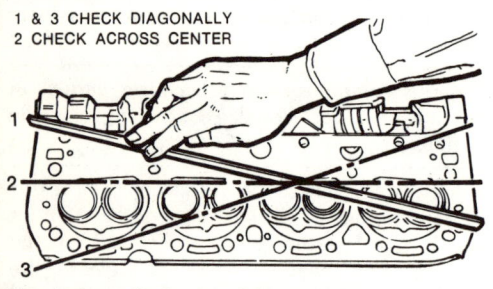

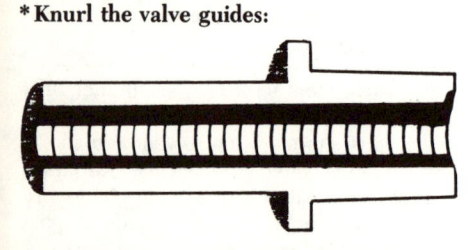

ENGINE AND ENGINE REBUILDING 81

Cylinder Head Reconditioning

Procedure	Method
	cases, the guides are replaced using a stepped drift (see illustration). Determine the height above the boss that the guide must extend, and obtain a stack of washers, their I.D. similar to the guide's O.D., of that height. Place the stack of washers on the guide, and insert the guide into the boss. NOTE: *Valve guides are often tapered or beveled for installation.* Using the stepped installation tool (see illustration), press or tap the guides into position. Ream the guides according to the size of the valve stem.

Valve guide installation tool using washers for installation

Replace valve seat inserts:	Replacement of valve seat inserts which are worn beyond resurfacing or broken, if feasible, must be done by a machine shop.
Resurface (grind) the valve face:	Using a valve grinder, resurface the valves according to specifications given earlier in this chapter. CAUTION: *Valve face angle is not always identical to valve seat angle.* A minimum margin of 1/32" should remain after grinding the valve. The valve stem top should also be squared and resurfaced, by placing the stem in the V-block of the grinder, and turning it while pressing lightly against the grinding wheel. NOTE: *Do not grind sodium filled exhaust valves on a machine. These should be hand lapped.*

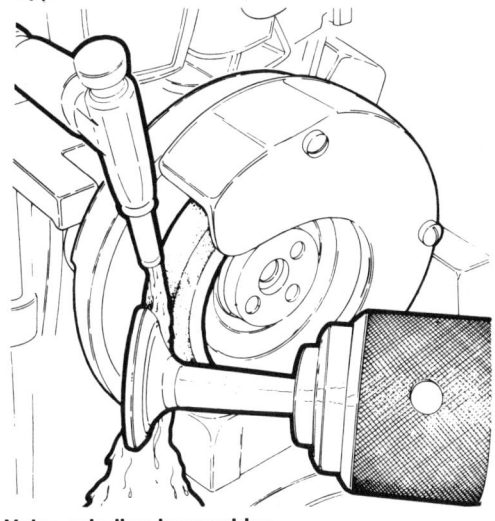

Critical valve dimensions

Valve grinding by machine

82 ENGINE AND ENGINE REBUILDING

Cylinder Head Reconditioning

Procedure	Method
Resurface the valve seats using reamers or grinder: *Valve seat width and centering* *Reaming the valve seat with a hand reamer*	Select a reamer of the correct seat angle, slightly larger than the diameter of the valve seat, and assemble it with a pilot of the correct size. Install the pilot into the valve guide, and using steady pressure, turn the reamer clockwise. **CAUTION**: *Do not turn the reamer counterclockwise.* Remove only as much material as necessary to clean the seat. Check the concentricity of the seat (following). If the dye method is not used, coat the valve face with Prussian blue dye, install and rotate it on the valve seat. Using the dye marked area as a centering guide, center and narrow the valve seat to specifications with correction cutters. **NOTE**: *When no specifications are available, minimum seat width for exhaust valves should be $5/64''$, intake valves $1/16''$.* After making correction cuts, check the position of the valve seat on the valve face using Prussian blue dye. To resurface the seat with a power grinder, select a pilot of the correct size and coarse stone of the proper angle. Lubricate the pilot and move the stone on and off the valve seat at 2 cycles per second, until all flaws are gone. Finish the seat with a fine stone. If necessary the seat can be corrected or narrowed using correction stones.
Check the valve seat concentricity: *Check the valve seat concentricity with a dial gauge*	Coat the valve face with Prussian blue dye, install the valve, and rotate it on the valve seat. If the entire seat becomes coated, and the valve is known to be concentric, the seat is concentric. *Install the dial gauge pilot into the guide, and rest of the arm on the valve seat. Zero the gauge, and rotate the arm around the seat. Run-out should not exceed .002''.

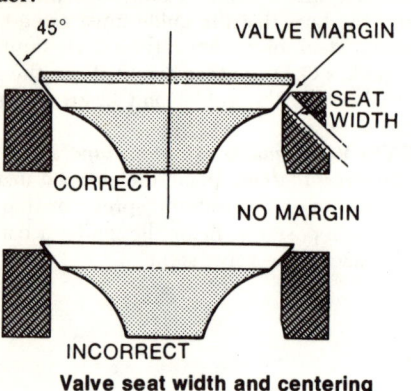

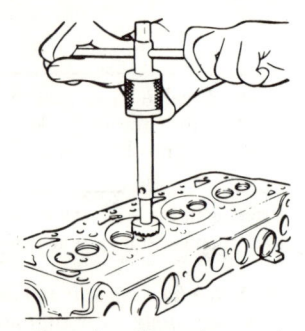

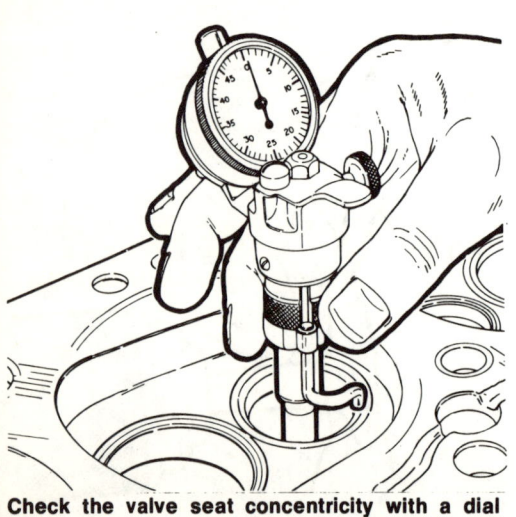

ENGINE AND ENGINE REBUILDING 83

Cylinder Head Reconditioning

Procedure	Method
*Lap the valves: NOTE: *Valve lapping is done to ensure efficient sealing of resurfaced valves and seats.* Lapping the valves by hand Home-made valve lapping tool	Invert the cyclinder head, lightly lubricate the valve stems, and install the valves in the head as numbered. Coat valve seats with fine grinding compound, and attach the lapping tool suction cup to a valve head. NOTE: *Moisten the suction cup.* Rotate the tool between the palms, changing position and lifting the tool often to prevent grooving. Lap the valve until a smooth, polished seat is evident. Remove the valve and tool, and rinse away all traces of grinding compound.
	**Fasten a suction cup to a piece of drill rod, and mount the rod in a hand drill. Proceed as above, using the hand drill as a lapping tool. CAUTION: *Due to the higher speeds involved when using the hand drill, care must be exercised to avoid grooving the seat.* Lift the tool and change direction of rotation often.
Check the valve springs: Check the valve spring free length and squareness Check the valve spring test pressure	Place the spring on a flat surface next to a square. Measure the height of the spring, and rotate it against the edge of the square to measure distortion. If spring height varies (by comparison) by more than $1/16''$ or if distortion exceeds $1/16''$, replace the spring.
	**In addition to evaluating the spring as above, test the spring pressure at the installed and compressed (installed height minus valve lift) height using a valve spring tester. Springs used on small displacement engines (up to 3 liters) should be $\mp$ 1 lb of all other springs in either position. A tolerance of $\mp$ 5 lbs is permissible on larger engines.

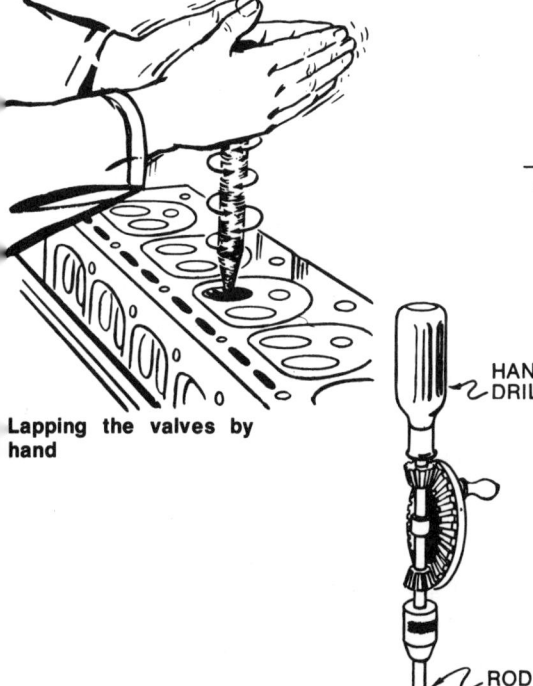

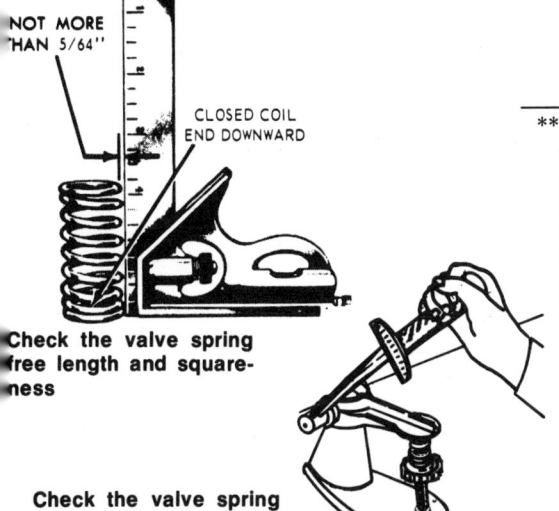

84 ENGINE AND ENGINE REBUILDING

Cylinder Head Reconditioning

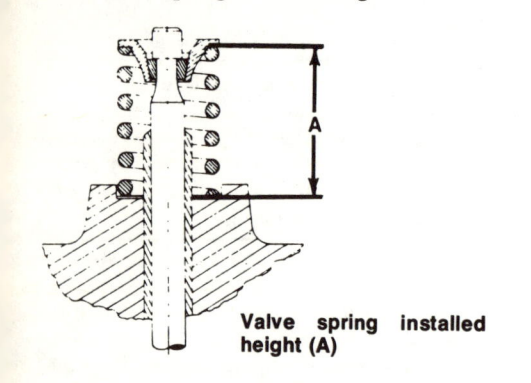

Procedure	Method
*Install valve stem seals: 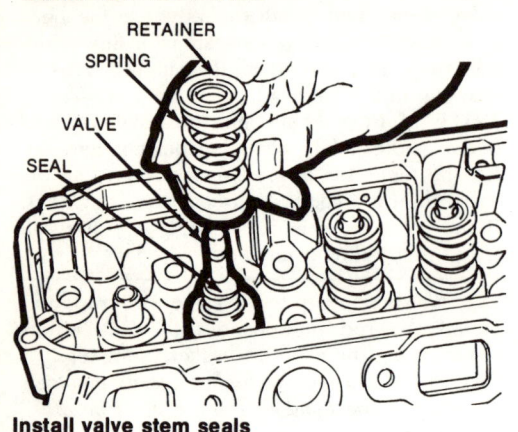 *Install valve stem seals* (RETAINER, SPRING, VALVE, SEAL)	*Due to the pressure differential that exists at the ends of the intake valve guides (atmospheric pressure above, manifold vacuum below), oil is drawn through the valve guides into the intake port. This has been alleviated somewhat since the addition of positive crankcase ventilation, which lowers the pressure above the guides. Several types of valve stem seals are available to reduce blow-by. Certain seals simply slip over the stem and guide boss, while others require that the boss be machined. Recently, Teflon guide seals have become popular. Consult a parts supplier or machinist concerning availability and suggested usages. NOTE: *When installing seals, ensure that a small amount of oil is able to pass the seal to lubricate the valve guides; otherwise, excessive wear may result.*
Install the valves:	See the engine service procedures earlier in this chapter for details concerning specific engines. Lubricate the valve stems, and install the valves in the cylinder head as numbered. Lubricate and position the seals (if used) and the valve springs. Install the spring retainers, compress the springs, and insert the keys using needlenose pliers or a tool designed for this purpose. NOTE: *Retain the keys with wheel bearing grease during installation.*
Check valve spring installed height: *Valve spring installed height (A)*	Measure the distance between the spring pad the lower edge of the spring retainer, and compare to specifications. If the installed height is incorrect, add shim washers between the spring pad and the spring. CAUTION: *Use only washers designed for this purpose.* 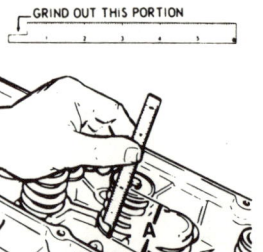 *Measure the valve spring installed height (A) with a modified steel rule* (GRIND OUT THIS PORTION)
Clean and inspect the camshaft:	Degrease the camshaft, using solvent, and clean out all oil holes. Visually inspect cam lobes and bearing journals for excessive wear. If a lobe is questionable, check all lobes as indicated below. If a journal or lobe is worn, the camshaft must be reground or replaced.

ENGINE AND ENGINE REBUILDING 85

Cylinder Head Reconditioning

Procedure	Method
	NOTE: *If a journal is worn, there is a good chance that the bushings are worn.* If lobes and journals appear intact, place the front and rear journals in V-blocks, and rest a dial indicator on the center journal. Rotate the camshaft to check straightness. If deviation exceeds .001″, replace the camshaft. *Check the camshaft lobes with a micrometer, by measuring the lobes from the nose to base and again at 90° (see illustration). The lift is determined by subtracting the second measurement from the first. If all exhaust lobes and all intake lobes are not identical, the camshaft must be reground or replaced.
Check the camshaft for straightness	**Camshaft lobe measurement**
Install the camshaft:	See the engine service procedures earlier in this chapter for details concerning specific engines.
Install the rocker arms:	See the engine service procedures earlier in this chapter for details concerning specific engines.

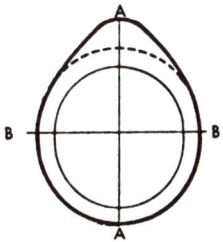

Cylinder Block Reconditioning

Procedure	Method
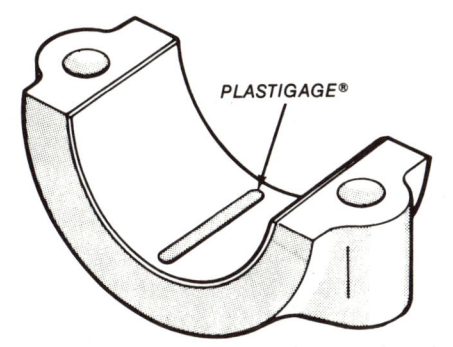 Checking the main bearing clearance:	Invert engine, and remove cap from the bearing to be checked. Using a clean, dry rag, thoroughly clean all oil from crankshaft journal and bearing insert. NOTE: *Plastigage® is soluble in oil; therefore, oil on the journal or bearing could result in erroneous readings.* Place a piece of Plastigage along the full length of journal, reinstall cap, and torque to specifications. NOTE: *Specifications are given in the engine specifications earlier in this chapter.* Remove bearing cap, and determine bearing clearance by comparing width of Plastigage to the scale on Plastigage envelope. Journal taper is determined by comparing width of the Plastigage strip near its ends. Rotate crankshaft 90° and retest, to determine journal eccentricity. NOTE: *Do not rotate crankshaft with Plastigage installed.* If bearing insert and journal appear in-
Plastigage® installed on the lower bearing shell	

ENGINE AND ENGINE REBUILDING

Cylinder Block Reconditioning

Procedure	Method
Measure Plastigage® to determine main bearing clearance	tact, and are within tolerances, no further main bearing service is required. If bearing or journal appear defective, cause of failure should be determined before replacement.
	*Remove crankshaft from block (see below). Measure the main bearing journals at each end twice (90° apart) using a micrometer, to determine diameter, journal taper and eccentricity. If journals are within tolerances, reinstall bearing caps at their specified torque. Using a telescope gauge and micrometer, measure bearing I.D. parallel to piston axis and at 30° on each side of piston axis. Subtract journal O.D. from bearing I.D. to determine oil clearance. If crankshaft journals appear defective, or do not meet tolerances, there is no need to measure bearings; for the crankshaft will require grinding and/or undersize bearings will be required. If bearing appears defective, cause for failure should be determined prior to replacement.
Check the connecting rod bearing clearance:	Connecting rod bearing clearance is checked in the same manner as main bearing clearance, using Plastigage. Before removing the crankshaft, connecting rod side clearance also should be measured and recorded.
	*Checking connecting rod bearing clearance, using a micrometer, is identical to checking main bearing clearance. If no other service is required, the piston and rod assemblies need not be removed.
Remove the crankshaft:	Using a punch, mark the corresponding main bearing caps and saddles according to position (i.e., one punch on the front main cap and saddle, two on the second, three on the third, etc.). Using number stamps, identify the corresponding connecting rods and caps, according to cylinder (if no numbers are present). Remove the main and connecting rod caps, and replace sleeves of plastic tubing or vacuum hose over the connecting rod bolts, to protect the journals as the crankshaft is removed. Lift the crankshaft out of the block.
Match the connecting rod to the cylinder with a number stamp	**Match the connecting rod and cap with scribe marks**

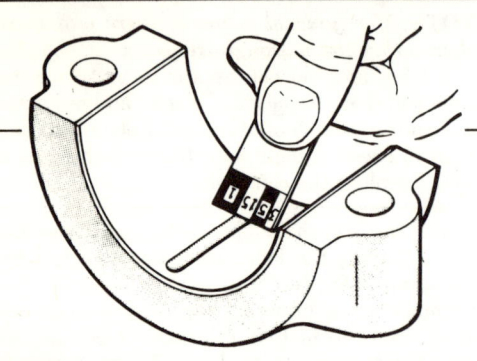

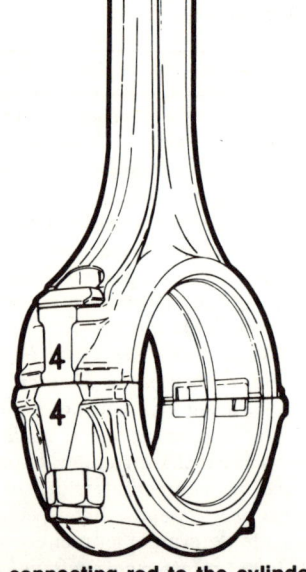

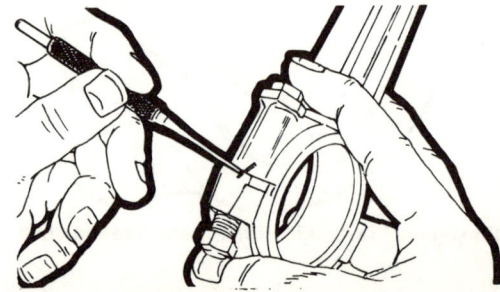

ENGINE AND ENGINE REBUILDING

Cylinder Block Reconditioning

Procedure	Method
Remove the ridge from the top of the cylinder: *Cylinder bore ridge* (RIDGE CAUSED BY CYLINDER WEAR / CYLINDER WALL / TOP OF PISTON)	In order to facilitate removal of the piston and connecting rod, the ridge at the top of the cylinder (unworn area; see illustration) must be removed. Place the piston at the bottom of the bore, and cover it with a rag. Cut the ridge away using a ridge reamer, exercising extreme care to avoid cutting too deeply. Remove the rag, and remove cuttings that remain on the piston. CAUTION: *If the ridge is not removed, and new rings are installed, damage to rings will result.*
Remove the piston and connecting rod: *Push the piston out with a hammer handle*	Invert the engine, and push the pistons and connecting rods out of the cylinders. If necessary, tap the connecting rod boss with a wooden hammer handle, to force the piston out. CAUTION: *Do not attempt to force the piston past the cylinder ridge* (see above).
Service the crankshaft:	Ensure that all oil holes and passages in the crankshaft are open and free of sludge. If necessary, have the crankshaft ground to the largest possible undersize.
	** Have the crankshaft Magnafluxed, to locate stress cracks. Consult a machinist concerning additional service procedures, such as surface hardening (e.g., nitriding, Tuftriding) to improve wear characteristics, cross drilling and chamfering the oil holes to improve lubrication, and balancing.
Removing freeze plugs:	Drill a small hole in the middle of the freeze plugs. Thread a large sheet metal screw into the hole and remove the plug with a slide hammer.
Remove the oil gallery plugs:	Threaded plugs should be removed using an appropriate (usually square) wrench. To remove soft, pressed in plugs, drill a hole in the plug, and thread in a sheet metal screw. Pull the plug out by the screw using pliers.
Hot-tank the block: NOTE: *Do not hot-tank aluminum parts.*	Have the block hot-tanked to remove grease, corrosion, and scale from the water jackets. NOTE: *Consult the operator to determine whether the camshaft bearings will be damaged during the hot-tank process.*

88 ENGINE AND ENGINE REBUILDING

Cylinder Block Reconditioning

Procedure	Method

Check the block for cracks:	Visually inspect the block for cracks or chips. The most common locations are as follows:
	    Adjacent to freeze plugs.
	    Between the cylinders and water jackets.
	    Adjacent to the main bearing saddles.
	    At the extreme bottom of the cylinders.
	Check only suspected cracks using spot check dye (see introduction). If a crack is located, consult a machinist concerning possible repairs.

	** Magnaflux the block to locate hidden cracks. If cracks are located, consult a machinist about feasibility of repair.
Install the oil gallery plugs and freeze plugs:	Coat freeze plugs with sealer and tap into position using a piece of pipe, slightly smaller than the plug, as a driver. To ensure retention, stake the edges of the plugs. Coat threaded oil gallery plugs with sealer and install. Drive replacement soft plugs into block using a large drift as a driver.
	* Rather than reinstalling lead plugs, drill and tap the holes, and install threaded plugs.
Check the bore diameter and surface:	Visually inspect the cylinder bores for roughness, scoring, or scuffing. If evident, the cylinder bore must be bored or honed oversize to eliminate imperfections, and the smallest possible oversize piston used. The new pistons should be given to the machinist with the block, so that the cylinders can be bored or honed exactly to the piston size (plus clearance). If no flaws are evident, measure the bore diameter using a telescope gauge and micrometer, or dial gauge, parallel and perpendicular to the engine centerline, at the top (below the ridge) and bottom of the bore. Subtract the bottom measurements from the top to determine taper, and the parallel to the centerline measurements from the perpendicular measurements to determine eccentricity. If the measurements are not within specifications, the cylinder must be bored or honed, and an oversize piston installed. If the measurements are within specifications the cylinder may

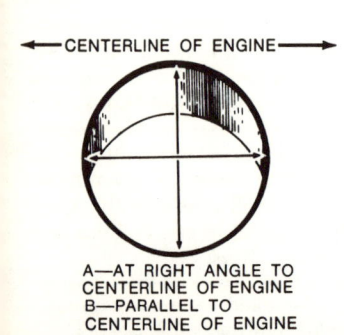

Measure the cylinder bore with a dial gauge

A—AT RIGHT ANGLE TO CENTERLINE OF ENGINE
B—PARALLEL TO CENTERLINE OF ENGINE

Cylinder bore measuring points

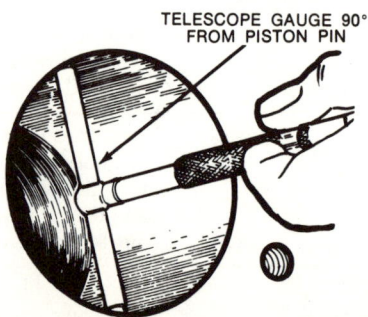

Measure the cylinder bore with a telescope gauge

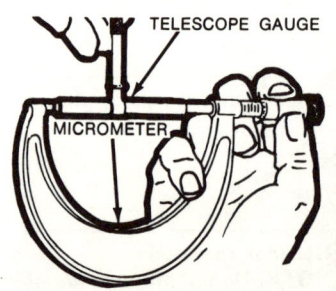

Measure the telescope gauge with a micrometer to determine the cylinder bore

ENGINE AND ENGINE REBUILDING

Cylinder Block Reconditioning

Procedure	Method
	be used as is, with only finish honing (see below). NOTE: *Prior to submitting the block for boring, perform the following operation(s).*
Check the cylinder block bearing alignment: **Check the main bearing saddle alignment**	Remove the upper bearing inserts. Place a straightedge in the bearing saddles along the centerline of the crankshaft. If clearance exists between the straightedge and the center saddle, the block must be alignbored.
*Check the deck height:	The deck height is the distance from the crankshaft centerline to the block deck. To measure, invert the engine, and install the crankshaft, retaining it with the center maincap. Measure the distance from the crankshaft journal to the block deck, parallel to the cylinder centerline. Measure the diameter of the end (front and rear) main journals, parallel to the centerline of the cylinders, divide the diameter in half, and subtract it from the previous measurement. The results of the front and rear measurements should be identical. If the difference exceeds .005″, the deck height should be corrected. NOTE: *Block deck height and warpage should be corrected at the same time.*
Check the block deck for warpage:	Using a straightedge and feeler gauges, check the block deck for warpage in the same manner that the cylinder head is checked (see Cylinder Head Reconditioning). If warpage exceeds specifications, have the deck resurfaced. NOTE: *In certain cases a specification for total material removal (cylinder head and block deck) is provided. This specification must not be exceeded.*
Clean and inspect the pistons and connecting rods: RING EXPANDER **Remove the piston rings**	Using a ring expander, remove the rings from the piston. Remove the retaining rings (if so equipped) and remove piston pin. NOTE: *If the piston pin must be pressed out, determine the proper method and use the proper tools; otherwise the piston will distort.* Clean the ring grooves using an appropriate tool, exercising care to avoid cutting too deeply. Thoroughly clean all carbon and varnish from the piston with solvent. CAUTION: *Do not use a wire brush or caustic solvent on pistons.* Inspect the pistons for scuffing, scoring, cracks, pitting, or excessive ringsgroove wear. If wear is evident, the piston must be replaced. Check the connecting rod length by measuring

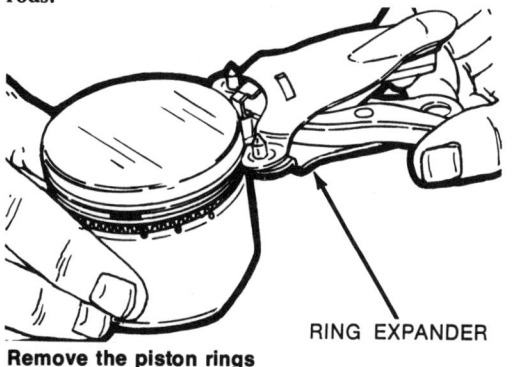

Cylinder Block Reconditioning

Procedure	Method
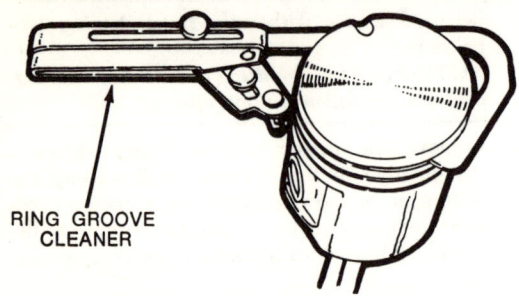 **Clean the piston ring grooves** (RING GROOVE CLEANER)	the rod from the inside of the large end to the inside of the small end using calipers (see illustration). All connecting rods should be equal length. Replace any rod that differs from the others in the engine.
	*Have the connecting rod alignment checked in an alignment fixture by a machinist. Replace any twisted or bent rods.
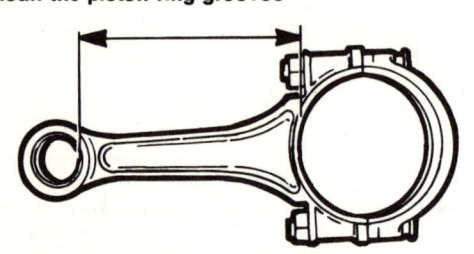 **Check the connecting rod length (arrow)**	*Magnaflux the connecting rods to locate stress cracks. If cracks are found, replace the connecting rod.
Fit the pistons to the cylinders: 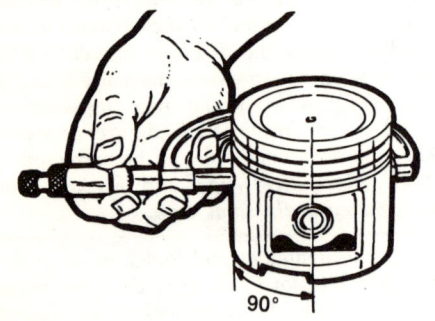 **Measure the piston prior to fitting**	Using a telescope gauge and micrometer, or a dial gauge, measure the cylinder bore diameter perpendicular to the piston pin, 2½" below the deck. Measure the piston perpendicular to its pin on the skirt. The difference between the two measurements is the piston clearance. If the clearance is within specifications or slightly below (after boring or honing), finish honing is all that is required. If the clearance is excessive, try to obtain a slightly larger piston to bring clearance within specifications. Where this is not possible, obtain the first oversize piston, and hone (of if necessary, bore) the cylinder to size.
Assemble the pistons and connecting rods: 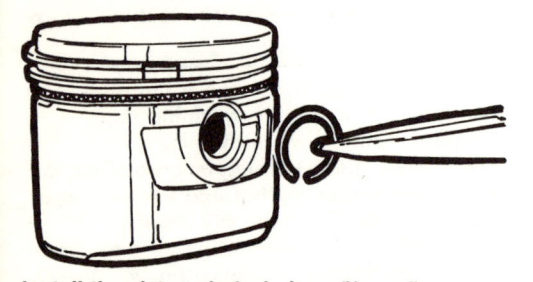 **Install the piston pin lock-rings (if used)**	Inspect piston pin, connecting rod small end bushing, and piston bore for galling, scoring, or excessive wear. If evident, replace defective part(s). Measure the I.D. of the piston boss and connecting rod small end, and the O.D. of the piston pin. If within specifications, assemble piston pin and rod. **CAUTION:** *If piston pin must be pressed in, determine the proper method and use the proper tools; otherwise the piston will distort.* Install the lock rings; ensure that they seat properly. If the parts are not within specifications, determine the service method for the type of engine. In some cases, piston and pin are serviced as an assembly when either is defective. Others specify reaming the piston and connecting rods for an oversize pin. If the connecting rod bushing is worn, it may in many cases be replaced. Reaming the piston and replacing the rod bushing are machine shop operations.

ENGINE AND ENGINE REBUILDING 91

Cylinder Block Reconditioning

Procedure	Method
Finish hone the cylinders: CROSS HATCH PATTERN 50°-60°	Chuck a flexible drive hone into a power drill, and insert it into the cylinder. Start the hone, and move it up and down in the cylinder at a rate which will produce approximately a 60° cross-hatch pattern. **NOTE:** *Do not extend the hone below the cylinder bore.* After developing the pattern, remove the hone and recheck piston fit. Wash the cylinders with a detergent and water solution to remove abrasive dust, dry, and wipe several times with a rag soaked in engine oil.
Check piston ring end-gap: Check the piston ring end gap	Compress the piston rings to be used in a cylinder, one at a time, into that cylinder, and press them approximately 1" below the deck with an inverted piston. Using feeler gauges, measure the ring end-gap, and compare to specifications. Pull the ring out of the cylinder and file the ends with a fine file to obtain proper clearance. **CAUTION:** *If inadequate ring end-gap is utilized, ring breakage will result.*
Install the piston rings: PISTON RING FEELER GAUGE RING GROOVE Check the piston ring side clearance	Inspect the ring grooves in the piston for excessive wear or taper. If necessary, recut the groove(s) for use with an overwidth ring or a standard ring and spacer. If the groove is worn uniformly, overwidth rings, or standard rings and spaces may be installed without recutting. Roll the outside of the ring around the groove to check for burrs or deposits. If any are found, remove with a fine file. Hold the ring in the groove, and measure side clearance. If necessary, correct as indicated above. **NOTE:** *Always install any additional spacers above the piston ring.* The ring groove must be deep enough to allow the ring to seat below the lands (see illustration). In many cases, a "go-no-go" depth gauge will be provided with the piston rings. Shallow grooves may be corrected by recutting, while deep

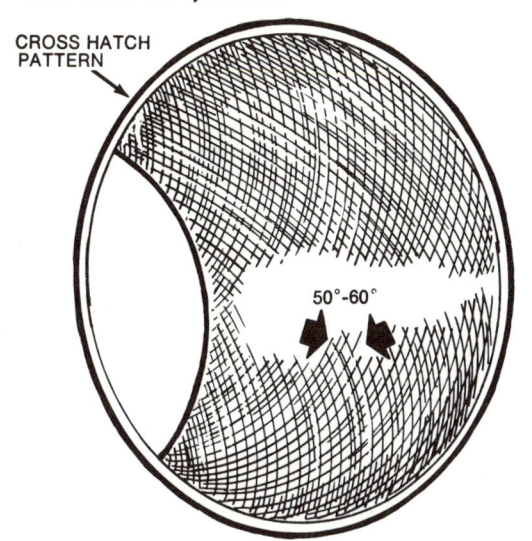

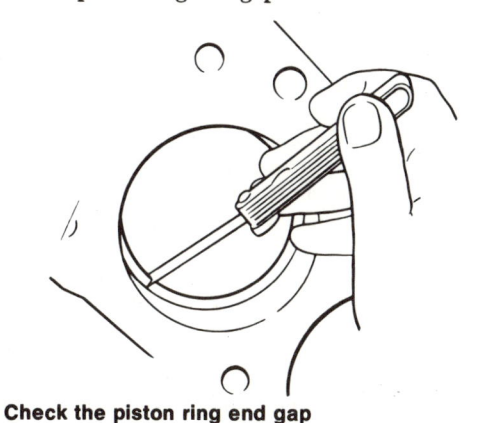

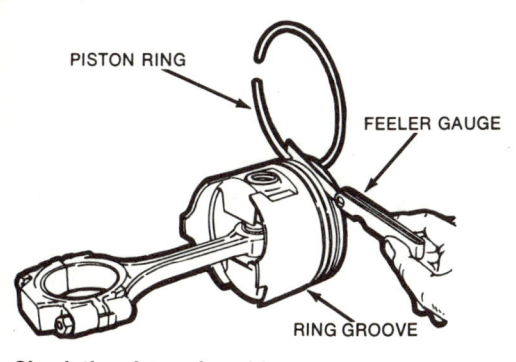

ENGINE AND ENGINE REBUILDING

Cylinder Block Reconditioning

Procedure	Method
	grooves require some type of filler or expander behind the piston. Consult the piston ring supplier concerning the suggested method. Install the rings on the piston, lowest ring first, using a ring expander. **NOTE:** *Position the rings as specified by the manufacturer.* Consult the engine service procedures earlier in this chapter for details concerning specific engines.
Install the rear main seal:	See the engine service procedures earlier in this chapter for details concerning specific engines.
Install the crankshaft: **Remove or install the upper bearing insert using a roll-out pin** **Home-made bearing roll-out pin**	Thoroughly clean the main bearing saddles and caps. Place the upper halves of the bearing inserts on the saddles and press into position. **NOTE:** *Ensure that the oil holes align.* Press the corresponding bearing inserts into the main bearing caps. Lubricate the upper main bearings, and lay the crankshaft in position. Place a strip of Plastigage on each of the crankshaft journals, install the main caps, and torque to specifications. Remove the main caps, and compare the Plastigage to the scale on the Plastigage envelope. If clearances are within tolerances, remove the Plastigage, turn the crankshaft 90°, wipe off all oil and retest. If all clearances are correct, remove all Plastigage, thoroughly lubricate the main caps and bearing journals, and install the main caps. If clearances are not within tolerance, the upper bearing inserts may be removed, without removing the crankshaft, using a bearing roll out pin (see illustration). Roll in a bearing that will provide proper clearance, and retest. Torque all main caps, excluding the thrust bearing cap, to specifications. Tighten the thrust bearing cap finger tight. To properly align the thrust bearing, pry the crankshaft the extent of its axial travel several times, the last movement held toward the front of the engine, and torque the thrust bearing cap to specifications. Determine the crankshaft end-play (see below), and bring within tolerance with thrust washers.

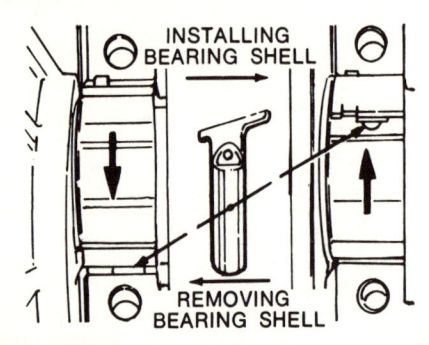

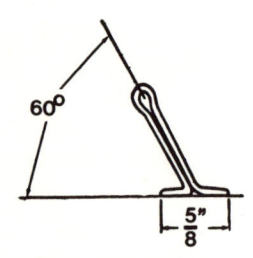

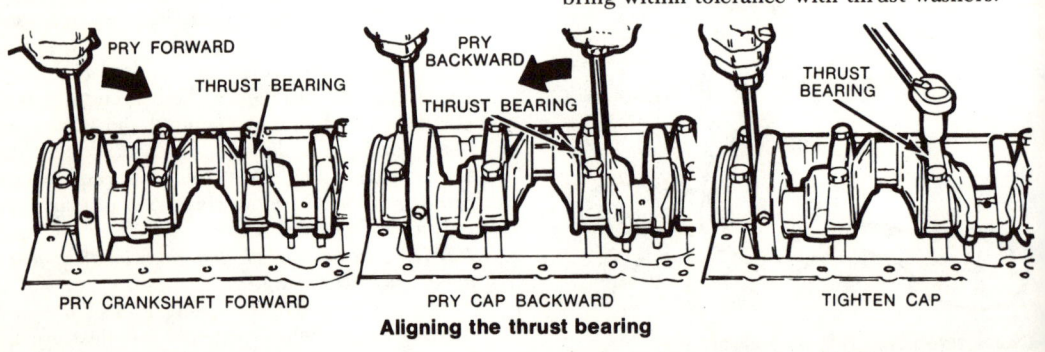

Aligning the thrust bearing
(PRY CRANKSHAFT FORWARD — PRY CAP BACKWARD — TIGHTEN CAP)

| Measure crankshaft end-play: | Mount a dial indicator stand on the front of the block, with the dial indicator stem resting on the |

ENGINE AND ENGINE REBUILDING 93

Cylinder Block Reconditioning

Procedure	Method

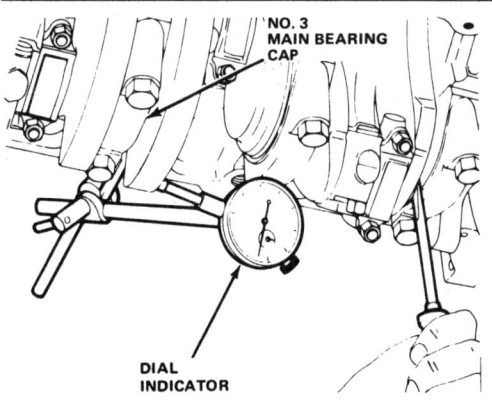

Method (continued):

nose of the crankshaft, parallel to the crankshaft axis. Pry the crankshaft the extent of its travel rearward, and zero the indicator. Pry the crankshaft forward and record crankshaft end-play.

NOTE: *Crankshaft end-play also may be measured at the thrust bearing, using feeler gauges (see illustration).*

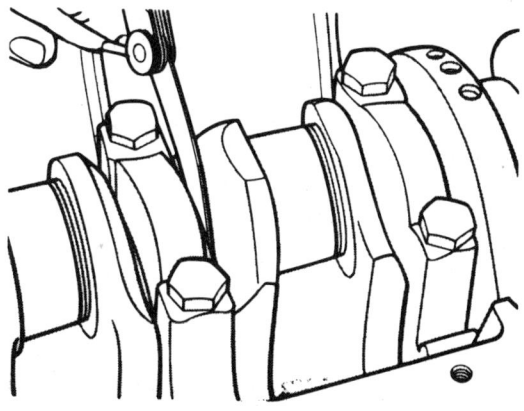

Check the crankshaft end-play with a dial indicator

Check the crankshaft end-play with a feeler gauge

Install the pistons:

Press the upper connecting rod bearing halves into the connecting rods, and the lower halves into the connecting rod caps. Position the piston ring gaps according to specifications (see car section), and lubricate the pistons. Install a ring compresser on a piston, and press two long (8") pieces of plastic tubing over the rod bolts. Using the tubes as a guide, press the pistons into the bores and onto the crankshaft with a wooden hammer handle. After seating the rod on the crankshaft journal, remove the tubes and install the cap finger tight. Install the remaining pistons in the same manner. Invert the engine and check the bearing clearance at two points (90° apart) on each journal with Plastigage.

NOTE: *Do not turn the crankshaft with Plastigage installed.*

If clearance is within tolerances, remove *all* Plastigage, thoroughly lubricate the journals, and torque the rod caps to specifications. If clearance is not within specifications, install different thickness bearing inserts and recheck.

CAUTION: *Never shim or file the connecting rods or caps.*

Always install plastic tube sleeves over the rod bolts when the caps are not installed, to protect the crankshaft journals.

Use lengths of vacuum hose or rubber tubing to protect the crankshaft journals and cylinder walls during piston installation

RING COMPRESSOR

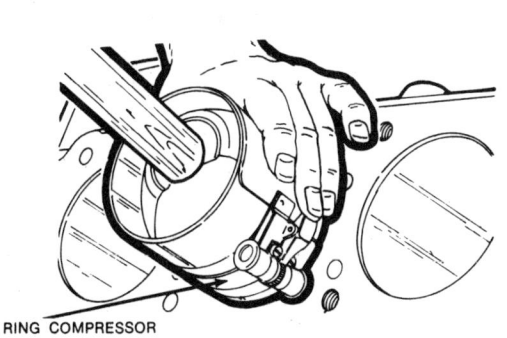

Install the piston using a ring compressor

Cylinder Block Reconditioning

Procedure	Method
Check connecting rod side clearance: Check the connecting rod side clearance with a feeler gauge	Determine the clearance between the sides of the connecting rods and the crankshaft using feeler gauges. If clearance is below the minimum tolerance, the rod may be machined to provide adequate clearance. If clearance is excessive, substitute an unworn rod, and recheck. If clearance is still outside specifications, the crankshaft must be welded and reground, or replaced.
Inspect the timing chain (or belt):	Visually inspect the timing chain for broken or loose links, and replace the chain if any are found. If the chain will flex sideways, it must be replaced. Install the timing chain as specified. Be sure the timing belt is not stretched, frayed or broken. NOTE: *If the original timing chain is to be reused, install it in its original position.* See the engine service procedures earlier in this chapter for details concerning specific engines.

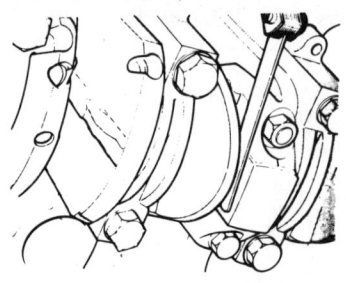

Completing the Rebuilding Process

Following the above procedures, complete the rebuilding process as follows:

Fill the oil pump with oil, to prevent cavitating (sucking air) on initial engine start up. Install the oil pump and the pickup tube on the engine. Coat the oil pan gasket as necessary, and install the gasket and the oil pan. Mount the flywheel and the crankshaft vibration damper or pulley on the crankshaft.

NOTE: *Always use new bolts when installing the flywheel.* Inspect the clutch shaft pilot bushing in the crankshaft. If the bushing is excessively worn, remove it with an expanding puller and a slide hammer, and tap a new bushing into place.

Position the engine, cylinder head side up. Install the cylinder head, and torque it as specified. Install the rocker arms and adjust the valves.

Install the intake and exhaust manifolds, the carburetor(s), the distributor and spark plugs. Adjust the point gap and the static ignition timing. Mount all accessories and install the engine in the car. Fill the radiator with coolant, and the crankcase with high quality engine oil.

Break-in Procedure

Start the engine, and allow it to run at low speed for a few minutes, while checking for leaks. Stop the engine, check the oil level, and fill as necessary. Restart the engine, and fill the cooling system to capacity. Check the point dwell angle and adjust the ignition timing and the valves. Run the engine at low to medium speed (800–2500 rpm) for approximately ½ hour, and retorque the cylinder head bolts. Road test the car, and check again for leaks.

Follow the manufacturer's recommended engine break-in procedure and maintenance schedule for new engines.

Emission Controls and Fuel System

EMISSION CONTROLS

All engines are equipped with Ford's Thermactor (air pump) system, positive crankcase ventilation (PCV), exhaust gas recirculation (EGR), Dura-Spark electronic ignition, a catalytic converter, a thermostatically-controlled air cleaner, and an evaporative emissions system (charcoal canister). No electronic engine controls are used on the Escort and Lynx engines.

The belt-driven air pump injects clean air either into the exhaust manifold, or downstream into the catalytic converter, depending on engine conditions. The oxygen contained in the injected air supports continued combustion of the hot carbon monoxide (CO) and hydrocarbon (HC) gases, reducing their release into the atmosphere.

No external PCV valve is necessary on the Escort and Lynx PCV system. Instead, an internal baffle and an orifice control the flow of crankcase gases.

The back-pressure modulated EGR valve is mounted next to the carburetor on the intake manifold. Vacuum applied to the EGR diaphragm raises the pintle valve from its seat, allowing hot exhaust gases to be drawn into the intake manifold with the intake charge. The exhaust gases reduce peak combustion temperature; lower temperatures reduce the formation of oxides of nitrogen (NO_x).

The dual brick catalytic converter is mounted in the exhaust system, ahead of the muffler. Catalytic converters use noble metals (platinum and palladium) and great heat (1200°F) to catalytically oxidize HC and CO gases into H_2O and CO_2. The Thermactor system is used as a fresh air (and therefore, oxygen) supply.

The thermostatically-controlled air cleaner housing is able to draw fresh air from two sources: cool air from outside the car (behind the grille), or warm air obtained from a heat stove encircling the exhaust manifold. A warm air supply is desirable during cold engine operation, because it promotes better atomization of the air/fuel mixture, while cool air promotes better combustion in a hot engine.

Instead of venting gasoline vapors from the carburetor float bowl into the atmosphere, an evaporative emission system captures the vapors and stores them in a charcoal-filled canister, located ahead of the left front wheel arch. When the engine is running, a purge control solenoid allows fresh air to be drawn through the canister; the fresh air and vapors are then routed to the carburetor, to be mixed with the intake charge.

EMISSION CONTROLS AND FUEL SYSTEM

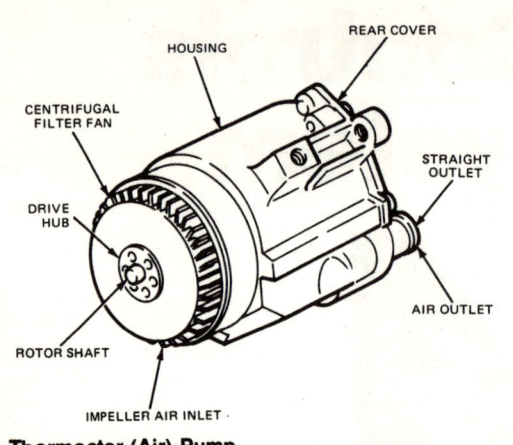

Thermactor (Air) Pump

Thermactor Emission Control System

OPERATION

A typical air injection system consists of an air supply pump and centrifugal filter, an air bypass valve, check valve, air manifold and air hoses.

Simply, the air pump injects air into the engine which reduces the hydrocarbon and carbon monoxide content of exhaust gases by continuing the combustion of the unburned gases after they leave the combustion chamber. Fresh air mixed with the hot exhaust gases promotes further oxidation of both the hydrocarbons and carbon monoxide, thereby reducing their concentration and converting some of them into harmless carbon dioxide and water.

Air for the Thermactor system is cleaned by means of a centrifugal filter fan mounted on the air pump driveshaft.

To prevent excessive pressure, the air pump is equipped with a pressure relief valve.

The air pump has sealed bearings which are lubricated for the life of the unit, and pre-set rotor vane and bearing clearances, which do not require any periodic adjustments.

The air supply from the pump is controlled by the air by-pass valve, sometimes a dump valve. During deceleration, the air by-pass valve opens, momentarily diverting the air supply into the atmosphere, thus preventing backfires within the exhaust system.

A check valve is incorporated in the air inlet side of the air manifold. Its purpose is to prevent the exhaust gases from backing up into the Thermactor system. The valve is especially important in the event of drive belt failure and during deceleration, when the air by-pass valve is dumping the air supply. The "air" manifold channel the air from the pump into the exhaust thus completing the cycle of the Thermactor system.

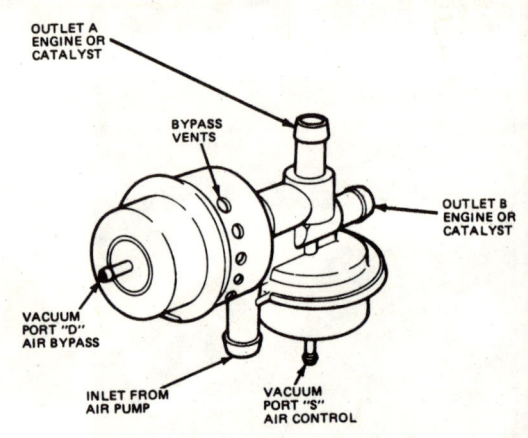

You car has a combination valve bypass and air control valve

COMBINATION AIR BYPASS-AIR CONTROL VALVE

The air bypass valve and the air control valve are combined on your car.

Functional Test

1. Disconnect the two hoses that go to the engine or converter (Outlet A and Outlet B; see illustration).
2. Disconnect and plug the vacuum line at port D.
3. With the engine operating at 1500 rpm, air flow should be coming out of the bypass vents.
4. Reconnect the vacuum line to port D. Disconnect and plug the vacuum line to port S. Make sure vacuum is present at vacuum port D.
5. Operate the engine at 1500 rpm, air flow should be detected at outlet B. No air flow should be at outlet A.
6. Use a hand vacuum pump and apply 8–10 inches of vacuum to port S. With the engine operating at 1500 rpm, air flow should be noted coming out of outlet A.
7. Replace the combination valve if any of the tests indicate a problem.

CHECK VALVE

The check valve is a one way valve. Pressure at the inlet allows air to flow past a viton disc. Vacuum at the outlet causes the reed to open,

EMISSION CONTROLS AND FUEL SYSTEM

Troubleshooting the Thermactor System

Condition	Possible Source	Resolution
• Excessive Belt Noise	• Loose belt	• Tighten to specification CAUTION: *Do not use a pry bar to move the air pump.*
	• Seized pump	• Replace pump.
	• Loose pulley	• Replace pulley and/or pump if damaged. Tighten bolts to specification 130–180 in. lbs.
	• Loose or broken mounting brackets or bolts	• Replace parts as required and tighten bolts to specification.
• Excessive Mechanical Clicking	• Over-tightened mounting bolt	• Tighten to 25 ft. lbs.
	• Excessive flash on the air pump adjusting arm boss.	• Remove flash from the boss.
	• Distorted adjusting arm.	• Replace adjusting arm.
• Excessive Thermactor System Noise (Putt-Putt, Whirling or Hissing)	• Leak in hose	• Locate source of leak using soap solution, and replace hoses as necessary.
	• Loose, pinched or kinked hose	• Reassemble, straighten, or replace hose and clamps as required.
	• Hose touching other engine parts	• Adjust hose to prevent contact with other engine parts.
	• Bypass valve inoperative	• Test the valve.
	• Check valve inoperative	• Test the valve.
	• Pump mounting fasteners loose	• Tighten fasteners to specification.
	• Restricted or bent pump outlet fitting	• Inspect fitting, and remove any flash blocking the air passage way. Replace bent fittings.
	• Air dumping through bypass valve (at idle only)	• On many vehicles, the thermactor system has been designed to dump air at idle to prevent overheating the catalyst. This condition is normal. Determine that the noise persists at higher speeds before proceeding further.
• Excessive Pump Noise (Chirps, Squeaks and Ticks)	• Insufficient break-in or worn or damaged pump	• Check the thermactor system for wear or damage and make any necessary corrections.

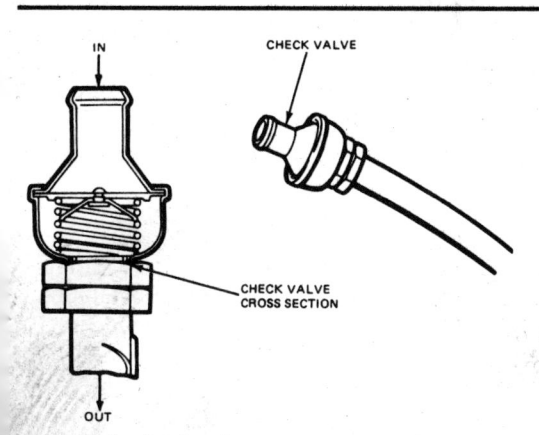

Typical air check valve

effecting one-way air flow in reed type valves. Air is prevented from passing through the valve if pressure at the outlet side of the valve is positive.

Functional Test

1. Disconnect the air supply at the pump side of the valve.
2. Blow through the check valve, toward the manifold, then attempt to suck back through the valve. Air should pass in the direction of the exhaust manifold only. Replace the valve if air flows both ways.

98 EMISSION CONTROLS AND FUEL SYSTEM

AIR PUMP
Removal and Installation

1. Loosen the pivot mounting and adjustment bolt. Relax the drive belt tension and remove the belt. Disconnect the air hoses.
2. Remove the adjuster and pivot nuts and bolts. Remove the air pump.
3. Installation is in the reverse order of removal. Adjust the belt to its proper tension.

Positive Crankcase Ventilation
SYSTEM OPERATION

A small amount of the fuel/air mixture in each cylinder escapes from the combustion chamber around the piston rings and enters the engine's crankcase, above the oil level. Since this material has been cooled by the lubricating oil and metal parts well below burning temperature, it is only partially burned and constitutes a large source of pollution. The PCV system allows outside air to be drawn in to the crankcase and to sweep this material back into the intake passages of the engine to be reburned before it either dirties the oil or escapes to the outside air. An internal baffle and an orifice control the flow of crankcase gases.

Exhaust Emission Control

All engines are equipped with a single muffler, a single catalytic converter and connecting pipes. The converter is of the dual brick type which uses both a three way catalyst and a conventional oxidation catalyst.

CONVERTER
Removal and Installation

1. Jack up the car and safely support it on jackstands.
2. Remove the front and rear converter mounting bolts. Separate the flange connections and remove the converter.
3. To install, align the flanges, install new gaskets and install the attaching bolts.
4. Align the exhaust system so that it won't rattle and tighten the mounting bolts.
5. Remove the car from the jackstands.

Thermostatically Controlled Air Cleaner

The air cleaner assembly intake duct is attached to a cold air intake as well as a heat shroud that surrounds the exhaust manifold. Air flow from these two sources is controlled by a door in the intake duct operated by a vacuum motor. The vacuum motor is controlled by a thermal sensor and a vacuum control system.

The thermal sensor is attached to the air valve actuating lever, along with the vacuum motor lever, both of which control the position of the air valve to supply either heated air from the exhaust manifold or cooler air from the engine compartment.

During the warm-up period, when the under-the-hood temperatures are low, the thermal sensor doesn't exert enough tension on the air valve actuating lever to close (heat off) the air valve. Thus, the carburetor receives heated air from around the exhaust manifold.

As the temperature of the air entering the air cleaner approaches approximately 110°F, the thermal sensor begins to push on the air valve actuating lever and overcome the spring tension which holds the air valve in the open (heat on) position. The air valve begins to move to the closed (heat off) position, allowing only under-the-hood air to enter the air cleaner.

The air valve in the air cleaner will also open, regardless of the air temperature, during heavy acceleration to obtain maximum airflow through the air cleaner. The extreme decrease in intake manifold vacuum during heavy acceleration permits the vacuum motor to override the thermostatic control. This opens the system to both heated air and air from the engine compartment.

HEATED AIR INTAKE TEST

1. With the engine completely cold, look inside the cold air duct and make sure that the valve plate is fully in the up position (closing the cold air duct).
2. Start the engine and bring it to operating temperature.
3. Stop the engine and look inside the cold air duct again. The valve plate should be down, allowing an opening from the cold air duct into the air cleaner.
4. If the unit appears to be malfunctioning, remove it and examine it to make sure that the springs are not broken or disconnected, and replace the thermostat if all other parts appear intact and properly connected.

Evaporative Emission Controls

Changes in atmospheric temperature cause fuel tanks to "breathe"; that is, the air within

EMISSION CONTROLS AND FUEL SYSTEM

the tank expands and contracts with outside temperature changes. As the temperature rises, air escapes through the tank vent tube or the vent in the tank cap. The air which escapes contains gasoline vapors. In a similar manner, the gasoline which fills the carburetor float bowl expands when the engine is stopped. Engine heat causes this expansion. The vapors escape through the carburetor and air cleaner.

The Evaporative Emission Control System provides a sealed fuel system with the capability to store and condense fuel vapors. The system has three parts: a fill control vent system; a vapor vent and storage system; and a pressure and vacuum relief system (special fill cap).

The fill control vent system is a modification to the fuel tank. It uses an air space within the tank which is 10–12% of the tank's volume. The air space is sufficient to provide for the thermal expansion of the fuel. The space also serves as part of the in-tank vapor vent system.

The in-tank vent system consists of the air space previously described and a vapor separator assembly. The separator assembly is mounted to the top of the fuel tank and is secured by a cam-lockring, similar to the one which secures the fuel sending unit. Foam material fills the vapor separator assembly. The foam material separates raw fuel and vapors, thus retarding the entrance of fuel into the vapor line.

The sealed filler cap has a pressure vacuum relief valve. Under normal operating conditions, the filler cap operates as a check valve, allowing air to enter the tank to replace the fuel consumed. At the same time, it prevents vapors from escaping through the cap. In case of excessive pressure within the tank, the filler cap valve opens to relieve the pressure.

Because the filler cap is sealed, fuel vapors have but one place through which they may escape—the vapor separator assembly at the top of the fuel tank. The vapors pass through the foam material and continue through a single vapor line which leads to a canister in the engine compartment. The canister is filled with activated charcoal.

Another vapor line runs from the top of the carburetor float chamber to the charcoal canister.

As the fuel vapors (hydrocarbons) enter the charcoal canister, they are absorbed by the charcoal. The air is dispelled through the open bottom of the charcoal canister, leaving the hydrocarbons trapped within the charcoal. When the engine is started, vacuum causes fresh air to be drawn into the canister from its open bottom. The fresh air passes through the charcoal picking up the hydrocarbons which are trapped there and feeding them into the carburetor for burning with the fuel mixture.

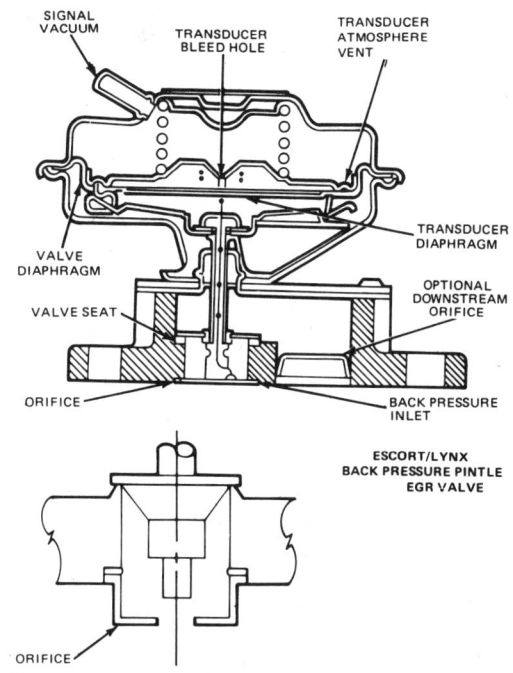

Cutaway view of a EGR valve

Exhaust Gas Recirculation (EGR)

The Exhaust Gas Recirculation System is designed to reintroduce small amounts of exhaust gas into the combustion cycle. Reintroducing the exhaust gas helps reduce the generation of nitrtus oxides (NO_x). The amount of exhaust gases reintroduced and the timing of the cycle varies as to engine speed, altitude, engine vacuum and exhaust system.

EGR MAINTENANCE REMINDER SYSTEM

Some models are equipped with an EGR Maintenance Reminder System that consists of a mileage sensor module, an instrument panel warning light and associated wiring harness. The system provides a visual warning to indicate EGR service at 30,000 miles. The sensor is a blue plastic box mounted on the dash panel in the passenger's compartment forward of the glove box. After

EMISSION CONTROLS AND FUEL SYSTEM

Troubleshooting the EGR System

Condition	Possible Source	Resolution
• Rough Idle and/or Stalling	• EGR valve receiving vacuum at idle, vacuum hoses misrouted	• Check EGR valve vacuum hose routing. Correct as required. Check vacuum supply at idle with engine at operating temperature.
	• EGR valve not closing fully or stuck open	• Remove EGR valve to inspect for proper closing and seating of valve components. Clean or replace valve as required.
	• EGR valve gasket blown, or valve attachment loose.	• Check EGR valve attaching bolts for tightness. Inspect gasket. Tighten valve or replace gasket as required.
	• EGR valve air bleeds plugged	• Check to see if valve holds vacuum with engine off. If so, replace valve.
• Rough running, surge, hesitation and general poor performance at part throttle when engine is cold	• EGR valve receiving vacuum. Vacuum hoses misrouted.	• Check EGR valve vacuum hose routing. Correct as required.
	• EGR valve not closing fully or stuck open	• Remove EGR valve to inspect for proper closing and seating of valve components. Clean or replace valve as required.
	• EGR valve gasket blown, or valve attachment loose.	• Check EGR valve attaching bolts for tightness. Inspect gasket. Tighten valve or replace gasket as required.
	• EGR valve air bleeds plugged (back pressure-type valve only)	• Check to see if valve holds vacuum with engine off. If so, replace valve.
• Rough running, surge, hesitation, and general poor performance at part-throttle when engine is hot or cold	Excessive EGR due to: • EGR valve stuck wide open	• Remove EGR valve to inspect for proper freedom of movement of valve components. Clean or replace as required.
• Engine stalls on deceleration	• EGR valve sticking open or not closing fully	• Remove EGR valve to inspect for proper closing and seating of valve components. Clean or replace as required.
• Part-throttle engine detonation	Insufficient EGR due to: • EGR valve stuck closed	• Check EGR valve for freedom of operation by pressing and releasing valve diaphragm to stroke the valve mechanism. Clean or replace valve if not operating smoothly.
	• Leaky valve diaphragm not actuating valve	• Check valve by applying vacuum. (Back pressure-type valves only—block tailpipe with drive socket of outside diameter approximately 1/16" less than inside diameter of tailpipe. DO NOT BLOCK FULLY. Idle engine while applying vacuum to valve. DO NOT RUN ENGINE FASTER THAN IDLE OR FOR PROLONGED PERIODS OF TIME. BE SURE TO REMOVE SOCKET FROM TAIL

CHILTON'S
FUEL ECONOMY & TUNE-UP TIPS

Tune-Up • Spark Plug Diagnosis • Emission Controls
Fuel System • Cooling System • Tires and Wheels
General Maintenance

55 WAYS TO IMPROVE FUEL ECONOMY

CHILTON'S FUEL ECONOMY & TUNE-UP TIPS

Fuel economy is important to everyone, no matter what kind of vehicle you drive. The maintenance-minded motorist can save both money and fuel using these tips and the periodic maintenance and tune-up procedures in this Repair and Tune-Up Guide.

There are more than 130,000,000 cars and trucks registered for private use in the United States. Each travels an average of 10-12,000 miles per year, and, in total they consume close to 70 billion gallons of fuel each year. This represents nearly 2/3 of the oil imported by the United States each year. The Federal government's goal is to reduce consumption 10% by 1985. A variety of methods are either already in use or under serious consideration, and they all affect your driving and the cars you will drive. In addition to "down-sizing", the auto industry is using or investigating the use of electronic fuel delivery, electronic engine controls and alternative engines for use in smaller and lighter vehicles, among other alternatives to meet the federally mandated Corporate Average Fuel Economy (CAFE) of 27.5 mpg by 1985. The government, for its part, is considering rationing, mandatory driving curtailments and tax increases on motor vehicle fuel in an effort to reduce consumption. The government's goal of a 10% reduction could be realized — and further government regulation avoided — if every private vehicle could use just 1 less gallon of fuel per week.

How Much Can You Save?

Tests have proven that almost anyone can make at least a 10% reduction in fuel consumption through regular maintenance and tune-ups. When a major manufacturer of spark plugs sur-

TUNE-UP

1. Check the cylinder compression to be sure the engine will really benefit from a tune-up and that it is capable of producing good fuel economy. A tune-up will be wasted on an engine in poor mechanical condition.

2. Replace spark plugs regularly. New spark plugs alone can increase fuel economy 3%.

3. Be sure the spark plugs are the correct type (heat range) for your vehicle. See the Tune-Up Specifications.

Heat range refers to the spark plug's ability to conduct heat away from the firing end. It must conduct the heat away in an even pattern to avoid becoming a source of pre-ignition, yet it must also operate hot enough to burn off conductive deposits that could cause misfiring.

The heat range is usually indicated by a number on the spark plug, part of the manufacturer's designation for each individual spark plug. The numbers in bold-face indicate the heat range in each manufacturer's identification system.

Manufacturer	Typical Designation
AC	R **45** TS
Bosch (old)	WA **145** T30
Bosch (new)	HR **8** Y
Champion	RBL **15** Y
Fram/Autolite	**415**
Mopar	P-**62** PR
Motorcraft	BRF-**42**
NGK	BP **5** ES-15
Nippondenso	W **16** EP
Prestolite	14GR **5** 2A

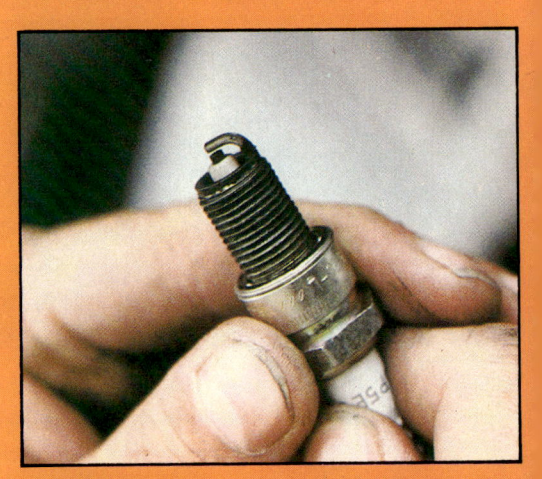

Periodically, check the spark plugs to be sure they are firing efficiently. They are excellent indicators of the internal condition of your engine.

On AC, Bosch (new), Champion, Fram/Autolite, Mopar, Motorcraft and Prestolite, a higher number indicates a hotter plug. On Bosch (old), NGK and Nippondenso, a higher number indicates a colder plug.

4. Make sure the spark plugs are properly gapped. See the Tune-Up Specifications in this book.

5. Be sure the spark plugs are firing efficiently. The illustrations on the next 2 pages show you how to "read" the firing end of the spark plug.

6. Check the ignition timing and set it to specifications. Tests show that almost all cars

veyed over 6,000 cars nationwide, they found that a tune-up, on cars that needed one, increased fuel economy over 11%. Replacing worn plugs alone, accounted for a 3% increase. The same test also revealed that 8 out of every 10 vehicles will have some maintenance deficiency that will directly affect fuel economy, emissions or performance. Most of this mileage-robbing neglect could be prevented with regular maintenance.

Modern engines require that all of the functioning systems operate properly for maximum efficiency. A malfunction anywhere wastes fuel. You can keep your vehicle running as efficiently and economically as possible, by being aware of your vehicles operating and performance characteristics. If your vehicle suddenly develops performance or fuel economy problems it could be due to one or more of the following:

PROBLEM	POSSIBLE CAUSE
Engine Idles Rough	Ignition timing, idle mixture, vacuum leak or something amiss in the emission control system.
Hesitates on Acceleration	Dirty carburetor or fuel filter, improper accelerator pump setting, ignition timing or fouled spark plugs.
Starts Hard or Fails to Start	Worn spark plugs, improperly set automatic choke, ice (or water) in fuel system.
Stalls Frequently	Automatic choke improperly adjusted and possible dirty air filter or fuel filter.
Performs Sluggishly	Worn spark plugs, dirty fuel or air filter, ignition timing or automatic choke out of adjustment.

Check spark plug wires on conventional point type ignition for cracks by bending them in a loop around your finger.

Be sure that spark plug wires leading to adjacent cylinders do not run too close together. (Photo courtesy Champion Spark Plug Co.)

have incorrect ignition timing by more than 2°.

7. If your vehicle does not have electronic ignition, check the points, rotor and cap as specified.

8. Check the spark plug wires (used with conventional point-type ignitions) for cracks and burned or broken insulation by bending them in a loop around your finger. Cracked wires decrease fuel efficiency by failing to deliver full voltage to the spark plugs. One misfiring spark plug can cost you as much as 2 mpg.

9. Check the routing of the plug wires. Misfiring can be the result of spark plug leads to adjacent cylinders running parallel to each other and too close together. One wire tends to pick up voltage from the other causing it to fire "out of time".

10. Check all electrical and ignition circuits for voltage drop and resistance.

11. Check the distributor mechanical and/or vacuum advance mechanisms for proper functioning. The vacuum advance can be checked by twisting the distributor plate in the opposite direction of rotation. It should spring back when released.

12. Check and adjust the valve clearance on engines with mechanical lifters. The clearance should be slightly loose rather than too tight.

SPARK PLUG DIAGNOSIS

Normal

APPEARANCE: This plug is typical of one operating normally. The insulator nose varies from a light tan to grayish color with slight electrode wear. The presence of slight deposits is normal on used plugs and will have no adverse effect on engine performance. The spark plug heat range is correct for the engine and the engine is running normally.

CAUSE: Properly running engine.

RECOMMENDATION: Before reinstalling this plug, the electrodes should be cleaned and filed square. Set the gap to specifications. If the plug has been in service for more than 10-12,000 miles, the entire set should probably be replaced with a fresh set of the same heat range.

Oil Deposits

APPEARANCE: The firing end of the plug is covered with a wet, oily coating.

CAUSE: The problem is poor oil control. On high mileage engines, oil is leaking past the rings or valve guides into the combustion chamber. A common cause is also a plugged PCV valve, and a ruptured fuel pump diaphragm can also cause this condition. Oil fouled plugs such as these are often found in new or recently overhauled engines, before normal oil control is achieved, and can be cleaned and reinstalled.

RECOMMENDATION: A hotter spark plug may temporarily relieve the problem, but the engine is probably in need of work.

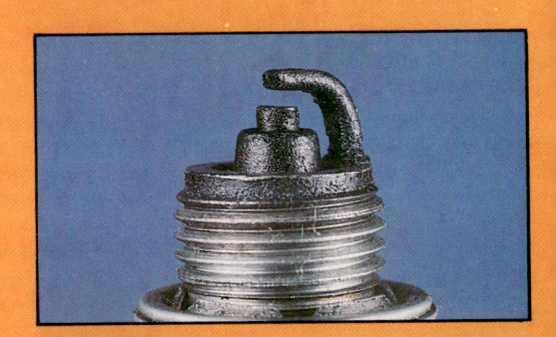

Incorrect Heat Range

APPEARANCE: The effects of high temperature on a spark plug are indicated by clean white, often blistered insulator. This can also be accompanied by excessive wear of the electrode, and the absence of deposits.

CAUSE: Check for the correct spark plug heat range. A plug which is too hot for the engine can result in overheating. A car operated mostly at high speeds can require a colder plug. Also check ignition timing, cooling system level, fuel mixture and leaking intake manifold.

RECOMMENDATION: If all ignition and engine adjustments are known to be correct, and no other malfunction exists, install spark plugs one heat range colder.

Carbon Deposits

APPEARANCE: Carbon fouling is easily identified by the presence of dry, soft, black, sooty deposits.

CAUSE: Changing the heat range can often lead to carbon fouling, as can prolonged slow, stop-and-start driving. If the heat range is correct, carbon fouling can be attributed to a rich fuel mixture, sticking choke, clogged air cleaner, worn breaker points, retarded timing or low compression. If only one or two plugs are carbon fouled, check for corroded or cracked wires on the affected plugs. Also look for cracks in the distributor cap between the towers of affected cylinders.

RECOMMENDATION: After the problem is corrected, these plugs can be cleaned and reinstalled if not worn severely.

Photos Courtesy Champion Spark Plug Co.

MMT Fouled

APPEARANCE: Spark plugs fouled by MMT (Methycyclopentadienyl Maganese Tricarbonyl) have reddish, rusty appearance on the insulator and side electrode.

CAUSE: MMT is an anti-knock additive in gasoline used to replace lead. During the combustion process, the MMT leaves a reddish deposit on the insulator and side electrode.

RECOMMENDATION: No engine malfunction is indicated and the deposits will not affect plug performance any more than lead deposits (see Ash Deposits). MMT fouled plugs can be cleaned, regapped and reinstalled.

High Speed Glazing

APPEARANCE: Glazing appears as shiny coating on the plug, either yellow or tan in color.

CAUSE: During hard, fast acceleration, plug temperatures rise suddenly. Deposits from normal combustion have no chance to fluff-off; instead, they melt on the insulator forming an electrically conductive coating which causes misfiring.

RECOMMENDATION: Glazed plugs are not easily cleaned. They should be replaced with a fresh set of plugs of the correct heat range. If the condition recurs, using plugs with a heat range one step colder may cure the problem.

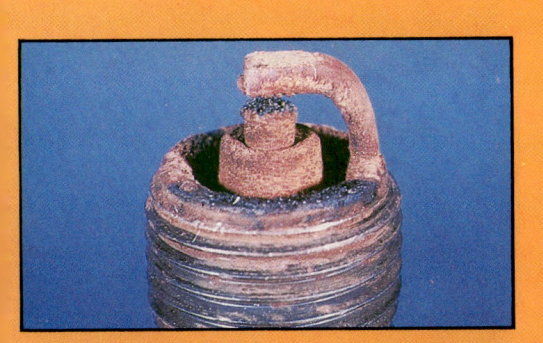

Ash (Lead) Deposits

APPEARANCE: Ash deposits are characterized by light brown or white colored deposits crusted on the side or center electrodes. In some cases it may give the plug a rusty appearance.

CAUSE: Ash deposits are normally derived from oil or fuel additives burned during normal combustion. Normally they are harmless, though excessive amounts can cause misfiring. If deposits are excessive in short mileage, the valve guides may be worn.

RECOMMENDATION: Ash-fouled plugs can be cleaned, gapped and reinstalled.

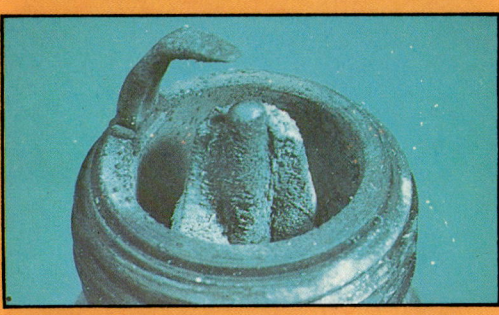

Detonation

APPEARANCE: Detonation is usually characterized by a broken plug insulator.

CAUSE: A portion of the fuel charge will begin to burn spontaneously, from the increased heat following ignition. The explosion that results applies extreme pressure to engine components, frequently damaging spark plugs and pistons.

Detonation can result by over-advanced ignition timing, inferior gasoline (low octane) lean air/fuel mixture, poor carburetion, engine lugging or an increase in compression ratio due to combustion chamber deposits or engine modification.

RECOMMENDATION: Replace the plugs after correcting the problem.

Photos Courtesy Fram Corporation

EMISSION CONTROLS

13. Be aware of the general condition of the emission control system. It contributes to reduced pollution and should be serviced regularly to maintain efficient engine operation.

14. Check all vacuum lines for dried, cracked or brittle conditions. Something as simple as a leaking vacuum hose can cause poor performance and loss of economy.

15. Avoid tampering with the emission control system. Attempting to improve fuel econ-

FUEL SYSTEM

Check the air filter with a light behind it. If you can see light through the filter it can be reused.

Extremely clogged filters should be discarded and replaced with a new one.

18. Replace the air filter regularly. A dirty air filter richens the air/fuel mixture and can increase fuel consumption as much as 10%. Tests show that ⅓ of all vehicles have air filters in need of replacement.

19. Replace the fuel filter at least as often as recommended.

20. Set the idle speed and carburetor mixture to specifications.

21. Check the automatic choke. A sticking or malfunctioning choke wastes gas.

22. During the summer months, adjust the automatic choke for a leaner mixture which will produce faster engine warm-ups.

COOLING SYSTEM

29. Be sure all accessory drive belts are in good condition. Check for cracks or wear.

30. Adjust all accessory drive belts to proper tension.

31. Check all hoses for swollen areas, worn spots, or loose clamps.

32. Check coolant level in the radiator or ex- pansion tank.

33. Be sure the thermostat is operating properly. A stuck thermostat delays engine warm-up and a cold engine uses nearly twice as much fuel as a warm engine.

34. Drain and replace the engine coolant at least as often as recommended. Rust and scale

TIRES & WHEELS

38. Check the tire pressure often with a pencil type gauge. Tests by a major tire manufacturer show that 90% of all vehicles have at least 1 tire improperly inflated. Better mileage can be achieved by over-inflating tires, but never exceed the maximum inflation pressure on the side of the tire.

39. If possible, install radial tires. Radial tires deliver as much as ½ mpg more than bias belted tires.

40. Avoid installing super-wide tires. They only create extra rolling resistance and decrease fuel mileage. Stick to the manufacturer's recommendations.

41. Have the wheels properly balanced.

omy by tampering with emission controls is more likely to worsen fuel economy than improve it. Emission control changes on modern engines are not readily reversible.

16. Clean (or replace) the EGR valve and lines as recommended.

17. Be sure that all vacuum lines and hoses are reconnected properly after working under the hood. An unconnected or misrouted vacuum line can wreak havoc with engine performance.

---

23. Check for fuel leaks at the carburetor, fuel pump, fuel lines and fuel tank. Be sure all lines and connections are tight.

24. Periodically check the tightness of the carburetor and intake manifold attaching nuts and bolts. These are a common place for vacuum leaks to occur.

25. Clean the carburetor periodically and lubricate the linkage.

26. The condition of the tailpipe can be an excellent indicator of proper engine combustion. After a long drive at highway speeds, the inside of the tailpipe should be a light grey in color. Black or soot on the insides indicates an overly rich mixture.

27. Check the fuel pump pressure. The fuel pump may be supplying more fuel than the engine needs.

28. Use the proper grade of gasoline for your engine. Don't try to compensate for knocking or "pinging" by advancing the ignition timing. This practice will only increase plug temperature and the chances of detonation or pre-ignition with relatively little performance gain.

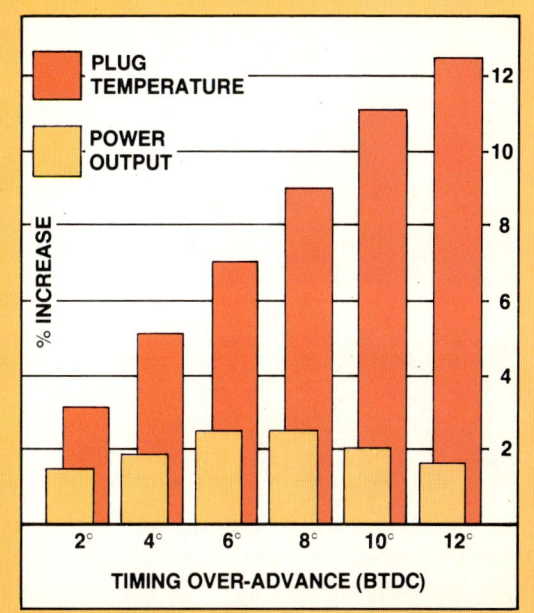

Increasing ignition timing past the specified setting results in a drastic increase in spark plug temperature with increased chance of detonation or preignition. Performance increase is considerably less. (Photo courtesy Champion Spark Plug Co.)

---

that form in the engine should be flushed out to allow the engine to operate at peak efficiency.

35. Clean the radiator of debris that can decrease cooling efficiency.

36. Install a flex-type or electric cooling fan, if you don't have a clutch type fan. Flex fans use curved plastic blades to push more air at low speeds when more cooling is needed; at high speeds the blades flatten out for less resistance. Electric fans only run when the engine temperature reaches a predetermined level.

37. Check the radiator cap for a worn or cracked gasket. If the cap does not seal properly, the cooling system will not function properly.

---

42. Be sure the front end is correctly aligned. A misaligned front end actually has wheels going in different directions. The increased drag can reduce fuel economy by .3 mpg.

43. Correctly adjust the wheel bearings. Wheel bearings that are adjusted too tight increase rolling resistance.

Check tire pressures regularly with a reliable pocket type gauge. Be sure to check the pressure on a cold tire.

GENERAL MAINTENANCE

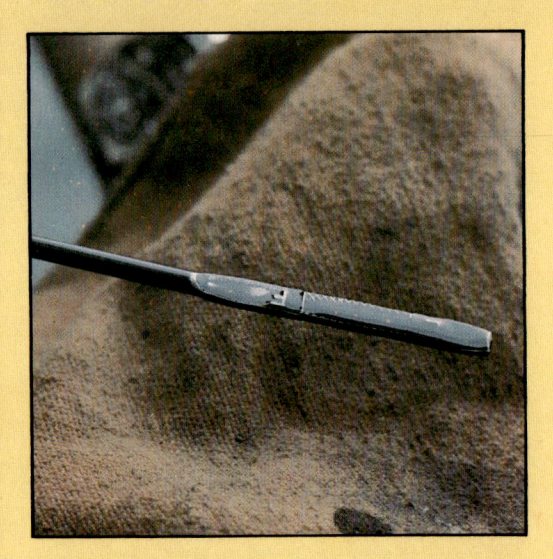

Check the fluid levels (particularly engine oil) on a regular basis. Be sure to check the oil for grit, water or other contamination.

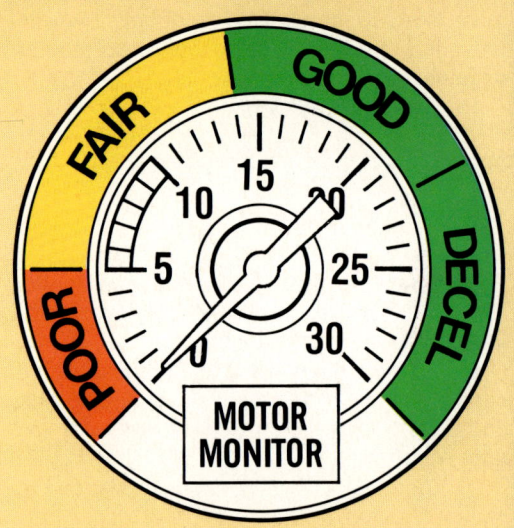

A vacuum gauge is another excellent indicator of internal engine condition and can also be installed in the dash as a mileage indicator.

44. Periodically check the fluid levels in the engine, power steering pump, master cylinder, automatic transmission and drive axle.

45. Change the oil at the recommended interval and change the filter at every oil change. Dirty oil is thick and causes extra friction between moving parts, cutting efficiency and increasing wear. A worn engine requires more frequent tune-ups and gets progressively worse fuel economy. In general, use the lightest viscosity oil for the driving conditions you will encounter.

46. Use the recommended viscosity fluids in the transmission and axle.

47. Be sure the battery is fully charged for fast starts. A slow starting engine wastes fuel.

48. Be sure battery terminals are clean and tight.

49. Check the battery electrolyte level and add distilled water if necessary.

50. Check the exhaust system for crushed pipes, blockages and leaks.

51. Adjust the brakes. Dragging brakes or brakes that are not releasing create increased drag on the engine.

52. Install a vacuum gauge or miles-per-gallon gauge. These gauges visually indicate engine vacuum in the intake manifold. High vacuum = good mileage and low vacuum = poorer mileage. The gauge can also be an excellent indicator of internal engine conditions.

53. Be sure the clutch is properly adjusted. A slipping clutch wastes fuel.

54. Check and periodically lubricate the heat control valve in the exhaust manifold. A sticking or inoperative valve prevents engine warm-up and wastes gas.

55. Keep accurate records to check fuel economy over a period of time. A sudden drop in fuel economy may signal a need for tune-up or other maintenance.

© 1980 Chilton Book Company, Radnor, PA 19089

EMISSION CONTROLS AND FUEL SYSTEM

Troubleshooting the EGR System (cont.)

Condition	Possible Source	Resolution
• Part-throttle engine detonation (cont'd)		PIPE AT END OF THIS TEST. IF THESE PRECAUTIONS ARE NOT OBSERVED, ENGINE AND/OR EXHAUST SYSTEM DAMAGE COULD OCCUR.) If valve leaks vacuum, replace it.
	• Vacuum restricted to EGR valve	• Check vacuum hoses, fittings, routing, and supply for blockage.
	• EGR disconnected	• Check connections and reconnect as required.
	• Load control valve venting	• Check for proper functioning. Vacuum should be present at load control valve vacuum port to EGR valve. Replace if damaged.
	• EGR passages blocked	• Check EGR passages for restrictions and blockage.
	• Insufficient exhaust back pressure (back pressure EGR valve only)	• Check for exhaust leaks ahead of muffler/catalyst or for blown-out muffler/catalyst. Also check for blockage to EGR valve. Service or replace all damaged components.
	• Vacuum hose leaking (cracked, split, broken, loose connections)	• Check all vacuum hoses for breaks and all connections for proper fit. Service or replace as required.

(NOTE: Detonation can also be due to carburetor or ignition malfunction.)

Condition	Possible Source	Resolution
• Abnormally low power at wide open throttle	• Load control valve not venting	• Check for proper functioning. Vacuum should not be present at vacuum port to EGR valve at wide-open throttle or heavy load. If vacuum is present, replace damaged valve.
• Engine starts but stalls immediately thereafter when cold	• EGR valve receiving vacuum, vacuum hoses misrouted • EGR valve not closing fully	• Check EGR valve hose routing. Correct as required. • Remove EGR valve to inspect for proper closing and seating of valve components. Clean or replace as required.

(NOTE: Stalling can also be due to carburetor malfunction.)

Condition	Possible Source	Resolution
• Engine hard to start, or no start condition	• EGR valve receiving vacuum. Vacuum hoses misrouted • EGR valve stuck open	• Check EGR valve hose routing. Correct as required. • Remove EGR valve to inspect for proper closing and seating of valve components. Clean or replace as required.
• Poor Fuel Economy	EGR related if: • Caused by detonation or other symptom of restricted or no EGR flow	• See Resolution for part-throttle engine detonation condition.

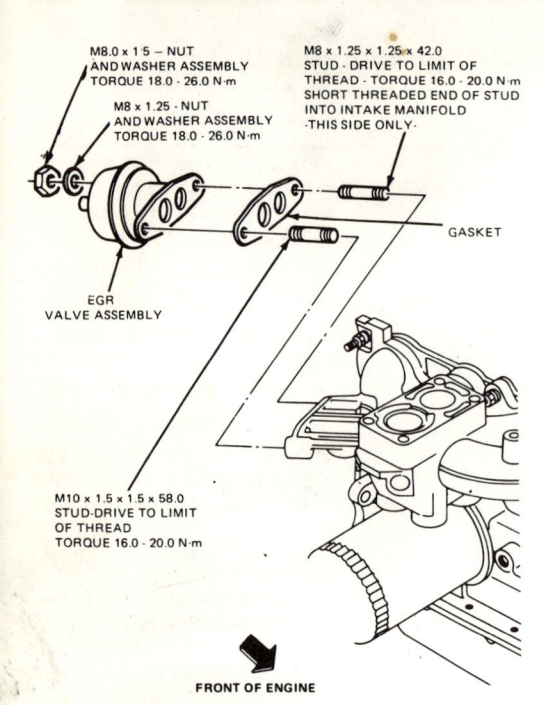

102 EMISSION CONTROLS AND FUEL SYSTEM

EGR valve installation

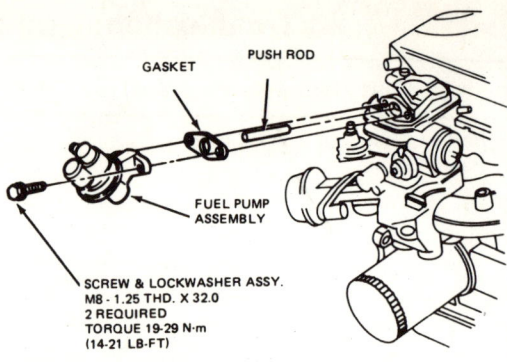

Fuel pump and push rod installation

Use a new mounting gasket, be sure the cam eccentric is in the lower position before installing the fuel pump.

NOTE: *The fuel pump push rod may come out when the fuel pump is removed; be sure to install the push rod before installing the fuel pump.*

6. After installing the pump, start the engine and check for fuel leaks.

FUEL PUMP CAPACITY CHECK

The fuel pump can fail in two ways; it can fail to provide a sufficient volume of gasoline under the proper pressure to the carburetor, or it can develop an internal or external leak. An external leak will be evident; not so with an internal leak. A quick check for an internal leak is to remove the oil dipstick and examine the oil on it. A fuel pump with an internal leak will leak fuel into the oil pan. If the oil on the dipstick is very thin and smells of gas, a defective fuel pump could be the cause.

To check the volume of gasoline from the fuel pump; disconnect the fuel pump line at the fuel filter. Connect a suitable rubber hose and clamp it to the fuel line. Insert it into a quart container. Start the engine. The fuel pump should provide one pint of gasoline in thirty seconds.

performing the required service the warning light is reset by installing a new sensor module.

FUEL SYSTEM

Fuel Pump

The mechanical fuel pump provides fuel for the engine from the gas tank. The lever arm is actuated by a pushrod driven by an eccentric on the camshaft. The pump lever arm actuates the internal diaphragm and provides fuel on demand of the carburetor when the engine is running.

REMOVAL AND INSTALLATION

1. Loosen the fuel outlet line using two flare wrenches. Loosen the fuel pump mounting bolts two turns.
2. Turn the engine until the fuel pump moves with just a little resistance on the mounting. The cam eccentric and pump lever are now in the low position.
3. Remove the rubber hose and clamp from the inlet side of the fuel pump.
4. Remove the outlet fuel line from the pump. Remove the mounting bolts and the fuel pump.
5. Installation is in the reverse order of removal. Mounting bolt torque is 14–21 ft. lbs.

Carburetor

Your car uses a staged two barrel unit; the second barrel is opened under heavy throttle situations.

The carburetor has five basic metering systems; they are the choke system, idle system, main metering system, acceleration system and the power enrichment system.

The choke system is used for cold starting. It incorporates a bi-metal spring and an electric heater for faster cold weather starts and improved drivability during warm-up.

EMISSION CONTROLS AND FUEL SYSTEM

The idle system is a separate and adjustable system for the correct air/fuel mixture at both idle and low speed operation.

The main metering system provides the necessary air/fuel mixture for normal driving speeds. A main metering system is provided for both primary and secondary stages of operation.

The accelerating system is operated from the primary stage throttle linkage. The system provides fuel to the primary stage during acceleration. Fuel is provided by a diaphragm pump located on the carburetor.

The power enrichment system consists of a vacuum-operated power valve and airflow-regulated pullover system for the secondary carburetor barrel. The system is used in conjunction with the main metering system to provide acceptable performance during mid and heavy acceleration.

REMOVAL AND INSTALLATION

1. Remove the air cleaner assembly. Disconnect the throttle control cable and speed control (if equipped). Disconnect the fuel line at the filter.
2. Label and disconnect all vacuum hoses, wires and linkage attached to the carburetor. If your car is equipped with an automatic transaxle, disconnect the TV linkage.
3. Remove the four mounting bolts that attach the carburetor to the intake manifold, remove the carburetor.
4. Installation is in the reverse order of removal. If your car is equipped with an automatic transaxle, a TV linkage adjustment may be required.

OVERHAUL NOTES

Generally, when a carburetor requires major service, a rebuilt one is purchased on an exchange basis, or a kit may be bought for overhauling the carburetor.

The kit contains the necessary parts (see below) and some form of instructions for carburetor rebuilding. The instructions may vary between a simple exploded view and detailed step-by-step rebuilding instructions. Unless you are familiar with carburetor overhaul, the latter should be used.

There are some general overhaul procedures which should always be observed:

Efficient carburetion depends greatly on careful cleaning and inspection during overhaul since dirt, gum, water, or varnish in or on the carburetor parts are often responsible for poor performance.

Overhaul your carburetor in a clean, dust-free area. Carefully disassemble the carburetor, referring often to the exploded views. Keep all similar and lookalike parts segregated during disassembly and cleaning to avoid accidental interchange during assembly. Make a note of all jet sizes.

When the carburetor is disassembled, wash all parts (except diaphragms, electric choke units, pump plunger, and any other plastic, leather, fiber, or rubber parts) in clean carburetor solvent. Do not leave parts in the solvent any longer than is necessary to sufficiently loosen the deposits. Excessive cleaning may remove the special finish from the float bowl and choke valve bodies, leaving these parts unfit for service. Rinse all parts in clean solvent and blow them dry with compressed air or allow them to air dry. Wipe clean all cork, plastic, leather, and fiber parts with a clean, lint-free cloth.

Blow out all passages and jets with compressed air and be sure that there are no restrictions or blockages. Never use wire or similar tools to clean jets, fuel passages, or air bleeds. Clean all jets and valves separately to avoid accidental interchange.

Check all parts for wear or damage. If wear or damage is found, replace the defective parts. Especially check the following:

1. Check the float needle and seat for wear. If wear is found, replace the complete assembly.
2. Check the float hinge pin for wear and the float(s) for dents or distortion. Replace the float if fuel has leaked into it.
3. Check the throttle and choke shaft bores for wear or an out-of-round condition. Damage or wear to the throttle arm, shaft, or shaft bore will often require replacement of the throttle body. These parts require a close tolerance; wear may allow air leakage, which could affect starting and idling.

NOTE: *Throttle shafts and bushings are usually not included in overhaul kits. They can be purchased separately.*

4. Inspect the idle mixture adjusting needles for burrs or grooves. Any such condition requires replacement of the needle, since you will not be able to obtain a satisfactory idle.
5. Test the accelerator pump check valves. They should pass air one way but not the other. Test for proper seating by blowing and sucking on the valve. Replace the valve if necessary. If the valve is satisfactory, wash the valve again to remove breath moisture.

104 EMISSION CONTROLS AND FUEL SYSTEM

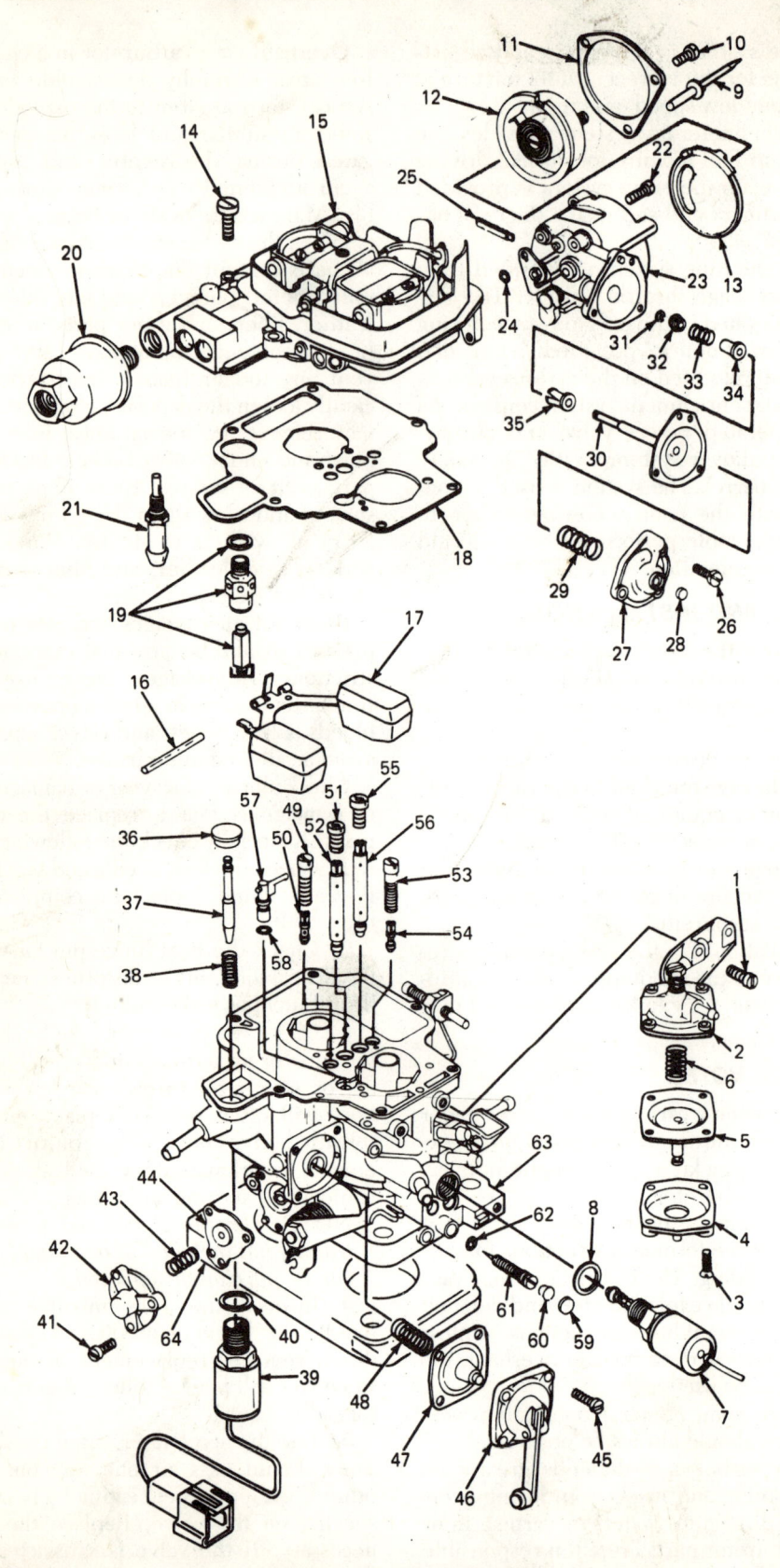

Exploded view of a carburetor

EMISSION CONTROLS AND FUEL SYSTEM

6. Check the bowl cover for warped surfaces with a straightedge.
7. Closely inspect the valves and seats for wear and damage, replacing as necessary.
8. After the carburetor is assembled, check the choke valve for freedom of operation.

Carburetor overhaul kits are recommended for each overhaul. These kits contain all gaskets and new parts to replace those that deteriorate most rapidly. Failure to replace all parts supplied with the kit (especially gaskets) can result in poor performance later.

Some carburetor manufacturers supply overhaul kits of three basic types: minor repair; major repair; and gasket kits. Basically, they contain the following:

Minor Repair Kits:
- All gaskets
- Float needle valve
- Volume control screw
- All diaphragms
- Spring for the pump diaphragm

Major Repair Kits:
- All jets and gaskets
- All diaphragms
- Float needle valve
- Volume control screw
- Pump ball valve
- Main jet carrier
- Float
- Other necessary items.
- Some cover hold-down screws and washers

Gasket Kits:
- All gaskets

After cleaning and checking all components, reassemble the carburetor, using new parts and referring to the exploded view. When reassembling, make sure that all screws and jets are tight in their seats, but do not overtighten, as the tips will be distorted. Tighten all screws gradually, in rotation. Do not tighten needle valves into their seats; uneven jetting will result. Always use new gaskets. Be sure to adjust the float level when reassembling.

DISASSEMBLY

NOTE: *All major and minor repair kits contain detailed instructions and illustrations. Refer to them for complete rebuilding instructions.*

NOTE: *To prevent damage to the throttle plates, make a stand using four bolts, eight flat washers and eight nuts. Place a washer and nut on the bolt, install through the carburetor base and secure with a nut.*

Always use a separate container to hold

1. Screw and lockwasher (2)—Throttle kicker
2. Throttle kicker assembly
3. Screw (4)—Cover
4. Cover—Diaphragm
5. Diaphragm assembly—Throttle kicker
6. Spring—Diaphragm
7. Solenoid—Idle shutoff
8. Gasket—Solenoid
9. Rivet (2)—Choke cover retainer
10. Screw (1)—Choke cover retainer
11. Retaining ring—Choke cover
12. Electric choke cover assembly
13. Dirt shield—choke housing
14. Screw and lockwasher (6)—Air horn
15. Air horn assembly
16. Pin—float
17. Float and lever assembly
18. Gasket—Air horn
19. Needle, seat and gasket assembly
20. Filter—Fuel inlet
21. Check valve—Fuel return
22. Screw (3)—Choke housing assembly
23. Choke housing assembly
24. O-ring—Choke housing
25. Retainer—Choke link seal
26. Screw (3)—Cover
27. Cover—Diaphragm
28. Plug—(Plastic) Adjusting Screw
29. Spring—Diaphragm
30. Diaphragm assembly—Choke Pulldown
31. E-clip—Bushing retainer
32. Bushing (small)—Bumper spring
33. Spring—Bumper
34. Bushing (large)—Bumper spring
35. Bushing—Guide
36. Seal—Bowl vent
37. Plunger—Bowl vent seal
38. Spring—Seal plunger
39. Solenoid—Bowl vent
40. Gasket—Bowl vent solenoid
41. Screw (3)—Cover
42. Cover—Power enrichment valve
43. Spring—Power enrichment valve diaphragm
44. Diaphragm assembly—Enrichment valve
45. Screw (4)—Cover
46. Cover—Pump diaphragm
47. Diaphragm assembly—Accelerator pump
48. Spring—Diaphragm return
49. Holder—primary idle jet
50. Jet—Primary idle
51. Air bleed—Primary
52. Tube—Primary main well
53. Holder—Secondary idle jet
54. Jet—Secondary idle
55. Air bleed—Secondary
56. Tube—Secondary main well
57. Nozzle assembly—accelerator pump discharge
58. O-ring—Pump nozzle
59. Plug—Idle fuel mixture needle
60. Plug (plastic)—Idle fuel mixture needle
61. Needle—Idle mixture adjustment
62. O-ring—Idle mixture adjustment needle
63. Main body assembly
64. Spacer and gasket assembly

EMISSION CONTROLS AND FUEL SYSTEM

parts from the same assembly so they cannot get lost or mixed up.

Air Horn

1. Remove the fuel filter. Remove the air horn mounting screws (six). Open the throttle enough to clear the fast idle screw and remove the air horn.
2. Turn the air horn over. Remove the float hinge pin, float and inlet needle.
3. Remove the inlet seat and gasket. Remove the air horn gasket. Remove the fuel return line check valve and fitting.

Automatic Electric Choke

NOTE: *Air horn removed.*
1. Remove the three rivets retaining the electric choke cover. They may be removed by driving them out with the proper size punch, or maybe drilled out with a ⅛ drill bit. If you use a drill, only drill the rivet head; use a punch to drive out the rest of the rivet. Use extreme care not to enlarge the existing hole.
2. Remove the choke cover retaining ring, electric unit and index shield.
3. Remove the three phillips screws that mount the choke housing to the carburetor. Slide the housing away from the carburetor and disengage the primary choke link. Remove the "O"-ring from the vacuum passage.
4. Disengage the choke assist spring from the choke housing, remove the bi-metal shaft nut. Remove the lockwasher and choke lever. Slide the shaft and lever outward.
5. Pull the choke pulldown diaphragm assembly outward until the shaft bottoms on the plastic retaining collar. Depress the plastic clip and slide the diaphragm assembly out.

Accelerator Pump

1. If your car is equipped with air conditioning or power steering, remove the "kicker". The "kicker" is located in front of the accelerator pump.
2. Remove the four accelerator pump cover screws, the accelerator pump cover, diaphragm and return spring.
3. Remove the pump nozzle from the main body with a pair of needle nose pliers. The pump cover must be removed before the nozzle can be taken from the main body.

Main Body

NOTE: *Air horn, choke, AC/PS "Kicker" and accelerator pump diaphragm and nozzle are removed.*
1. Remove the fuel shut-off solenoid and mounting washer. Remove the bowl vent solenoid and washer.
2. Remove the three power valve cover screws, cover, spring and diaphragm. If your car is equipped with a dashpot, remove it.
3. Remove the idle speed concealment plugs by center punching them and carefully drilling a 3/32 in. hole through both the hard-

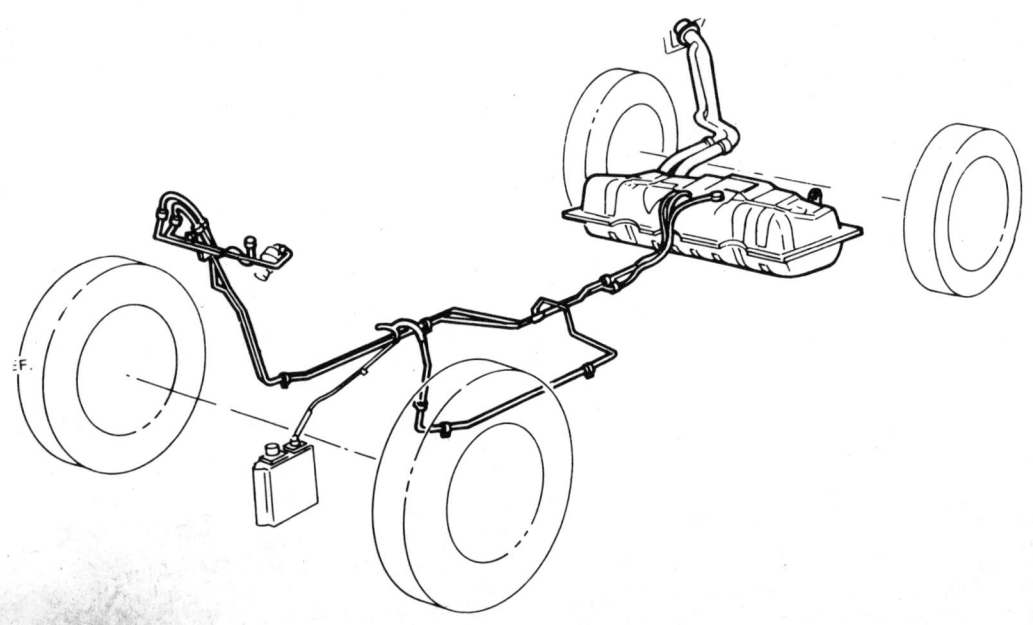

Fuel lines and hardware

EMISSION CONTROLS AND FUEL SYSTEM

ened steel plug and the plastic inner plug. Install an easy-out in the drilled hole and remove both plugs.

4. Turn the adjustment screw in while counting the number of turns necessary to lightly seat the screw. Remove the mixture screw, "O"-ring and spring.

5. Remove the primary and secondary fuel discharge nozzles. Note the difference, identify the nozzles as to location and reference top and bottom.

6. Remove the primary and secondary idle jet holder, the jet is pressed into the bottom. Identify the jets by referencing their numbers.

7. Remove the high speed air bleed. The bleeds contain the main well tubes and the main jets. The bleed may be disassembled by hand.

ASSEMBLY

Starting with the main body of the carburetor and working backwards, assembly is in the reverse order of disassembly. Remember to reinstall the mixture screws to the exact number of turns you recorded when they were removed. Refer to the instructions that came with the rebuilding kit for precise settings and adjustments.

Fuel Tank

REMOVAL AND INSTALLATION

CAUTION: *Have the tank as empty as possible. No smoking or open flame while working on the fuel system.*

1. Disconnect the negative battery cable from the battery.

2. Raise the rear of the car and safely support it on jackstands.

3. Disconnect the gas fill and breather lines from the tank. Disconnect the fuel feed, return and breather lines from the front of the tank, plug these lines.

4. Remove the two mounting bolts at the top rear of the tank while supporting the tank on a piece of wood and a floor tank. Lower and remove the gas tank.

5. Installation is in the reverse order of removal.

Chassis Electrical

The theory and basic troubleshooting of the chassis electrical system may be found in the "Troubleshooting" Chapter near the back of the book.

HEATER

NOTE: *In some cases removal of the instrument panel may be necessary.*

Heater Core

REMOVAL AND INSTALLATION

1. Disconnect the negative battery cable.
2. Drain the coolant.
3. Disconnect the heater hoses from the core tubes at the firewall, inside the engine compartment. Plug the core tubes to prevent coolant spillage when the core is removed.
4. Open the glove compartment. Remove the glove compartment liner.
5. Remove the core access plate screws and remove the access plate.
6. Remove the core through the glove compartment opening. Installation is the reverse.

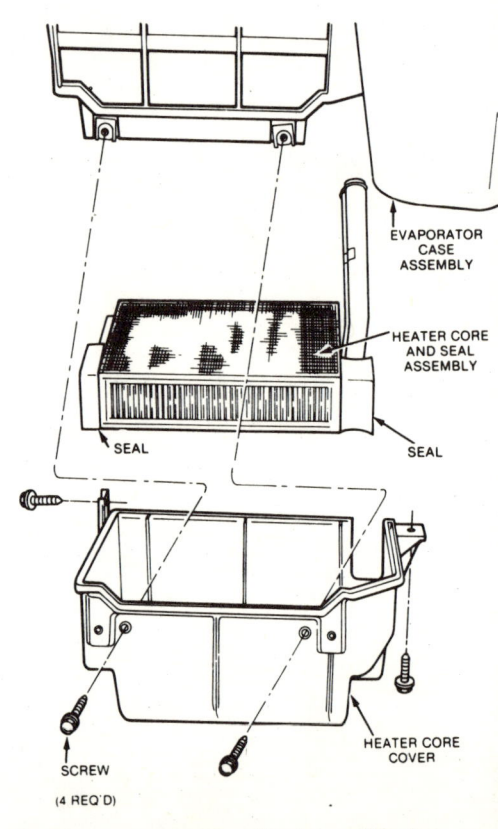

Heater core removal; with air conditioning

CHASSIS ELECTRICAL 109

Heater core removal; without air conditioning

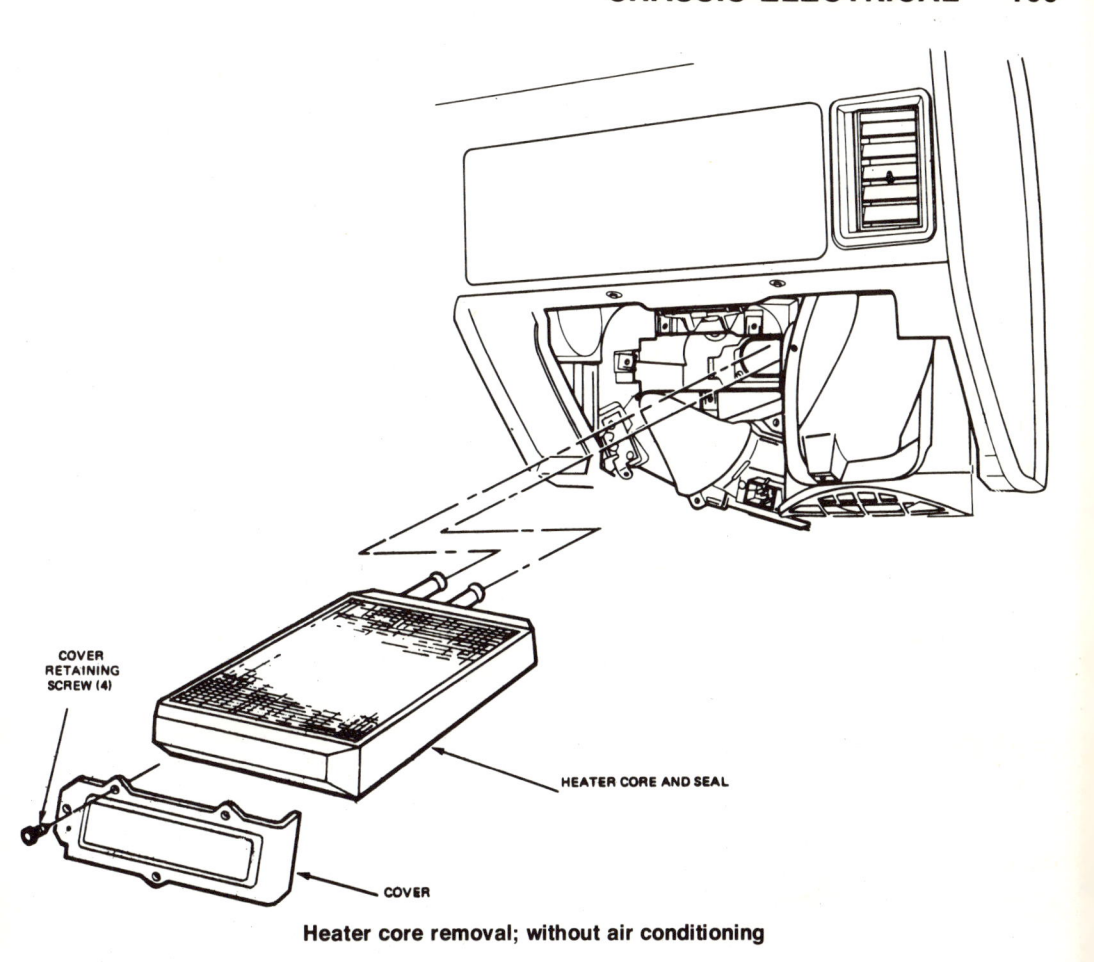

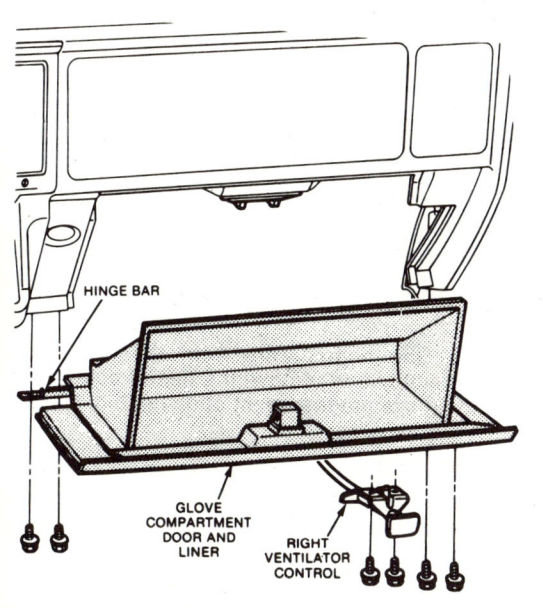

Typical glove box removal

Blower Motor

REMOVAL AND INSTALLATION

1. Disconnect the negative battery cable.
2. Remove the glove compartment and lower instrument panel reinforcing rail.
3. Disconnect the blower electrical connectors.
4. Remove the blower motor-to-case attaching screws. Remove the blower and fan as an assembly.
5. Installation is the reverse.

RADIO

For best FM reception, adjust the antenna to 31 inches in height. Fading or weak AM reception may be adjusted by means of the antenna trimmer control, located either on the right rear or front side of the radio chassis.

110 CHASSIS ELECTRICAL

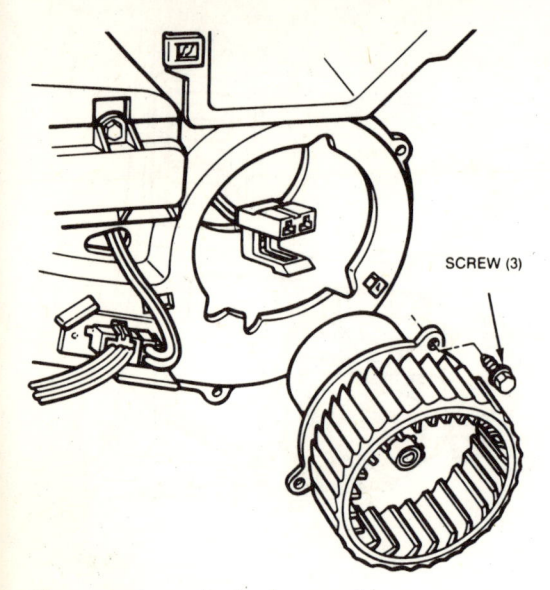

Blower motor and wheel removal

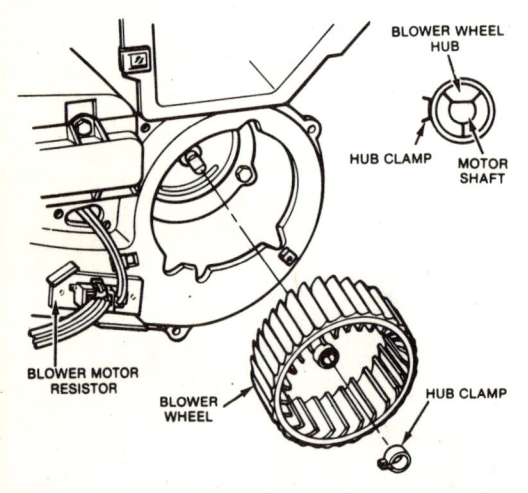

Blower wheel removal

See the owner's manual for position. To adjust the trimmer:

1. Extend the antenna to maximum height.
2. Tune the radio to a weak station around 1600 KC. Adjust the volume so that the sound is barely audible.
3. Adjust the trimmer to obtain maximum volume.

REMOVAL AND INSTALLATION

1. Disconnect the negative battery cable.
2. Pull the knobs from the shafts.
3. Working under the instrument panel, remove the support bracket nut from the radio chassis.
4. Remove the shaft nuts and washers.
5. Drop the radio down from behind the instrument panel. Disconnect the power lead, antenna, and speaker wires. Remove the radio.
6. Installation is the reverse.

WINDSHIELD WIPERS

Wiper Arm Assembly
REMOVAL AND INSTALLATION

1. Raise the blade end of the arm off the windshield and move the slide latch away from the pivot shaft.
2. The wiper arm should now be unlocked and can now be pulled off of the pivot shaft.
3. To install, position the auxiliary arm (if so equipped) over the pivot pin, hold it down and push the main arm head over the pivot shaft. Make sure the pivot shaft is in the park position.
4. Hold the main arm head on the pivot shaft while raising the blade end of the wiper arm and push the slide latch into the lock under the pivot shaft. Lower the blade to the windshield.

NOTE: *If the blade does not touch the windshield, the slide latch is not completely in place.*

Wiper Blade (Tridon Type)
REPLACEMENT

1. Pull up on the spring lock and pull the blade assembly from the pin.
2. To install, push the blade assembly onto the pin, so that the spring lock engages the pin.

Wiper Element (Tridon)
REPLACEMENT

1. Locate a $7/16''$ long notch approximately one inch from the end of the plastic backing strip, which is part of the rubber blade element assembly.
2. With the wiper blade removed from the arm place the blade assembly on a firm surface with the notched end of the backing strip visible.
3. Push down on one end of the wiper assembly until the blade is tightly bowed then grasp the tip of the backing strip firmly, pulling and twisting at the same time. The backing strip will then snap out of the retaining tab on the end of the wiper frame.
4. Lift the wiper blade assembly from the

CHASSIS ELECTRICAL 111

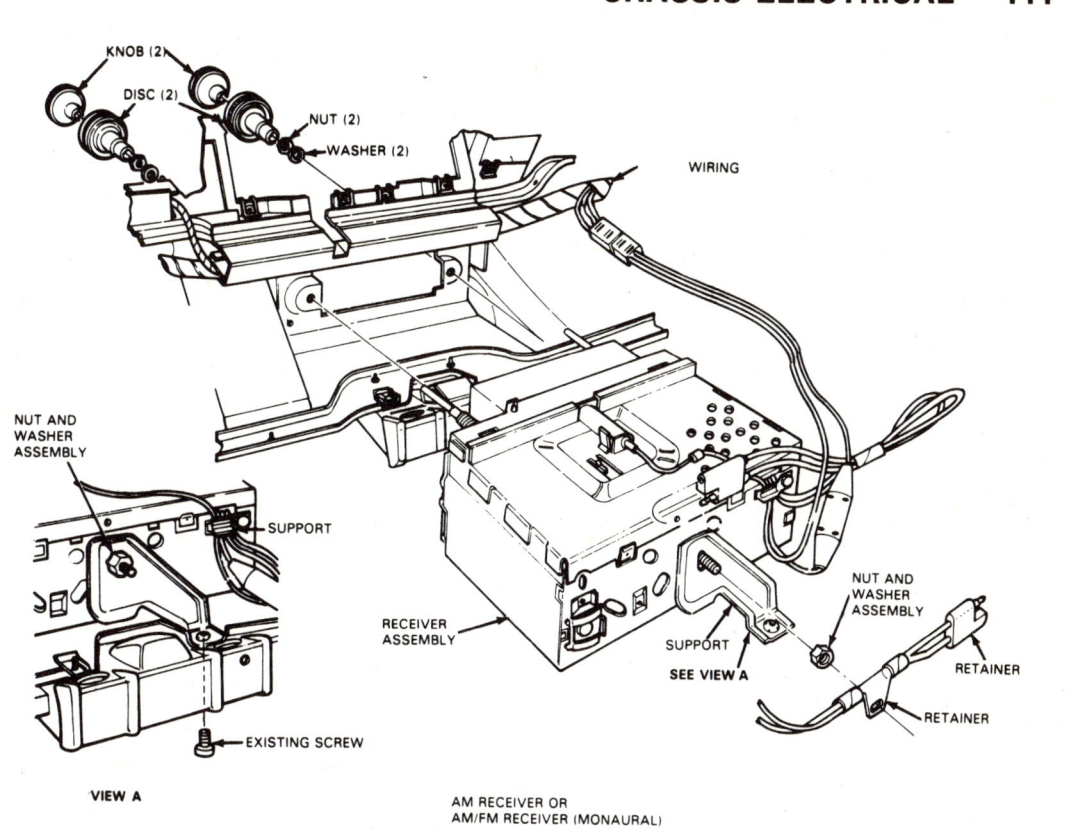

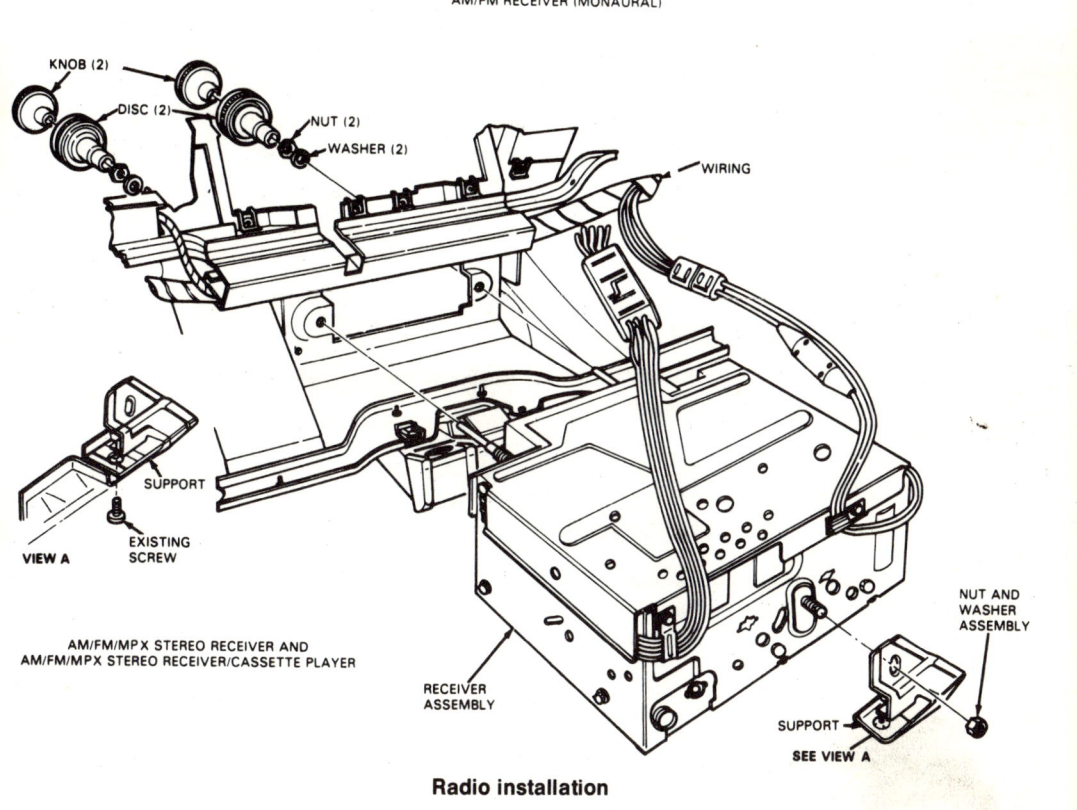

Radio installation

112 CHASSIS ELECTRICAL

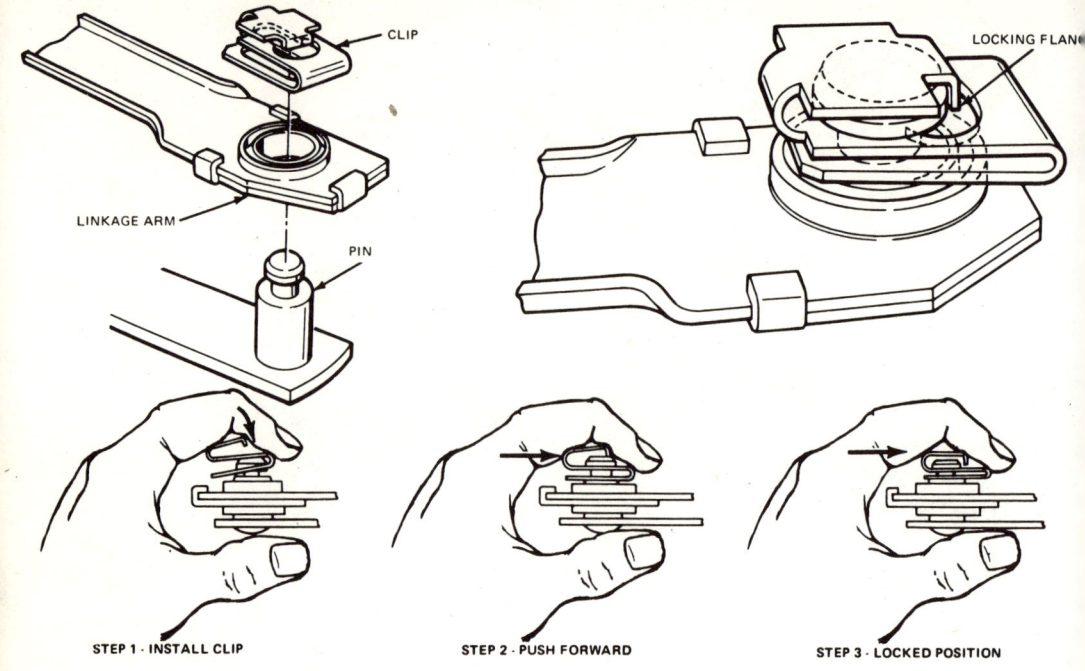

Removing and installing wiper linkage retaining clips

surface and slide the backing strip down the frame until the notch lines up with the next retaining tab then twist slightly and the backing strip will snap out. Follow this same procedure with the remaining tabs until the element is removed.

5. To install the blade element reverse the above procedure and make sure all six tabs are locked to the backing strip.

Motor

REMOVAL AND INSTALLATION

The motor is located in the right rear corner of the engine compartment, in the cowl area above the firewall.

1. Disconnect the negative battery cable.
2. Remove the plastic cowl cover.
3. Disconnect the motor electrical connector.
4. Remove the motor attaching bolts. Disengage the motor from the linkage and remove the motor. Installation is the reverse.

Linkage

REMOVAL AND INSTALLATION

The wiper linkage is mounted below the cowl top grille. The pivot shafts and linkage assemblies are connected together with nonremoveable plastic ball joints. The left- and right-hand pivot shafts and linkage are serviced as one unit.

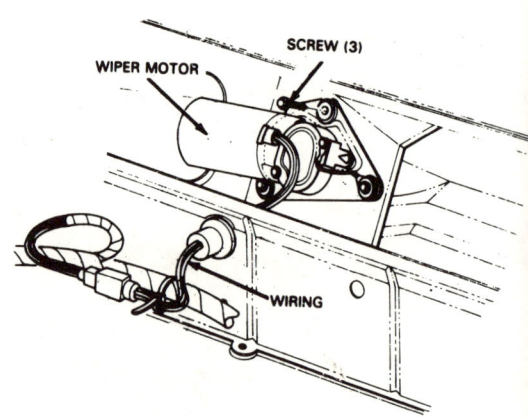

Wiper motor installation

1. Disconnect the negative battery cable.
2. Remove the cowl top grille attaching screws and the grille.
3. Remove the clip and disconnect the linkage drive arm from the motor crank pin.
4. Remove the two bolts retaining the right pivot shaft to the cowl, and remove the large nut, washer and spacer from the left pivot shaft.
5. To install reverse the removal procedure. Before installing the blade assemblies, make sure the motor is in PARK and the blades are set to the proper dimension. See the Arm and Blade Adjustment procedure.

CHASSIS ELECTRICAL 113

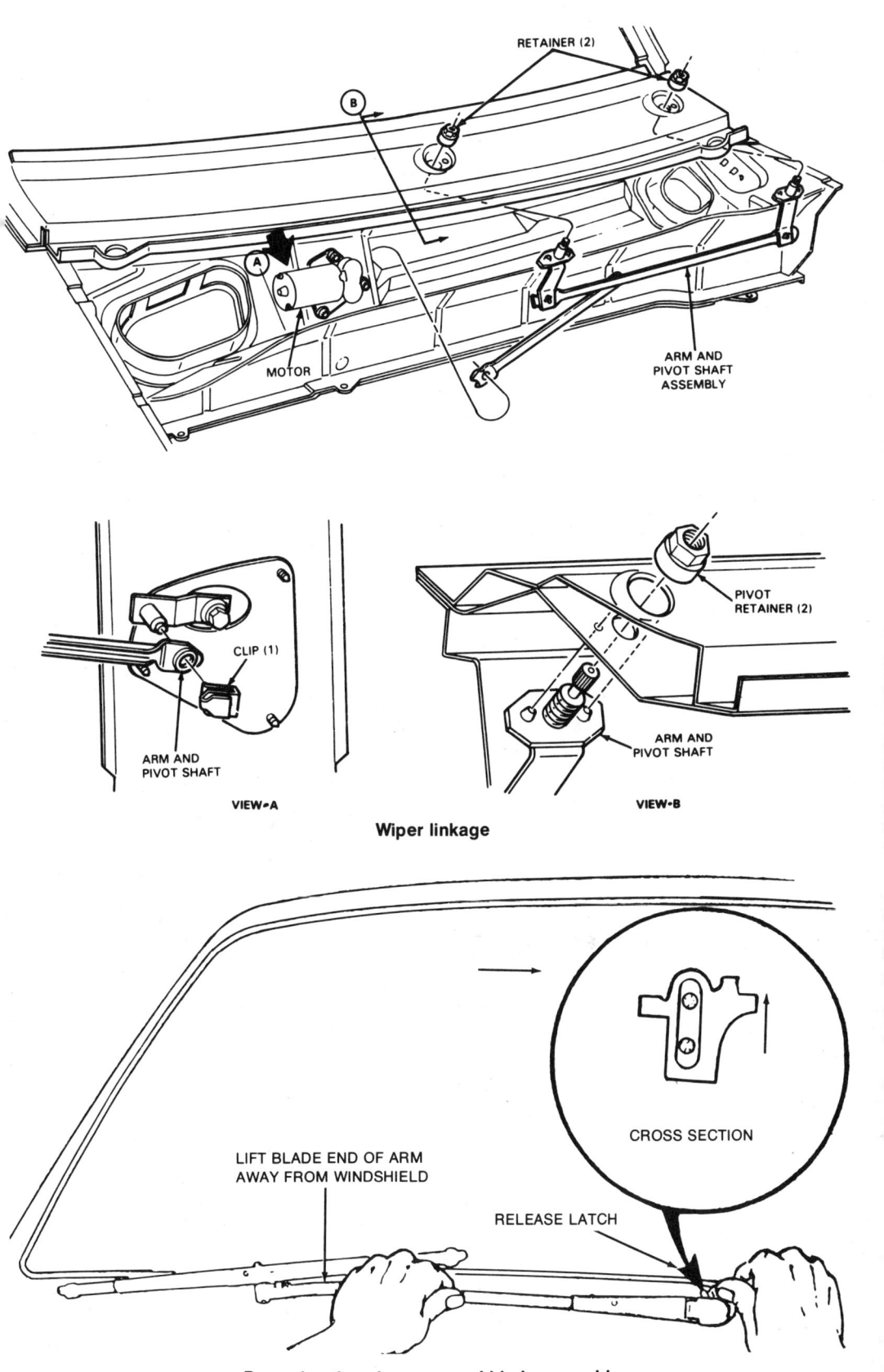

Wiper linkage

Removing the wiper arm and blade assembly

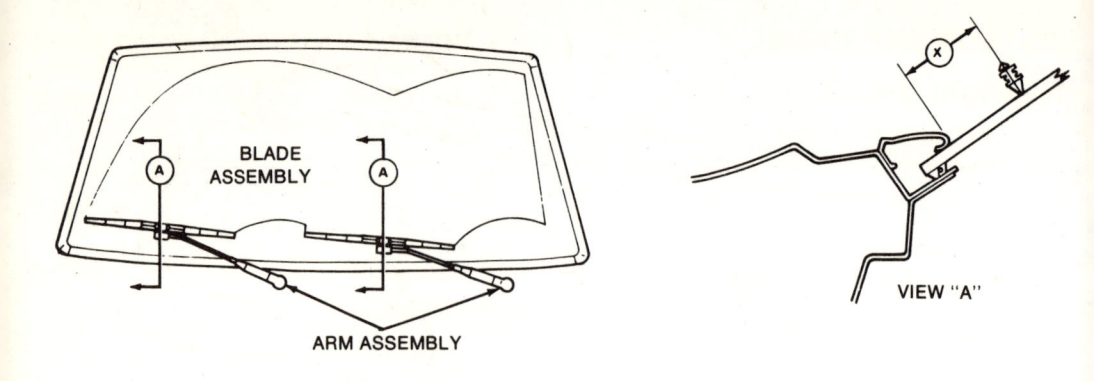

114 CHASSIS ELECTRICAL

Wiper arm adjustment

Vehicle	Dimension x (inches)	
	Driver's Side	Passenger Side
ESCORT AND LYNX FRONT 40-75 mm (1 5/8 — 3 in)		
THREE DOOR REAR 30-75 mm (1 1/8 — 3 in)		
FOUR DOOR REAR 20-60 mm (3/8 — 2 3/8 in)		

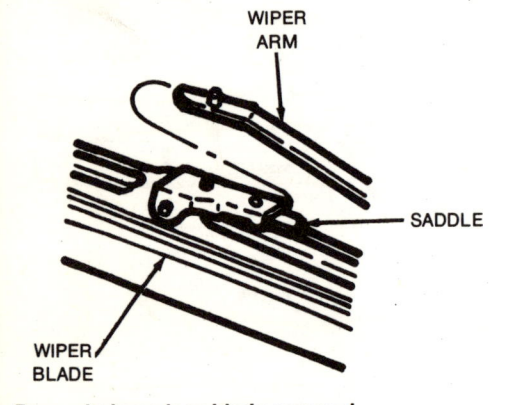

Rear window wiper blade removal

ARM AND BLADE ADJUSTMENT

1. With the arm and blade assemblies removed from pivot shafts turn on the wiper switch and allow the motor to move the pivot shafts three or four cycles, and then turn off the wiper switch. This will place the pivot shafts in the park position.

2. Install the arm and blade assemblies on the pivot shafts to the correct distance between the windshield lower moulding or weatherstrip and the blade saddle centerline.

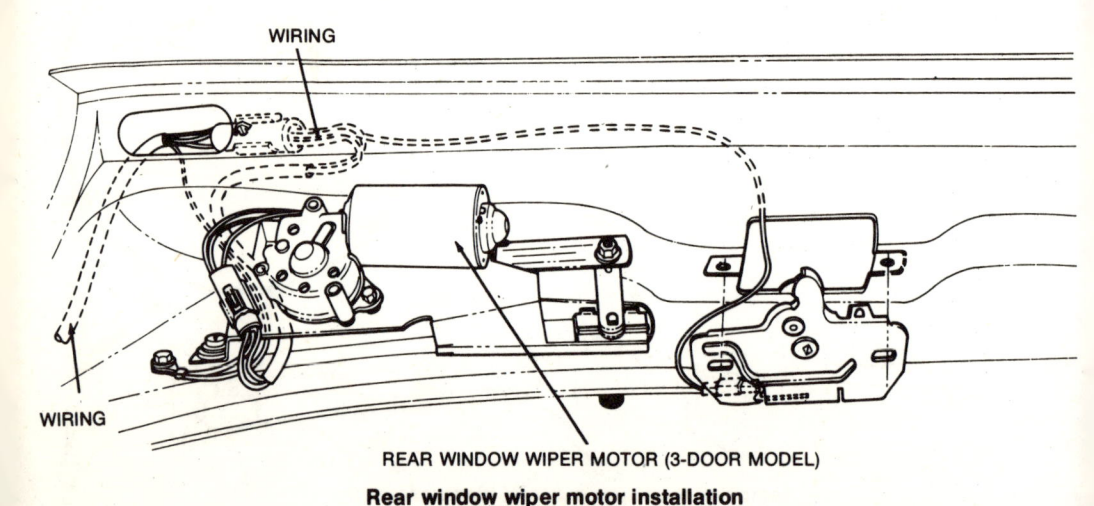

Rear window wiper motor installation

CHASSIS ELECTRICAL 115

INSTRUMENT PANEL
Headlight Switch
1. Disconnect the negative battery cable.
2. Reach behind the instrument panel and depress the knob release button on the switch housing, while at the same time pulling the knob and shaft from the switch.
3. Remove the switch retaining nut from the front of the instrument panel.
4. Lower the switch and remove the electrical connector.
5. Installation is the reverse.

Instrument Cluster
REMOVAL AND INSTALLATION
1. Disconnect the negative battery cable.
2. Remove the two lens screws at the upper corners of the cluster opening. Remove the lens.
3. Remove the four cluster retaining screws. Pull the cluster out slightly, disconnect the speedometer cable and electrical connectors, and remove the cluster.

Speedometer Cable
REPLACEMENT
1. Remove the instrument cluster.
2. Pull the speedometer cable from the casing. If the cable is broken, disconnect the casing from the transaxle and remove the broken piece from the transaxle end.
3. Lubricate the new cable with graphite lubricant. Feed the cable into the casing from the instrument panel end.
4. Attach the cable to the speedometer. Install the cluster.

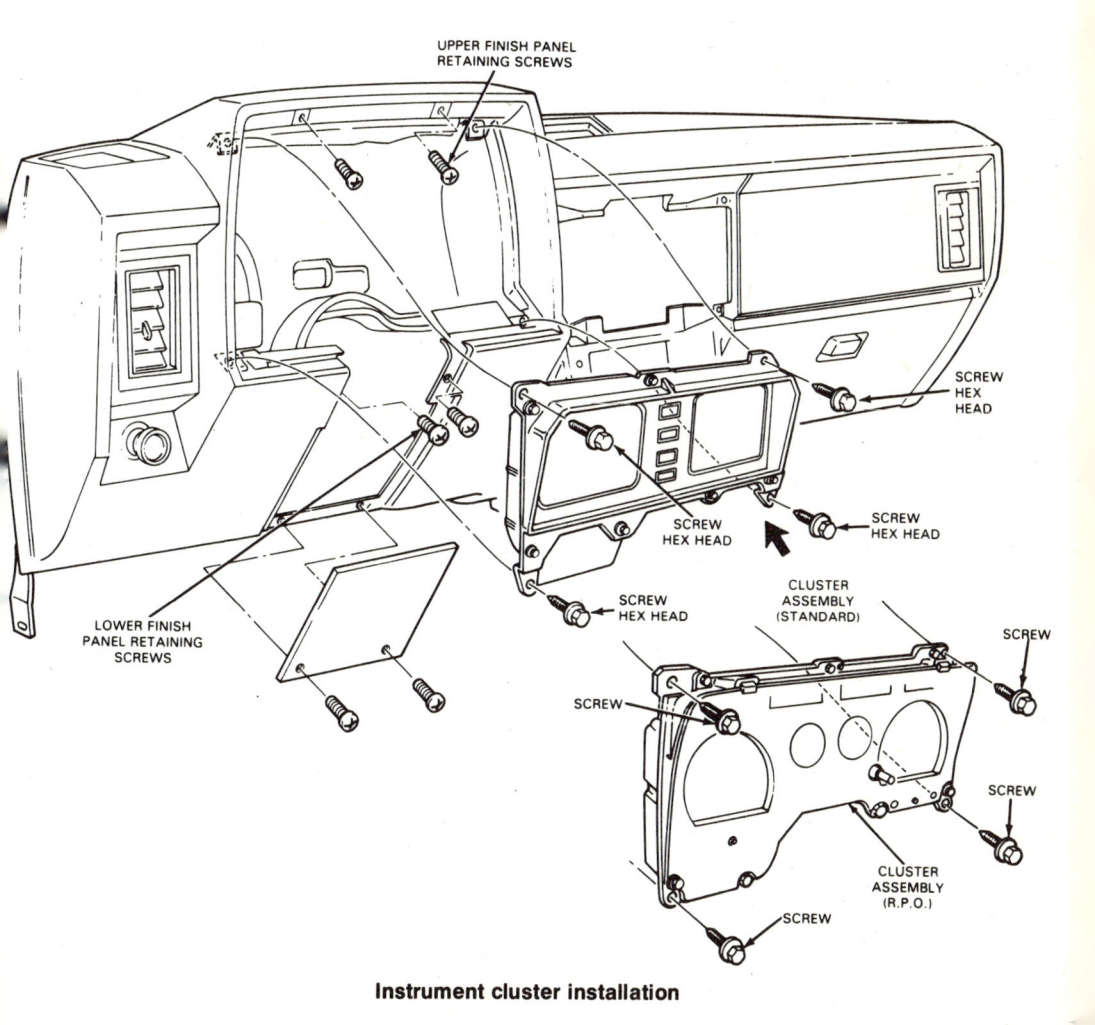

Instrument cluster installation

116 CHASSIS ELECTRICAL

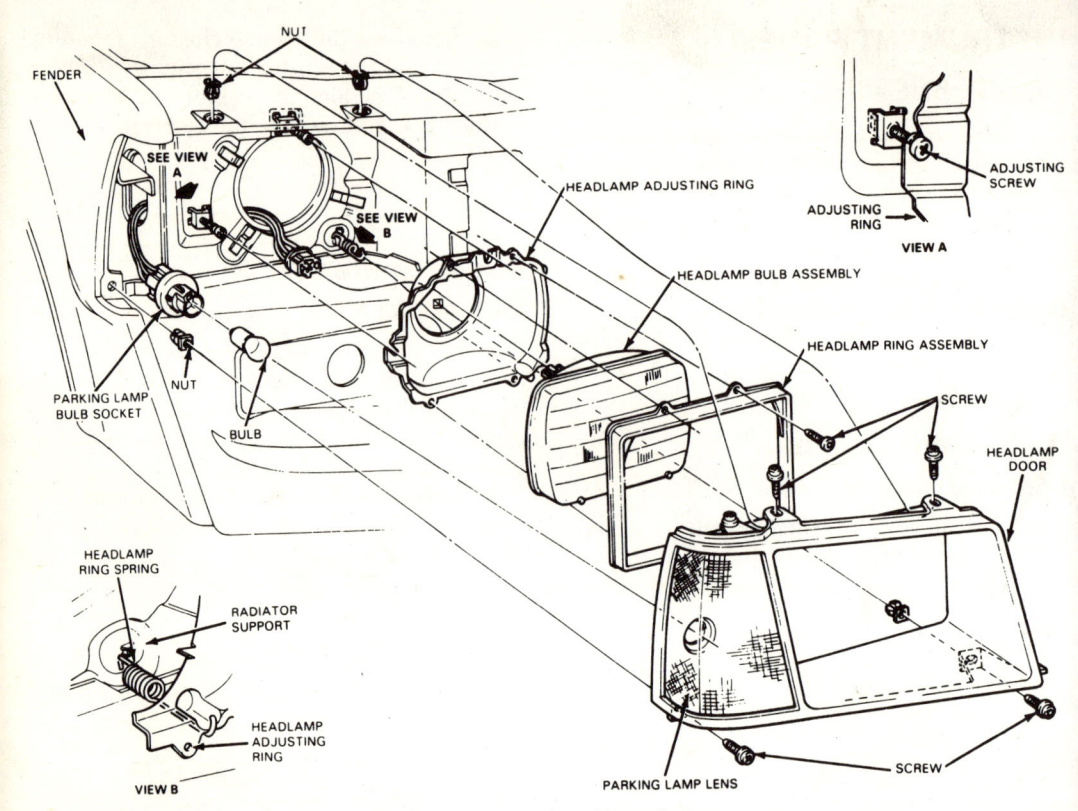

Headlamp removal and installation

LIGHTING

Headlights

Two rectangular dual beam headlamps are used on your car. A dash mounted switch controls them and the steering column dimmer switch controls the high and low beams.

REMOVAL AND INSTALLATION

1. Remove the headlamp door by removing the retaining screws. After the screws are removed, pull the "door" slightly forward and disconnect the parking light. Remove the headlight door.
2. Remove the lamp retaining ring screws, pull the headlamp from the connector.
3. Installation is in the reverse order of removal.

Turn Signal and Hazard Flasher

The turn signal flasher is located on the front side of the fuse panel (see illustration).
The hazard warning flasher is located on the rear side of the fuse panel.

CIRCUIT BREAKERS

Circuit breakers operate when a circuit overload exceeds its rated amperage. Once operated, they automatically reset after a certain period of time.
There are two kinds of circuit, as previously mentioned, one type will reset itself. The second will not reset itself until the problem in the circuit has been repaired.

FUSE PANEL

The fuse panel is located below and to the left of the steering column.
Fuses are a one-time circuit protection. If a circuit is overloaded or shorts, the fuse will "blow" thus protecting the circuit. A fuse will continue to "blow" until the circuit is repaired.

FUSE LINK

The fuse link is a short length of special, Hypalon (high temperature) insulated wire, in-

CHASSIS ELECTRICAL

Bulb Chart

Function	Number of Bulbs	Trade Number
Exterior Illumination		
Front Park/Turn Lamp	2	1157
Headlamps—Hi & Low Beam	2	H6054 ③
3-Door Hatchback		
Backup Lamp	2	1156
Rear License Plate Lamp	1	168
Rear Stop & Side Marker Lamp	2	1157
Rear Turn Lamp	2	1156
4-Door Liftgate		
Backup Lamp	2	1156
Rear License Plate Lamp	1	168
Rear Park Stop & Turn Lamp	2	1157
Rear Side Marker Lamp		Integral with Rear Lamp
Interior Illumination		
Cargo Lamp—4-Door	1	906
Dome Lamp	1	906
Dome/Map Lamp	1/1	906/1816
Engine Compartment Lamp	1	89
Luggage Compartment Lamp —3-Door (RPO)	1	906
"PRNDL" Illumination	1	1445
Instrument Panel Illumination		
A/C Control Nomenclature	1	161
Electric De-Ice Indicator	1	2162
Fan Nomenclature	1	1892
Glove Compartment	1	194
Heater Control Nomenclature	1	161
High Beam Indicator	1	194
I/P Ashtray Lamp	1	1892
I/P Gauge (Cluster)	3	194
R.P.O. Cluster	3	194
Stereo Indicator Light	1	②
Radio Pilot Lights	4	194
AM	1	1893
AM/FM/Mono	1	1893
AM/FM/MPX	1	1893
AM/FM/MPX/Cassette	1	②
Premium Sound Indicator	1	①
Turn Signal Indicator	2	194
Warning Lamps:		
Alternator	1	194
Brakes	1	194
Engine	1	194
Fasten Belts	1	194
Oil	1	194
Liftgate Open	1	194

① Replace with Ford Part Number D20B-18C622-AB or equivalent, if available. (Bulb is an integral part of assembly.)
② Replaceable at radio service centers.
③ Substitution of headlamp bulbs other than original equipment may result in no warning in the Graphic Display Warning Indicator System.

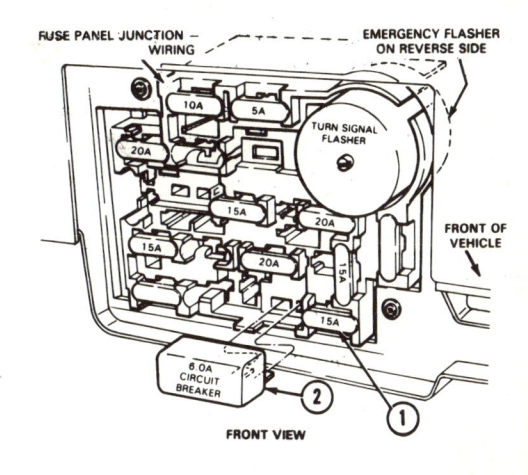

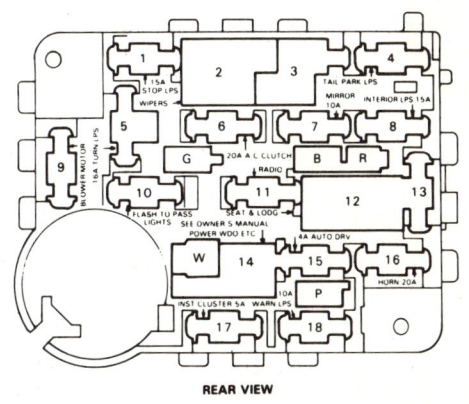

Fuse panel

Under no circumstances should a fuse link replacement repair be made using a length of standard wire cut from bulk stock or from another wiring harness.

To repair any blown fuse link use the following procedure:

1. Determine which circuit is damaged, its location and the cause of the open fuse link. If the damaged fuse link is one of three fed by a common No. 10 or 12 gauge feed wire, determine the specific affected circuit.

2. Disconnect the negative battery cable.

3. Cut the damaged fuse link from the wiring harness and discard it. If the fuse link is one of three circuits fed by a single feed wire, cut it out of the harness at each splice end and discard it.

4. Identify and procure the proper fuse link and butt connectors for attaching the fuse link to the harness.

5. To repair any fuse link in a 3-link group with one feed:

   a. After cutting the open link out of the harness, cut each of the remaining undamaged fuse links close to the feed wire weld.

tegral with the engine compartment wiring harness and should not be confused with standard wire. It is several wire gauges smaller than the circuit which it protects.

118 CHASSIS ELECTRICAL

REMOVE EXISTING VINYL TUBE SHIELDING REINSTALL OVER FUSE LINK BEFORE CRIMPING FUSE LINK TO WIRE ENDS

TYPICAL REPAIR USING THE SPECIAL #17 GA. (9.00" LONG-YELLOW) FUSE LINK REQUIRED FOR THE AIR/COND. CIRCUITS

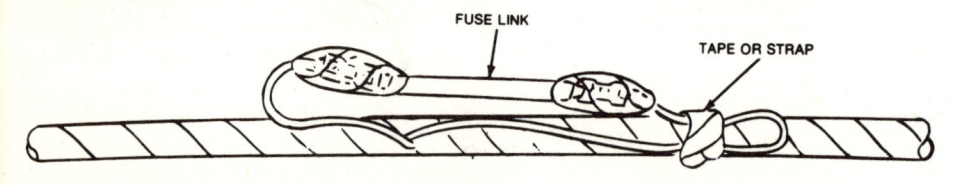

TYPICAL REPAIR FOR ANY IN-LINE FUSE LINK USING THE SPECIFIED GAUGE FUSE LINK FOR THE SPECIFIC CIRCUIT

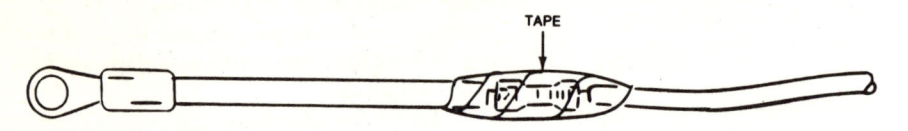

TYPICAL REPAIR USING THE EYELET TERMINAL FUSE LINK OF THE SPECIFIED GAUGE FOR ATTACHMENT TO A CIRCUIT WIRE END

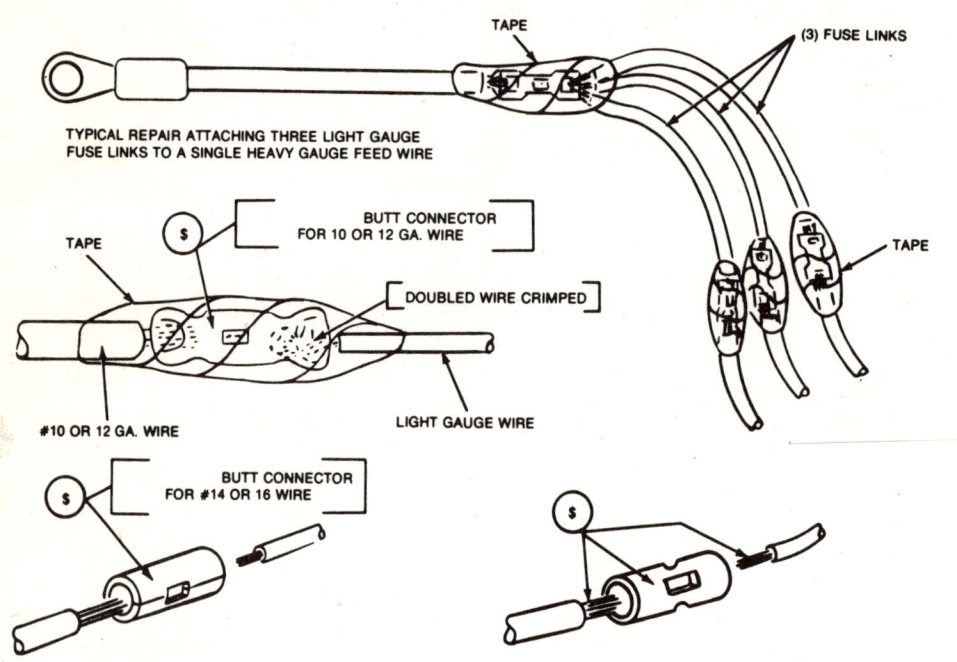

TYPICAL REPAIR ATTACHING THREE LIGHT GAUGE FUSE LINKS TO A SINGLE HEAVY GAUGE FEED WIRE

FUSIBLE LINK REPAIR PROCEDURE

General fuse link repair procedures

b. Strip approximately ½ inch of insulation from the detached ends of the two good fuse links. Then insert two wire ends into one end of a butt connector and carefully push one stripped end of the replacement fuse link into the same end of the butt connector and crimp all three firmly together.

NOTE: *Care must be taken when fitting the three fuse links into the butt connector as the internal diameter is a snug fit for three wires. Make sure to use a proper crimping*

CHASSIS ELECTRICAL

Fuse Panel Identification

Panel Fuse Cavity	Device	Systems
1	15 Amp Fuse	Stop Lamps, Hazard Warning Lamps
2	6 Amp C.B.	Windshield Wiper, Windshield Washer Pump, Intermittent Wiper, Low Washer Fluid Level Indicator
3	Spare Not Used	
4	15 Amp Fuse② 10 Amp Fuse	Tail Lamps, Parking Lamps, Cluster Illumination Lamps, License Lamps
5	15 Amp Fuse	Turn Signal Lamps, Back-Up Lamps
6	20 Amp Fuse	A/C Clutch, Misc. Accessory Systems ①
7	Spare Not Used	
8	15 Amp Fuse	Courtesy Lamps, Key Warning Buzzer, Clock
9	15 Amp Fuse 30 Amp Fuse	Heater Blower Motor A/C Blower Motor
10	20 Amp Fuse	Flash-to-pass
11	15 Amp Fuse	Radio, Tape Player, Premium Sound with 1 Amplifier
12-13-14-15	Spare Not Used	
16	20 Amp Fuse	Horn, Front Cigar Lighter
17	5 Amp Fuse	Instrument Cluster Illumination Lamps, Radio, Climate Control, Ash Tray Lamps
18	10 Amp Fuse	Warning Indicator Lamps, Throttle Solenoid Positioner, Low Fuel Module, Dual Timer Buzzer, Tachometer

① Heated Backlite Relay, Liftgate Release, Speed Control Module, Electronic Digital Clock Display, A/C Throttle Positioner

② 10 Amp Fuse used on Vehicles with Graphic Warning Display.

tool. Pliers, side cutters, etc. will not apply the proper crimp to retain the wires and withstand a pull test.

c. After crimping the butt connector to the three fuse links, cut the weld portion from the feed wire and strip approximately ½ inch of insulation from the cut end. Insert the stripped end into the open end of the butt connector and crimp very firmly.

d. To attach the remaining end of the replacement fuse link, strip approximately ½ inch of insulation from the wire end of the circuit from which the blown fuse link was removed, and firmly crimp a butt connector or equivalent to the stripped wire. Then, insert the end of the replacement link into the other end of the butt connector and crimp firmly.

e. Using rosin core solder with a consistency of 60 percent tin and 40 percent lead, solder the connectors and the wires at the repairs and insulate with electrical tape.

6. To replace any fuse link on a single circuit in a harness, cut out the damaged portion, strip approximately ½ inch of insulation from the two wire ends and attach the appropriate replacement fuse link to the stripped wire ends with two proper size butt connectors. Solder the connectors and wires and insulate with tape.

7. To repair any fuse link which has an eyelet terminal on one end such as the charging circuit, cut off the open fuse link behind the weld, strip approximately ½ inch of insulation from the cut end and attach the appropriate new eyelet fuse link to the cut stripped wire with an appropriate size butt connector. Solder the connectors and wires at the repair and insulate with tape.

8. Connect the negative battery cable to the battery and test the system for proper operation.

NOTE: *Do not mistake a resistor wire for a fuse link. The resistor wire is generally longer and has print stating, "Resistor-don't cut or splice."*

NOTE: *When attaching a single No. 16, 17, 18 or 20 gauge fuse link to a heavy gauge wire, always double the stripped wire end of the fuse link before inserting and crimping it into the butt connector for positive wire retention.*

WIRING DIAGRAMS

Wiring Diagrams have been left out of this book. Information on ordering wiring diagrams from the automobile manufacturer can be found in your owners manual or obtained from the dealer.

Clutch and Transaxle 6

TRANSAXLE

Your Escort, Lynx, EXP or LN7 uses a front wheel drive transmission called a "transaxle." The transaxle may either be manual or automatic.

A four-speed fully synchronized manual transaxle is standard equipment. The MTX (manual transaxle) is a wide-ratio unit; fourth gear is a 0.8:1 overdrive. An internally-gated shift mechanism and a single-rail shift linkage eliminate the need for periodic shift linkage adjustments. The MTX is designed to use Type F automatic transmission fluid as a lubricant. Never use gear oil (GL) in the place of Type F.

The optional automatic transaxle (ATX) is a wide-ratio three-speed unit. A unique feature is a patented split-path torque converter. The engine torque in second and third gears is divided, so that part of the engine torque is transmitted hydrokinetically through the torque converter, and part is transmitted mechanically by direct connection of the engine and transaxle. In third gear, 93% of the torque is transmitted mechanically, making the ATX highly efficient. Torque splitting is accomplished through a "splitter" gear set; a conventional compound gear set is also used.

Only one band is used in the ATX; no periodic adjustments are required. The unit is filled at the factory with type "CJ" fluid. No fluid changes are ever necessary in normal service. In service fluid additions may be made with Dexron® II or Dexron® II Series D fluid.

Half Shafts

The front wheel drive halfshafts are a one piece design. Constant velocity joints (CV) are used at each end. The left hand (driver's side) halfshaft is solid steel and is shorter than the right side halfshaft. The right hand (passenger's side) halfshaft is constructed of tubular steel. The automatic and manual transaxles use the same halfshafts.

The halfshafts can be replaced individually. The CV joint or boots can be cleaned or replaced. Individual parts of the CV joints are not available. The inboard and outboard joints differ in size. CV joint parts are fitted and should never be mixed or substituted with a part from another joint.

Inspect the boots periodically for cuts or splits. If a cut or split is found, inspect the joint, repack it with grease and install a new boot.

REMOVAL

NOTE: *Special tools are required for removing, installing and servicing halfshafts.*

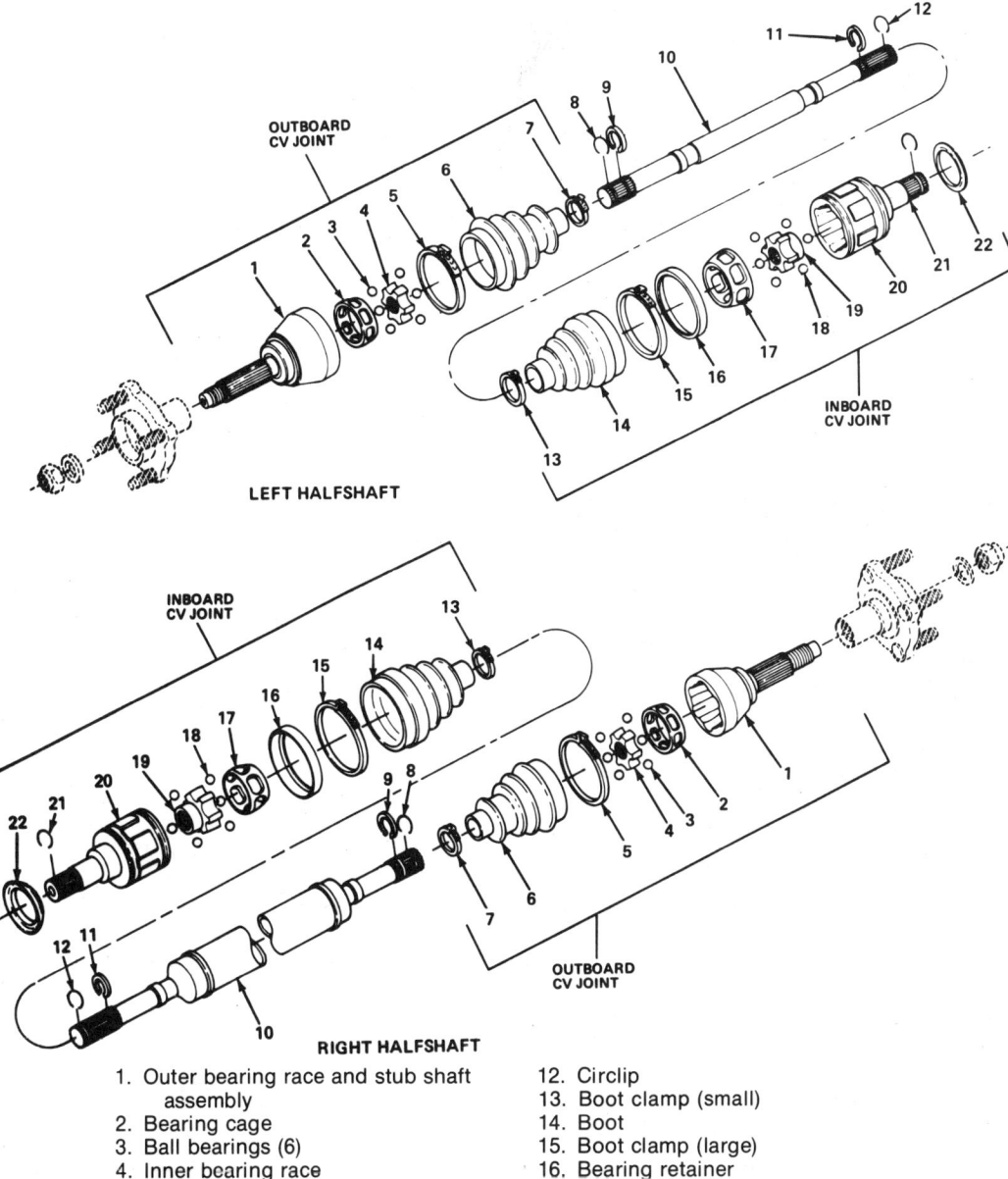

CLUTCH AND TRANSAXLE 121

1. Outer bearing race and stub shaft assembly
2. Bearing cage
3. Ball bearings (6)
4. Inner bearing race
5. Boot clamp (large)
6. Boot
7. Boot clamp (small)
8. Circlip
9. Stop ring
10. Interconnecting shaft
11. Stop ring
12. Circlip
13. Boot clamp (small)
14. Boot
15. Boot clamp (large)
16. Bearing retainer
17. Bearing cage
18. Ball bearings (6)
19. Inner bearing race
20. Outer bearing race and stub shaft assembly
21. Circlip
22. Dust deflector

Exploded view of the halfshafts

They are listed; descriptive name (Ford part number). Front Hub Installer Adapter (T81P1104A), Wheel Bolt Adapters (T81P1104B), CV Joint Separator (T81P3514A), Front Hub Installer/Remover (T81P1104C), Shipping Plug Tool (T81P1177B), Dust Deflector Installer CV Joint (T81P1177B), Differential Rotator (T81P4026A).

NOTE: *It is necessary to have on hand new hub nuts and new lower control arm to steering knuckle attaching nuts and bolts.*

CLUTCH AND TRANSAXLE

Once removed, these parts must not be reused. The torque holding ability is destroyed during removal.

1. Loosen the front hub nut and the wheel lugs.
2. Jack up the front of the car and safely support it on jackstands.
3. Remove the tire and wheel assembly. Remove and discard the front hub nut. Save the washers.

NOTE: *Halfshaft removal and installation are the same for Manual and Automatic transaxles—EXCEPT; The configuration of the ATX (automatic transaxle) differential case requires that the right hand halfshaft assembly be removed first. The differential service tool T81P4026A (Differential Rotator) is then inserted to drive the left hand halfshaft from the transaxle. If only the left hand halfshaft is to be serviced, remove the right hand halfshaft from the transaxle side and support it with a length of wire. Drive the left hand halfshaft assembly from the transaxle.*

4. Remove the bolt that retains the brake hose to the strut.
5. Remove the nut and bolt securing the lower ball joint and separate the joint from the steering knuckle by inserting a pry bar between the stabilizer and frame and pulling downward. Take care not to damage the ball joint boot. **Do not contact or pry on the lower control arm.**
6. Remove the halfshaft from the differential housing, using a pry bar. Position the pry bar between the case and the shaft and pry the joint away from the case. Do not damage the oil seal, the CV joint boot or the CV dust deflector. Install tool number T81P1177B (Shipping plug) to prevent fluid loss.
7. Support the end of the shaft with a piece of wire, suspending it from a chassis member.
8. Separate the shaft from the front hub using the special remover/installer tool and adapters. Instructions for the use of the tool may be found in Chapter 8 under the "Front Wheel Bearing" section.

CAUTION: *Never use a hammer to force the shaft from the wheel hub. Damage to the internal parts of the CV joint may occur.*

INSTALLATION

1. Install a new circlip on the inboard CV joint stub shaft. Align the splines of the inboard CV joint stub shaft with the splines in the differential. Push the CV joint into the differential until the circlip seats on the side gear. Some force may be necessary to seat.
2. Carefully align the splines of the outboard CV joint stub shaft with the splines in the front wheel hub. Push the shaft into the hub as far as possible. Install the remover/installer tool and pull the CV stub shaft through the hub.
3. Connect the control arm to the steering knuckle and install a new mounting bolt and nut.
4. Connect the brake line to the strut.
5. Install the front hub washer and new hub nut. Install the tire and wheel assembly.
6. Lower the car to the ground. Tighten the center hub nut to 180–200 ft. lbs. Stake the nut using a blunt chisel.
7. Torque the wheel lugs to 80–105 ft. lbs.

CV Joint and Boot

REMOVAL

1. Clamp the halfshaft in a vise equipped with jaw covers. Clamp below the boot, do not allow the vise to contact the boot or boot clamp.
2. Cut the large boot clamp using side cutters and peel the clamp away from the boot. Roll the boot back over the shaft. Check the grease for contamination by rubbing some between two fingers. If the grease feels gritty, it is contaminated and the joint will have to be disassembled, cleaned and inspected. If the grease is not contaminated and the CV joints are operating satisfactorily, repack them with grease and install a new boot.
3. Separate the CV joint from the shaft using Tool T81P3514A (CV Joint Separator). The boot can now be removed. Cut the remaining clamp and remove the boot.
4. Remove the circlip near the end of the shaft. The stop ring located further down the shaft should be removed only if inspection determines it to be damaged. A new circlip is included in the boot or CV joint replacement kit.
5. Clean the interconnecting shaft with a safe solvent.

INSTALLATION

1. If both joints have been removed from the intermediate shaft and some confusion exists as to which end of the shaft is which; the inboard CV joint is installed on the end with the longer splines.

CLUTCH AND TRANSAXLE

2. If you have removed the inner (lower) stop ring, install a new one. If not, be sure it is seated in the groove.

3. Install the new circlip, provided in the kit into the groove nearest the end of the shaft. Do not spread the circlip too far, nor twist it.

4. Install the new boot small end over the shaft until the end is over the mounting groove. Tighten the clamp securely but not enough to cut the boot. Peel back the boot and position the new CV joint on the shaft. Use a plastic tipped hammer and tap the joint onto the shaft. The CV joint is fully seated when the circlip locks into the groove cut into the CV joint bearing inner race. Check for seating by attempting to pull the joint off the shaft.

5. Pack the CV joint and boot with the grease supplied in the kit. On the outboard joint; fill the boot with 2/3rds of the grease and the CV joint with the remaining 1/3rd. The inboard requires one packet of grease in the bott and the other in the CV joint.

6. Wipe the excess grease from the outer parts of the CV joint and position the boot over the joint. After the sealing edge of the boot is in position, take a dull tipped screwdriver and lift the edge slightly. This allows any trapped air to escape. Move the joint up or down on the shaft until the total length of the axle shaft measures:

7. Make sure the boot is seated in its groove, attach the boot clamp and squeeze it closed by hand. Crimp the clamp with pliers; but not to the point that the boot is cut.

Service

NOTE: *Disassembly of the CV joints is necessary when the grease is contaminated. Contamination of the lubricant can damage the parts of the joint, an inspection is necessary to determine if replacement is required.*

Outboard Joint (Wheel Hub Side)

DISASSEMBLY

NOTE: *Two different bearing cage designs are used. One design uses four equal sized bearing cutouts and two elongated ones, the second design uses six equal sized cutouts. The step by step instructions will indicate the procedures necessary for the different designs.*

1. After the stub shaft has been removed from the axle, clamp in a soft jawed vise with the bearings facing up.

2. Press down on the inner race until it tilts enough to allow the removal of a ball bearing. If the bearing is tight, it might be necessary to tap the inner race with a plastic faced hammer. Tap on the race, do not hit the cage.

3. When the cage is tilted, remove a ball. Repeat until all six balls have been removed. If the balls are tight, take a blunt edged pry bar and pry the balls from the cage. Be careful not to scratch or damage the inner race or cage.

4. Pivot the bearing cage and inner race 90 degrees (straight up and down) to the center line of the outer race. Align the cage windows with the lands (grooves) in the outer race. When the windows are in alignment with the lands, lift the assembly from the outer race.

5. Separate the inner race from the cage. Six equal window type; rotate the inner race up and out of the cage.

Two elongated window type; Pivot the inner race until it is straight up and down in the cage. Align one of the inner race bands with one of the elongated windows. Put the land through the elongated window and rotate the inner race up and lift out of the cage.

6. Wash all of the parts in safe solvent. Inspect the parts for wear. If the components of the CV joint are worn, a complete kit must be installed. Do not replace a joint merely because the parts appear polished. Shiny areas in the ball races and on the curves of the cage are normal. A CV joint should be replaced only if a component is cracked, broken, severely pitted or otherwise unserviceable.

ASSEMBLY

1. Apply a light coating of grease on the inner and outer races. Install the inner race in the bearing cage by turning the inner race 90 degrees position the land through the cage window and rotate into position.

2. Install the inner race and cage assembly into the outer race. Install the assembly in the vertical position and pivot into position. The counterbores in the inner race must be facing upwards.

3. Align the bearing cage and inner race with the outer race. Tilt the inner race and cage and install a ball bearing. Repeat until all six bearings are installed.

4. Pack the CV joint with ⅓ of the packet of grease. Use only the specified grease; Ford

CLUTCH AND TRANSAXLE

Part Number D8RZ19590A or the equivalent. Pack the grease into the joint by forcing it through the splined hole in the inner race.

Inboard Joint (Transaxle Side)
DISASSEMBLY

1. Remove the circlip from the end of the CV joint stub shaft. Inspect the dust deflector. If it is cracked or damaged it must be replaced. Refer to the section that appears later in this chapter.
2. Use a pair of side cutters to cut the ball retainer and discard it. The retainer is not required for assembly of the CV joint.
3. Gently tap the CV joint on the bench until the bearing assembly comes loose and can be removed by hand.
4. Remove the balls from the cage by prying them out. Take care not to scratch or damage the inner ball race or cage.
5. Rotate the inner race until the cage windows are aligned with the lands. Lift from the cage through the wider side.
6. Clean all of the component parts in safe solvent and inspect for wear. If the components of the CV joint are worn, a complete kit must be installed. Do not replace a joint merely because the parts appear polished. Shiny areas in the ball races and on the curves of the cage are normal. A CV joint should be replaced only if a component is cracked, broken, severely pitted or otherwise unserviceable.

ASSEMBLY

1. Install a new circlip on the stub shaft. Do not over expand or twist the clip.
2. If the dust deflector needs replacing, do so now. See the next section for instructions.
3. Install the inner bearing race into the bearing cage. Install the race through the larger end of the cage with the inner race hub facing the large end of the cage.
4. Align the bearing cage and inner race. Install the ball bearings. Press the bearings into position with the heel of your hand.
5. Pack the outer race with grease. Use only the specified grease; Ford Part Number D8RZ1950A or the equivalent.
6. Position the inner race and bearing assembly into the outer race. The assembly should be installed with the inner hub facing the outer race.
7. Push the inner race and bearing assembly into the outer race.

DUST DEFLECTOR REPLACEMENT

NOTE: *The dust deflector should be replaced only if inspection determines it to be cracked, broken or deteriorated.*

Remove the old deflector. Soak the new dust deflector in a container of hot water and let it soak for five to ten minutes. Position the dust deflector over the sleeve with the ribbed side facing the CV joint. Tap the deflector into position with the Dust Deflector Installer (T81P3425A) and a hammer.

MANUAL TRANSAXLE

REMOVAL

1. Disconnect the negative battery cable from the battery.
2. Remove the two transaxle to engine top mounting bolts. Pull the clutch cable forward and disconnect it from the clutch release lever. Remove the clutch cable from the mounting rib on the top of the transaxle case.
3. Loosen the wheel lugs slightly. Raise the car and safely support on jackstands. Remove the front tire and wheel assemblies. Drain the transaxle lubricant.
4. Remove the bolt that mounts the brake hose to the strut bracket. Remove the pinch bolt and nut that secures the lower control arm to the steering knuckle assembly. Pry the lower control arm away from the knuckle. (Both sides).

NOTE: *Always install a new pinch nut and bolt when reassembling.*

NOTE: *It is necessary to bend the plastic dust shield slightly to provide clearance for the ball joint when disengaging the control arm from the steering knuckle.*

5. Use a pry bar and carefully pry the right side inboard CV joint assembly from the transaxle. Some loss of lubricant should be expected. Install the special tool TP81P1177B2 or the equivalent to seal the transaxle case. To free the CV joint from the transaxle case, pull the right hand steering knuckle and the shaft outward and away from the transaxle. Take special care not to damage the seal; when using the pry bar.
6. Wire the joint and shaft assembly to a chassis member (in a level position) so that it is out of the way.
7. Remove the left side CV joint and shaft assembly in a like manner. Wire it out of the way.
8. Disconnect the front stabilizer bar at

CLUTCH AND TRANSAXLE 125

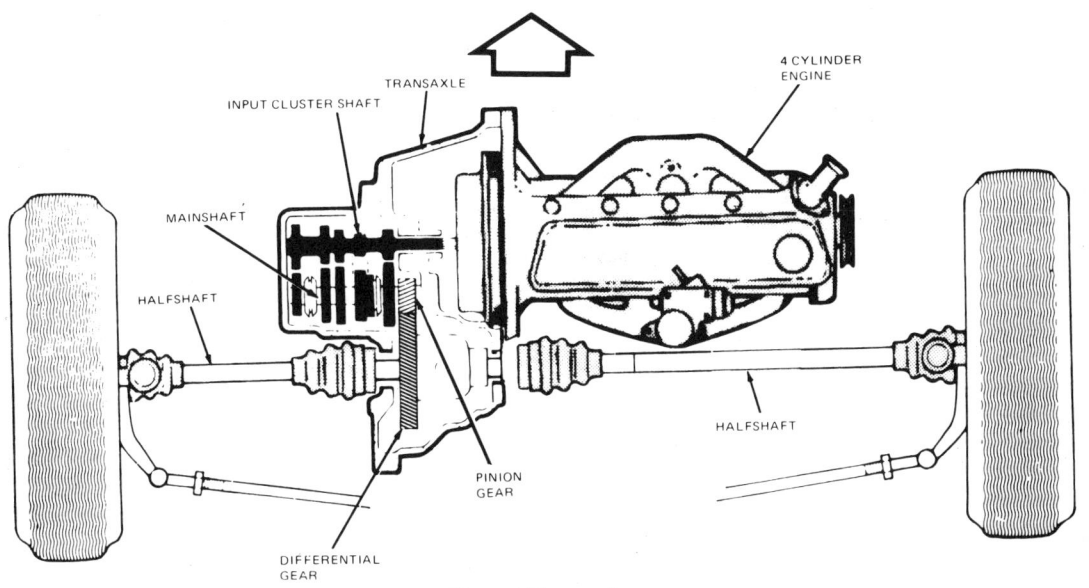

Manual Transaxle

both control arms. Remove the stabilizer bar mounting brackets; remove the stabilizer bar.

9. Disconnect the speedometer cable from the transaxle. Disconnect the backup light switch harness. The harness is fastened by two locking tabs. Lift up on the tabs to disconnect the harness.

10. Remove the three nuts from the starter mounting studs that mount the roll restrictor bracket. Remove the roll restrictor plate, the starter motor and the mounting studs.

11. Remove the two stiffener brace attaching bolts from the lower portion of the clutch housing. Remove the shift mechanism cross-

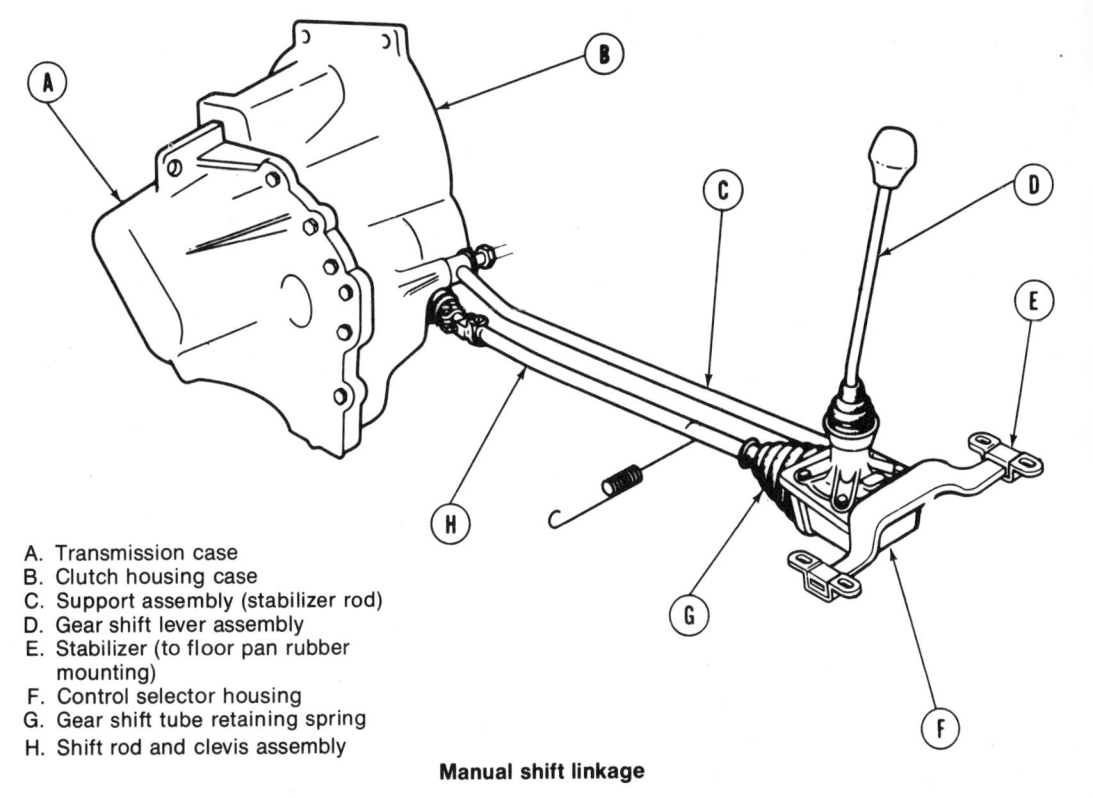

A. Transmission case
B. Clutch housing case
C. Support assembly (stabilizer rod)
D. Gear shift lever assembly
E. Stabilizer (to floor pan rubber mounting)
F. Control selector housing
G. Gear shift tube retaining spring
H. Shift rod and clevis assembly

Manual shift linkage

126 CLUTCH AND TRANSAXLE

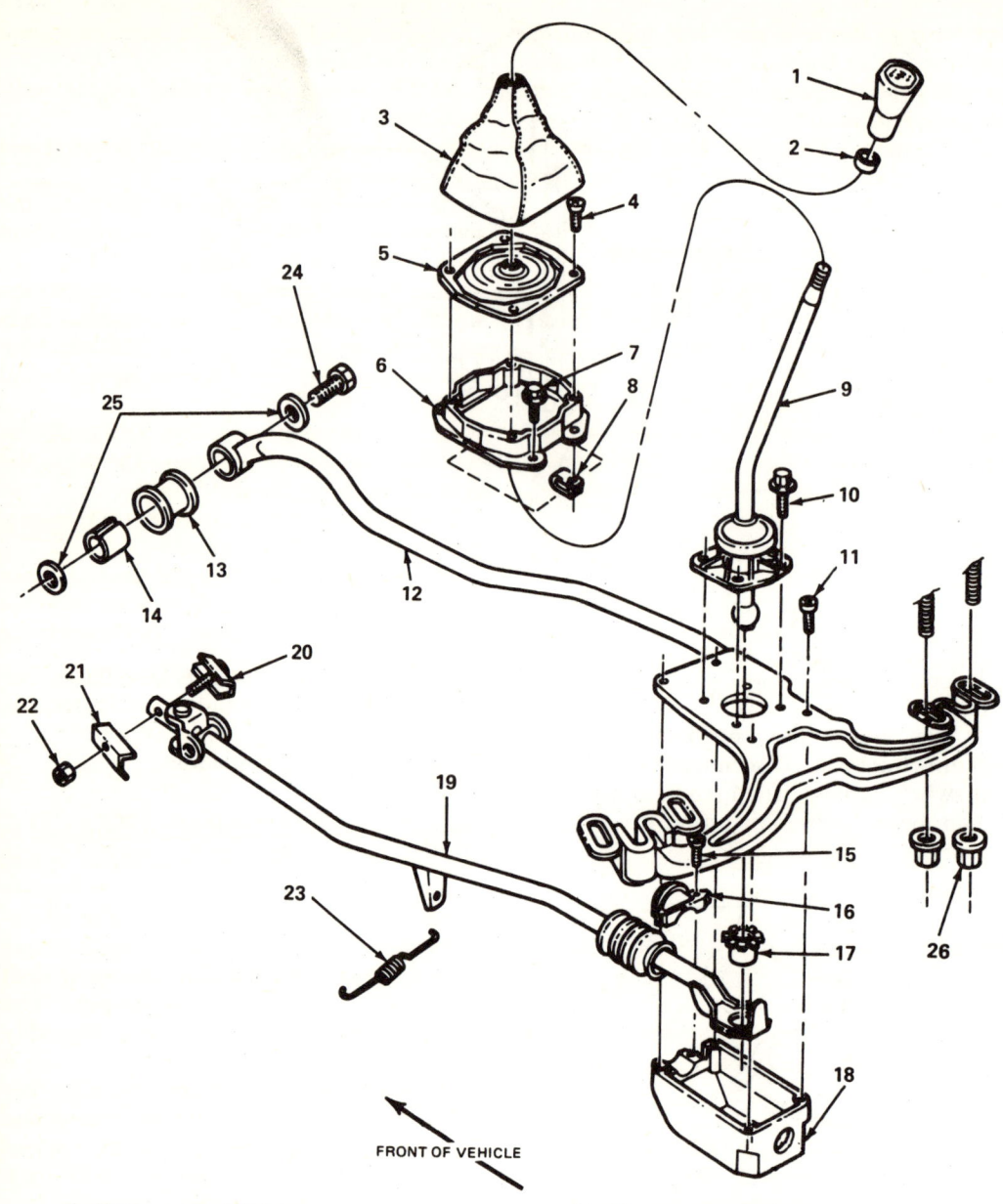

1. Knob—gear shift lever
2. Nut—shift knob locking
3. Upper boot assembly—gear shift lever
4. Screw—tapping (4 required)
5. Lower boot assembly—gear shift lever
6. Boot retainer assembly—gear shift lever
7. Bolt—boot retainer (4 required)
8. Nut—spring (4 required)
9. Lever assembly—gearshift
10. Bolt—tapping (4 required)
11. Screw—tapping (4 required)
12. Support assembly (shift stabilizer bar)
13. Bushing—gear shift stabilizer bar
14. Sleeve—gear shift rod
15. Screw—tapping (2 required)
16. Cover—control selector
17. Bushing—anti tizz
18. Housing—control selector
19. Assembly—shift rod and clevis
20. Assembly—clamp
21. Clamp—gear shift lever (2 required)
22. Nut—clamp assembly
23. Retaining spring—gear shift tube
24. Bolt—stabilizer bar attaching
25. Washer—flat (2 required)
26. Assembly—nut/washer (4 required)

Components parts of the manual shift linkage

CLUTCH AND TRANSAXLE 127

over spring. Remove the shift mechanism stabilizer bar to transaxle attaching bolt and the shift shaft attaching bolt. Remove the shift mechanism from the shift shaft.

12. Position a floor jack, that has a wide saddle, under the transaxle. Raise the jack until it just contacts the transaxle case.

13. Loosen the rear mount stud nut. Remove the bottom attaching bolt from the rear mount and loosen the two bolts at the top of the mount. Remove the three bolts holding the front mount to the transaxle case. Remove the rear stud mount nut.

14. Lower the jack supporting the transaxle until the transaxle clears the rear mount. Support the engine by placing a block of wood under the oil pan and on the top of another jack.

15. Remove the four engine to transaxle mounting bolts still attached.

16. Pull back slightly to disengage the drive spline and lower the transaxle to the ground. The transaxle case has sharp edges. Wear gloves while handling to help avoid cuts.

INSTALLATION

1. Raise the transaxle into position with the floorjack. Align the input shaft with the clutch disc. Work the transaxle into position and align it on the dowel pins.

2. Install the four engine to engine to transaxle mounting bolts (see Step 15 in the removal procedure).

3. Position the rear mount and install the mounting bolts and nut. The bolts are tightened to 40–50 ft. lbs. Tighten the nut to 38–41 ft. lbs.

4. Position the transaxle to align with the front mount bracket. Install the three mounting bolts and tighten to 40–50 ft. lbs. Install the two stiffener brace attaching bolts and tighten to 15–21 ft. lbs.

5. Position the starter motor against the engine rear cover plate. Make sure the starter motor is properly aligned and install the three mounting studs. The studs are tightened to 30–40 ft. lbs.

6. Install the engine roll restrictor plate. Tighten the nuts to 25–30 ft. lbs.

7. Install the shift mechanism. The stabilizer mounting bolt is tightened to 23–32 ft. lbs., while the input shift rail bolt is tightened to 7–10 ft. lbs. Install the shift crossover spring.

8. Install the speedometer cable and the backup light harness.

9. Remove the transaxle case sealing and install the halfshafts.

NOTE: *Install new circlips on the halfshafts.*

Refer to the section on halfshaft removal and installation.

10. Attach the lower ball joints to the steering knuckles using new pinch bolts and nuts. Tighten to 37–44 ft. lbs.

11. Connect the brake hoses to the struts. Install the stabilizer bar. The attaching bolts are tightened to 40–44 ft. lbs. The attaching nuts on the lower control arms are tightened to 59–73 ft. lbs.

12. Fill the transaxle with lubricant. Install the front wheels and lower the car to the ground. Connect the clutch cable.

13. Install the top engine to transaxle mounting bolts. Tighten to 28–31 ft. lbs.

14. Apply the clutch pedal several times to get the correct pedal adjustment. (See the clutch adjustment section). Reconnect the negative battery cable.

CLUTCH

The transmission and clutch are employed to vary the relationship between engine speed and the speed of the wheels so that adequate engine power can be produced under all circumstances. The clutch allows engine torque to be applied to the transmission input shaft gradually, due to mechanical slippage. The car can, consequently, be started smoothly from a full stop.

The transmission changes the ratio between the rotating speeds of the engine and the wheels by the use of gears. Three-speed or four-speed transmissions are most common. The lower gears allow full engine power to be applied to the rear wheels during acceleration at low speeds.

The clutch driven plate is a thin disc, the center of which is splined to the transmission input shaft. Both sides of the disc are covered with a layer of material which is similar to brake lining and which is capable of allowing slippage without roughness or excessive noise.

The clutch cover is bolted to the engine flywheel and incorporates a diaphragm spring which provides the pressure to engage the clutch. The cover also houses the pressure plate. The driven disc is sandwiched between the pressure plate and the smooth surface of the flywheel when the clutch pedal is

128 CLUTCH AND TRANSAXLE

Operation of the clutch components

1. TRANSMISSION HOUSING
2. CLUTCH DISC – AN ASSEMBLY ATTACHED TO THE TRANSMISSION SHAFT WITH A SPLINED HUB. THE DISC HAS FRICTION MATERIAL ON BOTH SIDES WHERE IT CONTACTS THE FLYWHEEL AND PRESSURE PLATE.
3. PRESSURE PLATE – APPLIES PRESSURE AGAINST THE CLUTCH DISC HOLDING IT TIGHT AGAINST THE SURFACE OF THE ENGINE FLYWHEEL.
4. COVER – PART OF PRESSURE PLATE ASSEMBLY.
5. RELEASE BEARING – CONSTANTLY ENGAGED WITH RELEASE FINGERS PROVIDE CONNECTION BETWEEN RELEASE FINGERS AND FORK.
6. RELEASE FORK
7. RELEASE LEVER (RELEASE FORK AND RELEASE LEVER IMPART PEDAL MOTION TO RELEASE BEARING LEVER IS CONNECTED TO CLUTCH CABLE.)
8. RELEASE FINGERS – PART OF THE BELLEVILLE LOAD SPRING. MOVEMENT TOWARD FLYWHEEL REMOVES CLAMP LOAD FROM CLUTCH DISC.
9. DAMPER SPRINGS PART OF THE DISC ASSEMBLY. AID IN ISOLATING ENGINE PULSES FROM POWER TRAIN.
10. ENGINE FLYWHEEL – BOLTED TO ENGINE CRANKSHAFT AND ROTATES WITH THE CRANKSHAFT. IT IS MACHINED TO PROVIDE A FRICTION OR FACE WHICH MEETS WITH THE FRICTION SURFACE OF THE CLUTCH DISC WHEN THE CLUTCH IS ENGAGED. THIS FORMS A CONTINOUS SYSTEM BY WHICH ENGINE POWER IS CONNECTED TO THE TRANSMISSION.

ENGINE CRANKSHAFT NOTE: THIS SYSTEM REQUIRES NO PILOT BEARING

TRANSMISSION INPUT SHAFT

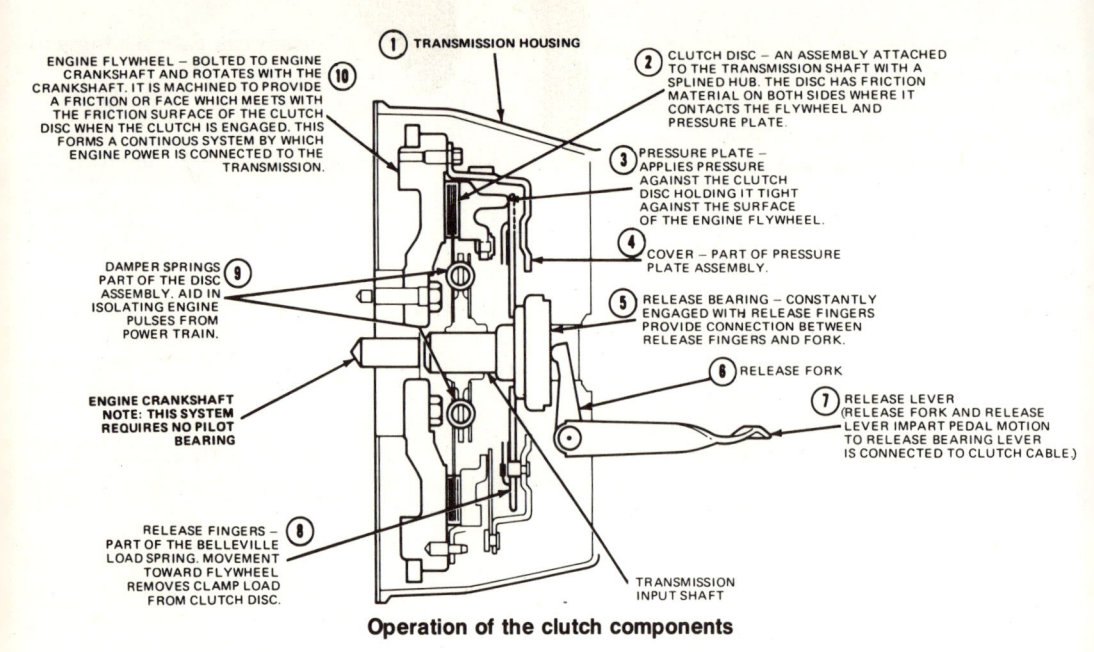

released, thus forcing it to turn at the same speed as the engine crankshaft.

The transmission contains a mainshaft which passes all the way through the transmission, from the clutch to the final drive gear in the transaxle. This shaft is separated at one point, so that front and rear portions can turn at different speeds.

Power is transmitted by a countershaft in the lower gears and reverse. The gears of the countershaft mesh with gears on the mainshaft, allowing power to be carried from one to the other. All the countershaft gears are integral with that shaft, while several of the mainshaft gears can either rotate independently of the shaft or be locked to it. Shifting from one gear to the next causes one of the gears to be freed from rotating with the shaft, and locks another to it. Gears are locked and unlocked by internal dog clutches which slide between the center of the gear and the shaft. The forward gears usually employ synchronizers: friction members which smoothly bring gear and shaft to the same speed before the toothed dog clutches are engaged.

The clutch is operating properly if:
1. It will stall the engine when released with the vehicle held stationary.
2. The shift lever can be moved freely between first and reverse gears when the vehicle is stationary and the clutch disengaged.

FREE PLAY ADJUSTMENT

The free play in the clutch is adjusted by a built in mechanism that allows the clutch

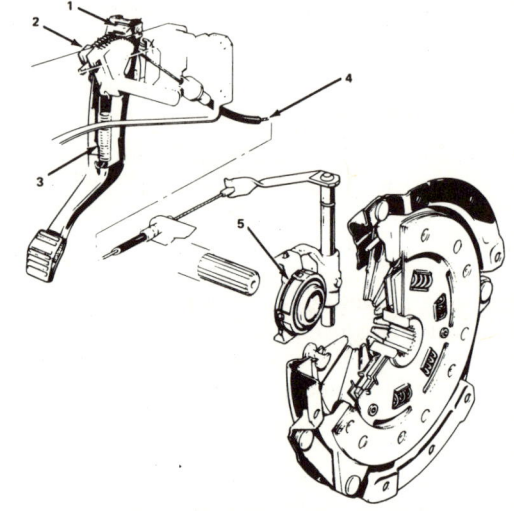

1. PAWL – IMPARTS PEDAL MOTION TO SECTOR DURING DOWNSTROKE. PAWL ENGAGES QUADRANT AT BEGINNING OF DOWNSTROKE.
2. QUADRANT – ACTUATES CABLE DURING PEDAL DOWNSTROKE FOLLOWING CABLE CORE AS CORE IS MOVED DURING DISC FACING WEAR.
3. ADJUSTER SPRING – KEEPS SECTOR IN FIRM CONTACT WITH CABLE. KEEPS RELEASE BEARING IN CONTACT WITH CLUTCH RELEASE FINGERS THROUGH CABLE LINKAGE WITH PEDAL IN UP POSITION.
4. CABLE
5. RELEASE BEARING

Identification of the clutch parts

controls to be self-adjusted during normal operation.

The self-adjusting feature should be checked every 5000 miles. This is accomplished by insuring that the clutch pedal travels to the top of its upward position. Grasp the clutch pedal with your hand or put your

CLUTCH AND TRANSAXLE

foot under the clutch pedal, pull up on the pedal until it stops. Very little effort is required (about 10 lbs.). During the application of upward pressure, a click may be heard which means an adjustment was necessary and has been accomplished.

Clutch Cable
REMOVAL

1. From under the hood, use a pair of pliers and grasp the extended tip of the clutch cable (on top of transaxle). Unhook the clutch cable from the clutch throwout bearing release lever.
2. From inside the car, remove the fresh air duct next to the clutch pedal (non-air conditioned cars). Remove the shield from the brake pedal support bracket.
3. Lift up on the clutch pedal to release the adjusting pawl. Rotate the adjustment gear quadrant forward. Unhook the clutch cable from the gear quadrant. Swing the quadrant to the rear.
4. Pull the clutch cable out from between the clutch pedal and the gear quadrant and from the isolator on the gear quadrant.
5. From under the hood, pull the clutch cable through the firewall and remove it from the car.

INSTALLATION

1. From under the hood, insert the clutch cable through the firewall into the drivers compartment.
2. Push the clutch cable through the isolator on the pedal stop bracket and through the recess between the clutch pedal and the adjusting gear quadrant.
3. Lift the clutch pedal to release the pawl and rotate the gear quadrant forward. Hook the clutch cable to the gear quadrant.
4. Install the fresh air duct. Install the shield on the brake pedal support.
5. Secure the clutch pedal in the up position. Use a piece of wire, tape, etc.
6. From under the hood, hook the cable to the clutch throwout bearing release lever.
7. Unfasten the clutch pedal and adjust the clutch by operating the clutch pedal several times. Pull up on the pedal to make sure it is reaching the maximum upward position.

Pressure Plate and Clutch Disc
REMOVAL AND INSTALLATION

1. Remove the transaxle (refer to the previous Transaxle Removal and Installation section).
2. Mark the pressure plate assembly and the flywheel so that they may be assembled

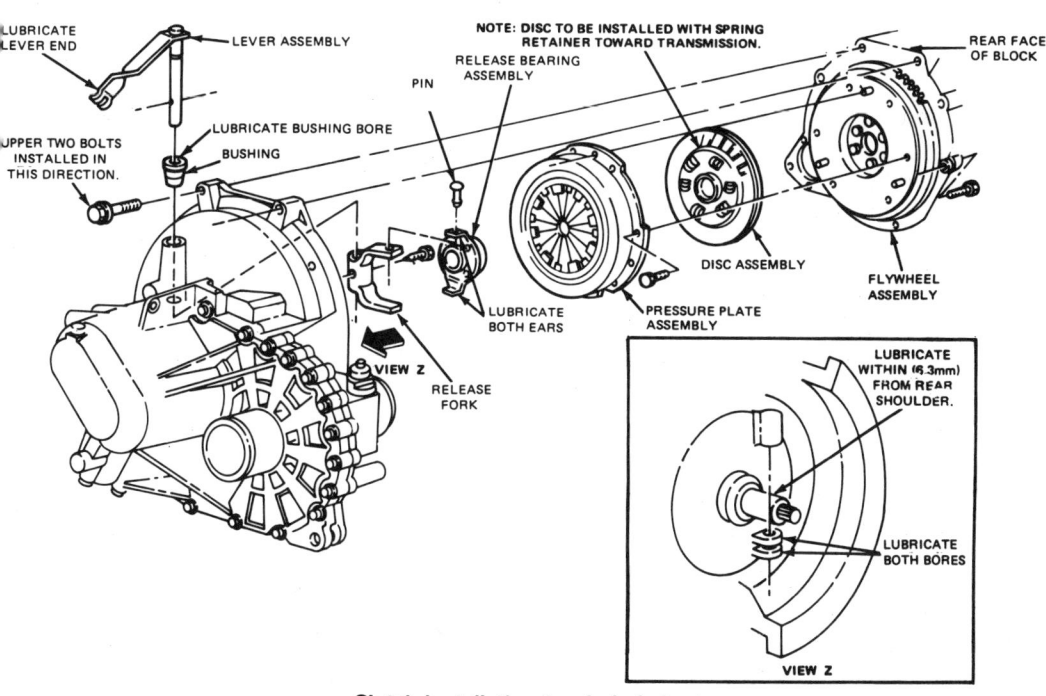

Clutch installation (exploded view)

130 CLUTCH AND TRANSAXLE

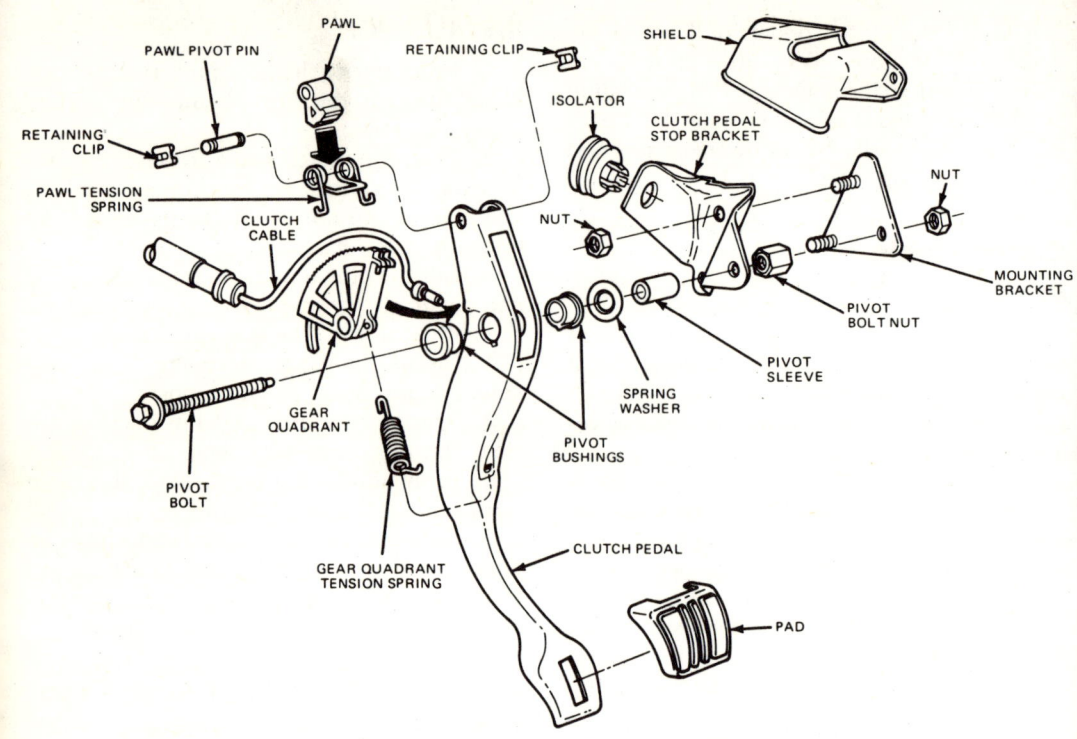

Self-adjusting clutch pedal components

in the same position if the original pressure plate is to be reused.

3. Loosen the attaching bolts one turn at a time, in sequence, until spring pressure is relieved.

4. Support the pressure plate and clutch disc and remove the bolts. Remove the pressure plate and disc.

5. Inspect the flywheel, clutch disc, pressure plate, throwout bearing and the clutch

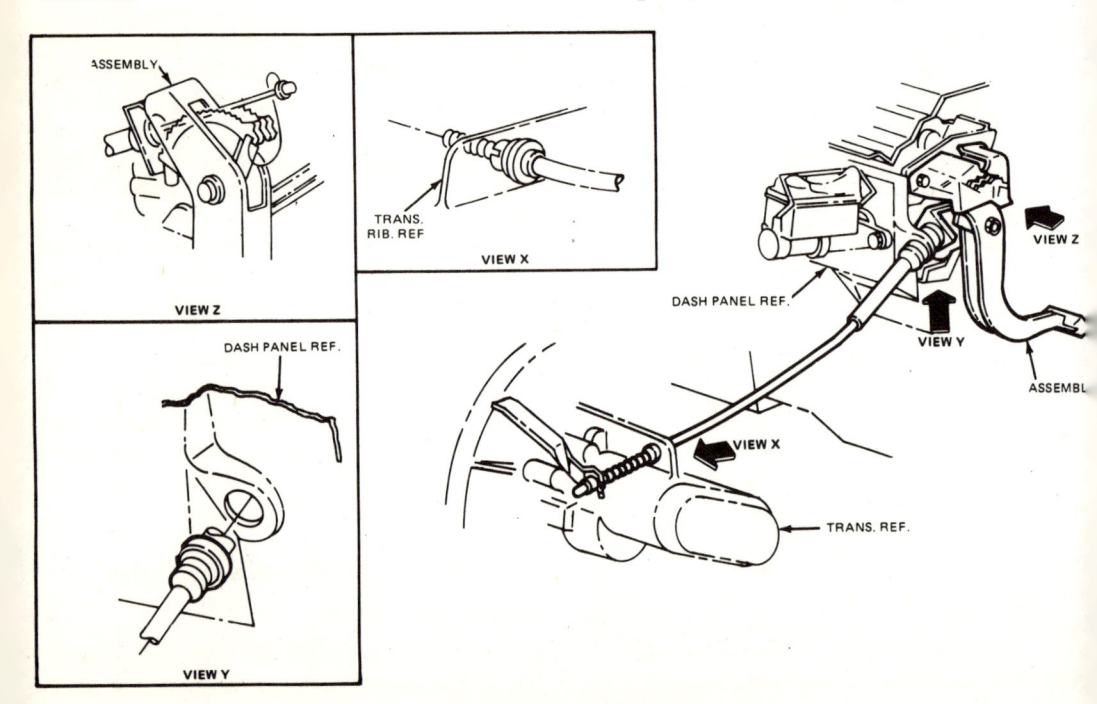

Clutch cable installation

CLUTCH AND TRANSAXLE   131

fork for wear. If the flywheel shows any sign of overheating (blue discoloration), or if it is badly scored or grooved, it should be refaced or replaced. Replace any other parts that are worn.

6. Clean the pressure plate (if it is to be reused) and the flywheel surfaces thoroughly. Position the clutch disc and pressure plate into the installed position.

NOTE: *The clutch disc must be assembled so that the flatter side is toward the flywheel.*

Align the match marks on the pressure plate and flywheel (when reusing the original pressure plate). Support the clutch disc and pressure plate with a dummy shaft or clutch aligning tool.

7. Install the pressure plate to flywheel bolts. Tighten them gradually in a criss-cross pattern. Remove the aligning tool. Mounting bolt torque is 12–24 ft. lbs.

8. Lubricate the release bearing and install it on the throwout fork.

9. Install the transaxle.

AUTOMATIC TRANSAXLE

REMOVAL AND INSTALLATION

1. Disconnect the negative battery cable from the battery.

2. From under the hood, remove the bolts that attach the air manage valve to the ATX (automatic transaxle) valve body cover. Disconnect the wiring harness connector from the neutral safety switch.

3. Disconnect the throttle valve linkage and the manual control lever cable. Remove the two transaxle to engine upper attaching bolts. The bolts are located below and on either side of the distributor.

4. Loosen the front wheel lugs slightly. Jack up the front of the car and safely support it on jackstands. Remove the tire and wheel assemblies.

5. Drain the transmission fluid. Disconnect the brake hoses from the strut brackets on both sides. Remove the pinch bolts that secure the lower control arms to the steering knuckles. Separate the ball joint from the steering knuckle. Remove the stabilizer bar attaching brackets. Remove the nuts that retain the stabilizer to the control arms. Remove the stabilizer bar. When removing the control arms from the steering knuckles, it will be necessary to bend the plastic shield slightly to gain ball joint clearance for removal.

6. Remove the tie rod ends from the steering knuckles. Use a special tie rod removing tool. Pry the right side halfshaft from the transaxle (see halfshaft removal section).

7. Remove the left side halfshaft from the transaxle. Support both right and left side halfshaft out of the way with wire.

8. Install sealing plugs or the equivalent into the transaxle halfshaft mounting holes.

9. Remove the starter support bracket. Disconnect the starter cable. Remove the starter mounting studs and the starter motor. Remove the transaxle support bracket.

10. Remove the lower cover from the transaxle. Turn the converter for access to the converter mounting nuts. Remove the nuts.

11. Remove the nuts that attach the left front insulator to the body bracket. Remove the bracket to body bolts and remove the bracket.

12. Remove the left rear insulator bracket attaching nut.

13. Disconnect the transmission cooler lines. Remove the bolts that attach the manual lever bracket to the transaxle case.

14. Position a floorjack with a wide saddle under the transaxle and remove the four remaining transaxle to engine attaching bolts.

15. The torque converter mounting studs must be clear of the engine flywheel before the transaxle can be lowered from the car. Take a small pry bar and place it between the flywheel and the convertor. Carefully move the transaxle away from the engine. When the convertor mounting studs are clear lower the ATX about three inches. Disconnect the speedometer cable from the ATX. Lower the transaxle to the ground.

NOTE: *When moving the transaxle away from the engine watch the mount insulator. If it interferes with the transaxle before the converter mounting studs clear the flywheel, remove the insulator.*

16. Installation is in the reverse order of removal. Be sure to install new circlips on the halfshaft before reinstalling. Always use new pinch bolts when connecting the lower control arms to the steering knuckles.

Transmission Fluid and Filter
DRAIN AND REFILL

In normal service it should not be necessary nor is it required to drain and refill the ATX fluid. However, under severe operation or

132 CLUTCH AND TRANSAXLE

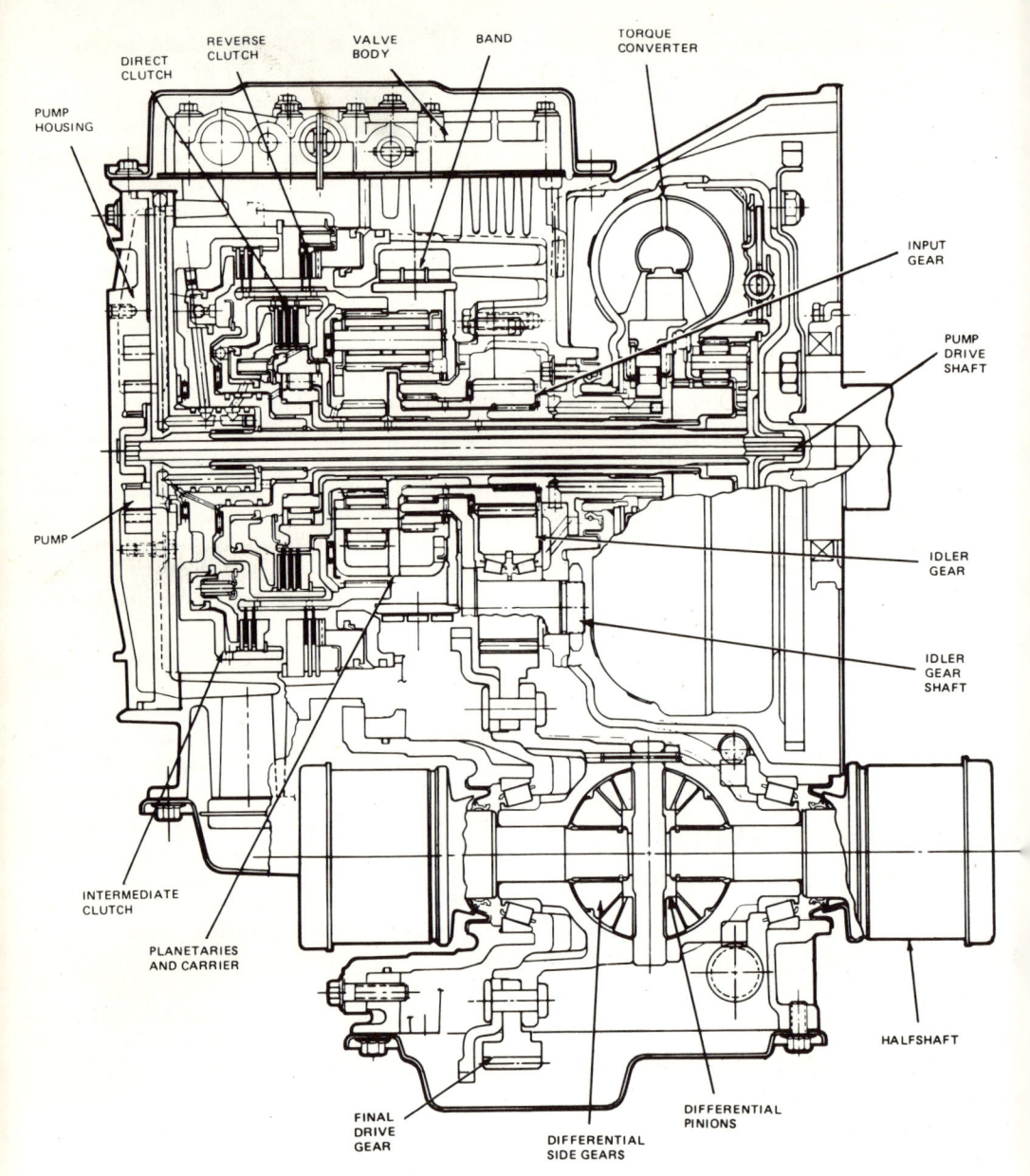

Automatic transaxle

dusty conditions the fluid should be changed every 20 months or 20,000 miles.

1. Raise the car and safely support it on jackstands.

2. Place a suitable drain pan underneath the transaxle oil pan. Loosen the oil pan mounting bolts and allow the fluid to drain until it reaches the level of the pan flange. Remove the attaching bolts, leaving one end attached so that the pan will tip and the rest of the fluid will drain.

3. Remove the oil pan. Thoroughly clean the pan. Remove the old gasket. Make sure that the gasket mounting surfaces are clean.

4. Remove the transmission filter screen retaining bolt. Remove the screen.

5. Install a new filter screen and "O" ring. Place a new gasket on the pan and install the pan to the transmission.

6. Fill the transmission to the correct level. Remove the jackstands and lower the car to the ground.

TRANSAXLE FLUID CONDITION

Pull the transmission dipstick out. Observe the color and odor of the transmission fluid. The color should be red not brown or black

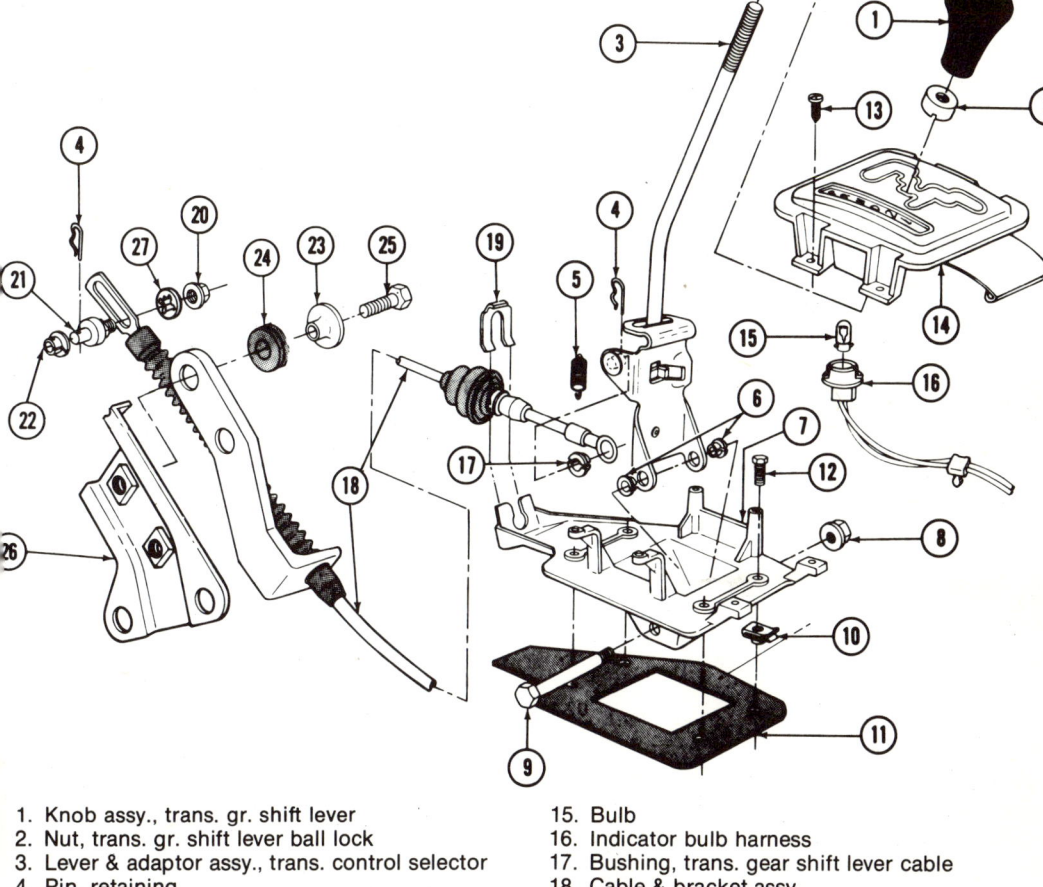

CLUTCH AND TRANSAXLE 133

1. Knob assy., trans. gr. shift lever
2. Nut, trans. gr. shift lever ball lock
3. Lever & adaptor assy., trans. control selector
4. Pin, retaining
5. Spring, trans. park gear lockout rtn.
6. Bushing, trans. gear shift lever shaft
7. Housing, trans. control selector
8. Nut, M8-1.25 hex flg.
9. Bolt, M8 x 1.25 x 82.0 hex flg. pilot
10. Nut, M6-1.00 "U"
11. Seal, trans. control selector housing
12. Bolt, M6-1.00 x 25.0 hex flg. hd.
13. Screw, 4.2 x 13.0 hex wa. hd. tap.
14. Bezel assy., trans. control sel. dial
15. Bulb
16. Indicator bulb harness
17. Bushing, trans. gear shift lever cable
18. Cable & bracket assy.
19. Clip, hand brake cable spring lock
20. Nut & washer assy.
21. Stud, trans. gr. shift connecting rod adjusting
22. Bushing, trans. control shift rod clevis
23. Spacer, trans. control cable bracket
24. Insulator, trans. control cable bracket
25. Bolt, M10-1.5 x 20.0 hex flg. hd.
26. Retainer assy., trans. control cable bracket
27. Nut, 5/16-18 round push on

Shift lever components, automatic transaxle

An odor can sometimes indicate an overheating condition, clutch disc or band failure.

Wipe the dipstick with a clean white rag. Examine the stain on the rag for specks of solids (metal or dirt) and for signs of contaminates (antifreeze-gum or varnish condition).

If examination shows evidence of metal specks or antifreeze contamination transaxle removal and inspection may be necessary.

Throttle Valve Control Linkage

The Throttle Valve (TV) Control Linkage System consists of a lever on the carburetor, linkage shaft assembly, mounting bracket assembly, control rod assembly, a control lever on the transaxle and a lever return spring.

The coupling lever follows the movement of the carburetor throttle lever and has an adjustment screw that is used for setting TV linkage adjustment when a line pressure gauge is used. If a pressure gauge is not available, a manual adjustment can be made.

A number of shift troubles can occur if the throttle valve linkage is not in adjustment. Some are;

1. **Symptom;** Excessively early and/or soft upshifts with or without slip-bump feel. No forced downshift (kickdown) function at appropriate speeds.

CLUTCH AND TRANSAXLE

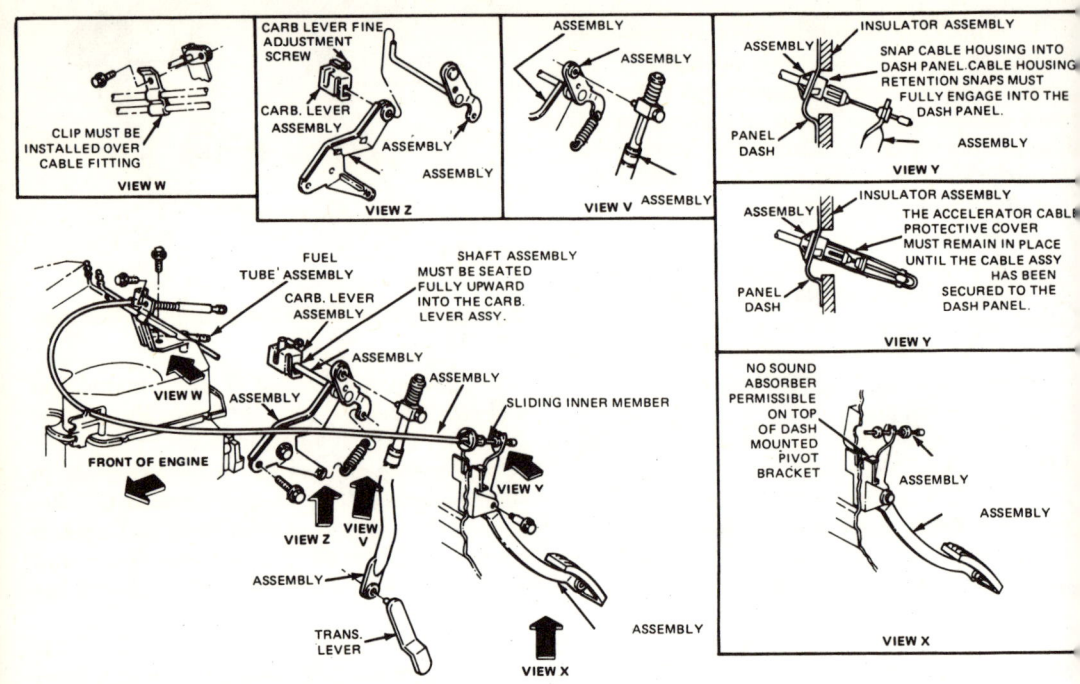

Throttle linkage cable and components; automatic transaxle

Cause; TV control linkage is set too short.
Remedy; Adjust linkage.

2. **Symptom**; Extremely delayed or harsh upshifts and harsh idle engagement.
Cause; TV control linkage is set too long.
Remedy; Adjust linkage.

3. **Symptom**; Harsh idle engagement after the engine is warmed up. Shift clunk when throttle is backed off after full or heavy throttle acceleration. Harsh coasting downshifts (automatic 3-2, 2-1 shifts in D range). Delayed upshifts at light acceleration.
Cause; Interference due to hoses, wires, etc. prevents return of TV control rod or TV linkage shaft. Excessive friction caused by binding grommets prevents the TV control linkage to return to its proper location.
Remedy; Correct the interference area, check for bent or twisted rods, levers or damaged grommets. Repair or replace whatever is necessary. Check and adjust linkage if necessary.

4. **Symptom**; Eratic/delayed upshifts, possibly no kickdown, harsh engagements.
Cause; Clamping bolt on trunnion at the upper end of the TV control rod is loose.
Remedy; Reset TV control linkage.

5. **Symptom**; No upshifts and harsh engagements.
Cause; TV control rod is disconnected or the linkage return spring is broken or disconnected.

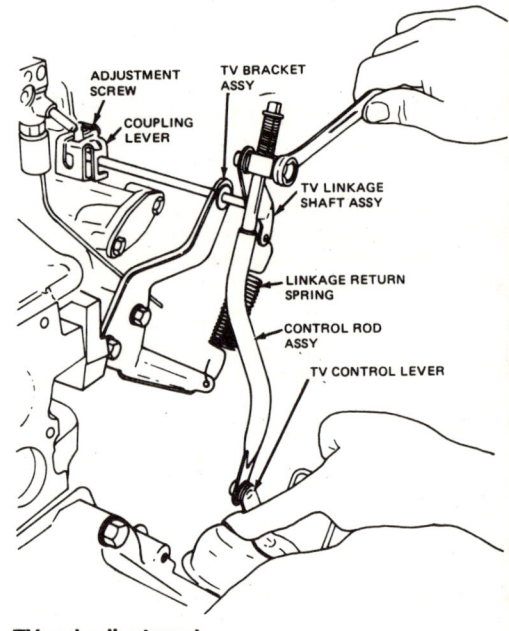

TV rod adjustment

Remedy; Reconnect TV control rod, check and replace the connecting grommet if necessary, reconnect or replace the TV return spring.

LINKAGE ADJUSTMENT

The TV control linkage is adjusted at the sliding trunnion block.

CLUTCH AND TRANSAXLE

1. Adjust the curb idle speed to specification as shown on the underhood decal.
2. After the curb idle speed has been set, shut off the engine. Make sure the choke is completely opened. Check the carburetor throttle lever to make sure it is against the hot engine curb idle stop.
3. Set the coupling lever adjustment screw at its approximate midrange. Make sure the TV linkage shaft assembly is fully seated upward into the coupling lever.
   CAUTION: *If adjustment of the linkage is necessary, allow the EGR valve to cool so you won't get burned.*
4. To adjust; loosen the bolt on the sliding block on the TV control rod a minimum of one turn. Clean any dirt or corrosion from the control rod, free-up the trunnion block so that it will slide freely on the control rod.
5. Rotate the transaxle TV control lever up using a finger and light force, to insure that the TV control lever is against its internal stop. With reducing the pressure on the control lever, tighten the bolt on the trunnion block.
6. Check the carburetor throttle lever to be sure it is still against the hot idle stop. If not, repeat the adjustment steps.

Transmission Control Lever

ADJUSTMENT

1. Position the selector lever in Drive against the rear stop.
2. Raise the car and support it safely on jackstands. Loosen the manual lever to control lever nut.
3. Move the transmission lever to the Drive position, second detent from the rearmost position. Tighten the attaching nut. Check the operation of the transmission in each selector position. Readjust if necessary. Lower the car.

Shift Lever Cable

REMOVAL AND INSTALLATION

1. Remove the shift knob, locknut, console, bezel assembly, control cable clip and cable retaining pin.
2. Disengage the rubber grommet from the floor pan by pushing it into the engine compartment. Raise the car and safely support it on jackstands.
3. Remove the retaining nut and control cable assembly from the transmission lever. Remove the control cable bracket bolts. Pull the cable through the floor.

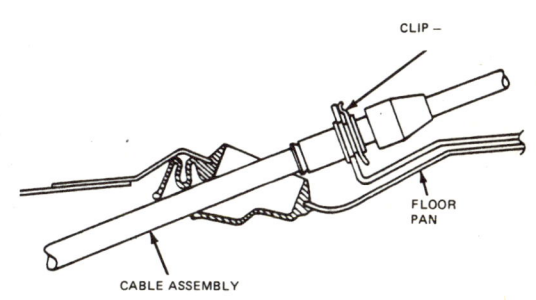

Shift cable (ATX) installation through the floor pan

4. To install the cable; feed the round end through the floor boards. Press the rubber grommet into its mounting hole.
5. Position the control cable assembly in the selector lever housing and install the spring clip. Install the bushing and control cable assembly on the selector lever and housing assembly shaft and secure it with the retaining pin.
   Install the bezel assembly, console, locknut and shift knob. Position the selector lever in the Drive position. The selector lever must be held in this position while attaching the other end of the control cable.
6. Position the control cable bracket on the retainer bracket and secure the two mounting bolts.
7. Shift the control lever into the second detent from full rearward (Drive position).
8. Place the cable end on the transmission

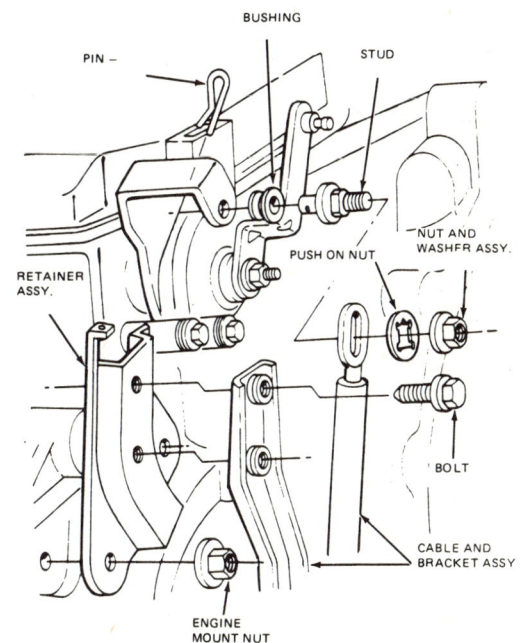

Exploded view of the installation of the shift cable and bracket

136 CLUTCH AND TRANSAXLE

lever stud. Align the flats on the stud with the slot in the cable. Make sure the transmission selector lever has not moved from the second detent position and tighten the retaining nut.

9. Lower the car to the ground. Check the operation of the transmission selector in all positions. Make sure the neutral safety switch is operating properly. (The engine should start only in Park or Neutral position).

Selector Indicator Bulb
REPLACEMENT

Remove the console and the four screws that mount the bezel. Lift the bezel assembly and disconnect the indicator bulb harness. Remove the indicator bulb. Install a new bulb and reverse the removal procedure.

Neutral Safety Switch
REMOVAL AND INSTALLATION

1. Disconnect the negative battery cable from the battery.

2. Remove the two hoses from the rear of the manage air valve. Remove all the vacuum hoses from the valve, label them for position before removal.

3. Remove the manage air valve supply hose band to intermediate shift control bracket attaching screw. Remove the air cleaner assembly.

4. Disconnect the neutral safety switch connector. Remove the two neutral safety switch retaining bolts and the neutral safety switch.

5. Installation is in the reverse order of removal.

ADJUSTMENT

When positioning the neutral safety switch a Number 43 drill (.089 inch) is used to align the hole in the switch and mount before the mounting bolts are tightened.

Suspension and Steering

07

Your Escort/Lynx, ESP or LN7 has fully independent four-wheel suspension. Because wheel movements are controlled independently, the suspension provides exceptional road-hugging and ride comfort advantages.

FRONT SUSPENSION

Your car is equipped with a MacPherson strut front suspension. The strut acts upon a cast steering knuckle, which pivots on a ball joint mounted on a forged lower control arm. A stabilizer bar, which also acts as a locating link, is standard equipment. To maintain good directional stability, negative scrub radius is designed into the suspension geometry; this means that an imaginary line extended from the strut intersects the ground outside the tire patch. Caster and camber are present and nonadjustable. The front suspension fittings are "lubed-for-life"; no grease fittings are provided.

The front suspension fasteners for the lower arm, tie rod and shock struts require only one wrench for loosening and tightening making them easier to work on.

The front strut is attached to a shear type upper mount to reduce engine, transaxle noise, vibration and harshness. The strut spring is contained between an offset lower spring seat fixed to the strut body and a rotating upper seat attached to the upper mount. The offset spring seat reduces friction in the strut to improve ride and decrease wear. The hydraulic damping (shock) system for the front strut has twin tubes with a single-acting piston attached to an 18mm rod.

Component Serviceability

The following components may be replaced individually or as components:
- Shock Absorber Struts (MacPherson):

The shock struts must be replaced as assemblies. They are not repairable.
- Strut Upper Mounts:

The upper strut mounts may be replaced individually.
- Coil Springs:

The front strut coil springs are replaceable.
- Ball Joints:

The ball joints are replaced with the lower control arm as an assembly.
- Lower Control Arm Bushing:

The lower control arm bushing may be replaced individually.
- Forged Lower Control Arm:

The lower control arm is replaceable with the ball joint, inner bushing and insulators as an assembly.

138 SUSPENSION AND STEERING

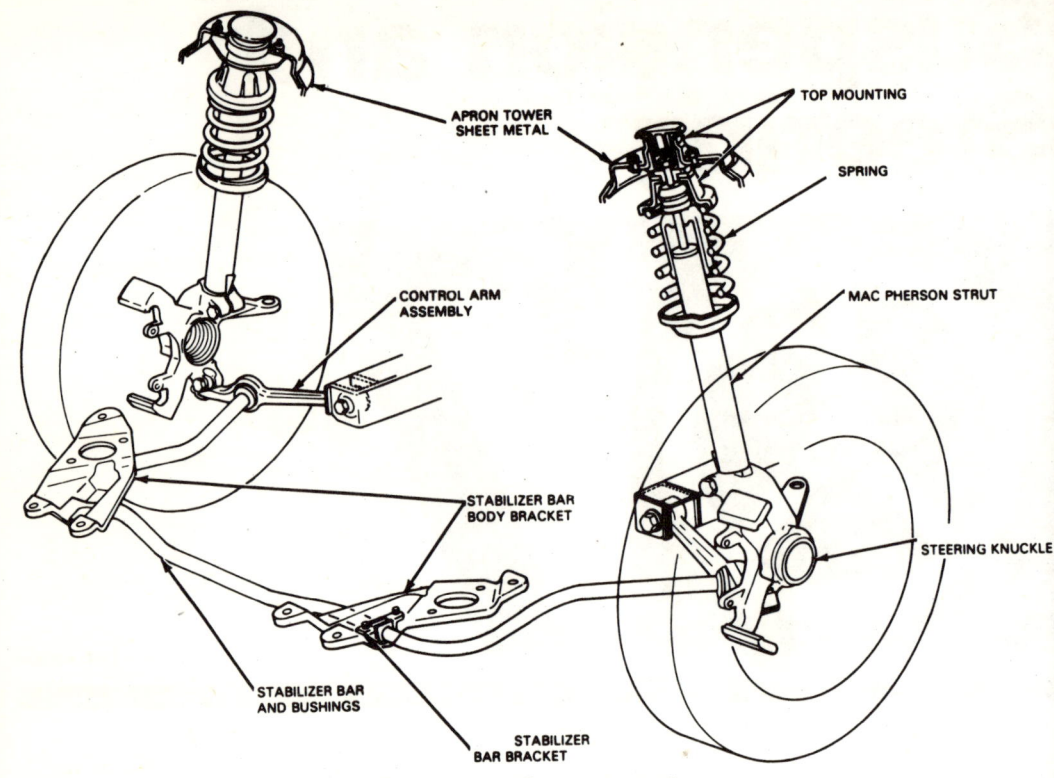

Front suspension components

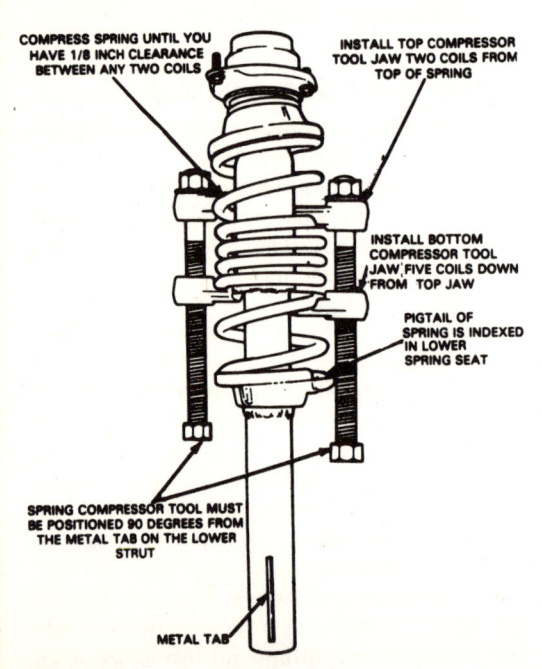

Coil spring compressor mounting

- Steering Knuckle:

The steering knuckle is replaceable.

- Stabilizer Bar:

The stabilizer bar is replaceable and contains the body mounting bushings. The stabilizer bar to lower arm insulator is replaceable as is the stabilizer bar to body bushing.

MacPherson Strut and Coil Spring

REMOVAL AND INSTALLATION

NOTE: *A coil spring compressor Ford Tool number T81P5310A or the equivalent is required when removing the strut and coil spring assembly.*

1. Loosen the wheel lugs, raise the front of the car and safely support it on jackstands. Locate the jackstands under the frame jack pads, slightly behind the front wheels.
2. Remove the tire and wheel assembly.
3. Remove the brake line from the strut mounting bracket.
4. Place a floor jack or small hydraulic jack under the lower control arm. Raise the lower arm and strut as far as possible without raising the car.
5. Install the coil spring compressors. Place the top jaw of the compressors on the second coil from the top of the spring. Install the bottom jaw so that five coils will be gripped. Compress the spring evenly, from side to side, until there is about 1/8 inch between any two spring coils.

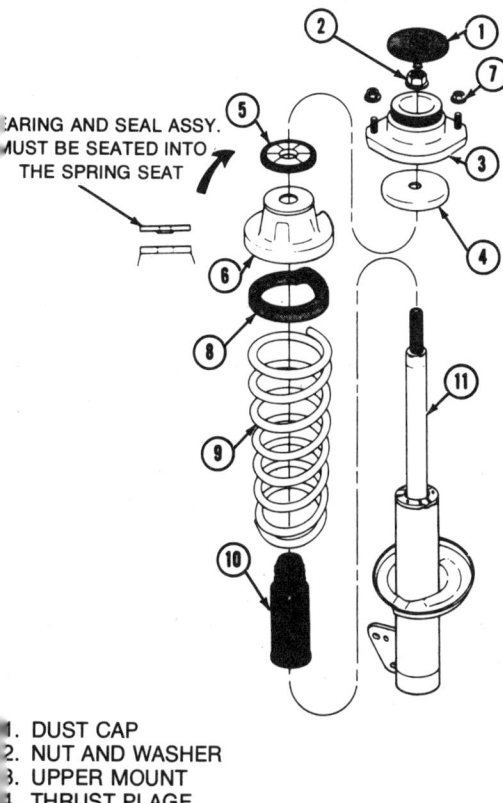

SUSPENSION AND STEERING 139

Top strut mounting

1. DUST CAP
2. NUT AND WASHER
3. UPPER MOUNT
4. THRUST PLAGE
5. BEARING AND SEAL
6. SPRING SEAT
7. NUT
8. SPRING INSULATOR
9. SPRING
10. JOUNCE BUMPER, FRONT
11. SHOCK ABSORBER STRUT

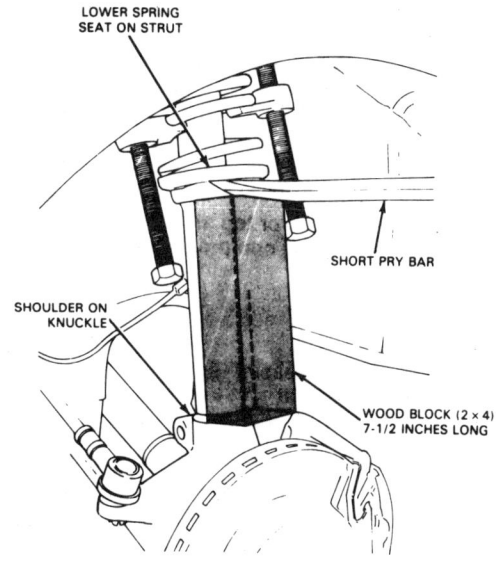

Block positioning

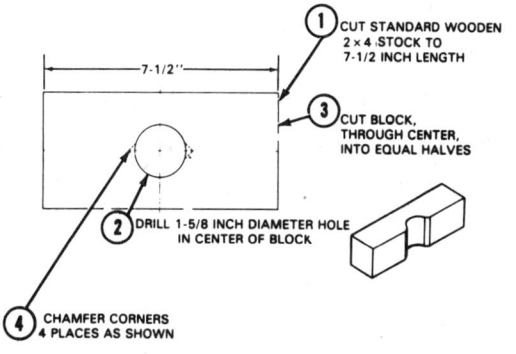

Strut holder construction

6. A pinch bolt retains the strut to the steering knuckle. Remove the pinch bolt.

7. Loosen, but do not remove, the two top mount to strut tower nuts. Lower the jack supporting the lower control arm.

8. Use a pry bar and slightly spread the pinch bolt joint (knuckle to strut connection).

9. Place a piece of (wooden) 2 x 4 by 7½ inches long against the shoulder on the steering knuckle. Use a short pry bar between the wooden block and the lower spring seat to separate the strut from the knuckle.

10. Remove the two strut upper mounting nuts.

11. Remove the MacPherson strut, spring and top mount assembly from the car.

12. Place an 18mm deep socket that has an external hex drive top (Ford tool number D81P18045A1) over the strut shaft center nut. Insert a 6mm allen wrench into the shaft end. With the edge of the strut mount clamped in a vise, remove the top shaft mounting nut from the shaft while holding the allen wrench. Use vise grips, if necessary or a suitable extension to hold the allen wrench.

NOTE: *Make a wooden holding device that will clamp the strut barrel into the bench vise. (See illustration). Do not clamp directly onto the strut barrel, damage may occur.*

13. Clamp the strut into a bench vise. Remove the strut upper mount and the coil spring. If only the strut is to be serviced, do not remove the coil spring compressor from the spring.

14. If the coil spring is to be replaced, remove the compressor from the old spring and install it on the new.

15. Mount the strut (if removed) in the vise using the wooden fixture. Position the coil spring in the lower spring seat. Be sure that the pigtail of the spring is indexed in the seat. That is; follows the groove in the seat and fits

140 SUSPENSION AND STEERING

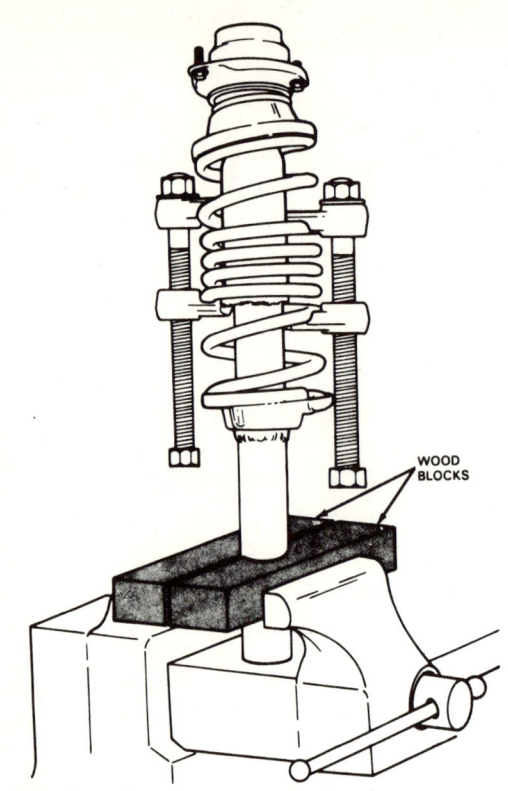

Mounting the strut in a bench vise

flush. Be sure that the spring compressors are positioned 90 degrees from the metal tab on the lower part of the strut.

16. Use a new nut and assemble the top mount to the strut. Tighten the shaft nut to 48–62 ft. lbs.

17. Install the assembled strut, spring and upper mount into the car. If you have installed a new coil spring, be sure it has been compressed enough.

18. Position the two top mounting studs through the holes in the tower and install two new mounting nuts. Do not tighten the nuts completely.

19. Install the bottom of the strut fully into the steering knuckle pinch joint.

20. Install a new pinch bolt and tighten it to 68–81 ft. lbs. Tighten the two upper mount nuts to 22–29 ft. lbs.

21. Remove the coil spring compressor. Make sure the spring is fitting properly between the upper and lower seats.

22. Install the brake line to the strut bracket. Install the front tire and wheel assembly. Lower the car and tighten the lugs.

Steering Knuckle

NOTE: *For illustrations refer to Chapter 8 under wheel bearings.*

REMOVAL

1. Loosen the wheel lugs, raise the front of the car and support safely on jackstands. Remove the tire and wheel assembly.

2. Remove the cotter pin from the tie rod end stud nut and remove the nut. Use a suitable removing tool and separate the tie rod end from the steering knuckle.

3. Remove the disc brake caliper, rotor and center hub as outlined in Chapter 8.

4. Remove the lower control arm to steering knuckle pinch bolt, slightly spread the connection after the bolt has been removed.

5. Remove the strut to steering knuckle pinch bolt, slightly spread the connection after the bolt has been removed.

6. Remove the steering knuckle from the strut.

7. Remove the wheel bearings and rotor splash shield. Refer to Chapter 8.

INSTALLATION

1. Install the rotor splash shield and wheel bearings. Refer to Chapter 8.

2. Install the steering knuckle onto the strut. Install a new pinch bolt and tighten to 66–81 ft. lbs.

3. Install the center hub onto the stub drive shaft as outlined in Chapter 8.

4. Install the lower control arm to the knuckle. Make sure the ball joint groove is aligned so the pinch bolt can slide through. Install a new pinch bolt and tighten to 37–4 ft. lbs.

5. Install the rotor and disc brake caliper (see Chapter 8). Position the tie rod end into the steering knuckle, install a new nut and tighten to 23–35 ft. lbs. Align the cotter pin slot and install a new cotter pin.

6. Install the tire and wheel assembly. Lower the car and tighten the wheel lugs.

Lower Control Arm and Ball Joint

REMOVAL AND INSTALLATION

1. Jack up the front of the car and safely support it on jackstands.

2. Remove the nut connecting the stabilizer bar to the control arm. Pull off the large dished washer located behind the nut.

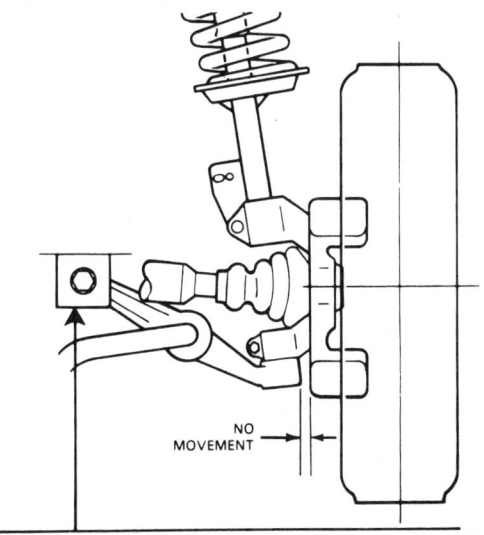

SUSPENSION AND STEERING 141

Checking the ball joint for excessive play

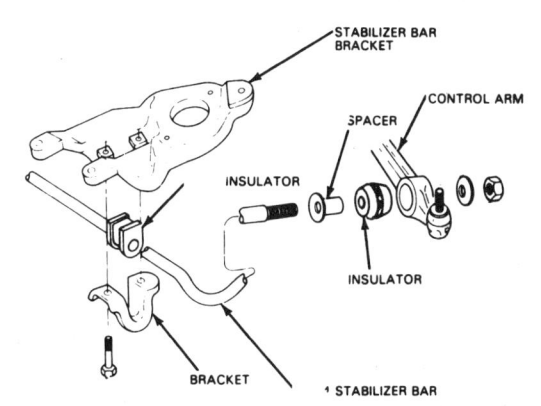

Stabilizer and related part mountings

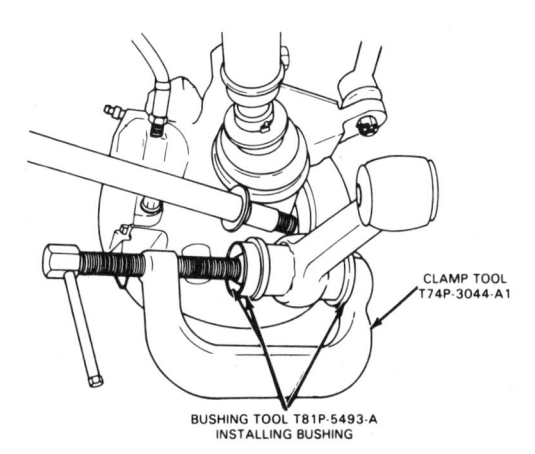

Using a "C"-clamp bushing tool

3. Remove the lower control arm inner pivot (frame mount) bolt and nut. Remove the pinch bolt from the ball joint to steering knuckle. It may be necessary to use a drift pin to drive out the pinch bolt. Spread the connection slightly after the bolt has been removed. Remove the lower control arm.

NOTE: *Be sure the steering wheel is in the unlocked position. DO NOT use a hammer to separate the ball joint from the steering knuckle.*

4. Installation is in the reverse order of removal. When installing the ball joint into the steering knuckle, make sure the stud groove is aligned so the pinch bolt may be installed. Tighten the pinch bolt to 37–44 ft. lbs. When tightening the inner control arm mounting bolt/nut the torque should be 44–55 ft. lbs. The stabilizer mounting nut is tightened to 59–73 ft. lbs.

Stabilizer Bar and/or Bushings
REMOVAL AND INSTALLATION

1. Raise the front of the car and safely support it on jackstands. The tire and wheel assembly may be removed for convenience.
2. Remove the stabilizer bar insulator mounting bracket bolts, end nuts and washers. Remove the bar assembly.
3. Carefully cut the center mounting insulators from the stabilizer.
  NOTE: *A "C"-Clamp type remover/installer tool is necessary to replace the control arm to stabilizer mounting bushings. The Ford part number of this tool is T81P5493A with T74P3044A1.*
4. Remove the control arm inner pivot nut and bolt. Pull the arm down from the inner mounting and away from the stabilizer bar (if still mounted on car).
5. Remove the old bar to control arm insulator bushing with the clamp type tool.
6. Use vegetable oil and saturate the new control arm bushing. Install the bushing with the clamp type tool. Coat the center stabilizer bar bushings with Ruglyde or an equivalent lubricant. Slide the bushings into place. Install the inner control arm mounting. Tighten to 60–75 ft. lbs.
7. Install the stabilizer bar using new insulator mounting bracket bolts. Tighten to 50–60 ft. lbs. Install new end nuts with the old dished washers. Tighten to 59–73 ft. lbs.
8. Install tire and wheel assembly if removed. Lower the car.

Lower Control Arm Inner Pivot Bushing

REMOVAL AND INSTALLATION

NOTE: *A special "C"-Clamp type removal/installation tool is required. See note under Stabilizer Bar for the Ford part number of this tool.*

1. Raise the front of the car and safely support it on jackstands.
2. Remove the stabilizer bar to control arm nut and the dished washer.
3. Remove the inner control arm pivot nut and bolt. Pull the arm down from its mounting and away from the stabilizer bar.
4. Carefully cut away the retaining lip of the bushing. Use the special clamp type tool and remove the bushing.
5. Saturate the new bushing with vegetable oil and install the bushing using the special tool.
6. Position the lower control arm over the stabilizer bar and install into the inner body mounting using a new bolt and nut. Tighten the inner nut and bolt to 44–53 ft. lbs. Tighten the stabilizer nut to 59–73 ft. lbs. Be sure to install the dished washer ahead of the nut.

Front End Alignment

CASTER AND CAMBER

Caster and camber angles on your car are preset at the factory and cannot be adjusted in the field. Improper caster and camber can be corrected only through replacement of worn or bent parts. The measurements given in the chart are for reference only.

TOE ADJUSTMENT

Toe is the difference in distance between the front and the rear of the front wheels.

1. Loosen and slide off the small outer boot clamp so the boot will not twist during adjustment.
2. Loosen the locknuts on the outer tie rod ends.

Alignment Specifications Wheelbase And Tread Width—Inches

Wheelbase	Tread Width	
	Front	Rear
94.2	54.7	55.6

Front Wheel Alignment

Alignment Factors	Normal	Minimum	Maximum
Caster	+1.65°	+ .9°	+2.4°
Left Camber	+1.75°	+1.0°	+2.5°
Right Camber	+1.3°	+ .55°	+2.05°
Toe	0.1" out	0.02" in	0.22" out

3. Rotate both (right and left) tie rods in exactly equal amounts during adjustment. This will keep the steering wheel centered.
4. Tighten the locknuts when the adjustment has been made. Install and tighten the boot clamps.

Front Suspension Tips and Inspection

• Maintain the correct tire pressures.
• Raise the front of the car and support on jackstands. Grasp the upper and lower edges of the tire. Apply up and downward movement to the tire and wheel. Check for looseness in the front ball joints. See previous ball joint inspection illustration. Inspect the various mounting bushings for wear. Tighten all loose nuts and bolts to "specs".
Replace all worn parts found as soon as possible.
• Check the steering gear and assembly for looseness at its mountings. Check the tie rod ends for looseness.
• Check the shock absorbers. If any dampness from fluid leakage is observed, the shock should be replaced. Check the damping action of the shock by pushing up and down on each corner. If the damping effect is not uniform and smooth the shock should be suspect.

REAR SUSPENSION

Your car features a completely new modified MacPherson strut type independent rear suspension. Each side has a shock absorber (strut), lower control (tranverse) arm, tie rod, forged spindle and a coil spring mounted between the lower control arm and the body crossmember side rail.

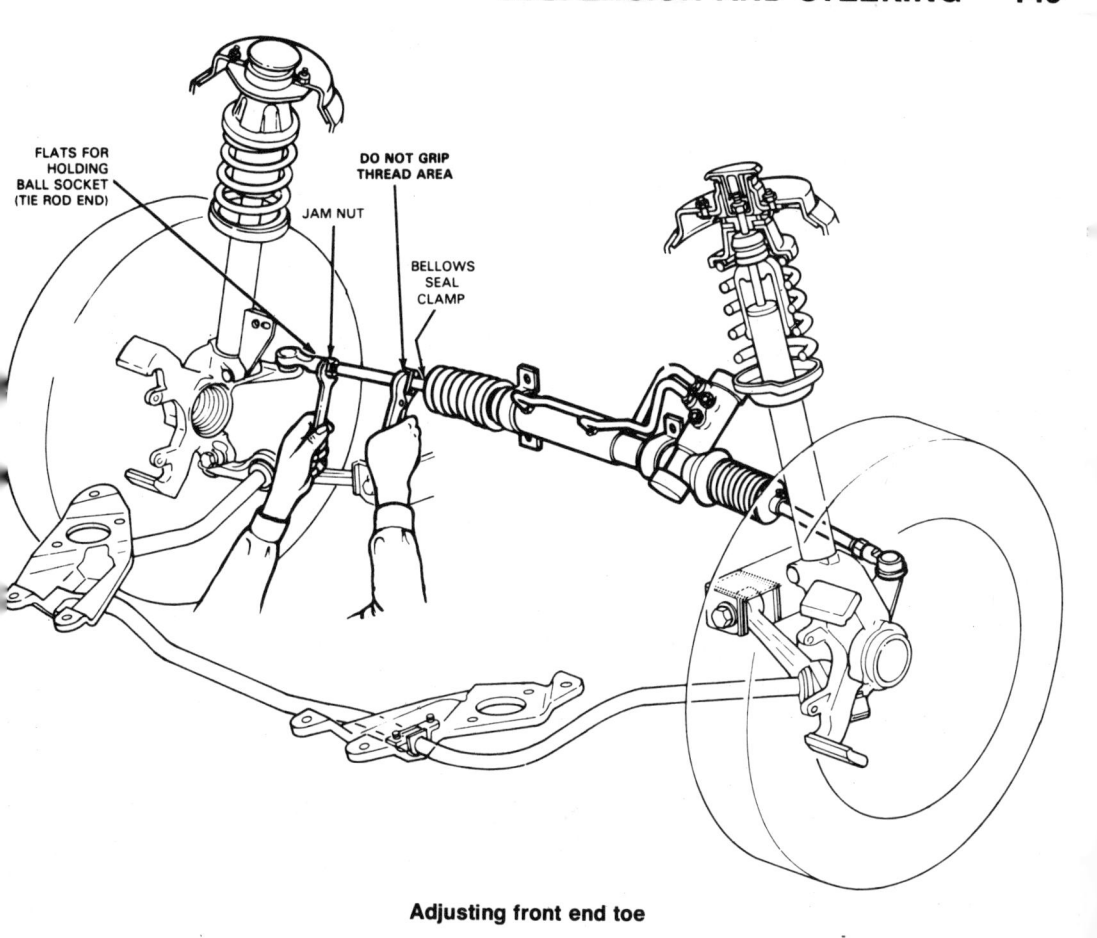

SUSPENSION AND STEERING 143

Adjusting front end toe

The lower control (transverse) arm and the tie rod provide lateral and longitudinal control. The shock strut counters braking forces and provides the necessary suspension damping. The coil is mounted on the lower control arm and acts as a metal to metal jounce stop in case of heavy bottoming (going over bumps with weight in the back).

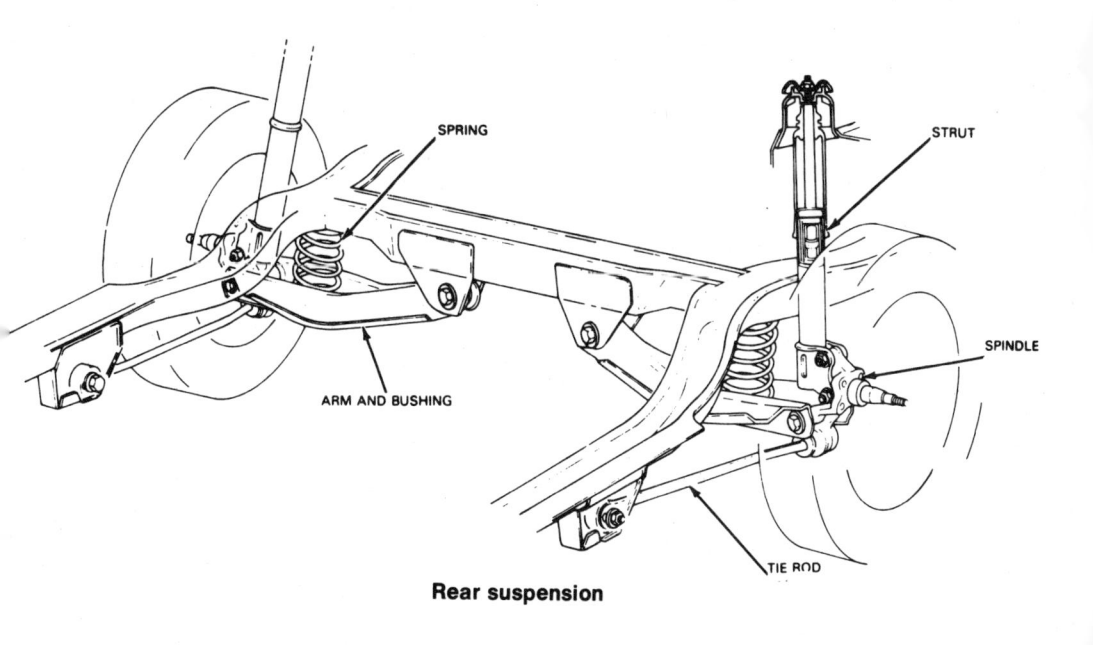

Rear suspension

SUSPENSION AND STEERING

The unique independent rear suspension provides exceptional road hugging ability and adds to ride comfort.

Component Description and Serviceability

- Rear Coil Spring:

Controls the suspension travel, provides rideheight control and acts as a metal to metal jounce stop. The coil springs are replaceable, however the upper spring insulator must be replaced at the same time.

- Lower Control (Transverse) Arm:

Controls the side to side movement of each wheel and has the lower coil spring seat built in. The lower control arm is replaceable, however the control arm bushings are not. If the bushings are worn the control arm must be replaced.

- Shock Absorber Strut:

Counters the braking forces and provides the necessary damping action to rear suspension travel caused by road conditions. The assembly is not repairable and must be replaced as a unit. The upper mounting may be serviced separately.

- Tie Rod:

Controls the fore and aft wheel movement and holds the rear toe-in adjustment. The tie rod may be replaced as an assembly. Mounting bushings may be replaced separately, but new ones should be installed if the tie rod is replaced.

- Wheel Spindle:

The one piece forged spindle attached to the lower arm, tie rod, shock strut and brake assembly. The rear wheel is mounted on the spindle. It may be replaced as a unit.

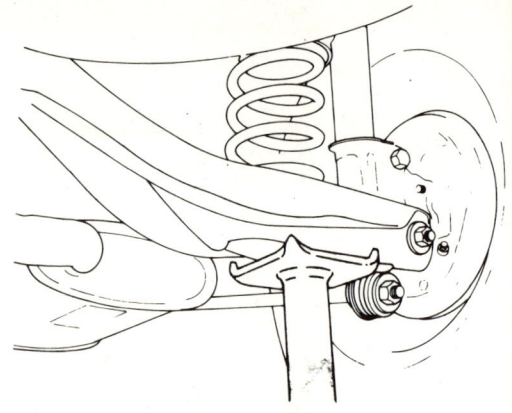

Supporting the rear suspension

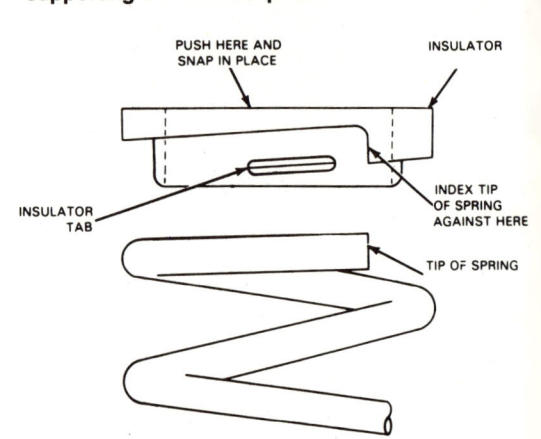

Rear spring insulator installation

Rear Coil Spring

REMOVAL AND INSTALLATION

1. Jack up the rear of the car and safely support it on jackstands. The jackstand location should be on the frame pads slightly in front of the rear wheels.
2. Place a floor jack or small hydraulic jack under the rear control arm. Raise the control arm to its normal height with the jack, do not lift the car frame from the jackstands.
3. Remove the tire and wheel assembly. Remove the nut, bolt and washer that mounts the lower control arm to the wheel spindle.
4. Slowly lower the jack under the control arm. The coil spring will relax as the control arm is lowered. Lower the control arm until the spring can be removed.
5. Install a new upper spring insulator onto the top of the coil spring. Install the new spring on the control arm and slowly jack into position. Be sure the spring is properly seated (indexed) in place on the control arm.
6. Jack up the control arm and position the top of the spring (insulator attached) into the body pocket.
7. Use a new attaching bolt, washers and nut to attach the control arm to the spindle. Tighten the nut and bolt to 90–100 ft. lbs.
8. Install the tire and wheel assembly. Remove the car from the jackstands and lower to the ground.

Rear Shock Absorber Strut

REMOVAL

1. From inside the car, remove the rear compartment access panels (over the upper strut mount). On four door models, remove the quarter trim panels.

SUSPENSION AND STEERING 145

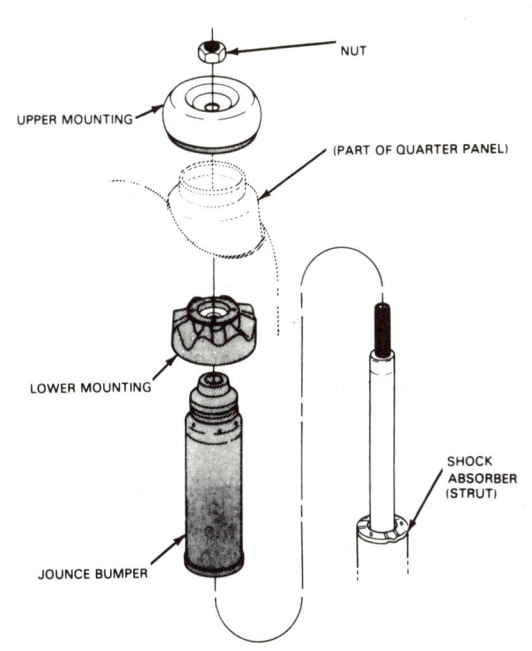

Rear strut top mounting

2. Loosen, but do not remove the upper shock mounting nut.

NOTE: *A special 18mm deep socket is required, the socket should have a hex drive outer head so that it can be turned with an open-end wrench, as well as a ratchet. A 6mm Allen wrench is also required.*

To loosen the upper nut, place the socket over the nut, insert the Allen wrench through the center of the socket and into the upper strut rod. Hold the Allen wrench and loosen the nut by turning the socket with an open-end wrench. Use an extension to hold the Allen wrench, if necessary.

3. Jack up the rear of the car and support it safely on jackstands. Remove the rear tire and wheel assembly.

4. Remove the clip that holds the rear brake line to the shock. Locate the brake hose out of the way.

5. Loosen the two nuts and bolts that hold the shock to the wheel spindle. DO NOT REMOVE THEM at this time.

6. Remove the upper mounting nut, washer and rubber insulator.

7. Remove the two lower nuts and bolts and remove the shock strut assembly from the car.

INSTALLATION

1. Extend the shock to its maximum length. Install the new (upper mount) lower washer and insulator assembly. Lubricate the insulator with a tire lubricant. Position the upper part of the shock shaft through the upper mount.

2. Slow push upwards on the shock until the lower mounting holes align with the mounting holes in the spindle. Install new lower mounting bolts and nuts, but do not completely at this time. The heads of the mounting bolts must face the rear of the car.

3. Install the new top rubber insulator and washer. Tighten the mounting nut to 60–70 ft. lbs.

4. Tighten the two lower mounting nuts and bolts to 90–100 ft. lbs.

5. Install the brake hose with the retaining clip. Put the tire and wheel assembly back on. Remove the jackstands and lower the car.

6. Reinstall the access or trim panels.

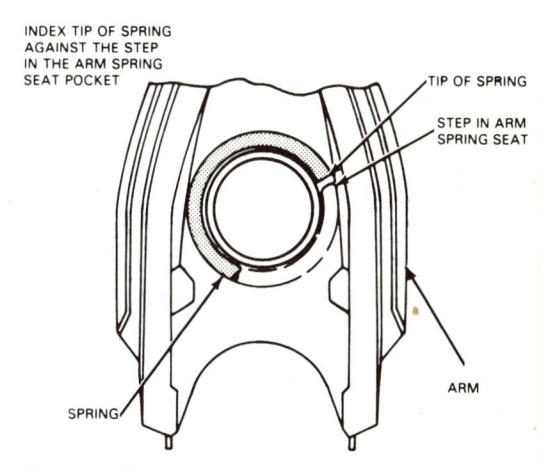

Indexing the rear coil spring

Lower Control Arm
REMOVAL AND INSTALLATION

1. Perform Steps 1–4 of the Coil Spring Removal section.

2. After the spring and insulator have been removed. Take out the inner mounting bolt and nut. Remove the control arm.

3. Installation is in the reverse order of removal. Be sure that the coil is properly indexed (seated) when jacking into position.

Tie Rod End
REMOVAL AND INSTALLATION

1. Jack up the rear of the car and safely support it on jackstands. Remove the tire and wheel assembly.

2. At the front mounting bracket of the tie rod, take a sharp tool and scribe a vertical

SUSPENSION AND STEERING

mark at the mounting bolt head center. This is so the tie rod can be mounted in the same position.

3. Remove the nut, washer and insulator that mount the rear of the tie rod to the wheel spindle.

4. Remove the front mounting nut and bolt that attach the tie rod to the front bracket. Remove the tie rod.

NOTE: *It may be necessary to separate the front body bracket slightly apart with a pry bar to remove the tie rod.*

5. Install new mounting bushings on the spindle end of the tie rod (reverse the removal order). Install the tie rod through the spindle and install the bushings, washer and nut. Tighten the nut to 65–75 ft. lbs.

6. Use a floor jack or a small hydraulic jack and slowly raise the rear control arm to its curb height.

7. Line up the new front mounting bolt with the mark you scribed on the mounting bracket. Install the bolt and nut (bolt head facing inward). Tighten the nut and bolt to 90–100 ft. lbs.

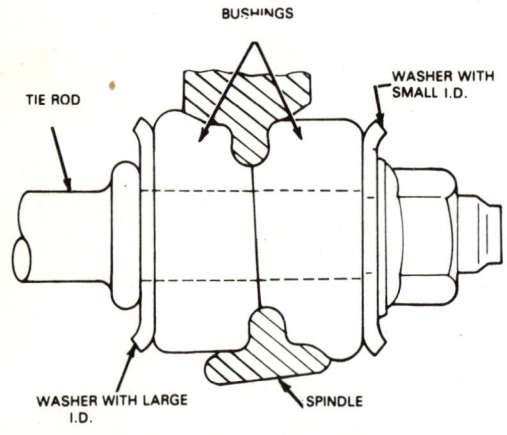

NOTE: WASHERS N801336 AND N801335 MUST BE INSTALLED IN THIS POSITION WITH DISH AWAY FROM BUSHINGS.

Rear tie rod installation

8. Install tire and wheel assembly. Lower the car.

Tie Rod Bushings

The tie rod bushings (body mount) can be replaced after removing the tie rod. A special "C"-clamp type remover/installer tool is used. Refer to the front suspension section of this Chapter under Stabilizer Bushings for the Ford part number of the puller required.

Rear Wheel Spindle

REMOVAL AND INSTALLATION

1. Raise the rear of the car and safely support it on jackstands. Remove the tire and wheel assembly.

2. Remove the rear brake drum, shoe assembly and brake backing plate. Refer to Chapter 8 for instructions on drum, shoe assembly and wheel cylinder removal. The backing plate is retained by four bolts, loosen and remove the bolts, and the backing plate.

3. Remove the tie rod to spindle retaining nut, washer and insulator. Remove the shock (strut) lower mounting nuts and bolts. Remove the nut and bolt retaining the lower control arm to the spindle. Remove the spindle.

4. Installation is in the reverse order of removal. Torque the mounting bolts and nuts; Shock mount; 90–100 ft. lbs.; Control arm; 90–100 ft. lbs.; Tie rod; 65–75 ft. lbs.

Rear Suspension Inspection

Check the rear suspension at regular intervals for the following;
- Rear shock struts for leakage. A slight seepage is alright, heavy leakage requires that the shock be replaced.
- Check shock operation. Push up and

Rear Wheel Alignment (At Curb Position)

Factor	Left Nom.	Left Total	Right Nom.	Right Total	Side-Side Nom.	Side-Side Total
Camber (Degrees)	−1.0	±.85	−1.0	±.85	0	±1.20 ①
Toe (Inches)	+.09	±.15	+.09	±.15	+.18	± .15 ②

① Left minus right.   ② Total toe, left plus right.

SUSPENSION AND STEERING 147

down on a rear corner, if the car bounces and feels spongy the shock might need replacement.
• Inspect the condition of the various mounting bushings. If they show signs of deterioration or looseness they must be replaced.
• Condition of the tire tread. If it shows unusual wear the caster, camber or toe could be out.

Rear End Alignment

Rear toe is adjustable but requires special equipment and procedures. If you suspect an alignment problem have it checked by a qualified repair shop. The alignment chart in this section is for factory setting reference.

STEERING

Rack and pinion steering in either manual or power versions gives your car precise steering control. The manual rack and pinion gear is smaller and about seven and one half pounds lighter than that in any other Ford or Mercury small cars. The increased use of aluminum and the use of a one piece valve sleeve make this weight reduction possible.

Lightweight, sturdy bushings are used to mount the steering, these are long lasting and lend to quieter gear operation. The steering also features lifetime lubricated outer tie rod ends, eliminating the need for scheduled maintenance.

The power steering gear shares a common body mounting system with the manual gear. The power steering pump is of a smaller displacement than current pumps, it requires less power to operate and has streamlined inner porting to provide more efficient fluid flow characteristics.

The steering column geometry uses a double universal joint shaft system and separate column support brackets for improved energy-absorbing capabilities.

Steering Wheel

REMOVAL AND INSTALLATION

1. Disconnect the negative (ground) battery cable from the battery.
2. Remove the steering wheel center hub cover (See illustration). Lift up on the outer edges, do not use a sharp tool or remove the screws from behind the steering wheel cross spoke. Loosen and remove the center mounting nut.
3. Remove the steering wheel with a

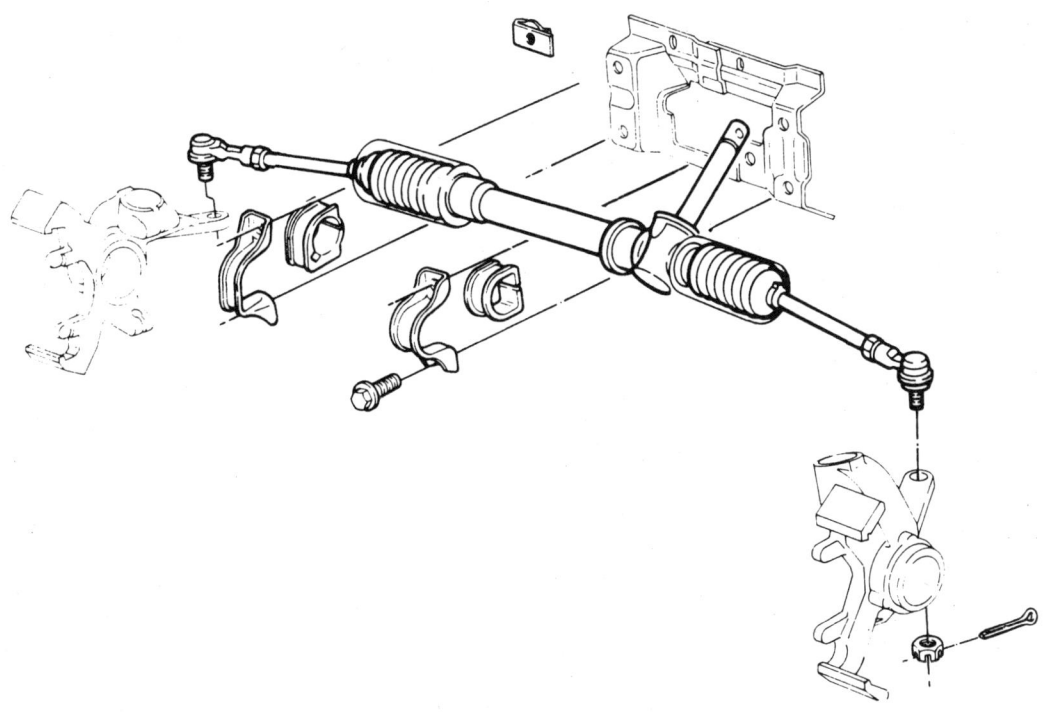

Manual rack and pinion steering

148 SUSPENSION AND STEERING

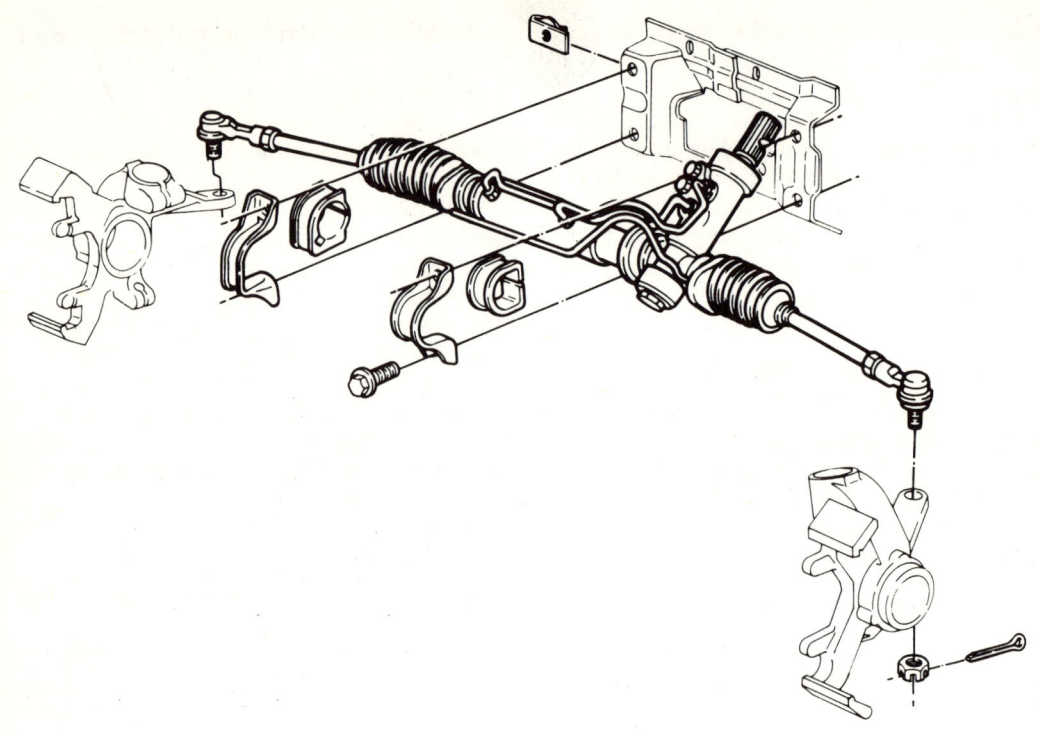

Power rack and pinion steering

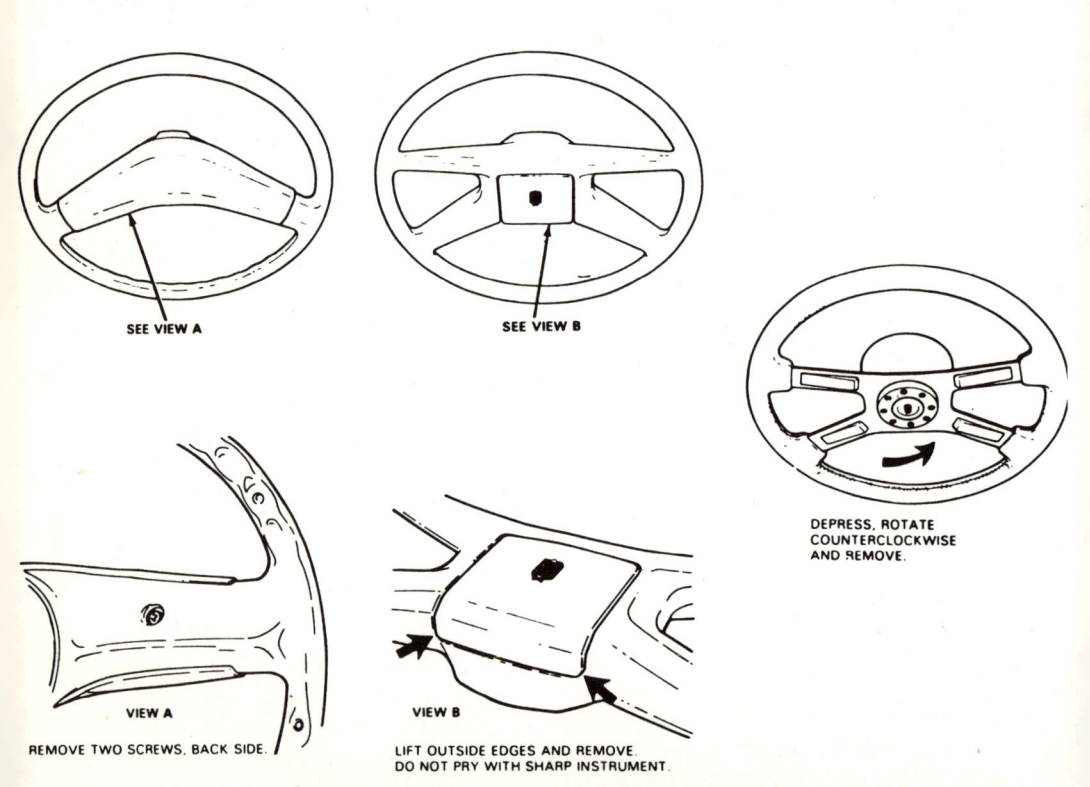

SEE VIEW A

SEE VIEW B

DEPRESS, ROTATE
COUNTERCLOCKWISE
AND REMOVE.

VIEW A
REMOVE TWO SCREWS, BACK SIDE.

VIEW B
LIFT OUTSIDE EDGES AND REMOVE.
DO NOT PRY WITH SHARP INSTRUMENT.

Steering wheel horn pad removal and installation

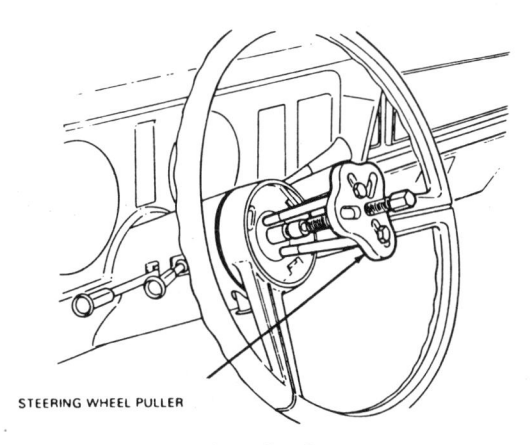

SUSPENSION AND STEERING 149

Removing the steering wheel

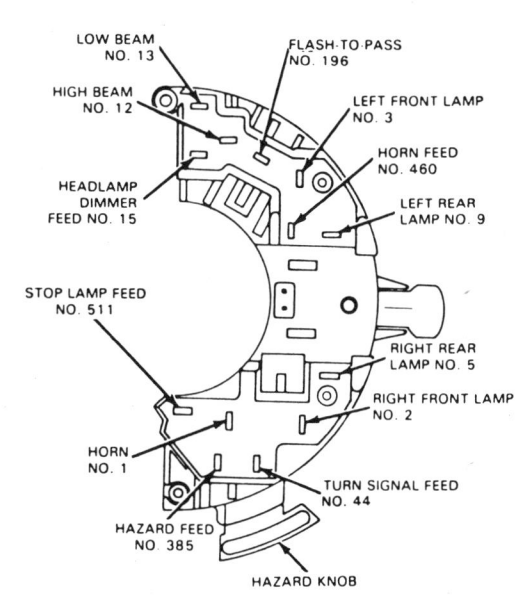

Combination switch electrical check points

"crowsfoot" steering wheel puller. DO NOT USE a knock-off type puller it will cause damage to the collapsible steering column.

4. To reinstall the steering wheel, align the marks on the steering shaft and steering wheel. Place the wheel onto the shaft. Install a new center mounting nut. Tighten the nut to 30–40 ft. lbs.

5. Install the center cover on the steering wheel. Connect the negative battery cable.

Turn Signal (Combination Switch)

The turn signals, emergency (hazard) warning, horn, flash-to-pass and the headlight dimmer are all together on a combination switch. On the following pages are an illustration and troubleshooting tests for the switch.

REMOVAL AND INSTALLATION

1. Disconnect the negative (ground) cable from the battery.
2. Remove the steering column shroud by taking out the five mounting screws. Remove both halves of the shroud.
3. Remove the switch lever by using a twisting motion while pulling the lever straight out from the switch.
4. Peel back the foam cover to expose the switch.
5. Disconnect the two electrical connectors. Remove the two self-tapping screws that attach the switch to the lock cylinder housing. Disengage the switch from the housing.
6. Transfer the ground brush located in the turn signal switch cancelling cam to the new switch, if your car is equipped with speed control.

7. To install the new switch; align the switch with the holes in the lock cylinder housing. Install the two self-tapping screws.
8. Install the foam covering the switch. Install the handle by aligning the key on the lever with the keyway in the switch. Push the lever into the switch until it is fully engaged.
9. Reconnect the two electrical connectors. Install the upper and lower steering column shrouds.
10. Connect the negative battery cable. Test the switch operation.

Ignition Switch
CONTINUITY TEST

Remove the lower and upper steering column shrouds by removing the five mounting screws. Disconnect the electrical connector from the ignition switch. To disconnect, spread apart the fingers on each end of the connector shell and pull away from the igni-

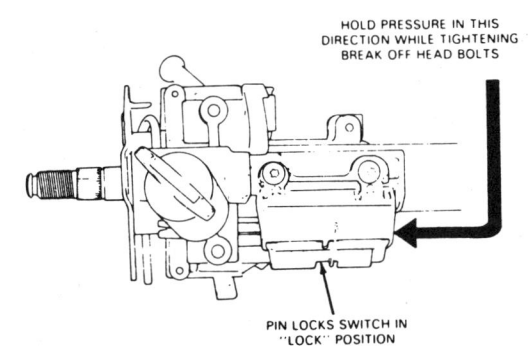

Ignition switch installation

150 SUSPENSION AND STEERING

Turn Signal/Hazard/Horn/Flash-to-Pass/Dimmer Switch Diagnosis (Continuity Tests)

Switch Function	Circuit Continuity
1. Lever in neutral position (Brake lights inoperative)	Continuity from #511 to 5 & 9 (brake circ.) Open circuit #511 to ground (casting) Open circuit #44 to 2, 3, 5, 9 (turn signal)
2. Left lane change & turn position (Left turn signal lights inoperative) (Right brake light inoperative)	Continuity from #44 to 3 & 9 (turn signal) Continuity from #511 to 5 (brake) Open circuit #44 to ground (casting) Open circuit #44 to 5 (turn signal to brake)
3. Right lane change & turn signal position (Right turn signal lights inoperative) (Left brake lights inoperative)	Continuity from #44 to 2 & 5 (turn signal) Continuity from #511 to 9 (brake) Open circuit #44 to ground (casting) Open circuit #44 to #9 (turn signal to brake)
4. Horn ON position—lever pushed in (Horn inoperative)	Continuity from #460 to ground (casting) Note: Lever must return to OFF position automatically. If lever sticks on ON position, replace lever.
5. Emergency warning—ON position (Emergency warning lights inoperative)	Continuity from #385 to 2, 3, 5, 9 Continuity from #511 to 2, 3, 5 & 9 (brake) Open circuit #385 to ground (casting) and #44
6. Headlamp dimmer • Low beam (Low beam inoperative)	Continuity from 15 to 13 Open circuit 15 to 12 Open circuit #196 to 13 & 12
• High beam (High beam inoperative)	Continuity 15 to 12 Open circuit 15 to 13 Open circuit #196 to 13 & 12
• Flash-to-pass (Lever held up column)	Closed circuit #196 to 12 Open circuit #196 to 13

tion switch. Connect a self-powered test lamp or an ohmmeter between the blade terminals of the connector. In the "START" position only (of the key switch) no continuity between any connector blade and chassis ground should exist. The exception being in the "proof" circuits #39 and #977 (see illustration).

If your car is equipped with an automatic transaxle and a "dead battery" condition is experienced, determine if the condition exists when the selector lever is in either PARK or NEUTRAL. If the engine "starts" in one selector position and not the other, the problem is probably in the transmission mounted neutral start switch.

MECHANICAL TEST

Rotate the lock cylinder key switch through all of its positions. The movement should be smooth with no sticking or binding. If the

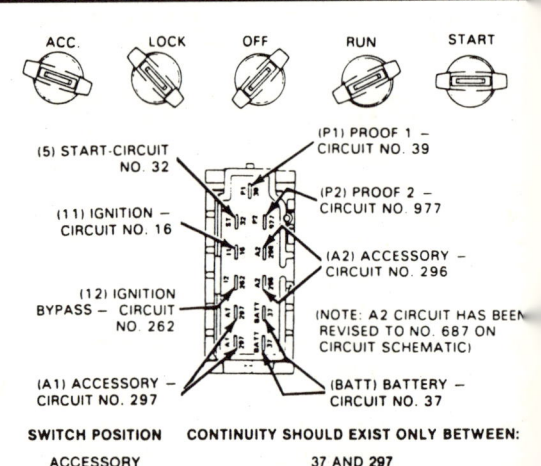

ACC. LOCK OFF RUN START

(5) START-CIRCUIT NO. 32
(11) IGNITION — CIRCUIT NO. 16
(12) IGNITION BYPASS — CIRCUIT NO. 262
(A1) ACCESSORY — CIRCUIT NO. 297
(P1) PROOF 1 — CIRCUIT NO. 39
(P2) PROOF 2 — CIRCUIT NO. 977
(A2) ACCESSORY — CIRCUIT NO. 296
(NOTE: A2 CIRCUIT HAS BEEN REVISED TO NO. 687 ON CIRCUIT SCHEMATIC)
(BATT) BATTERY — CIRCUIT NO. 37

SWITCH POSITION	CONTINUITY SHOULD EXIST ONLY BETWEEN:
ACCESSORY	37 AND 297
LOCK	NO CONTINUITY
OFF	NO CONTINUITY
RUN	37-16-296-297
START	39-977-CHASSIS GROUND 37-32-262-(POSSIBLY 16)

NOTE: CIRCUIT PAIRS 37, 296, AND 297 ARE CONNECTED TOGETHER INTERNALLY IN THE SWITCH.

Ignition switch continuity test points

SUSPENSION AND STEERING 151

Turn Signal, Hazard/Horn/Flash-to-Pass/Dimmer Switch (Chart for Determining Cause of Blown Fuse)

Remove wire harness from switch.
Test continuity from ground (casting) to corresponding feed circuit in switch. Continuity between feed circuit and ground indicates switch is shorted. Replace switch if short is indicated.

Brake Circuit
Check #511 to ground. Operate switch from left turn to right turn to neutral. Continuity between #511 and ground in any position indicates a short in the switch.

Turn Signal Circuit
Check #44 to ground. Operate switch from left turn to right turn to neutral. Continuity between #44 and ground in any position indicates a short in the switch.

Emergency Warning Circuit
Check #385 to ground. Operate hazard from "ON" to "OFF". Continuity in any position indicates a short in the switch.

Horn Circuit
Check #460 to ground. Push the turn signal lever to horn "ON" position and release lever. Lever must automatically return to "OFF". Continuity in either position indicates short in switch.

Headlamp Circuit
Check #15 to ground. Operate turn signal lever to both "HIGH" and "LOW" beam positions. Continuity in either position indicates a short in the switch.

Flash-to-Pass Circuit
Check #196 to ground, operate through-signal lever to flash-to-pass position. Continuity indicates a short in the switch.

Turn Signal/Hazard/Horn/Flash-to-Pass/Dimmer Switch (Mechanical)

Switch Component—Condition	Correction Procedure
Turn signal lever binds—horn blows continuously	Replace lever. To remove lever grasp lever and apply force away from switch and in line with lever. To install lever, align tang on lever with slot in hub of turn signal switch and push into mating hole.
No turn signal lever retention in mating hole.	Switch defective—retaining pin in switch missing—replace switch.
No headlamp transfer between bright and dim	Binding—jammed dimmer—replace switch.
No cancel	Remove switch and examine cancel cam for retention on steering column shaft, cracks and position on shaft. If cancel cam found to be satisfactory, replace switch.
Lever won't stay in turn position	Switch defective—replace switch

SUSPENSION AND STEERING

Ignition Switch Diagnosis

Condition	Possible Source	Verification	Action
High key efforts	Casting/actuator binds, sticks, grabs, with key rotation.	Inspect actuator, lock housing casting contact surfaces for "proper fit" and burrs. Actuator must be free to slide through entire length of lock housing casting.	If improper fit between casting and actuator exists, replace parts. If burrs are found on actuator surfaces which contact the casting during key travel, gently file these surfaces until smooth. At no time attempt to file teeth of actuator. If serious burrs are found on casting surface which contact actuator during key travel, replace the casting. If gear/actuator teeth show excessive wear or are burred, replace them. Assemble lock housing assembly taking care to thoroughly lube all internal components and check key efforts. If still high, replace lock housing as an assembly.
	Shrouds mis-aligned.	Check to see if lock cylinder rubs shroud	Align shroud to fit properly.
	Defective ignition switch.	Check ignition switch for travel ease ("off" to "on" position).	If ignition switch efforts are excessive, replace the ignition switch. NOTE: *When assembling a lock housing, care should be taken to bias the ignition switch.*

switch is binding or sticking check for the following;
- Burrs on the ignition key
- Binding lock cylinder
- Shroud rubbing against the lock cylinder
- Burrs in the column mounted activator
- Burrs in the lock cylinder housing

REMOVAL AND INSTALLATION

1. Disconnect the negative (ground) battery cable from the battery.
2. Remove the upper and lower steering column shrouds by taking out the five retaining screws.
3. Disconnect the electrical harness at the ignition switch.
4. Remove the nuts and bolts retaining the steering column mounting brackets and lower the steering wheel and column to the front seat.
5. Use an ⅛" drill bit and drill out the "break-off head" bolts mounting the ignition switch.
6. Take a small screw extractor (Easy Out®) and remove the bolts.
7. Remove the ignition switch by disconnecting it from the actuator pin.
NOTE: *If reinstalling the old switch, it must be adjusted to the "Lock" position. Slide the carrier of the switch to the "Lock" position and insert a 1/16" drill bit or pin through the switch housing into the carrier. This keeps the carrier from moving when the switch is connected to the actuator. It may be necessary to wiggle the carrier back and forth to line up the holes when installing the drill or pin. New switches come with a pin in place.*
8. When installing the ignition switch, rotate the key lock cylinder to the "Lock" position.
9. Install the ignition switch by connect-

Ignition Switch Diagnosis (cont.)

Condition	Possible Source	Verification	Action
	Defective lock cylinder	Check lock cylinder for ease of operation.	If lock cylinder effort is excessive, lubricate cylinder and check for burrs on key. If effort is still excessive, replace lock cylinder.
Key release mechanism is hard to activate.	Key release actuator rod holes in lock housing casting too small.	Remove upper and lower shrouds and visually inspect key release mechanism action.	Disassemble key release mechanism and open up key release hole in casting taking care not to open holes excessively. Test operation of key release mechanism. If operation is poor, replace entire rod assembly. It will be necessary to remove the steering wheel assembly and upper bearing retainer plate.
	Key release rod bent.	Remove upper and lower shrouds and visually inspect key release mechanism action.	If problem is not severe, try to manually straighten rod. Test operation of key release mechanism. If operation is poor, replace entire rod assembly. It will be necessary to remove the steering wheel assembly and upper brearing retainer plate.

ing it to the actuator and loosely installing the two new mounting screws.

10. Move the switch up the steering column until it reaches the end of its elongated screw slots. Hold the switch in position, tighten the mounting screws until the heads break off (special "break-off bolts").

11. Remove the pin or drill bit that is locking the actuator carrier in position.

12. Raise the steering column and secure the mounting brackets.

13. Connect the wiring harness to the ignition switch. Install the upper and lower steering column shrouds.

14. Connect the negative battery cable.

15. Check the ignition for operation. Make sure the car will start in Neutral and Park, if equipped with an automatic transaxle, but be sure it will not start in Drive or Reverse. Make sure the steering (wheel) locks when the key switch is in the LOCK position.

Ignition Lock Cylinder Assembly
REMOVAL AND INSTALLATION

1. Disconnect the negative (ground) battery cable from the battery.

2. Remove the steering column lower shroud.

3. Disconnect the warning buzzer electrical connector. Turn the key cylinder to the Run position.

4. Take a 1/8" diameter pin or small punch and push on the cylinder retaining pin. The pin is visible through a hole in the mounting surrounding the key cylinder. As you push on the pin pull out on the lock cylinder.

5. To reinstall the switch, make sure it is in the RUN position. Push in on the retaining pin and insert the cylinder into the casting. Be sure it is fully seated and aligned with the interlocking washer. Turn the key cylinder to the OFF position. When the lock cylinder is

154 SUSPENSION AND STEERING

turned to the OFF position, the retaining pin locks the cylinder into the casting.

6. Rotate the lock cylinder through the different positions to make sure it is working freely.

7. Connect the wire to the buzzer, mount the lower shroud, connect the battery cable and test the operation of the lock cylinder.

Manual Rack and Pinion Steering

If your car is equipped with manual steering, it is of the rack and pinion type. The gear input shaft is connected to the steering shaft by a double U-joint. A pinion gear, machined on the input shaft, engages the rack. The rotation of the input shaft pinion causes the rack to move laterally. The rack has two tie rods whose ends are connected to the front wheels. When the rack moves so do the front wheel knuckles. Toe adjustment is made by turning the outer tie-rod ends; in or out equally as required.

REMOVAL AND INSTALLATION

1. Disconnect the negative battery cable from the battery. Jack up the front of the car and support it safely on jackstands.

2. Turn the ignition switch to the ON position. Remove the lower access (kick) panel from below the steering wheel.

3. Remove the intermediate shaft bolts at the gear input shaft and at the steering column shaft.

4. Spread the slots of the clamp to loosen the intermediate shaft at both ends. The next steps must be performed before the intermediate shaft and gear input shaft can be separated.

5. Turn the steering wheel full left so the tie rod will clear the shift linkage. Separate the outer tie rod ends from the steering knuckle by using a tie rod end remover.

6. Remove the left tie rod end from the tie rod (wheel must be at full left position). Disconnect the speedometer cable from the transmission if the car is equipped with an automatic transaxle. Disconnect the secondary air tube at the check valve. Disconnect the exhaust pipe from the exhaust manifold and wire it out of the way to allow enough room to remove the steering gear.

7. Remove the exhaust hanger bracket from below the steering gear. Remove the steering gear mounting brackets and rubber mounting insulators.

8. Have someone help by holding the gear from the inside of the car. Separate the intermediate shaft from the input shaft.

9. Make sure the gear is still in the full left turn position. Rotate the gear forward and down to clear the input shaft through the opening. Move the gear to the right to clear the splash panel and other linkage that interferes with the removal. Lower the gear and remove from under the car.

10. Installation is in the reverse order of removal. Have the toe adjustment checked after installing a new rack and pinion assembly.

Integral Power Rack and Pinion Steering

Power steering is optional on Escort/Lynx. A rotary design control valve uses relative rotational motion of the input shaft and valve sleeve to direct fluid flow. When the steering wheel is turned, resistance of the wheels and the weight of the car cause a "torsion" bar to twist. The twisting causes the valve to move in the sleeve and aligns fluid passages for right/left and straight ahead position. The pressure forces on the valve and helps move the rack to assist in the turning effort. The piston is attached directly to the rack. The housing tube functions as the power cylinder. The hydraulic areas of the gear assembly are always filled with fluid. The mechanical gears are filled with grease making periodic lubrication unnecessary. The fluid and grease act as a cushion to absorb road shock.

REMOVAL AND INSTALLATION

Removal and installation is basically the same as the manual rack and pinion steering. However, the pressure and return lines must be disconnected at the intermediate connectors and drained of fluid. It is necessary to remove the pressure switch from the pressure line.

Brakes

BRAKE SYSTEM

Understanding the Brakes Hydraulic System

BASIC OPERATING PRINCIPLES

Hydraulic systems are used to actuate the brakes of all modern automobiles. The system transports the power required to force the frictional surfaces of the braking system together from the pedal to the individual brake units at each wheel. A hydraulic system is used for two reasons. First, fluid under pressure can be carried to all parts of an automobile by small hoses—some of which are flexible—without taking up a significant amount of room or posing routing problems. Second, a great mechanical advantage can be given to the brake pedal end of the system, and the foot pressure required to actuate the brakes can be reduced by making the surface area of the master cylinder pistons smaller than that of any of the pistons in the wheel cylinders or calipers.

The master cylinder consists of a double reservoir and piston assembly as well as other springs, fittings etc. Double (dual) master cylinders are designed to separate two wheels from the others. Your car's braking system is separated diagonally. That is; the right front and left rear use one reservoir and the left front and right rear use the other.

Steel lines carry the brake fluid to a point on the car's frame near each wheel. A flexible hose usually carries the fluid to the disc caliper or wheel cylinder. The flexible line allows for suspension and steering movements.

The rear wheel cylinders contain two pistons each, one at either end, which push outward in opposite directions. The front disc brake calipers contain one piston each.

All pistons employ some type of seal, usually made of rubber, to minimize fluid leakage. A rubber dust boot seals the outer end of the cylinder against dust and dirt. The boot fits around the outer end of the piston on disc brake calipers, and around the brake actuating rod on wheel cylinders.

The hydraulic system operates as follows: When at rest, the entire system, from the piston(s) in the master cylinder to those in the wheel cylinders or calipers, is full of brake fluid. Upon application of the brake pedal, fluid trapped in front of the master cylinder piston(s) is forced through the lines to the wheel cylinders. Here, it forces the pistons outward, in the case of drum brakes, and inward toward the disc, in the case of disc brakes. The motion of the pistons is opposed by return springs mounted outside the cyl-

156 BRAKES

inders in drum brakes, and by internal springs or spring seals, in disc brakes.

Upon release of the brake pedal, a spring located inside the master cylinder immediately returns the master cylinder pistons to the normal position. The pistons contain check valves and the master cylinder has compensating ports drilled in it. These are uncovered as the pistons reach their normal position. The piston check valves allow fluid to flow toward the wheel cylinders or calipers as the pistons withdraw. Then, as the return springs force the brake pads or shoes into the released position, the excess fluid reservoir through the compensating ports. It is during the time the pedal is in the released position that any fluid that has leaked out of the system will be replaced from the reservoirs through the compensating ports.

The dual master cylinder has two pistons, located one behind the other. The primary piston is actuated directly by mechanical linkage from the brake pedal. The secondary piston is actuated by fluid trapped between the two pistons. If a leak develops in front of the secondary piston, it moves forward until it bottoms against the front of the master cylinder. The fluid trapped between the pistons will operate one side of the diagonal system. If the other side of the system develops a leak, the primary piston will move forward until direct contact with the secondary piston takes place, and it will force the secondary piston to acuate the other side of the diagonal system. In either case the brake pedal drops closer to the floor board and less braking power is available.

The brake system uses a switch to warn the driver when only half of the brake system is operational. This switch is located in a valve body which is mounted on the firewall or the frame below the master cylinder. A hydraulic piston receives pressure from both circuits, each circuit's pressure being applied to one end of the piston. When the pressures are in balance, the piston remains stationary. When one circuit has a leak, however, the greater pressure in that circuit during application of the brakes will push the piston to one side, closing the switch and activating the brake warning light.

In disc brake systems, this valve body contains a metering valve and, in some cases, a proportioning valve or valves. The metering valve keeps pressure from traveling to the disc brakes on the front wheels until the brake shoes on the rear wheels have contacted the drums, ensuring that the front brakes will never be used alone. The proportioning valve controls the pressure to the rear brakes to avoid rear wheel lock-up during very hard braking.

Warning lights may be tested by depressing the brake pedal and holding it while opening one of the wheel cylinder bleeder screws. If this does not cause the light to go on, substitute a new lamp, make continuity checks, and, finally, replace the switch as necessary.

The hydraulic system may be checked for leaks by applying pressure to the pedal gradually and steadily. If the pedal sinks very slowly to the floor, the system as a leak. This is not to be confused with a springy or spongy feel due to the compression of air within the lines. If the system leaks, there will be a gradual change in the position of the pedal with a constant pressure.

Check for leaks along all lines and at wheel cylinders or calipers. If no external leaks are apparent, the problem is inside the master cylinder.

Disc Brakes
BASIC OPERATING PRINCIPLES

Instead of the traditional expanding brakes that press outward against a circular drum, disc brake systems utilize a disc (rotor) with brake pads positioned on either side of it. Braking effect is achieved in a manner similar to the way you would squeeze a spinning phonograph record between your fingers. The disc (rotor) is a casting with cooling fins between the two braking surfaces. This enables air to circulate between the braking surfaces making them less sensitive to heat buildup and more resistant to fade. Dirt and water do not affect braking action since contaminants are thrown off by the centrifugal action of the rotor or scraped off by the pads. Also, the equal clamping action of the two brake pads tends to ensure uniform, straightline stops. Disc brakes are inherently self-adjusting.

Your car uses a pin slider front wheel caliper. The brake pad on the inside of the brake rotor is moved in contact with the rotor by hydraulic pressure. The caliper, which is not held in a fixed position, moves slightly, bringing the outside brake pad into contact with the disc rotor.

Drum Brakes (Rear)
BASIC OPERATING PRINCIPLES

Drum brakes employ two brake shoes mounted on a stationary backing plate. These shoes are positioned inside a circular drum which rotates with the wheel assembly. The shoes are held in place by springs; this allows them to slide toward the drums (when they are applied) while keeping the linings and drums in alignment. The shoes are actuated by a wheel cylinder which is mounted at the top of the backing plate. When the brakes are applied, hydraulic pressure forces the wheel cylinder's actuating links outward. Since these links bear directly against the top of the brake shoes, the tops of the shoes are then forced against the inner side of the drum. This action forces the bottoms of the two shoes to contact the brake drum by rotating the entire assembly slightly (known as servo action). When pressure within the wheel cylinder is relaxed, return springs pull the shoes back away from the drum.

The rear drum brakes on your car are designed to self-adjust themselves during application. Motion causes both shoes to rotate very slightly with the drum, rocking an adjusting lever, thereby causing rotation of the adjusting screw or lever.

Power Brake Boosters

Power brakes operate just as standard brake systems except in the actuation of the master cylinder pistons. A vacuum diaphragm is located on the front of the master cylinder and assists the driver in applying the brakes, reducing both the effort and travel he must put into moving the brake pedal.

The vacuum diaphragm housing is connected to the intake manifold by a vacuum hose. A check valve is placed at the point where the hose enters the diaphragm housing, so that during periods of low manifold vacuum brake assist vacuum will not be lost.

Depressing the brake pedal closes off the vacuum source and allows atmospheric pressure to enter on one side of the diaphragm. This causes the master cylinder pistons to move and apply the brakes. When the brake pedal is released, vacuum is applied to both sides of the diaphragm, and return springs return the diaphragm and master cylinder pistons to the released position. If the vacuum fails, the brake pedal rod will butt against the end of the master cylinder actuating rod, and direct mechanical application will occur as the pedal is depressed.

The hydraulic and mechanical problems that apply to conventional brake systems also apply to power brakes, and should be checked for if the tests below do not reveal the problem.

Test for a system vacuum leak as described below:

1. Operate the engine at idle without touching the brake pedal for at least one minute.
2. Turn off the engine, and wait one minute.
3. Test for the presence of assist vacuum by depressing the brake pedal and releasing it several times. Light application will produce less and less pedal travel, if vacuum was present. If there is no vacuum, air is leaking into the system somewhere.

Test for system operation as follows:

1. Pump the brake pedal (with engine off) until the supply vacuum is entirely gone.
2. Put a light, steady pressure on the pedal.
3. Start the engine, and operate it at idle. If the system is operating, the brake pedal should fall toward the floor if constant pressure is maintained on the pedal.

Power brake systems may be tested for hydraulic leaks just as ordinary systems are tested.

Brake Adjustment
FRONT DISC BRAKES

Front disc brakes require no adjustment. Hydraulic pressure maintains the proper pad-to-disc contact at all times.

REAR DRUM BRAKES

The rear drum brakes, on your car, are self-adjusting. The only adjustment necessary is an initial one after new brake shoes have been installed or some type of service work has been done on the rear brake system.

> NOTE: *After any brake service, obtain a firm brake pedal before moving the car. Adjusted brakes must not drag; the wheel must turn freely. Be sure the parking brake cables are not too tightly adjusted.*

> NOTE: *A special brake shoe gauge is necessary, if your car is equipped with 8 inch brakes, for making an accurate adjustment after installing new brake shoes. The spe-*

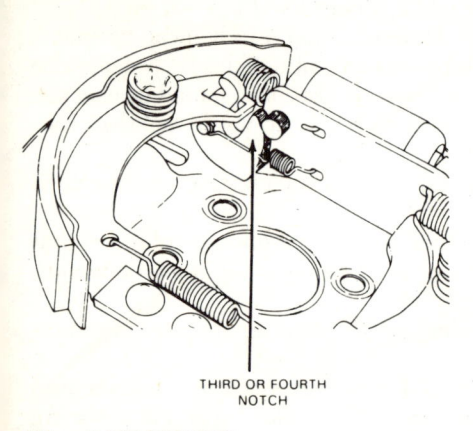

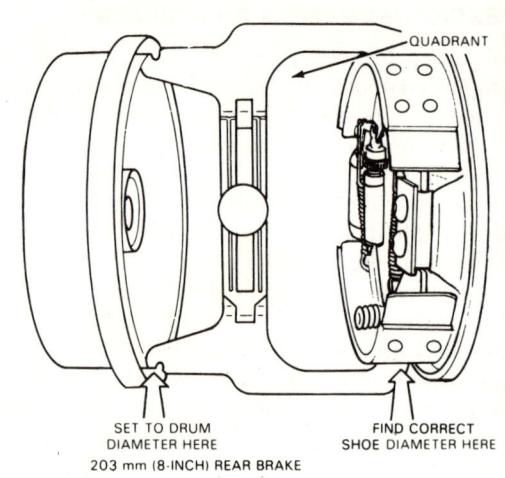

158 BRAKES

Rear brake shoe adjustment

cial gauge measures both the drum diameter and the brake shoe setting.

Since no adjustment is necessary except when service work is done on the rear brakes, we will assume that the car is jacked up and safely supported by jackstands, and that the rear drums have been removed. (If not, refer to the appropriate sections of this Chapter for the procedures necessary).

Cars Equipped With 7 Inch Brakes (Three-Door Models)

Pivot the adjuster quadrant (see illustration) until the third or fourth notch from the outer end of the quadrant meshes with the knurled pin on the adjuster strut. Install the hub and drum.

Cars Equipped With 8 Inch Brakes (Four-Door and Sport Models)

Measure and set the special brake gauge to the inside diameter of the brake drum. Lift the adjuster lever from the starwheel teeth. Turn the starwheel until the brake shoes are adjusted out to the shoe setting fingers of the brake gauge. Install the hub and drum.

NOTE: *Complete the adjustment (7 or 8 inch brakes) by applying the brakes several times. After the brakes have been properly adjusted, check their operation by making several stops from varying forward speeds.*

Master Cylinder

The fluid reservoir of the master cylinder has a large and small compartment. The larger serves the right front and left rear brakes, while the smaller serves the left front and right rear brakes.

Always be sure that the fluid level of the reservoirs is within ¼ inch of the top. Use only DOT 3 approved brake fluid.

MODELS WITHOUT POWER BRAKES
Removal

1. Disconnect the negative (ground) battery cable from the battery.
2. From under the dash panel, disconnect the wires to the stoplight switch. Remove the spring clip that retains the stoplight switch and the master cylinder pushrod to the brake pedal.
3. Slide the stoplight switch off the brake pedal pin. Remove the switch.
4. From under the hood; loosen the two retaining nuts mounting the master cylinder to the firewall. Disconnect the brake lines from the master cylinder.
5. Slide the master cylinder pushrod, washers and bushings from the brake pedal pin.

NOTE: *Models with speed control have an adapter instead of a washer on the brake pedal mounting pin.*

6. Remove the cylinder mounting nuts. Lift the cylinder out and away from the firewall.

CAUTION: *Take care not to spill any brake fluid on the painted surfaces of your car. If you spill any on your car, flush off with water as soon as possible. Brake fluid will act like a paint remover.*

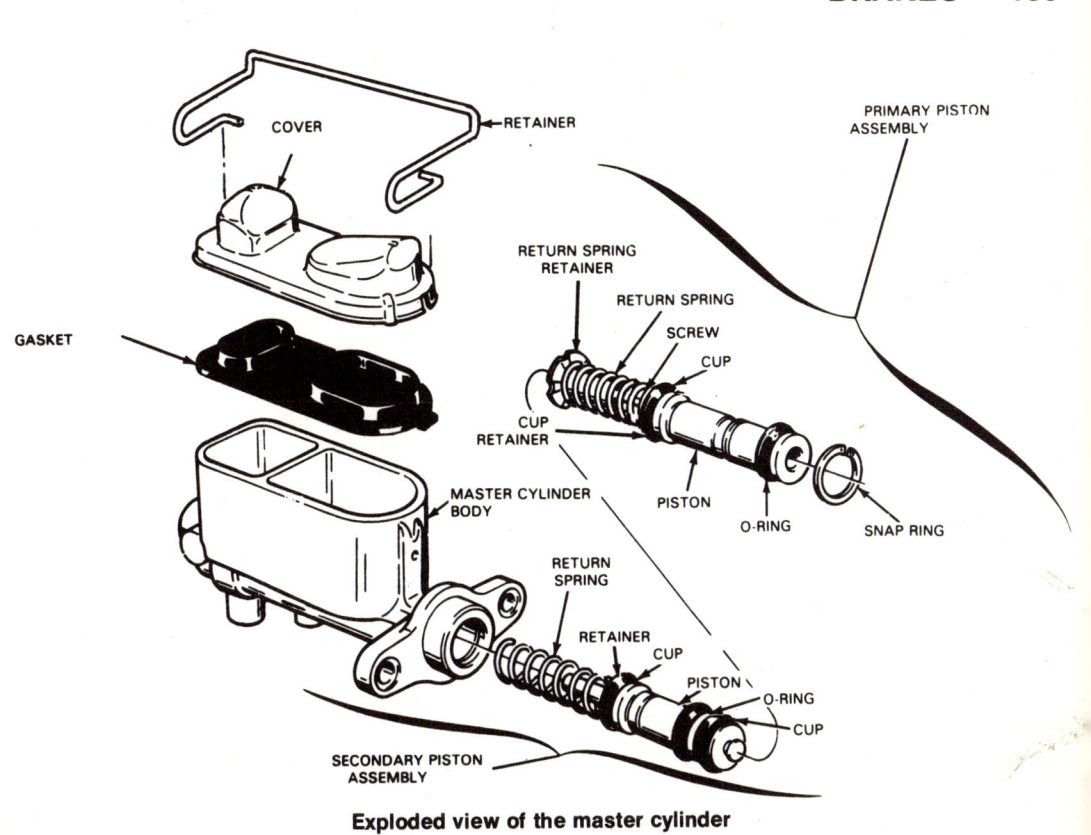

BRAKES 159

Exploded view of the master cylinder

Installation

1. Insert the master cylinder pushrod through the opening in the firewall. Place the cylinder mounting flange over the studs on the firewall and loosely install the mounting nuts.
2. Coat the nylon pushrod mounting bushing with oil. Install the washer, pushrod and bushing on the brake pedal shaft. (Speed control models use a snap-on adapter instead of a washer).
3. Position the stoplight switch on the brake pedal pin. Install the nylon bushing and washer and secure with the spring pin.
4. Connect the wires to the stoplight switch.
5. Connect the brake lines to the master cylinder, but do not tighten them completely.
6. Secure the cylinder mounting nuts. Fill the master cylinder to within ¼ inch of the top. Slowly pump the brake pedal to help evacuate the air in the master cylinder.
   NOTE: *Cover the brake line connections (at the master cylinder) with a rag to prevent brake fluid spray.*
7. Tighten the brake lines at the master cylinder. Add brake fluid if necessary.
8. Connect the negative battery cable. Bleed the entire brake system. Centralize the pressure differential valve (refer to the following sections).
8. Check for hydraulic leaks. Road test the car.

POWER BRAKE MODELS

Removal

1. Disconnect the brake lines from the master cylinder.
2. Remove the two nuts that mount the master cylinder to the brake booster.
3. Pull the master cylinder forward and away from the booster.
   CAUTION: *Brake fluid acts like a paint remover. If you spill any on the finish of your car; flush off with water.*

Installation

1. Slip the master cylinder base over the pushrod at the power brake booster. Align the mounting flange and place over the mounting studs on the booster. Loosely secure with the two mounting nuts.
2. Connect the brake lines to the master cylinder. Tighten the mounting nuts. Tighten the brake lines.

3. Fill the master cylinder to within ¼ inch of the top. Bleed the brake system. Centralize the pressure differential valve (refer to the following sections). Check for system leaks. Road test the car.

MASTER CYLINDER OVERHAUL

Referring to the exploded view of the dual master cylinder components, disassemble the unit as follows: Clean the exterior of the cylinder and remove the filler cover and diaphragm. Any brake fluid remaining in the cylinder should be poured out and discarded. Remove the secondary piston stop bolt from the bottom of the cylinder and remove the bleed screw, if required. With the primary piston depressed, remove the snap-ring from its retaining groove at the rear of the cylinder bore. Withdraw the pushrod and the primary piston assembly from the bore.

NOTE: *Do not remove the screw that retains the primary return spring retainer, return spring, primary cup and protector on the primary piston. The assembly is adjusted at the factory and should not be disassembled.*

Remove the secondary piston assembly.

NOTE: *Do not remove the outlet tube seats, outlet check valves and outlet check valve springs from the cylinder body.*

All components should be cleaned in clean isopropyl alcohol or clean brake fluid and inspected for chipping, excessive wear and damage. Check to ensure that all recesses, openings and passageways are clear and free of foreign matter. Dirt and cleaning solvent may be removed by using compressed air. After cleaning, keep all parts on a clean surface. Inspect the cylinder bore for etching, pitting, scoring or rusting. If necessary, the cylinder bore may be honed to repair damage, but never to a diameter greater than the original diameter plus 0.003 in.

During the assembly operation, be sure to use all parts supplied with the master cylinder repair kit. With the exception of the master cylinder body, submerge all parts in extra heavy duty brake fluid. Carefully insert the complete secondary piston and return spring assembly into the cylinder bore and install the primary piston assembly into the bore. With the primary piston depressed, install the snap-ring into its groove in the cylinder bore. Install the pushrod, boot and retainer (if equipped), then install the pushrod assembly into the primary piston. Be sure that the retainer is properly seated and is holding the pushrod securely. Position the inner end of the pushrod boot (if equipped) in the master cylinder body retaining groove. Install the secondary piston stop bolt and O-ring at the bottom of the master cylinder body. Install the bleed screw (if equipped) and position the gasket on the master cylinder filler cover. Be sure that the gasket is securely seated. Reinstall the master cylinder and fill with brake fluid. Install the cover and secure with the retainer. Bleed the brake system and road test the car.

VACUUM BOOSTER REMOVAL AND INSTALLATION

1. Working from inside the car, beneath the instrument panel, remove the booster pushrod from the brake pedal.
2. Disconnect the stop light switch wires and remove the switch from the brake pedal. Use care not to damage the switch during removal.
3. Raise the hood and remove the master cylinder from the booster.
4. Remove the manifold vacuum hose from the booster.
5. Remove the booster to firewall attaching bolts and remove the booster from the car.
6. Reverse above procedure to reinstall.

TESTING THE POWER BRAKE BOOSTER

The power brake booster depends on vacuum produced by the engine for proper operation.

If you suspect problems in the power brake system, check the following:

1. Inspect all hoses and hose connections. All unused vacuum connectors should be sealed. Hoses and connections should be tightly secured and in good condition. The hoses should be pliable with no holes or cracks and no collapsed areas.
2. Inspect the check valve which is located in line between the intake manifold and booster. Disconnect the hose on the intake manifold side of the valve. Attempt to blow through the valve. If air passes through the valve, it is defective and must be replaced.
3. Check the level of brake fluid in the master cylinder. If the level is low, check the system for fluid leaks.
4. Idle the engine briefly and then shut it off. Pump the brake pedal several times to exhaust all of the vacuum stored in the booster. Keep the brake pedal depressed and

start the engine. The brake pedal should drop slightly, if vacuum is present after the engine is started less pressure should be necessary on the brake pedal. If no drop, or action is felt the power brake booster should be suspect.

5. With the parking brake applied and the wheels blocked, start the engine and allow to idle in Neutral (Park if automatic). Disconnect the vacuum line to the check valve on the intake manifold side. If vacuum is felt, connect the hose and repeat Step 4. Once again, if no action is felt on the brake pedal, suspect the booster.

6. Operate the engine at a fast idle for about ten seconds, shut off the engine. Allow the car to sit for about ten minutes. Depress the brake pedal with moderate force (about 20 pounds). The pedal should feel about the same as when the engine was running. If the brake pedal feels hard (no power assist) suspect the power booster.

Valves

CONTROL VALVE

The brake system of your car contains a control valve assembly that consists of a pressure differential and dual proportioning valve (separate valves control the left and right rear brakes).

PRESSURE DIFFERENTIAL VALVE

If a loss of brake fluid occurs on either side of the diagonally split system when the brakes are applied, a piston mounted in the valve moves off center allowing the brakes on the non-leaking side of the split system to operate. When the piston moves off center a brake warning switch, located in the center of the valve body, will turn on a dash mounted warning light indicating brake problems.

After repairs are made on the brake system and the system bled, the warning switch will reset itself when you pump the brake pedal and the dash light will turn off.

PROPORTIONING VALVE

The dual proportioning valve, located between the rear brake system inlet and outlet ports, controls the rear brake system hydraulic pressure. When the brakes are applied, the dual proportioning valve reduces pressure to the rear wheels and provides balanced braking.

TROUBLESHOOTING THE PROPORTIONING VALVE

If the rear brakes lock-up during light brake application or do not lock-up under heavy braking the problem could be with the dual proportioning valve.

1. Check tires and tire pressures.
2. Check the brake linings for thickness, and for contamination by fluid, grease etc.
3. Check the brake system hoses, steel lines, calipers and wheel cylinders for leaks.
4. If none of the proceeding checks have uncovered any problems, suspect the proportioning valve.

NOTE: *Take the car to a qualified service center and ask them to do a pressure test on the valve. If a pressure test is not possible, replace the control valve.*

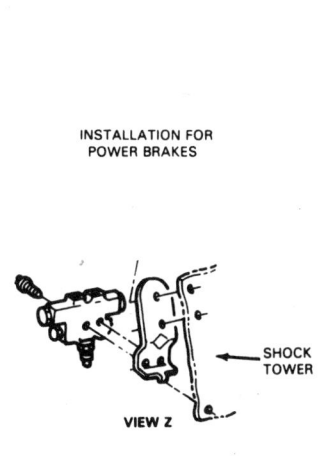

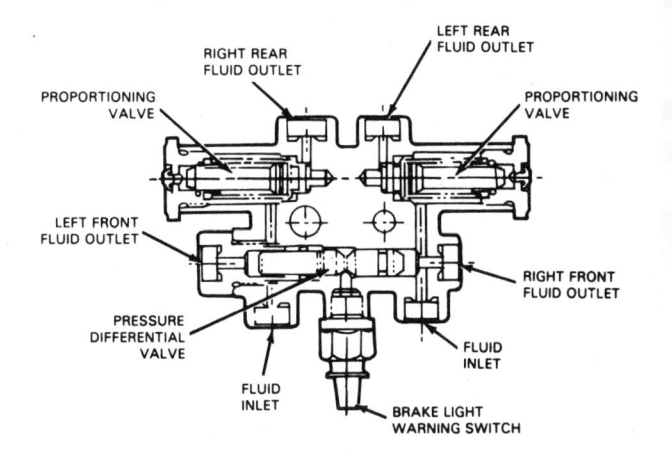

Combination brake valve

Brake Control Valve Replacement

The brake control valve is located to the left and below the master cylinder and mounted to the shock (strut) tower by a removable bracket. Use the proper size flare wrench and disconnect the brake lines to the valve. Disconnect the warning switch wire. Remove the bolt(s) retaining the valve to the mount and remove the valve. Installation is in the reverse order of removal. Bleed the brake system after installing the new valve.

Bleeding the Brake System

It is necessary to bleed the brake system of air whenever a hydraulic component, of the system, has been rebuilt or replaced, or if the brakes feel spongy during application.

Your car has a diagonally split brake system. Each side of this system must be bled as an individual system. **Bleed the right rear brake, left front brake, left rear brake and right front brake—always start with the longest line from the master cylinder first.**

CAUTION: *When bleeding the system(s) never allow the master cylinder to run completely out of brake fluid. Always use DOT 3 heavy duty brake fluid or the equivalent. Never reuse brake fluid that has been drained from the system or that has been allowed to stand in an opened container for an extended period of time. If your car is equipped with power brakes, remove the reserve vacuum stored in the booster by pumping the brake pedal several times before bleeding the brakes.*

1. Clean all of the dirt away from the master cylinder filler cap.
2. Raise and support the car on jackstands. Make sure your car is safely supported and it is raised evenly front and back.
3. Starting with the right rear wheel cylinder. Remove the dust cover from the bleeder screw. Place the proper size box wrench over the bleeder fitting and attach a piece of rubber tubing (about three feet long and snug fitting) over the end of the fitting.
4. Submerge the free end of the rubber tube into a container half filled with clean brake fluid.
5. Have a friend pump up the brake pedal and then push down to apply the brakes while you loosen the bleeder screw. When the pedal reaches the bottom of its travel close the bleeder fitting before your friend releases the brake pedal.
6. Repeat Step 5 until air bubbles cease to appear in the container in which the tubing is submerged. Tighten the fitting, remove the rubber tubing and replace the dust cover.
7. Repeat Steps 3 through 6 to the left front wheel, then to the left rear and right front.

NOTE: *Refill the master cylinder after each wheel cylinder or caliper is bled. Be sure the master cylinder top gasket is mounted correctly and the brake fluid level is within ¼ inch of the top.*

8. After bleeding the brakes, pump the brake pedal several times; this ensures proper seating of the rear linings and the front caliper pistons.

FRONT DISC BRAKES

Disc Brake Pads

INSPECTION

1. Loosen the front wheel lugs slightly, then raise the front of the car and safely support it on jackstands.
2. Remove the front wheel and tire assemblies.
3. The cut out in the top of the front brake caliper allows visual inspection of the disc brake pad. If the lining is worn to within ⅛ inch of the metal disc shoe (check local inspection requirements) replace all four pads (both sides).
4. While you are inspecting the brake pads, visually inspect the caliper for hydraulic fluid leaks. If a leak is visible the caliper will have to be rebuilt or replaced.

PAD REMOVAL AND INSTALLATION

1. Loosen the front wheel lugs slightly, then raise the front of the car and safely support it on jackstands.
2. Remove the front wheel and tire assemblies.
3. Remove the master cylinder cap. Siphon off some fluid from each reservoir until they are half full. Replace the cap.
4. Remove the anti-rattle spring from the bottom of the caliper by pushing up on the center until the tabs are free of the mounting holes.
5. Backout the Torx headed caliper locating pins. DO NOT REMOVE THEM ALL THE WAY. If removed, the pins are difficult to install and require new guide bushings.
6. Lift the caliper assembly from the knuckle, anchor plate and rotor.

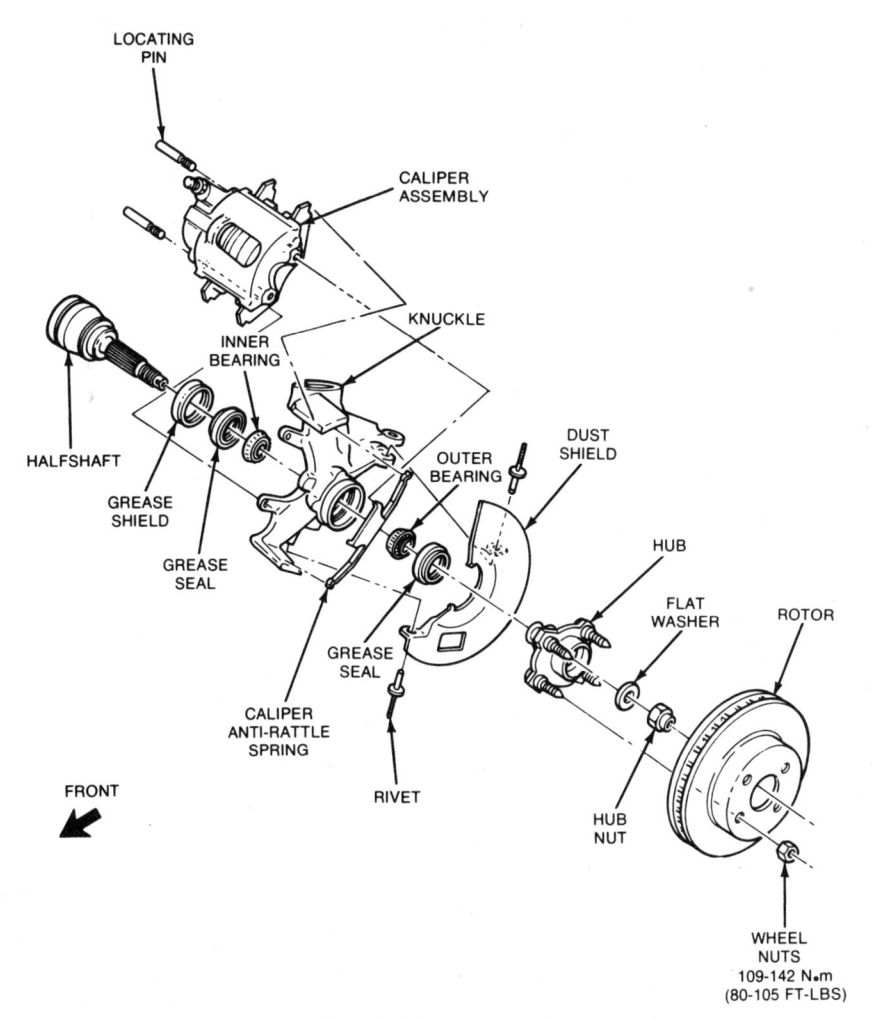

Disc brake components

7. Remove the outer and inner disc brake pads. The outer pad has two clips that fit into the bosses on the outer edge of the caliper. The inner pad uses a three point clip that fits inside the caliper piston.

8. Suspend the caliper, with wire, inside the fender housing.

CAUTION: *Do not suspend in such a way to put stress on the brake hose.*

9. Use a 4 inch "C" clamp and a block of 2¾ inch by 1 inch piece of wood to seat the caliper piston back in its bore. Place the wood against the face of the piston, attach the clamp and slowly close it pushing the piston into the caliper. Extra care must be taken during this procedure to prevent damage to the aluminum piston.

NOTE: *The piston must be fully seated in its bore to provide clearance for the caliper with the new pads to fit over the disc rotor.*

10. Install the inner brake pad with the mounting clips onto the caliper piston. Install the outer pad, make sure the clips are properly seated on the caliper bosses.

11. Unwire the caliper from the fender well. Mount the caliper over the rotor and fasten the Torx headed pins. Reinstall the anti-rattle spring making sure it is firmly located in the mounting holes.

12. Refill the master cylinder to correct levels.

13. Pump the brakes several times to position the new pads.

14. Install the wheels and tighten the lugs snugly.

164 BRAKES

15. Lower the car from the jackstands. Tighten the lug nuts to 80–105 ft. lbs.

16. Road test the car.

Overhauling the Caliper

1. Follow Steps 1–3 of the Pad Removal and Installation procedure.

2. Disconnect the hydraulic brake hose from the caliper. To disconnect the hose, loosen the tube fitting at the frame bracket. Remove the horseshoe clip from between the hose and bracket. Remove the hollow bolt fastening the hose to the caliper and remove the hose. Do not loosen the two gaskets used in mounting the brake hose to the caliper.

3. Follow Steps 4–7 of the Pad Removal and Installation procedure.

4. The next step requires a controllable air source. If you have one fine, if not take the caliper(s) to your local gas station and ask them to do Step 5 for you.

5. Place a folded cloth, shop rag, etc. over the caliper piston. Apply air pressure through the brake line fitting hole with a rubber tipped air blow gun. The air pressure will force the caliper piston from its bore. If the piston is seized, tap lightly on the caliper with a plastic hammer while applying air pressure.

CAUTION: *Apply air pressure slowly. Pressure can build up inside the caliper and the piston may come out with considerable force.*

6. Remove the dust boot and piston seal from the caliper. Clean all parts with alcohol or clean brake fluid. Blow out the passageways in the caliper. Check the condition of the caliper bore and piston. If they are pitted or scored or show excessive wear, replacement will be necessary. Slight scoring in the caliper bore may be cleaned up by light honing. Replace the piston if it is scored or gaulded.

7. Apply a coating of brake fluid to the new caliper piston seal and caliper bore. Some rebuilding kits provide a lubricant for this purpose. Install the seal in the caliper bore

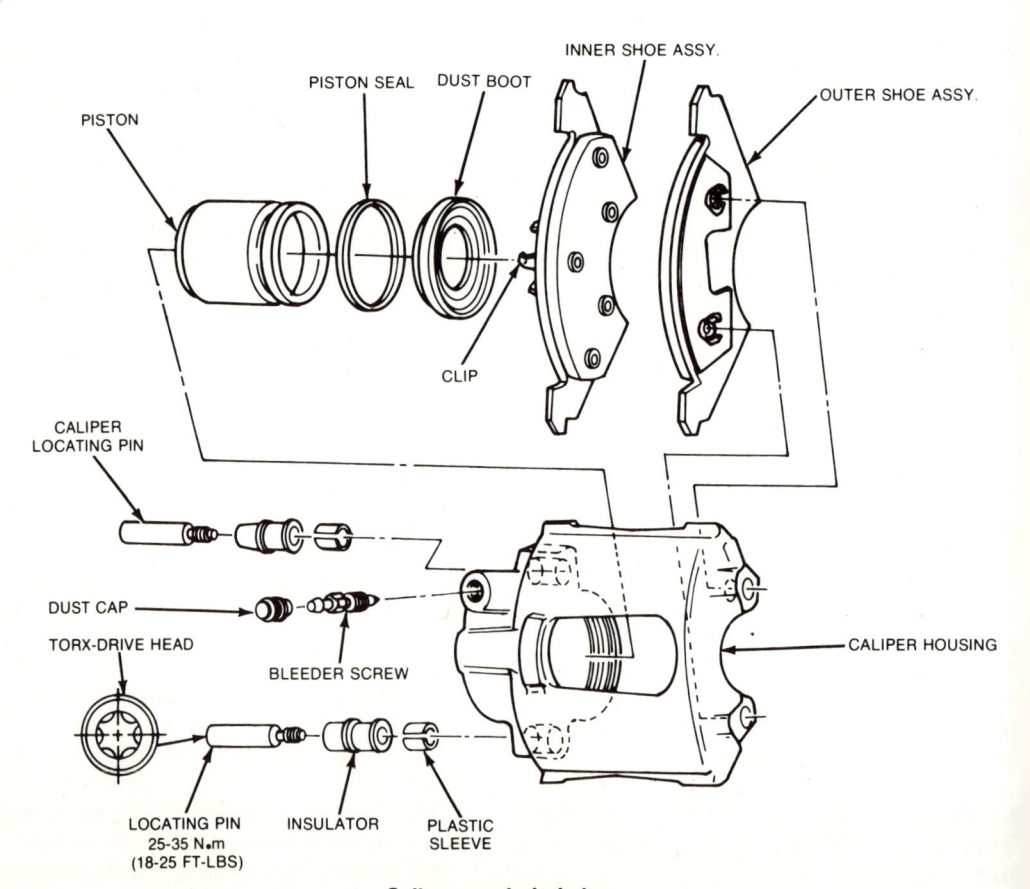

Caliper, exploded view

BRAKES 165

make sure it is not twisted and is firmly seated in the groove.

8. Install the new dust seal in the caliper mounting groove, be sure it is mounted firmly.

9. Coat the piston with clean brake fluid or the special lubricant and install it in the caliper bore, make sure it is firmly seated to the bottom of the caliper bore. Spread the dust boot over the piston and seat in the piston groove.

10. Install the brake pads as outlined in the previous section.

11. Install the caliper over the rotor. Mount the caliper as described in the previous section.

12. Install the brake hose to the caliper. Be sure to use a new gasket on each side of the hose fitting. Position and install the upper end of the hose, remember to put the horseshoe clip in place, take care not to twist the hose.

13. Bleed the brake system and centralize the brake warning switch.

14. Fill the master cylinder to the correct level. Refer to Steps 12–15 of the Pad Removal and Installation for the remaining procedures.

Front Brake Rotor

REMOVAL AND INSTALLATION

1. Follow Steps 1–6 of the Pad Removal and Installation omitting Step 3 (it is not necessary to siphon off any brake fluid).

2. Suspend the caliper with a piece of wire from the fender support, do not put any stress on the brake hose.

3. Pull the rotor outward from the wheel hub.

4. Installation is in the reverse order of removal.

Front Wheel Bearings

The front wheel bearings of your Escort/Lynx are Timken "Set-Right." The bearing design relies on component stack-up and deformation/torque at assembly to determine bearing setting. The bearings, therefore, cannot be adjusted after assembly. There is no scheduled maintenance required.

The front bearings are located in the front suspension knuckle, not in the rotor or wheel hub. Two inner and one outer seal protect the bearings (the seal closer to the CV joint is a shield). The wheel hub is installed with a close slip fit through the wheel bearings and an interference fit over the splines of the halfshaft's constant velocity stub shaft. A flat washer and a staked hub nut maintain the correct endplay and prevent the wheel bearing inner races from spinning on the wheel hub.

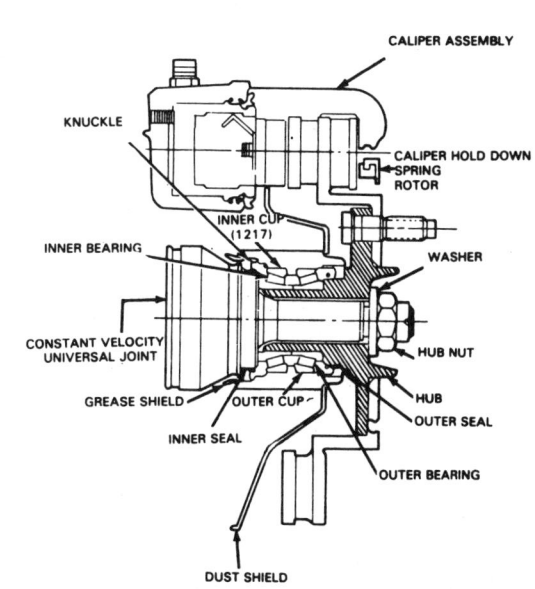

Cross section view of the front wheel bearings

REMOVAL

NOTE: *The wheel hub and knuckle must be removed for bearing replacement or servicing. A special puller is required to remove and install the hub. (Ford Part Number T81P1104A, T81P1104C and adaptors T81P1104B). The adaptors screw over the lugs and attach to the puller, which uses a long screw attached to the end of the stub shaft to pull off or install the hub.*

1. Remove wheel cover and slightly loosen the lugs.

2. Remove the hub retaining nut and washer. The nut is crimped staked to the shaft. Use a socket and sufficient torque to overcome the locking force of the crimp.

3. Raise the front of the car and support safely with jackstands. Remove the tire and wheel assembly.

4. Remove the brake caliper and disc rotor. Refer to the proceeding sections in this Chapter for the necessary procedures.

5. Install the hub remover/installer tool and remove the hub. If the outer bearing is seized on the hub remove it with a puller.

6. Remove the front suspension knuckle.

7. After the front knuckle is removed, pull

166 BRAKES

REMOVAL

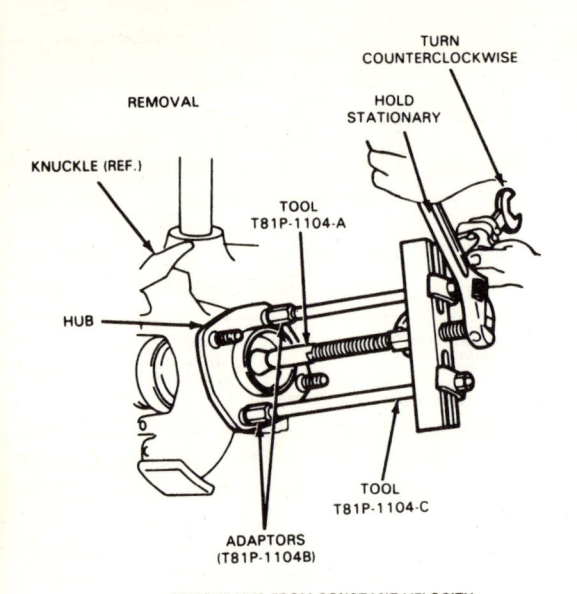

- KNUCKLE (REF.)
- HUB
- TOOL T81P-1104-A
- TURN COUNTERCLOCKWISE
- HOLD STATIONARY
- TOOL T81P-1104-C
- ADAPTORS (T81P-1104B)

REMOVE HUB FROM CONSTANT VELOCITY UNIVERSAL JOINT SPLINED STUB SHAFT AS SHOWN

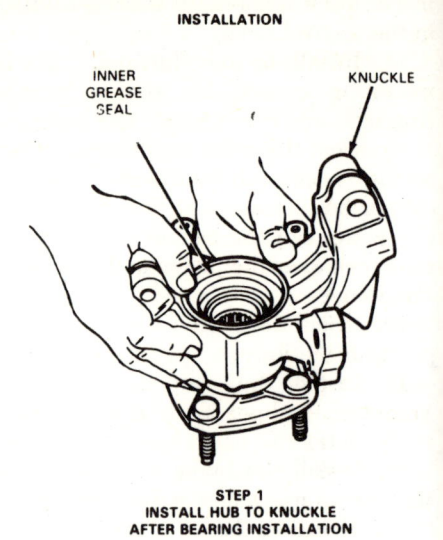

INSTALLATION

- INNER GREASE SEAL
- KNUCKLE

**STEP 1
INSTALL HUB TO KNUCKLE
AFTER BEARING INSTALLATION**

KNUCKLE MUST BE POSITIONED AS SHOWN AND HUB MUST BE INSERTED THROUGH BEARINGS USING HAND PRESSURE ONLY

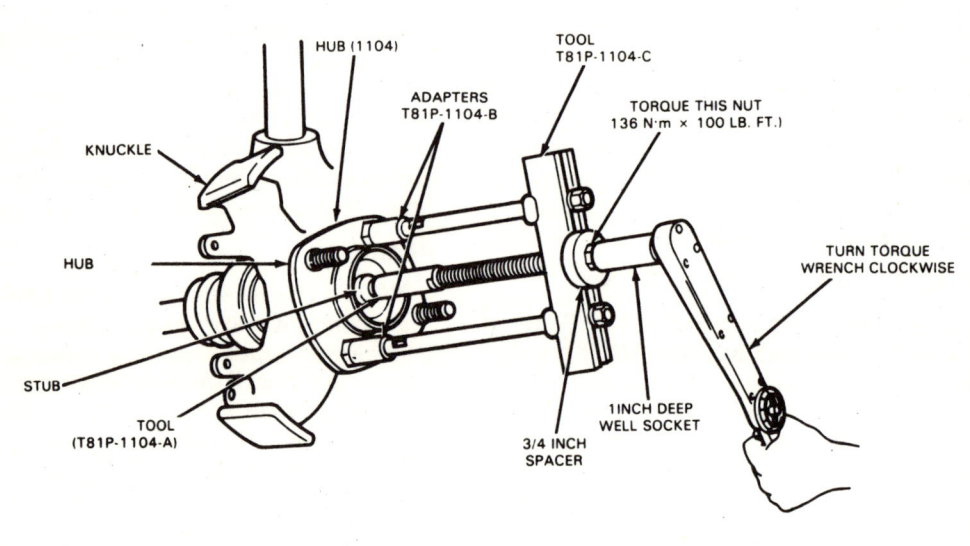

- KNUCKLE
- HUB
- STUB
- TOOL (T81P-1104-A)
- HUB (1104)
- ADAPTERS T81P-1104-B
- TOOL T81P-1104-C
- TORQUE THIS NUT 136 N·m × 100 LB. FT.)
- TURN TORQUE WRENCH CLOCKWISE
- 1 INCH DEEP WELL SOCKET
- 3/4 INCH SPACER

**STEP 2
INSTALL HUB TO CONSTANT
VELOCITY UNIVERSAL JOINT
SPLINED STUB SHAFT**

TIGHTEN TOOL NUT TO 150 N·m (110 lb-ft) USING TORQUE WRENCH TO SEAT HUB

Using the front stub shaft remover/installer tool

out the inner grease shield, the inner seal and bearing.

8. Remove the outer grease seal and bearing.

9. If you hope to reuse the bearings, clean them in a safe solvent. After cleaning the bearings and races, carefully inspect them for damage, pitting, heat coloring etc. If damage etc. has occurred, replace all components (bearings, cups and seals). If the bearings are acceptable repack them. **Always replace the seals with new ones. Always use a new hub nut whenever the old one has been removed.**

10. If new bearings are to be used, remove the inner and outer races from the knuckle. A three jawed puller on a slide hammer will do the job.

11. Clean the interior bore of the knuckle.

INSTALLATION

1. Install the new bearing cups using a suitable driver. Be sure the cups are fully seated in the knuckle bore.

2. Pack the wheel bearings with multi-purpose lubricant (Ford part number C1AZ19590B or the equivalent). If a bearing packer is not available, place a large portion of grease into the palm of your hand and slide the edge of the roller cage through the grease with your other hand. Work as much grease as you can between the bearing rollers.

3. Put a sufficient amount of grease between the bearing cups in the center of the knuckle. Apply a thin film of grease on the beariang cups.

4. Place the outer bearing and new grease seal into the knuckle. Place a thin film of grease on all three lips of the new outer seal.

5. Turn the knuckle over and install the inner bearing and seal. Once again, apply a thin film of grease to the three lips of the seal.

6. Install the inner grease shield; a small block of wood may be used to tap the seal into the knuckle bore.

7. Keep the knuckle in the vertical position or the inner bearing will fall out. Start the wheel hub into the outer knuckle bore and push the hub as far as possible through the outer and inner bearings by hand.

NOTE: *Prior to installing the hub, make sure it is clean and free from burrs. Use crocus cloth to polish the hub if necessary. It is important to use only hand pressure when installing the hub, make sure the hub is through both the outer and inner bearings.*

8. With the hub as fully seated as possible through the bearings, position the hub and knuckle to the front strut. Refer to Chapter 1 for instructions on attaching the strut and knuckle.

9. Lubricate the stub shaft splines with a thin film of SAE 20 motor oil. Use hand pressure only and insert the splines into the knuckle and hub as far as possible.

NOTE: *Do not allow the hub to back out of the bearings while installing the stub shaft, otherwise it will be necessary to start all over from Step 7.*

10. Complete the installation of the suspension parts as described in Chapter 7.

11. Install the hub remover/installer tool and tighten the center adapter to 120 foot pounds, this ensures the hub is fully seated.

12. Remove the installer tool and install the hub washer and nut. Tighten the hub nut finger tight.

13. Install the disc rotor, caliper etc. in reverse order of removal. Refer to the proceeding sections of this Chapter, if necessary, for procedures.

14. Install the tire and wheel assembly and snug the wheel lugs.

15. Lower the car to the ground, set the parking brake and block the wheels.

16. Tighten the wheel lugs to 80–105 ft. lbs.

17. Tighten the center hub nut to 180–200 ft. lbs. DO NOT USE A POWER WRENCH TO TIGHTEN THE HUB NUT.

18. Stake the hub nut using a rounded, dull chisel. DO NOT USE A SHARP CHISEL.

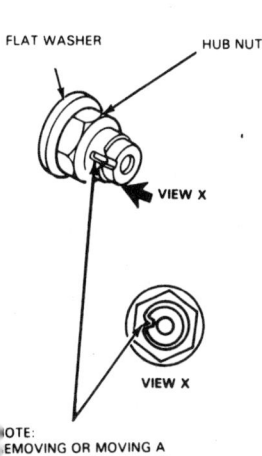

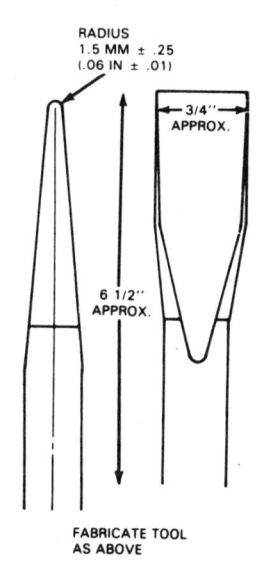

How to stake the front wheel retainer nut

BRAKES

REAR BRAKES

The rear brakes used on your car are of the non-servo leading-trailing shoe design. This means that the leading shoe does the majority of the braking when the car is going forward and the trailing shoe does the majority of the braking when the car is backing up.

The brakes are self-adjusting. The only time any adjustment is necessary is during servicing or brakeshoe replacement.

If your Escort/Lynx is a sedan, it is equipped with 7 inch diameter brakes. If it is a EXP/LN7 or a station wagon, it uses 8 inch brakes. There are sections covering both sizes in this Chapter.

Brake Shoe Inspection

Two access holes, covered by a rubber plug, are provided in the brake backing plate. By removing the plugs the brake lining thickness and condition can be inspected.

Rear Brake Drum

REMOVAL AND INSTALLATION (ALL MODELS)

1. Remove the wheel cover, loosen the lugs, jack up the rear end of your car and safely support it on jackstands.
2. Remove the wheel lugs and the tire and wheel assembly.

Front Disc Brake Dimensions

Components	All Models
Lining Size	(0.48 in.) 12.16mm thick
Lining Wear Limit (from shoe surface)	.3175mm (.0125 in.)
Caliper Cylinder Bore Diameter	54mm (2.125 in.)
Front Rotor Nominal Thickness	24.0mm (0.945 in.)
Front Rotor Minimum Thickness ①	23.88 mm (0.940 in.)
Front Rotor Diameter	236.0mm (9.29 in.)
Front Rotor Allowable Runout	0.05mm max. (0.002 in.)
Front Rotor Finish (Micro-inches)	40-0.8 vc 31-160 rms
Front Rotor Thickness Variation	.01mm max. (0.0004 in.)

① Minimum safe thickness is shown on each rotor 22.4mm (0.882 in.)

Rear Drum Brake Lining Dimensions

Model	Brake Shoe	Brake Diameter	Lining Size
3-Door	Leading	180 mm (7 inch)	32 mm (1.26 in.)
	Trailing	180 mm (7 inch)	32 mm (1.26 in.)
4-Door	Leading	203 mm (8 inch)	34 mm (1.34 in.)
	Trailing	203 mm (8 inch)	34 mm (1.34 in.)

BRAKES 169

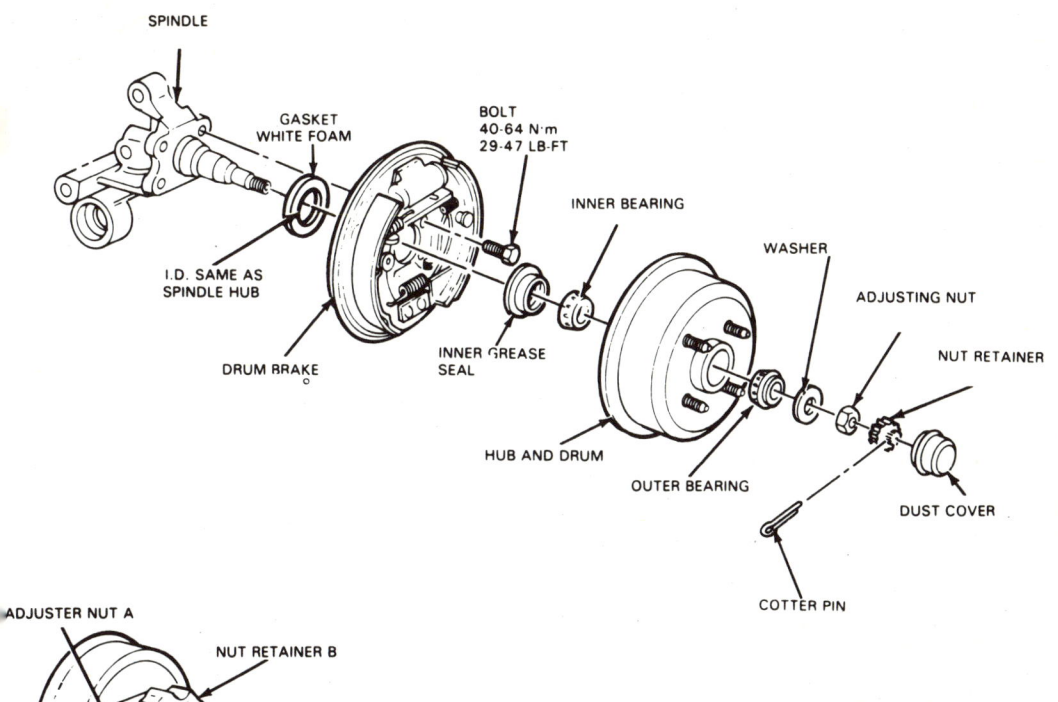

BEARING ADJUSTMENT:
TIGHTEN ADJUSTING NUT "A" TO 23-34 N·m (17-25 LB-FT) WHILE ROTATING HUB AND DRUM ASSEMBLY. BACK OFF ADJUSTING NUT APPROXIMATELY 100 DEGREES. POSITION NUT RETAINER "B" OVER ADJUSTING NUT SO SLOTS ARE IN LINE WITH COTTER PIN HOLE WITHOUT ROTATING ADJUSTING NUT. INSTALL COTTER PIN.

NOTE: THE SPINDLE HAS A PREVAILING TORQUE FEATURE THAT PREVENTS ADJUSTING THE NUT BY HAND.

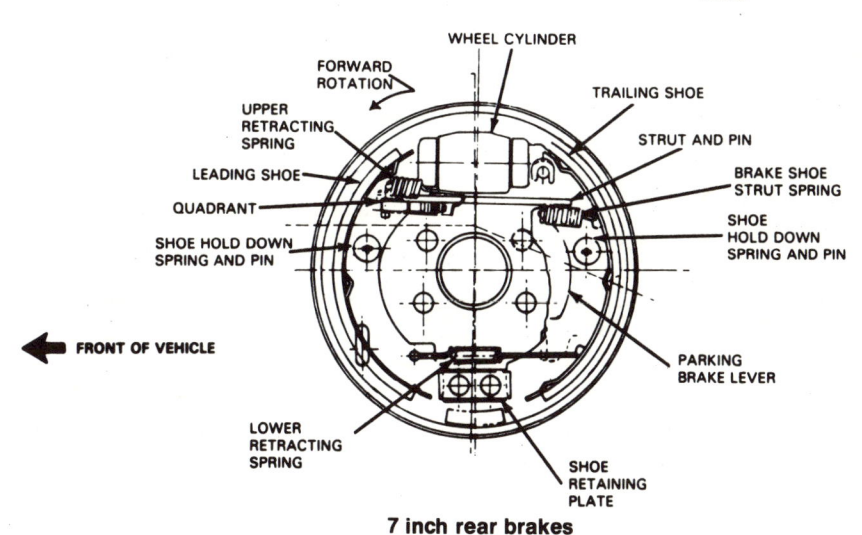

7 inch rear brakes

3. Remove the center grease cap from the brake drum hub. Remove the cotter pin, nut retainer, spindle nut, and keyed flat washer.

4. Make sure the parking brake is completely released. Slide the brake drum off of the spindle. Be careful not to drop the outer bearing. Make sure that you keep the drum straight and not drag the inner grease seal across the spindle threads.

NOTE: *If the hub and drum assembly will not slide off of the spindle, the brake shoe adjustment will have to be backed off.*

On 7 inch brakes:

Insert a thin blade screwdriver in to the inspection slot until it contacts the adjuster assembly pivot. Apply side pressure on the pivot point to allow the adjuster quadrant to ratchet and release the brake adjustment.

On 8 inch brakes:

Remove the brake line to axle bracket to gain enough room so a thin bladed screwdriver and brake adjusting tool may be inserted in the inspection slot. Push the adjuster lever away from the adjuster screw wheel. Back off the starwheel with the adjusting tool.

5. Inspect the brake drum for scoring etc. Have the drum turned if necessary. Perform any necessary brake work. Pack the wheel bearings if required. Reinstall the brake drum in the reverse order of removal. Consult the next section on rear wheel bearing service for proper bearing adjustment when reinstalling the brake drum.

Rear Wheel Bearings
REMOVAL, PACKING, INSTALLATION AND ADJUSTMENT

The rear wheel bearings are located in the brake drum hub. The inner wheel bearing is protected by a grease seal. A washer and spindle nut retain the hub/drum assembly and control the bearing endplay.

1. Complete Steps 1–4 in the proceeding Drum Removal section.

2. The outer bearing will be loose when the drum is removed and may be lifted out by hand. The inner bearing is retained by a grease seal. To remove the inner bearing, insert a wooden dowel or soft drift through the hub from the outer bearing side and carefully drive out the inner bearing and grease seal.

3. Clean the bearings, cups and hubs with a suitable solvent. Inspect the bearings and cups for damage or heat discoloring. Replace as a set if necessary. Always install a new grease seal.

4. If new bearings are to be used, use a three jawed slide-hammer puller to remove the cups from the drum hub. Install the new bearing cups using a suitable driver. Make sure they are fully seated in the hub.

5. Pack the bearings with a multi-purpose grease. (See the front wheel bearing section for packing instructions.)

6. Coat the cups with a thin film of grease. Install the inner bearing and grease seal.

7. Coat the bearing surfaces of the spindle with a thin film of grease. Slowly and carefully slide the drum and hub over the spindle and brake shoes. Install the outer bearing over the spindle and into the hub.

8. Install the keyed flat washer and adjusting nut on the spindle.

9. Tighten the adjusting nut to between 17–25 ft. lbs.

10. Back-off the adjusting nut ½ turn. Then retighten it to between 10–15 ft. lbs.

11. Position the nut retainer on the nut and install the cotter pin. Do not tighten the nut to install the cotter pin.

12. Spread the ends of the cotter pin and bend them around the nut retainer. Install the center grease cap.

13. Install the tire and wheel assembly. Lower the car and tighten the wheel lugs.

Rear Brake Shoes
TIPS

After any brake service work, obtain a firm brake pedal before moving the car. Adjusted brakes must not put a drag on the wheel, the wheel must turn freely.

The rear brakes are self-adjusting and require adjustment only after new shoes have been installed or service work has been done which required the disassembly of the brake shoes.

When adjusting the rear brake shoes, make sure the parking brake cables are not adjusted too tightly.

After the brakes have been installed and adjusted, check the operation of the brakes by making several stops from varying speeds. Readjust if necessary.

7 INCH REAR BRAKES
Removal

1. Perform Steps 1–4 of the Brake Drum Removal section.

2. Remove the holddown pins and springs by pushing down on and rotating the outer

BRAKES 171

SPINDLE
I.D. SAME AS SPINDLE HUB
GASKET
DRUM BRAKE
INNER GREASE SEAL
INNER BEARING
OUTER BEARING ASSY
HUB AND DRUM
WASHER
ADJUSTING NUT
NUT RETAINER
COTTER PIN
DUST COVER

ADJUSTING NUT A
NUT RETAINER B
SPREAD ENDS AND BEND AROUND NUT RETAINER
COTTER PIN C

BEARING ADJUSTMENT:
TIGHTEN ADJUSTING NUT "A" TO 23-34 N·m (17-25 LB-FT) WHILE ROTATING HUB AND DRUM ASSEMBLY. BACK OFF ADJUSTING NUT APPROXIMATELY 100 DEGREES. POSITION NUT RETAINER "B" OVER ADJUSTING NUT SO SLOTS ARE IN LINE WITH COTTER PIN HOLE WITHOUT ROTATING ADJUSTING NUT. INSTALL COTTER PIN.

NOTE: THE SPINDLE HAS AS PREVAILING TORQUE FEATURE THAT PREVENTS ADJUSTING THE NUT BY HAND.

FORWARD ROTATION
ADJUSTER SCREW RETRACTING SPRING
WHEEL CYLINDER
ADJUSTER WASHER
ADJUSTER LEVER
LEADING SHOE AND LINING
ADJUSTING SOCKET
ADJUSTING NUT AND SCREW
SHOE HOLD DOWN PIN AND SPRING
PARKING BRAKE LEVER
TRAILING SHOE AND LINING
SHOE HOLD DOWN PIN AND SPRING
BACKING PLATE
LOWER RETRACTING SPRING
SHOE RETAINING PLATE

8 inch rear brakes

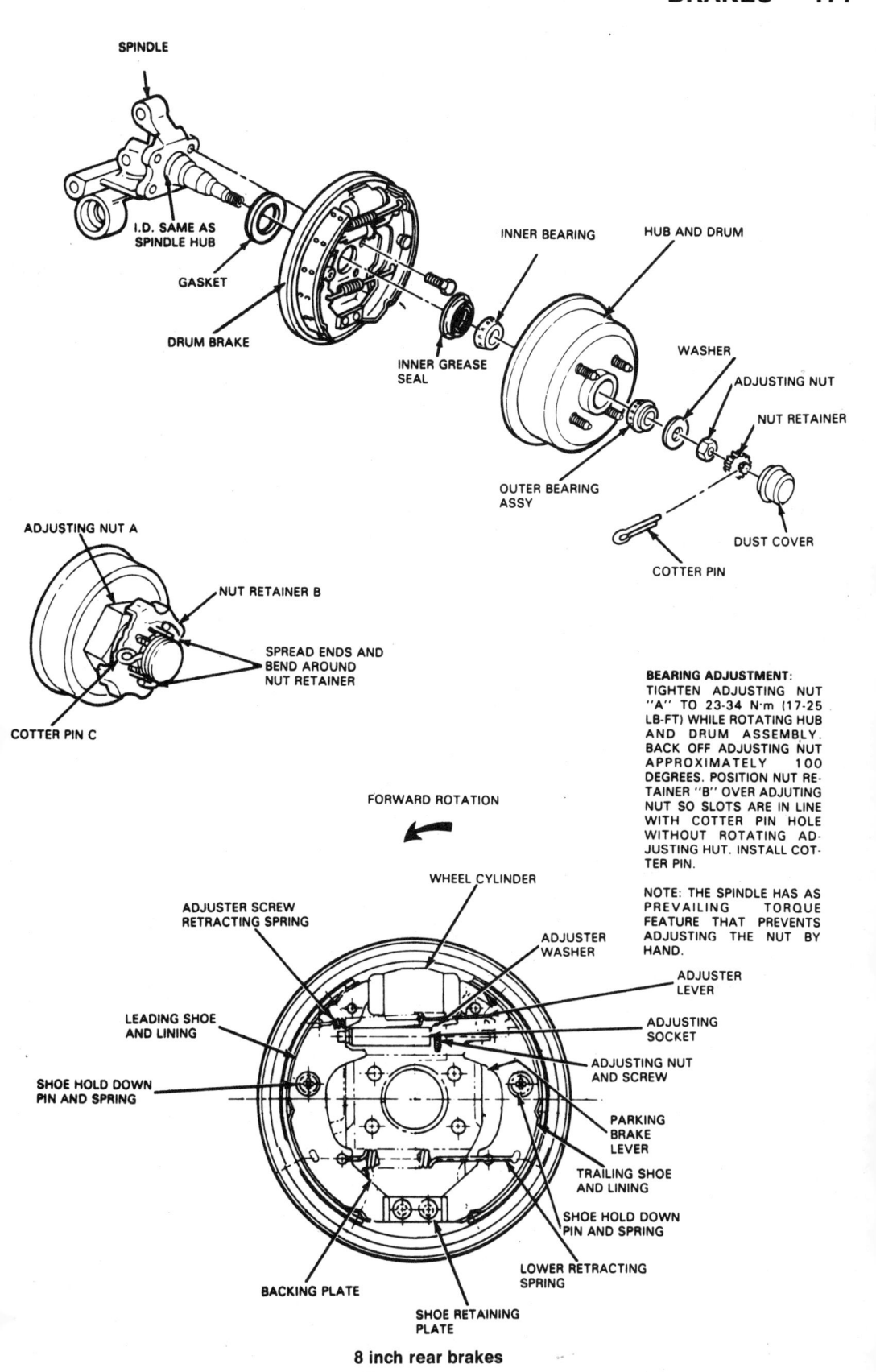

172 BRAKES

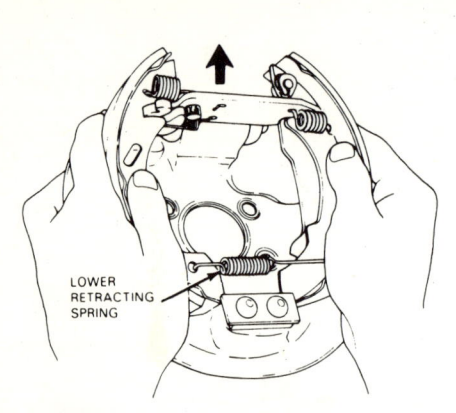

STEP 1

a. Remove holddown springs and pins.
b. Lift assembly off backing plate.
c. Disengage parking brake cable.
d. Remove lower retracting spring.

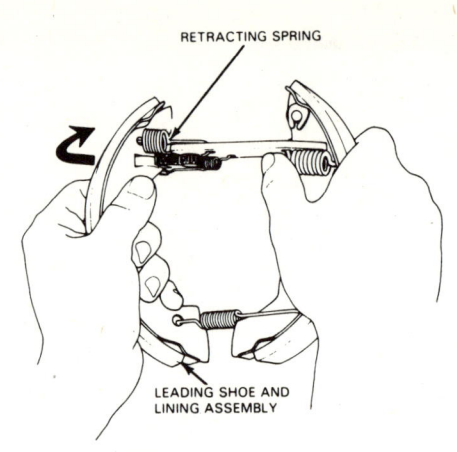

STEP 2

Remove leading shoe retracting spring by rotating shoe as shown to release spring tension. Do not pry spring off shoe.

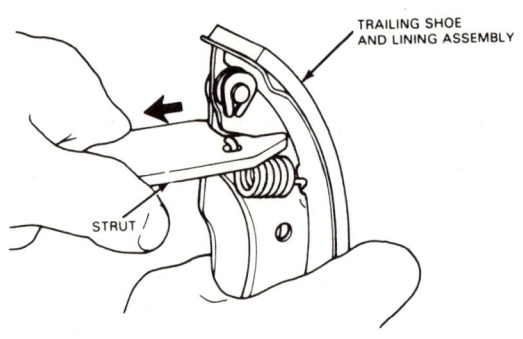

STEP 3a

Remove strut to trailing shoe and lining assembly by pulling strut away from shoe and...

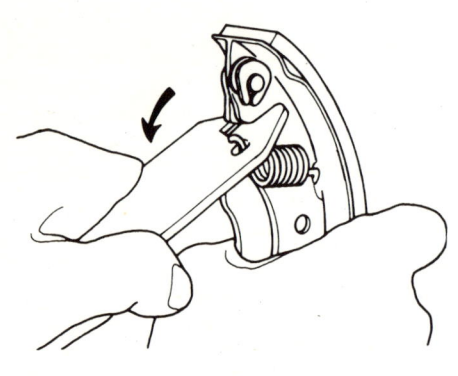

STEP 3b

...twisting strut downward

STEP 3c

...toward technician until spring tension is released. Remove spring from slots.

Removing the 7 inch rear brake shoes

washer 90 degrees. It may be necessary to hold the back of the pin (behind the backing plate) while pressing down and turning the washer.

3. After the holddown pins and springs have been removed from both brake shoes, remove both shoes and the adjuster assembly by lifting up and away from the bottom anchor plate and shoe guide. Take care not to damage the wheel cylinder boots when removing the shoes from the wheel cylinder.

4. Remove the parking brake cable from the brake lever to allow the removal of the shoes and adjuster assembly.

REMOVAL PROCEDURE

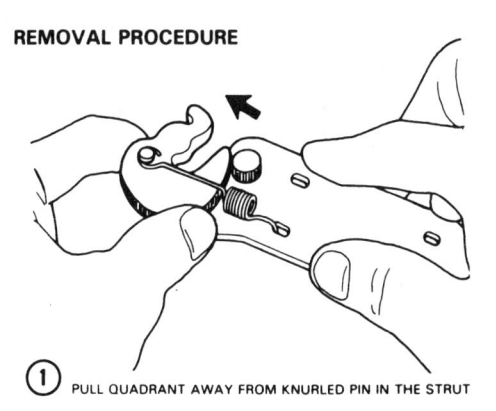

① PULL QUADRANT AWAY FROM KNURLED PIN IN THE STRUT

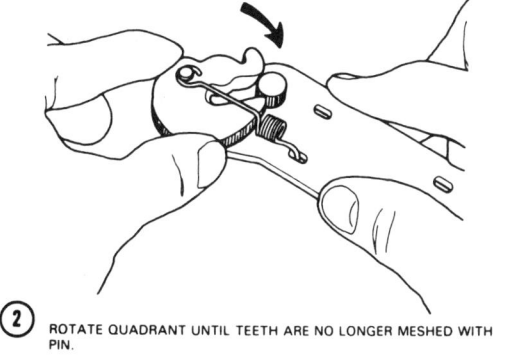

② ROTATE QUADRANT UNTIL TEETH ARE NO LONGER MESHED WITH PIN.

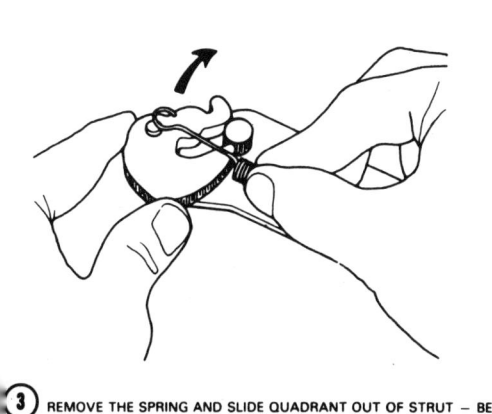

INSTALLATION PROCEDURE

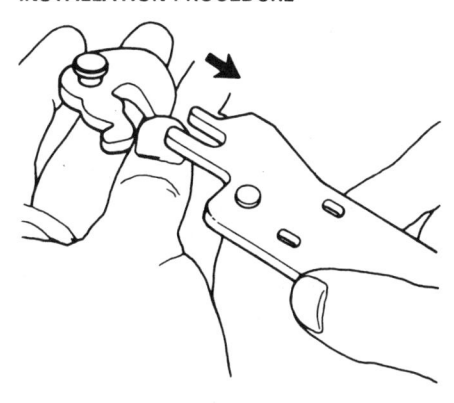

③ REMOVE THE SPRING AND SLIDE QUADRANT OUT OF STRUT — BE CAREFUL NOT TO OVERSTRESS SPRING.

INSTALL ADJUSTER QUADRANT PIN INTO SLOT IN STRUT. TURN ASSEMBLY OVER AND INSTALL SPRING.

7 inch brakes; quadrant removal and installation

5. Remove the lower shoe to shoe spring by rotating the leading brake shoe to release the spring tension. Do not pry the spring from the shoe.

6. Remove the adjuster strut from the trailing shoe by pulling the strut away from the shoe and twisting it downward toward yourself until the spring tension is released. Remove the spring from the slot.

7. Remove the parking brake lever from the trailing shoe by disconnecting the horseshoe clip and spring washer and pulling the lever from the shoe.

8. If for any reason the adjuster assembly must be taken apart, do the following: pull the adjuster quadrant (U-shaped lever) away from the knurled pin on the adjuster strut by rotating the quadrant in either direction until the teeth are no longer engaged with the pin. Remove the spring and slide the quadrant out of the slot on the end of the adjuster strut. Do not put too much stress on the spring during disassembly.

Installation

1. Clean the brake backing (mounting) plate with a soft paint brush or vacuum cleaner.

CAUTION: *Never inhale the dust from the brake linings. Asbestos dust when inhaled can be injurious to your health. Use a vacuum cleaner. Do not blow off the dust with air pressure.*

2. Apply a thin film of high temperature grease at the points on the backing plate where the brake shoes make contact.

3. Apply a thin film of multi-purpose grease to the adjuster strut at the point between the quadrant and strut.

4. If the adjuster has been disassembled; install the quadrant mounting pin into the slot on the adjuster strut and install the adjuster spring.

5. Assemble the parking brake lever to the trailing shoe. Install the spring washer and a new horseshoe clip, squeeze the clip with pliers until the lever is secured on the shoe.

174 BRAKES

6. Install the adjuster strut attaching spring on to the trailing shoe. Attach the adjusting strut by fastening the spring in the slot and pivoting the strut into position. This will tension the spring. Make sure the end of the spring where the hook is parallel to the center line of the spring coils is hooked into the web of the brake shoe. The installed spring should be flat against the web and parallel to the adjuster strut.

7. Install the shoe to shoe spring with the longest hook attached to the trailing shoe.

8. Install the leading shoe to adjuster strut spring by installing the spring to both parts and pivoting the leading shoe over the quadrant and into position, this will tension the spring.

9. Place the shoes and adjuster assembly onto the backing plate. Spread the shoes slightly and position them into the wheel cylinder piston inserts and anchor plate. Take care not to damage the wheel cylinder boots.

10. Attach the parking brake cable to the parking brake lever.

11. Install the holddown pins, springs and washers.

12. Adjust the brakes as described in the proceeding brake adjustment section.

13. Install the rear drums and adjust the bearings as described in the previous section.

8 INCH REAR BRAKES

Removal

1. Perform Steps 1-4 of the Brake Drum Removal section.

2. Remove the holddown pins and springs by pushing down on and rotating the outer washer 90 degrees. It may be necessary to hold the back of the pin (behind the backing plate) while pressing down and turning the washer.

3. After the holddown pins and springs have been removed, remove both shoes and the adjuster assembly by lifting up and away from the anchor plate and wheel cylinder. Take care not to damage the wheel cylinder boots or bend the adjusting lever.

4. Disconnect the parking brake cable from the parking brake lever.

5. Remove the lower shoe to shoe spring and the upper spring attaching the adjusting lever to the brake shoe. This will separate the brake shoes and disengage the adjuster.

6. Spread the horseshoe clip and remove the parking brake lever from the trailing shoe.

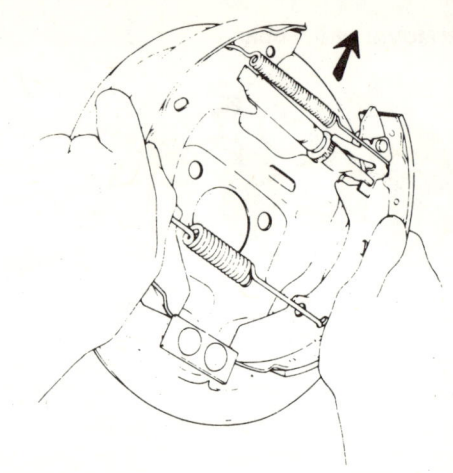

REMOVAL PROCEDURE:
1. REMOVE BRAKE SHOE HOLDDOWN SPRINGS AND PINS.
2. LIFT ASSEMBLY OFF THE BACKING PLATE.
3. REMOVE PARKING BRAKE CABLE FROM THE PARKING BRAKE
4. REMOVE RETRACTING SPRINGS AND ADJUSTING LEVER.

8 inch brakes; removal

Installation

1. Clean the brake backing (mounting) plate with a soft paint brush or vacuum cleaner.

CAUTION: *Never inhale the dust from the brake linings. Asbestos dust when inhaled can be injurious to your health. Use a vacuum cleaner. Do not blow off the dust with air pressure.*

2. Apply a thin film of high temperature grease at the points on the backing plate where the brake shoes make contact.

3. Apply a thin film of multi-purpose grease to the threads of the adjuster screw and to the socket end of the adjuster. Turn the adjuster screw into the socket and then back off from bottom a number of threads.

4. Install the parking brake lever on the trailing shoe. Use a new horseshoe clip. Be sure to put the spring washer in position. Connect the parking brake cable to the parking brake lever.

5. Attach the lower retracting spring between the two brake shoes and install the shoes on the backing plate. It will be necessary to spread the shoes apart to mount them on the anchor plate and wheel cylinder.

6. Install the adjuster screw assembly between the slot in the leading shoe and the slots in the trailing shoe and parking brake lever. Lengthen the screw if necessary. The adjuster socket blades are marked L for left

BRAKES 175

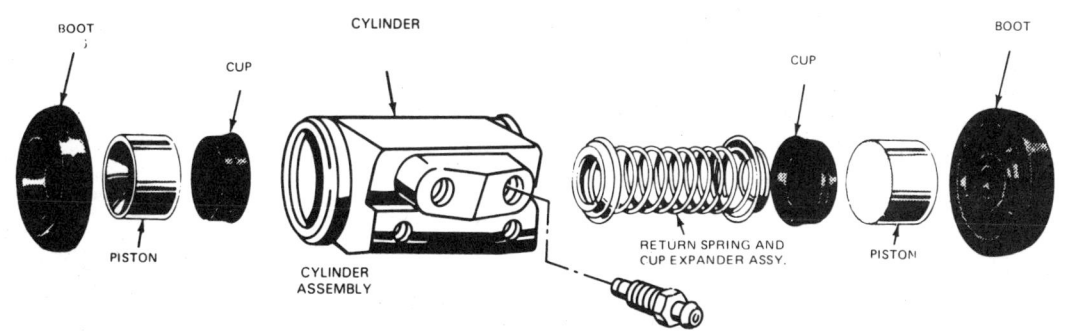

Exploded view of a rear wheel brake cylinder

side or R for right side and fit onto the trailing shoe and the parking brake lever (slots provided). The letter (L or R) must face up toward the wheel cylinder when the blade is installed. This permits the deeper of the two slots to fit onto the parking brake lever.

7. Install the adjusting lever (also marked L or R) by sliding the groove over the parking brake lever pin slot and into a groove on the starwheel.

8. Attach the upper retracting spring to the leading shoe anchor hole. Use a pair of brake spring pliers, stretch the spring and attach the other end onto the adjuster lever notch.

NOTE: *If the adjuster lever does not contact the starwheel after installing the spring, make sure that the adjuster socket is installed correctly.* (see Step 6).

9. Install the holddown pins, springs and washers.

10. Adjust the brakes, using a brake adjusting tool as described in the brake adjustment section. Do not adjust with shoe drag on the drum. The wheel must turn freely.

11. Install the brake drum and adjust the wheel bearings.

12. Lower the car and road test.

Rear Wheel Cylinders

REMOVAL AND INSTALLATION

1. Remove the rear wheel, brake drum and brake shoes as described in the proceeding sections.

2. Disconnect the rear brake line from the back of the wheel cylinder.

3. Remove the bolts that attach the wheel cylinder to the brake backing (mounting) plate.

4. Remove the wheel cylinder.

5. Installation is in the reverse order of removal.

OVERHAULING THE WHEEL CYLINDER

Wheel cylinders need not be rebuilt unless they are leaking. To check the wheel cylinder for leakage, carefully pull the lower edge of the rubber end boot away from the cylinder. Excessive brake fluid in the boot or running out of the boot, when the edges are pulled away from the cylinder, denotes leakage. A certain (slight) amount of fluid in the boot is normal.

1. It is not necessary to remove the cylinder from the brake backing (mounting) plate to rebuild the cylinder, however removal makes the job easier.

2. Disengage and remove the rubber boots from both ends of the wheel cylinder. The piston should come out with the boot. If not, remove the piston by applying finger pressure inward on one piston, the piston on the opposite end should come out. Take care not to splash brake fluid all over yourself when the piston pops from the cylinder.

3. Remove the rubber cups, center expander and spring from the wheel cylinder. Remove the bleeder screw from the back of the cylinder.

4. Discard all rubber boots and cups. Wash the pistons and cylinder in denatured alcohol or clean brake fluid.

5. Inspect the pistons for scratches, scoring or other visible damage. Inspect the cylinder bore for score marks or rust. The cylinder may be honed (with a brake cylinder hone) if necessary. Do not hone more than .003 inch beyond original diameter. If the scoring or pitting is deeper, replace the cylinder.

6. After honing the cylinder, wash again with alcohol or clean brake fluid. Check the bleeder screw hole to make sure it is opened. Wipe the cylinder bore with a clean cloth. Install the bleeder screw.

7. Never reuse the old rubber parts. Al-

176 BRAKES

ways use all of the parts supplied in the rebuilding kit.

8. Apply a light coat of brake fluid, or the special lubricant if supplied with the rebuilding kit, on the pistons, rubber cups and cylinder bore.

9. Insert the spring and expander assembly into the cylinder bore. Put the cups, facing in, and the pistons into the cylinder. Install the boots and fit the outer lips into the retaining grooves on the outer edges of the wheel cylinder.

10. Install the wheel cylinder onto the backing plate. Be sure that the inlet port (where the brake hose connects) is toward the rear of the car. Install the brake shoes, drum and wheel assembly. Adjust and bleed the brake system. Road test the car.

PARKING BRAKE

The parking brake control is hand operated and mounted on the floor between the front seats. When the control lever is pulled up (from the floor) an attached cable applies the rear brakes.

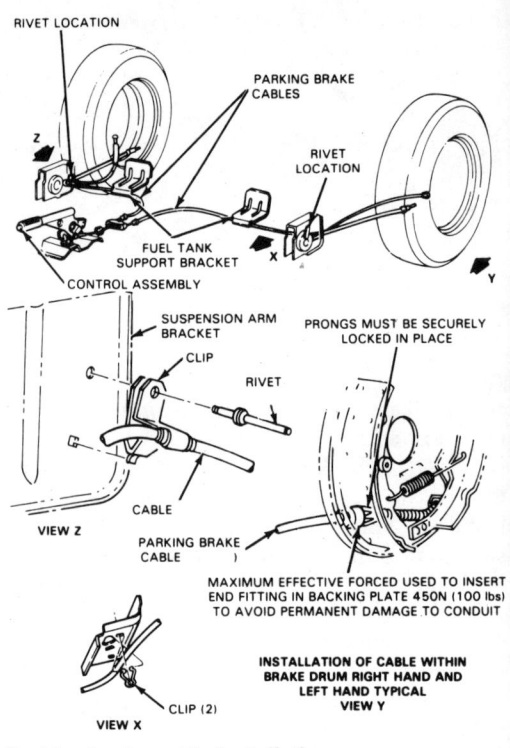

Parking brake cable installation

Cable Removal and Installation

1. Pull up slowly on the control lever and stop at the seventh notch position, count the clicks as you pull up on the handle. The adjusting nut is now accessable. Remove the adjusting nut. Completely release the control handle (push the release button and lower to the floor.

2. Raise the car and safely support on jackstands.

3. Disconnect the rear parking brake cables from the front equalizer and rod assembly.

4. If the front equalizer and rod assembly is to be replaced; drill out the rivets that hold the cable guide to the floor pan. Remove the equalizer and rod assembly from the parking brake control lever and withdraw it through the floor pan.

5. To install the front equalizer and rod assembly; feed the adjusting rod end of the assembly through the floor pan and into the parking control lever clevis. Attach the cable guide to the floor pan using new pop rivets. Borrow a pop rivet gun from a friend.

6. If the rear parking brake cable is to be replaced; first disconnect from the front equalizer and rod assembly. Remove the hairpin clip that holds the cable to the floor pan tunnel bracket.

7. Remove the wire retainer that hold the cable to the fuel tank mounting bracket. Remove the cable from the retaining clip.

8. Remove the rear tire and wheel assemblies and the brake drums.

9. Disconnect the parking brake cable from the trailing shoe parking brake levers. Depress the cable prongs that hold the cable in the backing plate hole. Remove the cable through the holes.

10. Installation is in the reverse order of removal.

11. Adjust the parking brake cable as per instructions in the next section.

Cable Adjustment

1. If a new cable has been installed, the parking brake lever control should be in the seventh notch and the adjusting nut run down to the approximate position it was removed from. Release the hand brake and pump the brake pedal several times. If your car has power brakes, start the engine and allow it to idle when pumping the brakes. Shut off the engine.

2. Place the control lever in the twelfth

notch, two notches before complete application. Tighten the adjusting nut until the rear brakes have a slight drag when the parking brake control lever is completely released. Repeat the parts of this step as necessary.

3. Loosen the adjusting nut until there is no rear brake drag when the control lever is completely released.

4. Lower the car and test the parking brake application.

Body 9

You can repair most minor auto body damage yourself. Minor damage usually falls into one of several categories: (1) small scratches and dings in the paint that can be repaired without the use of body filler, (2) deep scratches and dents that require body filler, but do not require pulling, or hammering metal back into shape and (3) rust-out repairs. The repair sequences illustrated in this chapter are typical of these types of repairs. If you want to get involved in more complicated repairs including pulling or hammering sheet metal back into shape, you will probably need more detailed instructions. Chilton's *Minor Auto Body Repair, 2nd Edition* is a comprehensive guide to repairing auto body damage yourself.

TOOLS AND SUPPLIES

The list of tools and equipment you may need to fix minor body damage ranges from very basic hand tools to a wide assortment of specialized body tools. Most minor scratches, dings and rust holes can be fixed using an electric drill, wire wheel or grinder attachment, half-round plastic file, sanding block, various grades of sandpaper (#36, which is coarse through #600, which is fine) in both wet and dry types, auto body plastic, primer, touch-up paint, spreaders, newspaper and masking tape.

Most manufacturers of auto body repair products began supplying materials to professionals. Their knowledge of the best, most-used products has been translated into body repair kits for the do-it-yourselfer. Kits are available from a number of manufacturers and contain the necessary materials in the required amounts for the repair identified on the package.

Kits are available for a wide variety of uses, including:
- Rusted out metal
- All purpose kit for dents and holes
- Dents and deep scratches
- Fiberglass repair kit
- Epoxy kit for restyling.

Kits offer the advantage of buying what you need for the job. There is little waste and little chance of materials going bad from not being used. The same manufacturers also merchandise all of the individual products used—spreaders, dent pullers, fiberglass cloth, polyester resin, cream hardener, body filler, body files, sandpaper, sanding discs and holders, primer, spray paint, etc.

CAUTION: *Most of the products you will be using contain harmful chemicals, so be extremely careful. Always read the complete label before opening the containers. When*

BODY 179

you put them away for future use, be sure they are out of children's reach!

Most auto body repair kits contain all the materials you need to do the job right in the kit. So, if you have a small rust spot or dent you want to fix, check the contents of the kit before you run out and buy any additional tools.

ALIGNING BODY PANELS

Doors

There are several methods of adjusting doors. Your vehicle will probably use one of those illustrated.

Whenever a door is removed and is to be reinstalled, you should matchmark the position of the hinges on the door pillars. The holes of the hinges and/or the hinge attaching points are usually oversize to permit alignment of doors. The striker plate is also moveable, through oversize holes, permitting up-and-down, in-and-out and fore-and-aft movement. Fore-and-aft movement is made by adding or subtracting shims from behind the striker and pillar post. The striker should be adjusted so that the door closes fully and remains closed, yet enters the lock freely.

Door hinge adjustment

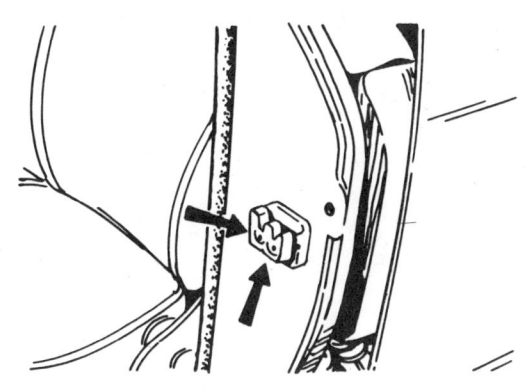

DOOR HINGES

Don't try to cover up poor door adjustment with a striker plate adjustment. The gap on each side of the door should be equal and uniform and there should be no metal-to-metal contact as the door is opened or closed.

1. Determine which hinge bolts must be loosened to move the door in the desired direction.
2. Loosen the hinge bolt(s) just enough to allow the door to be moved with a padded pry bar.
3. Move the door a small amount and check the fit, after tightening the bolts. Be sure that there is no bind or interference with adjacent panels.
4. Repeat this until the door is properly positioned, and tighten all the bolts securely.

Move the door striker as indicated by arrows

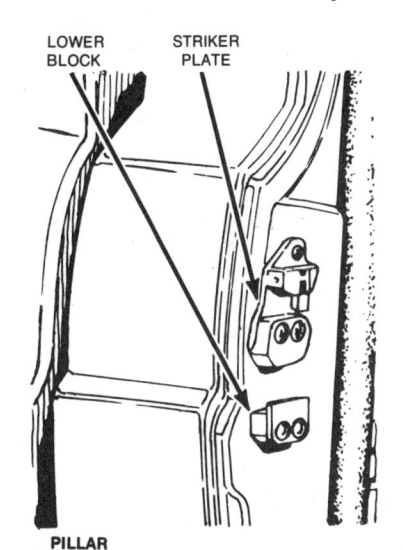

Hood, Trunk or Tailgate

As with doors, the outline of hinges should be scribed before removal. The hood and trunk can be aligned by loosening the hinge bolts in their slotted mounting holes and moving the hood or trunk lid as necessary.

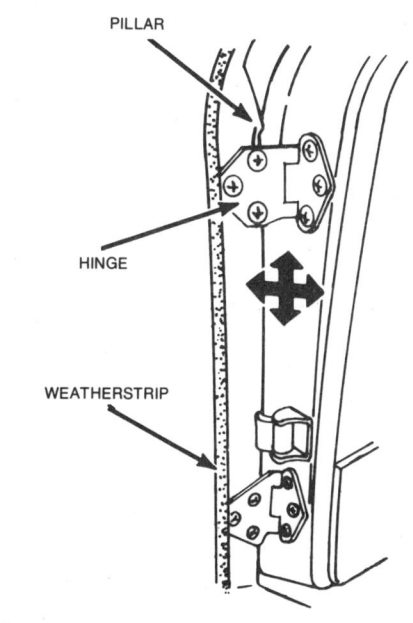

Striker plate and lower block

180 BODY

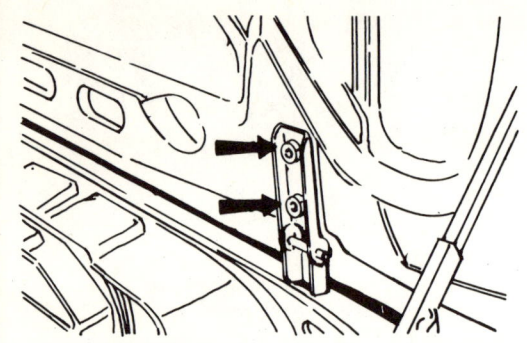

Loosen the hinge boots to permit fore-and-aft and horizontal adjustment

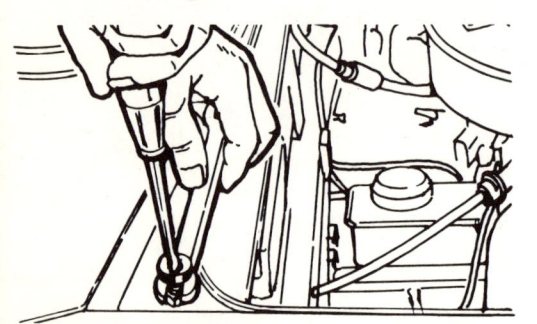

The hood is adjusted vertically by stop-screws at the front and/or rear

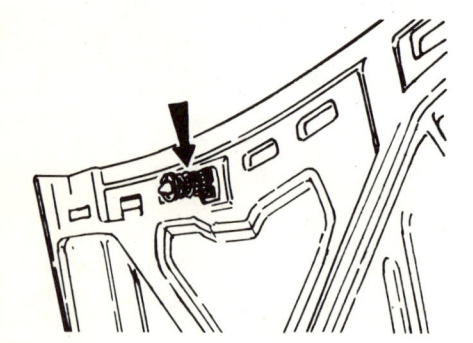

The hood pin can be adjusted for proper lock engagement

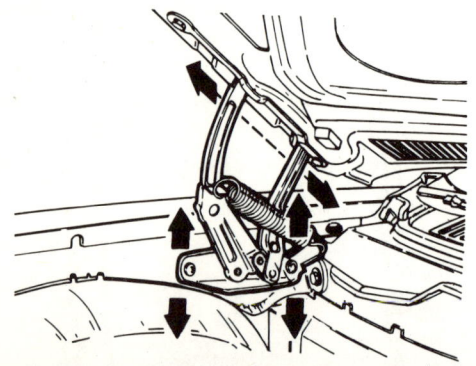

The height of the hood at the rear is adjusted by loosening the bolts that attach the hinge to the body and moving the hood up or down

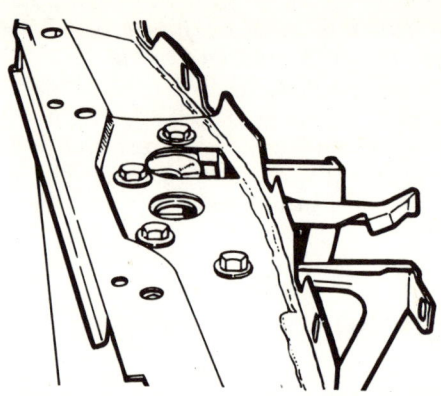

The base of the hood lock can also be repositioned slightly to give more positive lock engagement

The hood and trunk have adjustable catch locations to regulate lock engagement. Bumpers at the front and/or rear of the hood provide a vertical adjustment and the hood lockpin can be adjusted for proper engagement.

The tailgate on the station wagon can be adjusted by loosening the hinge bolts in their slotted mounting holes and moving the tailgate on its hinges. The latchplate and latch striker at the bottom of the tailgate opening can be adjusted to stop rattle. An adjustable bumper is located on each side.

RUST, UNDERCOATING, AND RUSTPROOFING

Rust

Rust is an electrochemical process. It works on ferrous metals (iron and steel) from the inside out due to exposure of unprotected surfaces to air and moisture. The possibility of rust exists practically nationwide—anywhere humidity, industrial pollution or chemical salts are present, rust can form. In coastal areas, the problem is high humidity and salt air; in snowy areas, the problem is chemical salt (de-icer) used to keep the roads clear, and in industrial areas, sulphur dioxide is present in the air from industrial pollution and is changed to sulphuric acid when it rains. The rusting process is accelerated by high temperatures, especially in snowy areas, when vehicles are driven over slushy roads and then left overnight in a heated garage.

Automotive styling also can be a contributor to rust formation. Spot welding of panels

BODY

creates small pockets that trap moisture and form an environment for rust formation. Fortunately, auto manufacturers have been working hard to increase the corrosion protection of their products. Galvanized sheet metal enjoys much wider use, along with the increased use of plastic and various rust retardant coatings. Manufacturers are also designing out areas in the body where rust-forming moisture can collect.

To prevent rust, you must stop it before it gets started. On new vehicles, there are two ways to accomplish this.

First, the car or truck should be treated with a commercial rustproofing compound. There are many different brands of franchised rustproofers, but most processes involve spraying a waxy "self-healing" compound under the chassis, inside rocker panels, inside doors and fender liners and similar places where rust is likely to form. Prices for a quality rustproofing job range from $100–$250, depending on the area, the brand name and the size of the vehicle.

Ideally, the vehicle should be rustproofed as soon as possible following the purchase. The surfaces of the car or truck have begun to oxidize and deteriorate during shipping. In addition, the car may have sat on a dealer's lot or on a lot at the factory, and once the rust has progressed past the stage of light, powdery surface oxidation rustproofing is not likely to be worthwhile. Professional rustproofers feel that once rust has formed, rustproofing will simply seal in moisture already present. Most franchised rustproofing operations offer a 3–5 year warranty against rust-through, but will not support that warranty if the rustproofing is not applied within three months of the date of manufacture.

Undercoating should not be mistaken for rustproofing. Undercoating is a black, tar-like substance that is applied to the underside of a vehicle. Its basic function is to deaden noises that are transmitted from under the car. It simply cannot get into the crevices and seams where moisture tends to collect. In fact, it may clog up drainage holes and ventilation passages. Some undercoatings also tend to crack or peel with age and only create more moisture and corrosion attracting pockets.

The second thing you should do immediately after purchasing the car is apply a paint sealant. A sealant is a petroleum based product marketed under a wide variety of brand names. It has the same protective properties as a good wax, but bonds to the paint with a chemically inert layer that seals it from the air. If air can't get at the surface, oxidation cannot start.

The paint sealant kit consists of a base coat and a conditioning coat that should be applied every 6–8 months, depending on the manufacturer. The base coat must be applied before waxing, or the wax must first be removed.

Third, keep a garden hose handy for your car in winter. Use it a few times on nice days during the winter for underneath areas, and it will pay big dividends when spring arrives. Spraying under the fenders and other areas which even car washes don't reach will help remove road salt, dirt and other build-ups which help breed rust. Adjust the nozzle to a high-force spray. An old brush will help break up residue, permitting it to be washed away more easily.

It's a somewhat messy job, but worth it in the long run because rust often starts in those hidden areas.

At the same time, wash grime off the door sills and, more importantly, the under portions of the doors, plus the tailgate if you have a station wagon or truck. Applying a coat of wax to those areas at least once before and once during winter will help fend off rust.

When applying the wax to the under parts of the doors, you will note small drain holes. These holes often are plugged with undercoating or dirt. Make sure they are cleaned out to prevent water build-up inside the doors. A small punch or penknife will do the job.

Water from the high-pressure sprays in car washes sometimes can get into the housings for parking and taillights, so take a close look. If they contain water merely loosen the retaining screws and the water should run out.

182 BODY

Repairing Scratches and Small Dents

Step 1. This dent (arrow) is typical of a deep scratch or minor dent. If deep enough, the dent or scratch can be pulled out or hammered out from behind. In this case no straightening is necessary

Step 2. Using an 80-grit grinding disc on an electric drill grind the paint from the surrounding area down to bare metal. This will provide a rough surface for the body filler to grab

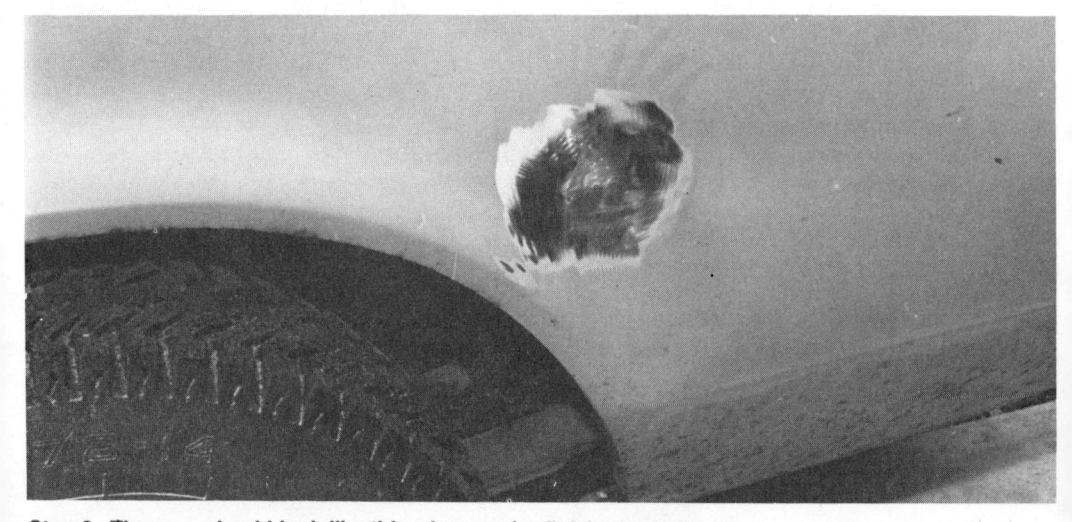

Step 3. The area should look like this when you're finished grinding

BODY   183

Step 4. Mix the body filler and cream hardener according to the directions

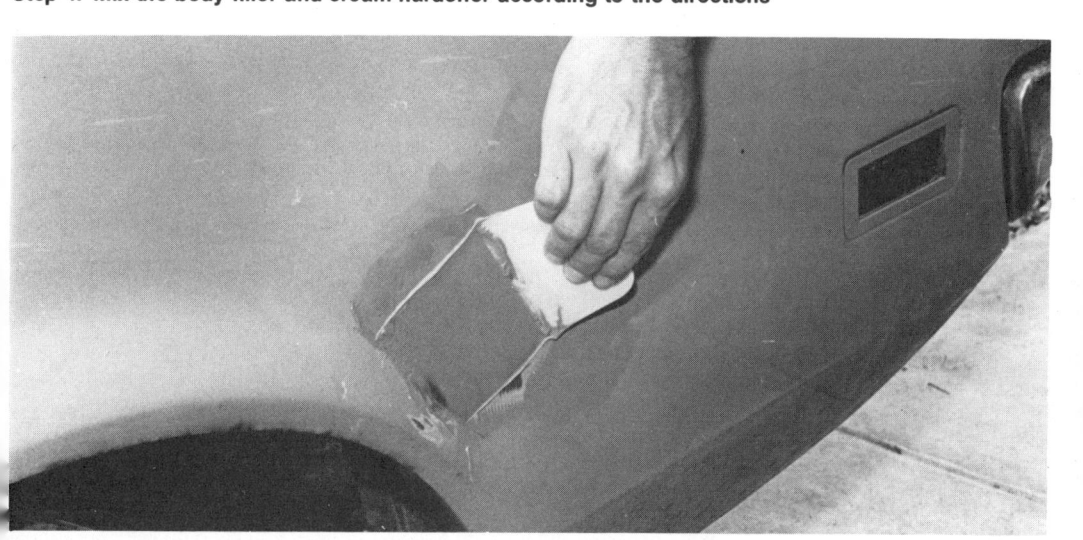

Step 5. Spread the body filler evenly over the entire area. Be sure to cover the area completely

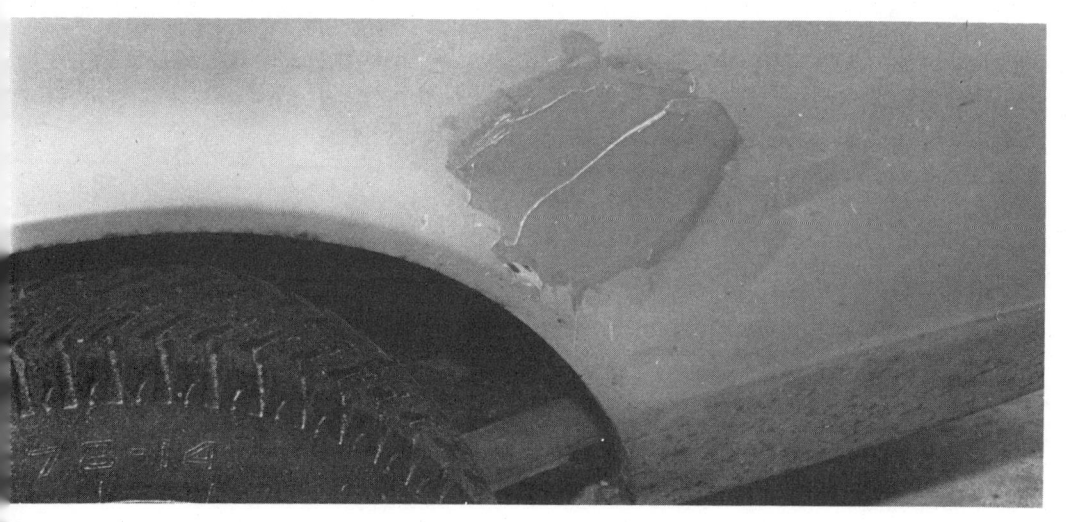

Step 6. Let the body filler dry until the surface can just be scratched with your fingernail

184 BODY

Step 7. Knock the high spots from the body filler with a body file

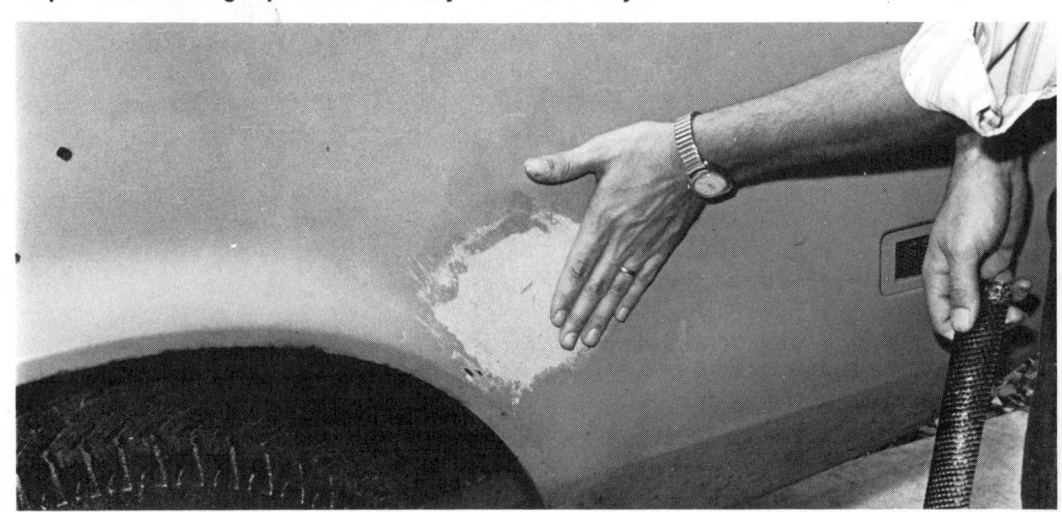

Step 8. Check frequently with the palm of your hand for high and low spots. If you wind up with low spots, you may have to apply another layer of filler

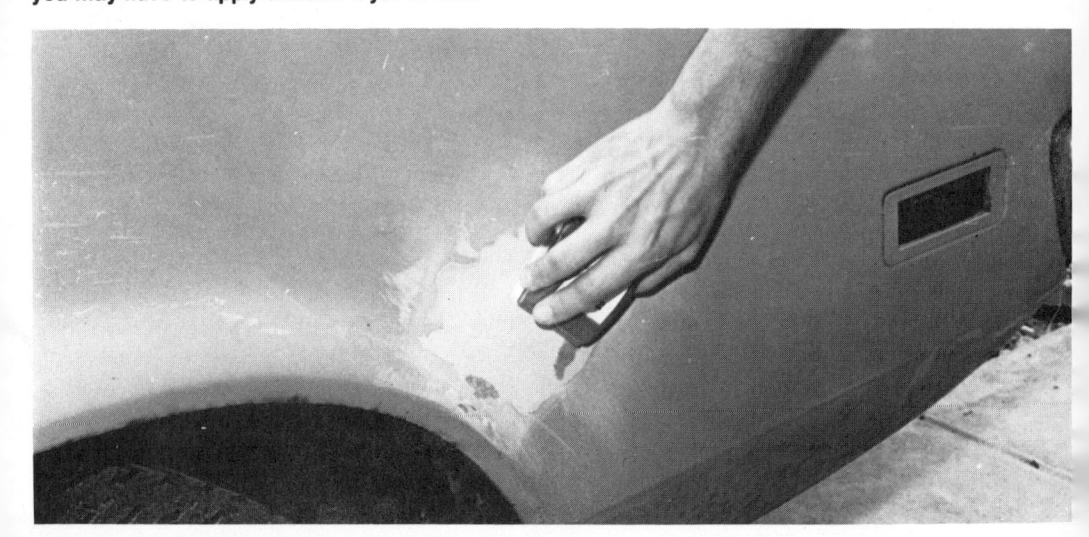

Step 9. Block sand the entire area with 320 grit paper

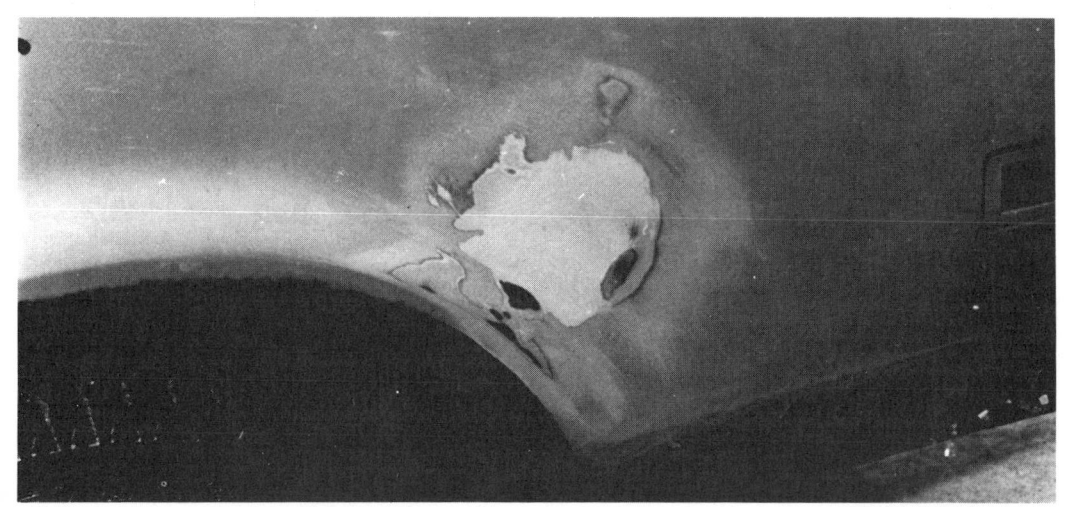

BODY 185

Step 10. When you're finished, the repair should look like this. Note the sand marks extending 2—3 inches out from the repaired area

Step 11. Prime the entire area with automotive primer

Step 12. The finished repair ready for the final paint coat. Note that the primer has covered the sanding marks (see Step 10). A repair of this size should be able to be spotpainted with good results

REPAIRING RUST HOLES

One thing you have to remember about rust: even if you grind away all the rusted metal in a panel, and repair the area with any of the kits available, *eventually* the rust will return. There are two reasons for this. One, rust is a chemical reaction that causes pressure under the repair from the inside out. That's how the blisters form. Two, the back side of the panel (and the repair) is wide open to moisture, and unpainted body filler acts like a sponge. That's why the best solution to rust problems is to remove the rusted panel and install a new one or have the rusted area cut out and a new piece of sheet metal welded in its place. The trouble with welding is the expense; sometimes it will cost more than the car or truck is worth.

One of the better solutions to do-it-yourself rust repair is the process using a fiberglass cloth repair kit (shown here). This will give a strong repair that resists cracking and moisture and is relatively easy to use. It can be used on large or small holes and also can be applied over contoured surfaces.

Step 1. Rust areas such as this are common and are easily fixed

Step 2. Grind away all traces of rust with a 24-grit grinding disc. Be sure to grind back 3—4 inches from the edge of the hole down to bare metal and be sure all traces of rust are removed

BODY 187

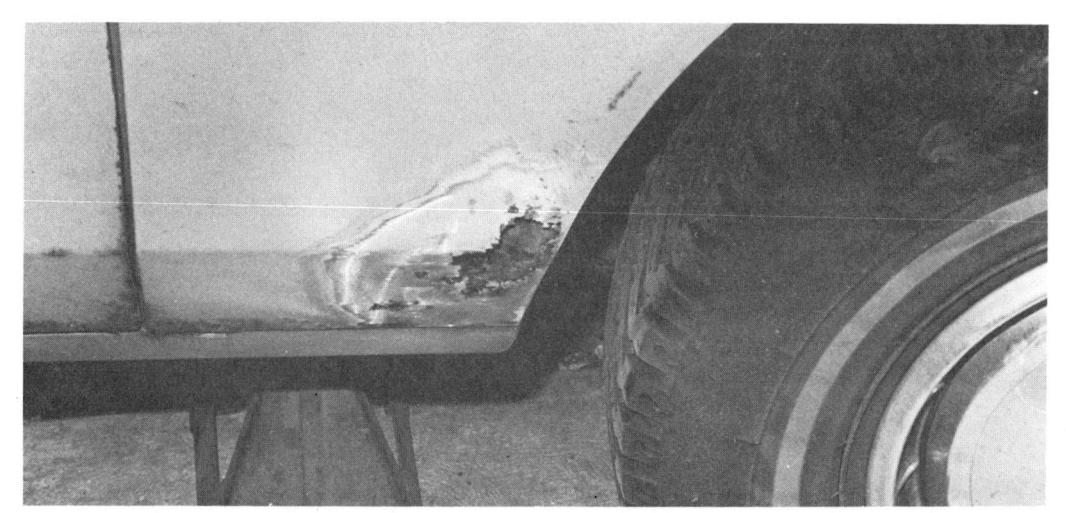

Step 3. Be sure all rust is removed from the edges of the metal. The edges must be ground back to un-rusted metal

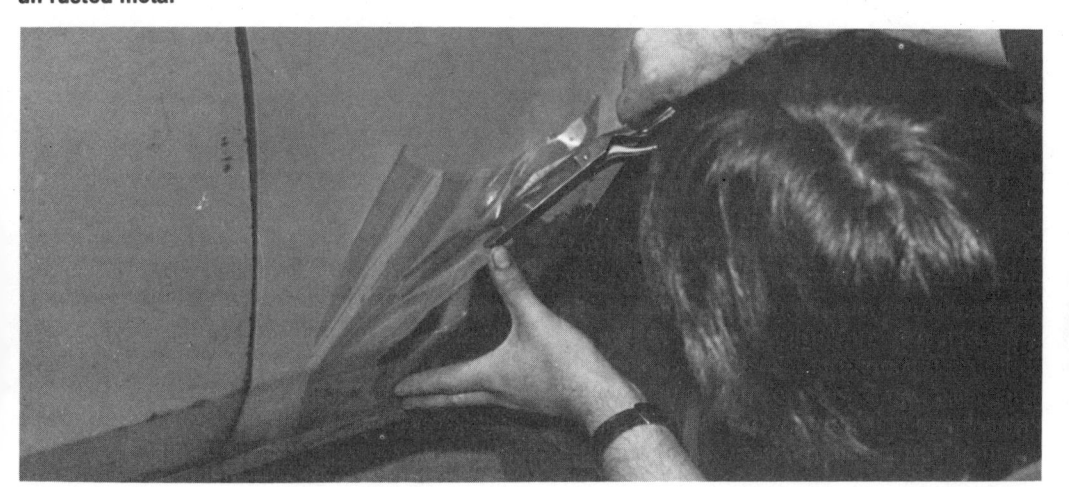

Step 4. If you are going to use release film, cut a piece about 2" larger than the area you have sanded. Place the film over the repair and mark the sanded area on the film. Avoid any unnecessary wrinkling of the film

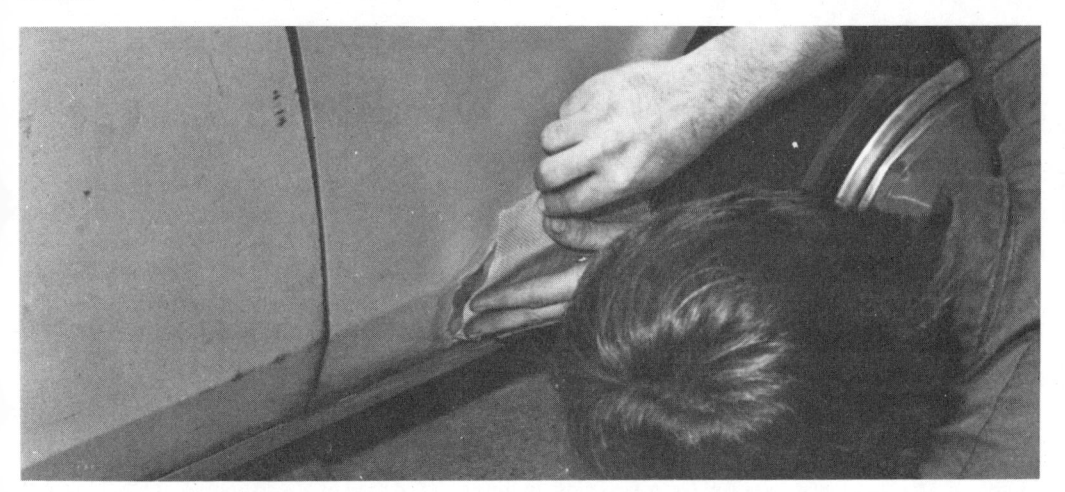

Step 5. Cut 2 pieces of fiberglass matte. One piece should be about 1" smaller than the sanded area and the second piece should be 1" smaller than the first. Use sharp scissors to avoid loose ends

188　BODY

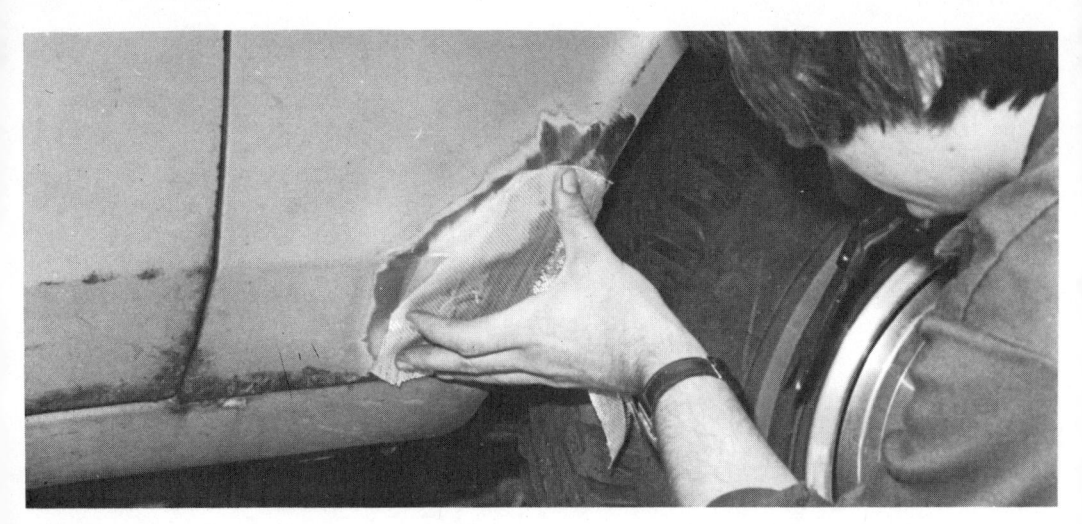

Step 6. Check the dimensions of the release film and cloth by holding them up to the repair area

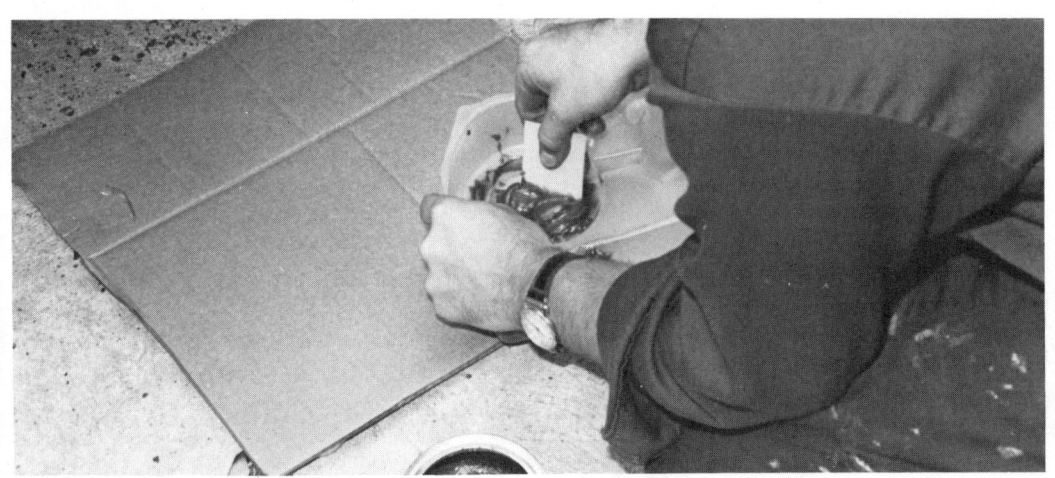

Step 7. Mix enough repair jelly and cream hardener in the mixing tray to saturate the fiberglass material or fill the repair area. Follow the directions on the container

Step 8. Lay the release sheet on a flat surface and spread an even layer of filler, large enough to cover the repair. Lay the smaller piece of fiberglass cloth in the center of the sheet and spread another layer of repair jelly over the fiberglass cloth. Repeat the operation for the larger piece of cloth. If the fiberglass cloth is not used, spread the repair jelly on the release film, concentrated in the middle of the repair

BODY 189

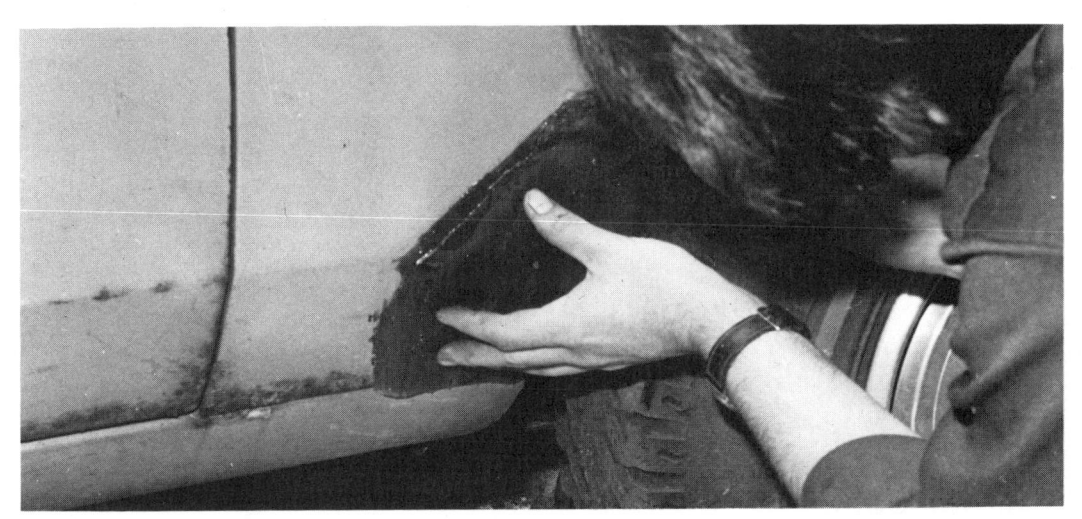

Step 9. Place the repair material over the repair area, with the release film facing outward

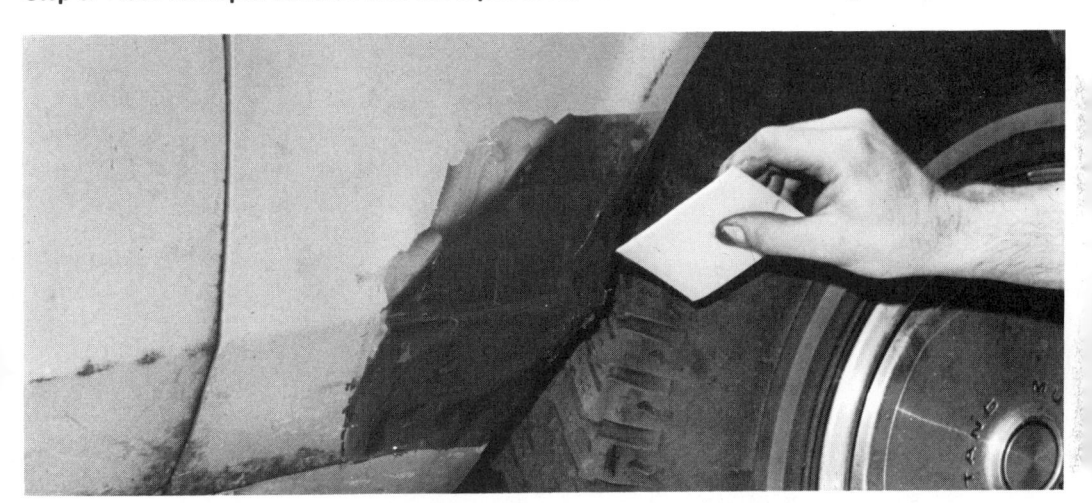

Step 10. Use a spreader and work from the center outward to smooth the material, following the body contours. Be sure to remove all air bubbles

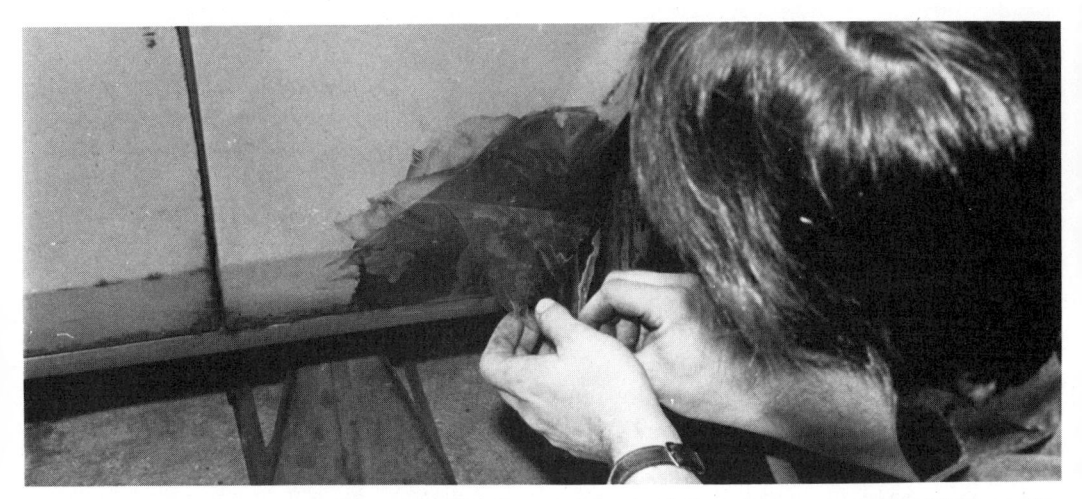

Step 11. Wait until the repair has dried tack-free and peel off the release sheet. The ideal working temperature is 65—90° F. Cooler or warmer temperatures or high humidity may require additional curing time

190 BODY

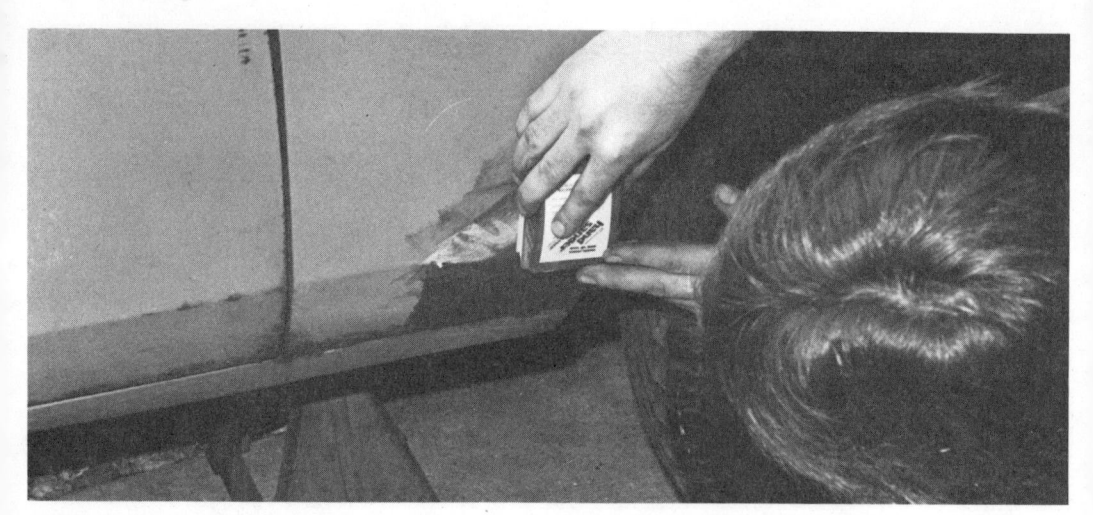

Step 12. Sand and feather-edge the entire area. The initial sanding can be done with a sanding disc on an electric drill if care is used. Finish the sanding with a block sander

Step 13. When the area is sanded smooth, mix some topcoat and hardener and apply it directly with a spreader. This will give a smooth finish and prevent the glass matte from showing through the paint

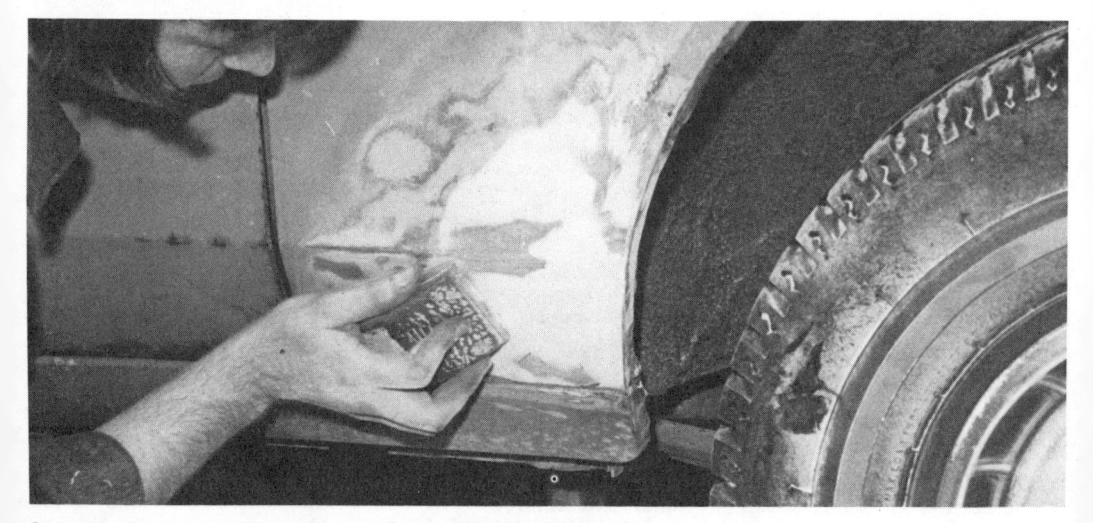

Step 14. Block sand the topcoat with finishing sandpaper

BODY 191

Step 15. To finish this repair, grind out the surface rust along the top edge of the rocker panel

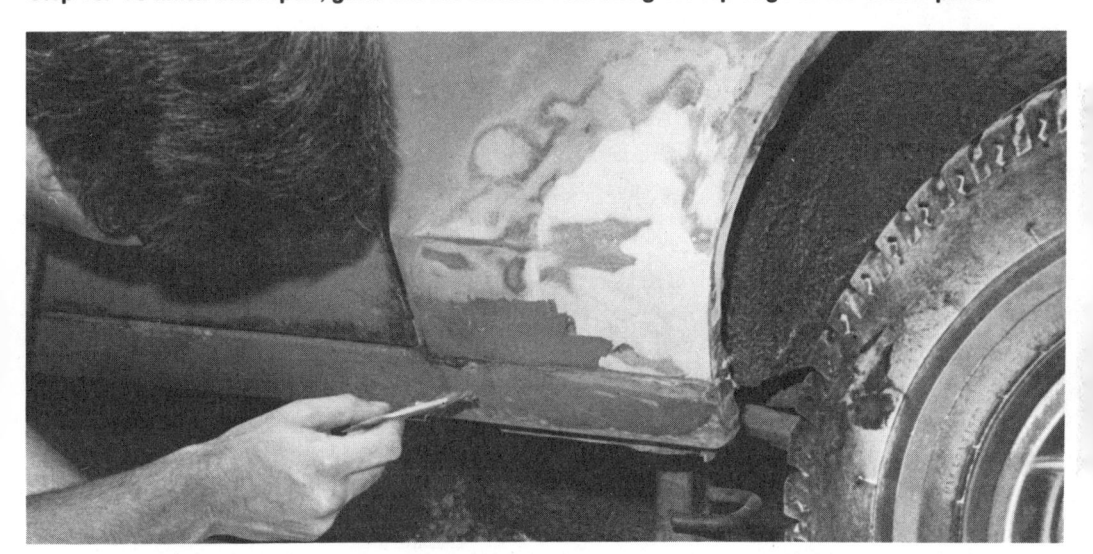

Step 16. Mix some more repair jelly and cream hardener and apply it directly over the surface

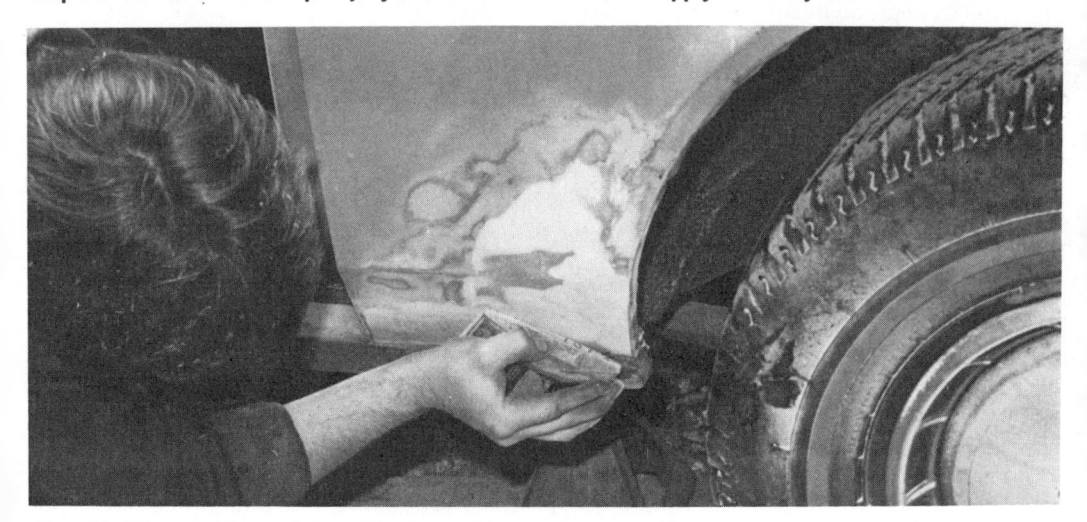

Step 17. When it dries tack-free, block sand the surface smooth

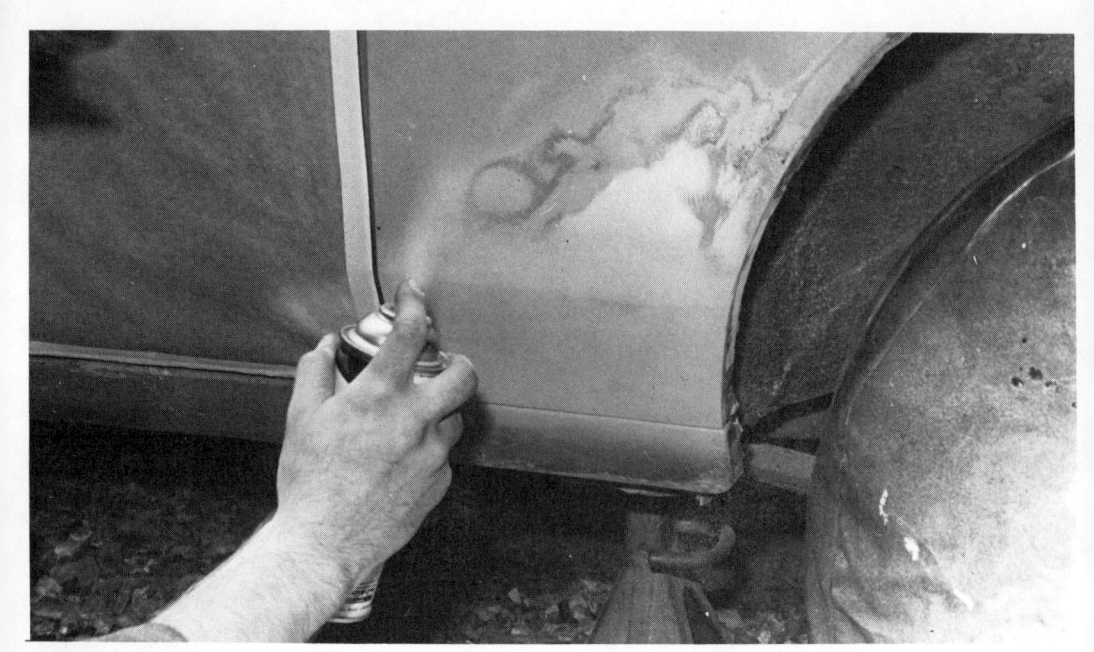

Step 18. If necessary, mask off adjacent panels and spray the entire repair with primer. You are now ready for a color coat

AUTO BODY CARE

There are hundreds—maybe thousands—of products on the market, all designed to protect or aid your car's finish in some manner. There are as many different products as there are ways to use them, but they all have one thing in common—the surface must be clean.

Washing

The primary ingredient for washing your car is water, preferably "soft" water. In many areas of the country, the local water supply is "hard" containing many minerals. The little rings or film that is left on your car's surface after it has dried is the result of "hard" water.

Since you usually can't change the local water supply, the next best thing is to dry the surface before it has a chance to dry itself.

Into the water you usually add soap. Don't use detergents or common, coarse soaps. Your car's paint never truly dries out, but is always evaporating residual oils into the air. Harsh detergents will remove these oils, causing the paint to dry faster than normal. Instead use warm water and a non-detergent soap made especially for waxed surfaces or a liquid soap made for waxed surfaces or a liquid soap made for washing dishes by hand.

Other products that can be used on painted surfaces include baking soda or plain soda water for stubborn dirt.

Wash the car completely, starting at the top, and rinse it completely clean. Abrasive grit should be loaded off under water pressure; scrubbing grit off will scratch the finish. The best washing tool is a sponge, cleaning mitt or soft towel. Whichever you choose, replace it often as each tends to absorb grease and dirt.

Other ways to get a better wash include:

• Don't wash your car in the sun or when the finish is hot.

• Use water pressure to remove caked-on dirt.

• Remove tree-sap and bird effluence immediately. Such substances will eat through wax, polish and paint.

One of the best implements to dry your car is a turkish towel or an old, soft bath towel. Anything with a deep nap will hold any dirt in suspension and not grind it into the paint.

Harder cloths will only grind the grit into the paint making more scratches. Always start drying at the top, followed by the hood and trunk and sides. You'll find there's always more dirt near the rocker panels and wheelwells which will wind up on the rest of the car if you dry these areas first.

Cleaners, Waxes and Polishes

Before going any farther you should know the function of various products.

Cleaners—remove the top layer of dead pigment or paint.

Rubbing or polishing compounds—used to remove stubborn dirt, get rid of minor scratches, smooth away imperfections and partially restore badly weathered paint.

Polishes—contain no abrasives or waxes; they shine the paint by adding oils to the paint.

Waxes—are a protective coating for the polish.

CLEANERS AND COMPOUNDS

Before you apply any wax, you'll have to remove oxidation, road film and other types of pollutants that washing alone will not remove.

The paint on your car never dries completely. There are always residual oils evaporating from the paint into the air. When enough oils are present in the paint, it has a healthy shine (gloss). When too many oils evaporate the paint takes on a whitish cast known as oxidation. The idea of polishing and waxing is to keep enough oil present in the painted surface to prevent oxidation; but when it occurs, the only recourse is to remove the top layer of "dead" paint, exposing the healthy paint underneath.

Products to remove oxidation and road film are sold under a variety of generic names—polishes, cleaner, rubbing compound, cleaner/polish, polish/cleaner, self-polishing wax, pre-wax cleaner, finish restorer and many more. Regardless of name there are two types of cleaners—abrasive cleaners (sometimes called polishing or rubbing compounds) that remove oxidation by grinding away the top layer of "dead" paint, or chemical cleaners that dissolve the "dead" pigment, allowing it to be wiped away.

Abrasive cleaners, by their nature, leave thousands of minute scratches in the finish, which must be polished out later. These should only be used in extreme cases, but are usually the only thing to use on badly oxidized paint finishes. Chemical cleaners are much milder but are not strong enough for severe cases of oxidation or weathered paint.

The most popular cleaners are liquid or paste abrasive polishing and rubbing compounds. Polishing compounds have a finer abrasive grit for medium duty work. Rubbing compounds are a coarser abrasive and for heavy duty work. Unless you are familiar with how to use compounds, be very careful. Excessive rubbing with any type of compound or cleaner can grind right through the paint to primer or bare metal. Follow the directions on the container—depending on type, the cleaner may or may not be OK for your paint. For example, some cleaners are not formulated for acrylic lacquer finishes.

When a small area needs compounding or heavy polishing, it's best to do the job by hand. Some people prefer a powered buffer for large areas. Avoid cutting through the paint along styling edges on the body. Small, hand operations where the compound is applied and rubbed using cloth folded into a thick ball allow you to work in straight lines along such edges.

To avoid cutting through on the edges when using a power buffer, try masking tape. Just cover the edge with tape while using power. Then finish the job by hand with the tape removed. Even then work carefully. The paint tends to be a lot thinner along the sharp ridges stamped into the panels.

Whether compounding by machine or by hand, only work on a small area and apply the compound sparingly. If the materials are spread too thin, or allowed to sit too long, they dry out. Once dry they lose the ability to deliver a smooth, clean finish. Also, dried out polish tends to cause the buffer to stick in one spot. This in turn can burn or cut through the finish.

WAXES AND POLISHES

Your car's finish can be protected in a number of ways. A cleaner/wax or polish/cleaner followed by wax or variations of each all provide good results. The two-step approach (polish followed by wax) is probably slightly better but consumes more time and effort. Properly fed with oils, your paint should never need cleaning, but despite the best polishing job, it won't last unless it's protected with wax. Without wax, polish must be renewed at least once a month to prevent oxidation. Years ago (some still swear by it today), the best wax was made from the Brazilian palm, the Carnuba, favored for its vegetable base and high melting point. However, modern synthetic waxes are harder, which means they protect against moisture better, and chemically inert silicone is used for a long lasting protection. The only problem with silicone wax is that it penetrates all layers of paint. To repaint or touch up a panel or car protected by silicone wax, you have to completely strip the finish to avoid "fisheyes."

Under normal conditions, silicone waxes will last 4–6 months, but you have to be careful of wax build-up from too much waxing. Too thick a coat of wax is just as bad as no wax at all; it stops the paint from breathing.

Combination cleaners/waxes have become popular lately because they remove the old layer of wax plus light oxidation, while putting on a fresh coat of wax at the same time. Some cleaners/waxes contain abrasive cleaners which require caution, although many cleaner/waxes use a chemical cleaner.

Applying Wax or Polish

You may view polishing and waxing your car as a pleasant way to spend an afternoon, or as a boring chore, but it has to be done to keep the paint on your car. Caring for the paint doesn't require special tools, but you should follow a few rules.

1. Use a good quality wax.
2. Before applying any wax or polish, be sure the surface is completely clean. Just because the car looks clean, doesn't mean it's ready for polish or wax.
3. If the finish on your car is weathered, dull, or oxidized, it will probably have to be compounded to remove the old or oxidized paint. If the paint is simply dulled from lack of care, one of the non-abrasive cleaners known as polishing compounds will do the trick. If the paint is severely scratched or really dull, you'll probably have to use a rubbing compound to prepare the finish for waxing. If you're not sure which one to use, use the polishing compound, since you can easily ruin the finish by using too strong a compound.
4. Don't apply wax, polish or compound in direct sunlight, even if the directions on the can say you can. Most waxes will not cure properly in bright sunlight and you'll probably end up with a blotchy looking finish.
5. Don't rub the wax off too soon. The result will be a wet, dull looking finish. Let the wax dry thoroughly before buffing it off.
6. A constant debate among car enthusiasts is how wax should be applied. Some maintain pastes or liquids should be applied in a circular motion, but body shop experts have long thought that this approach results in barely detectable circular abrasions, especially on cars that are waxed frequently. They advise rubbing in straight lines, especially if any kind of cleaner is involved.
7. If an applicator is not supplied with the wax, use a piece of soft cheesecloth or very soft lint-free material. The same applies to buffing the surface.

SPECIAL SURFACES

One-step combination cleaner and wax formulas shouldn't be used on many of the special surfaces which abound on cars. The one-step materials contain abrasives to achieve a clean surface under the wax top coat. The abrasives are so mild that you could clean a car every week for a couple of years without fear of rubbing through the paint. But this same level of abrasiveness might, through repeated use, damage decals used for special trim effects. This includes wide stripes, wood-grain trim and other appliques.

Painted plastics must be cleaned with care. If a cleaner is too aggressive it will cut through the paint and expose the primer. If bright trim such as polished aluminum or chrome is painted, cleaning must be performed with even greater care. If rubbing compound is being used, it will cut faster than polish.

Abrasive cleaners will dull an acrylic finish. The best way to clean these newer finishes is with a non-abrasive liquid polish. Only dirt and oxidation, not paint, will be removed.

Taking a few minutes to read the instructions on the can of polish or wax will help prevent making serious mistakes. Not all preparations will work on all surfaces. And some are intended for power application while others will only work when applied by hand.

Don't get the idea that just pouring on some polish and then hitting it with a buffer will suffice. Power equipment speeds the operation. But it also adds a measure of risk. It's very easy to damage the finish if you use the wrong methods or materials.

Caring for Chrome

Read the label on the container. Many products are formulated specifically for chrome, but others contain abrasives that will scratch the chrome finish. If it isn't recommended for chrome, don't use it.

Never use steel wool or kitchen soap pads to clean chrome. Be careful not to get chrome cleaner on paint or interior vinyl surfaces. If you do, get it off immediately.

Troubleshooting 10

This section is designed to aid in the quick, accurate diagnosis of automotive problems. While automotive repairs can be made by many people, accurate troubleshooting is a rare skill for the amateur and professional alike.

In its simplest state, troubleshooting is an exercise in logic. It is essential to realize that an automobile is really composed of a series of systems. Some of these systems are interrelated; others are not. Automobiles operate within a framework of logical rules and physical laws, and the key to troubleshooting is a good understanding of all the automotive systems.

This section breaks the car or truck down into its component systems, allowing the problem to be isolated. The charts and diagnostic road maps list the most common problems and the most probable causes of trouble. Obviously it would be impossible to list every possible problem that could happen along with every possible cause, but it will locate MOST problems and eliminate a lot of unnecessary guesswork. The systematic format will locate problems within a given system, but, because many automotive systems are interrelated, the solution to your particular problem may be found in a number of systems on the car or truck.

USING THE TROUBLESHOOTING CHARTS

This book contains all of the specific information that the average do-it-yourself mechanic needs to repair and maintain his or her car or truck. The troubleshooting charts are designed to be used in conjunction with the specific procedures and information in the text. For instance, troubleshooting a point-type ignition system is fairly standard for all models, but you may be directed to the text to find procedures for troubleshooting an individual type of electronic ignition. You will also have to refer to the specification charts throughout the book for specifications applicable to your car or truck.

TOOLS AND EQUIPMENT

The tools illustrated in Chapter 1 (plus two more diagnostic pieces) will be adequate to troubleshoot most problems. The two other tools needed are a voltmeter and an ohmmeter. These can be purchased separately or in combination, known as a VOM meter.

In the event that other tools are required, they will be noted in the procedures.

TROUBLESHOOTING

Troubleshooting Engine Problems
See Chapters 2, 3, 4 for more information and service procedures.

Index to Systems

System	To Test	Group
Battery	Engine need not be running	1
Starting system	Engine need not be running	2
Primary electrical system	Engine need not be running	3
Secondary electrical system	Engine need not be running	4
Fuel system	Engine need not be running	5
Engine compression	Engine need not be running	6
Engine vacuum	Engine must be running	7
Secondary electrical system	Engine must be running	8
Valve train	Engine must be running	9
Exhaust system	Engine must be running	10
Cooling system	Engine must be running	11
Engine lubrication	Engine must be running	12

Index to Problems

Problem: Symptom	Begin at Specific Diagnosis, Number ___
Engine Won't Start:	
Starter doesn't turn	1.1, 2.1
Starter turns, engine doesn't	2.1
Starter turns engine very slowly	1.1, 2.4
Starter turns engine normally	3.1, 4.1
Starter turns engine very quickly	6.1
Engine fires intermittently	4.1
Engine fires consistently	5.1, 6.1
Engine Runs Poorly:	
Hard starting	3.1, 4.1, 5.1, 8.1
Rough idle	4.1, 5.1, 8.1
Stalling	3.1, 4.1, 5.1, 8.1
Engine dies at high speeds	4.1, 5.1
Hesitation (on acceleration from standing stop)	5.1, 8.1
Poor pickup	4.1, 5.1, 8.1
Lack of power	3.1, 4.1, 5.1, 8.1
Backfire through the carburetor	4.1, 8.1, 9.1
Backfire through the exhaust	4.1, 8.1, 9.1
Blue exhaust gases	6.1, 7.1
Black exhaust gases	5.1
Running on (after the ignition is shut off)	3.1, 8.1
Susceptible to moisture	4.1
Engine misfires under load	4.1, 7.1, 8.4, 9.1
Engine misfires at speed	4.1, 8.4
Engine misfires at idle	3.1, 4.1, 5.1, 7.1, 8.4

Sample Section

Test and Procedure	Results and Indications	Proceed to
4.1—Check for spark: Hold each spark plug wire approximately ¼" from ground with gloves or a heavy, dry rag. Crank the engine and observe the spark.	If no spark is evident:	4.2
	If spark is good in some cases:	4.3
	If spark is good in all cases:	4.6

TROUBLESHOOTING 197

Specific Diagnosis

This section is arranged so that following each test, instructions are given to proceed to another, until a problem is diagnosed.

Section 1—Battery

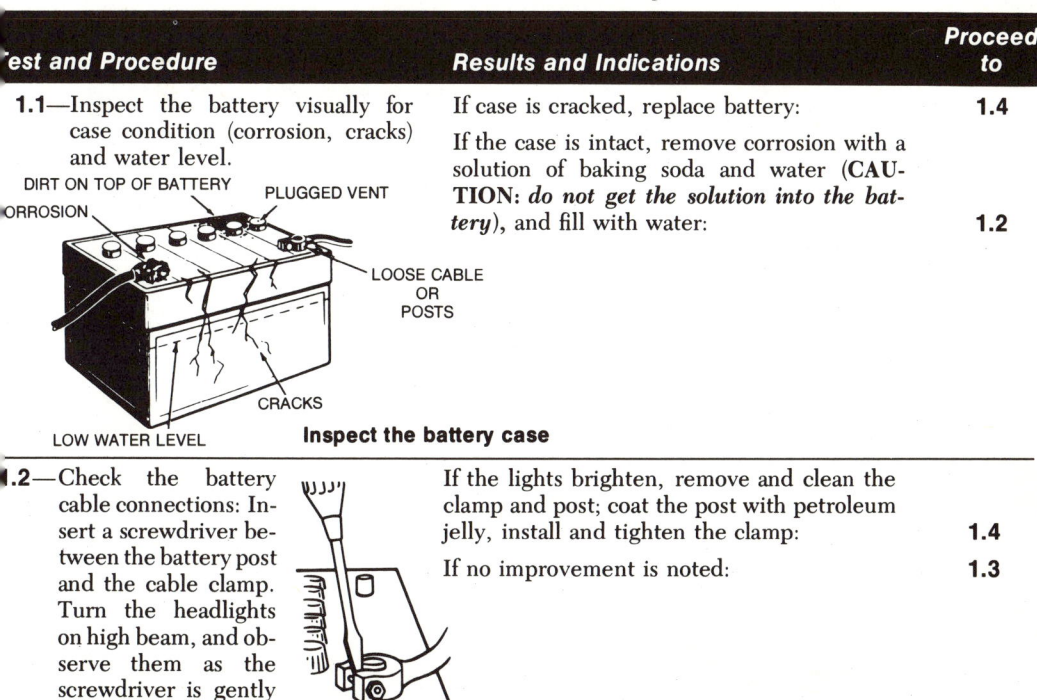

Test and Procedure	Results and Indications	Proceed to
1.1—Inspect the battery visually for case condition (corrosion, cracks) and water level.	If case is cracked, replace battery:	1.4
	If the case is intact, remove corrosion with a solution of baking soda and water (**CAUTION:** *do not get the solution into the battery*), and fill with water:	1.2
1.2—Check the battery cable connections: Insert a screwdriver between the battery post and the cable clamp. Turn the headlights on high beam, and observe them as the screwdriver is gently twisted to ensure good metal to metal contact.	If the lights brighten, remove and clean the clamp and post; coat the post with petroleum jelly, install and tighten the clamp:	1.4
	If no improvement is noted:	1.3
1.3—Test the state of charge of the battery using an individual cell tester or hydrometer.	If indicated, charge the battery. **NOTE:** *If no obvious reason exists for the low state of charge (i.e., battery age, prolonged storage),* proceed to:	1.4

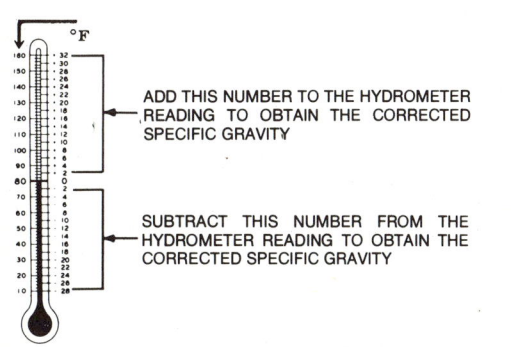

Specific Gravity (@ 80° F.)

Minimum		Battery Charge
1.260	....	100% Charged
1.230	....	75% Charged
1.200	....	50% Charged
1.170	....	25% Charged
1.140	....	Very Little Power Left
1.110	....	Completely Discharged

The effects of temperature on battery specific gravity (left) and amount of battery charge in relation to specific gravity (right)

1.4—Visually inspect battery cables for cracking, bad connection to ground, or bad connection to starter.	If necessary, tighten connections or replace the cables:	2.1

TROUBLESHOOTING

Section 2—Starting System
See Chapter 3 for service procedures

Test and Procedure	Results and Indications	Proceed to
Note: Tests in Group 2 are performed with coil high tension lead disconnected to prevent accidental starting.		
2.1—Test the starter motor and solenoid: Connect a jumper from the battery post of the solenoid (or relay) to the starter post of the solenoid (or relay).	If starter turns the engine normally:	2.2
	If the starter buzzes, or turns the engine very slowly:	2.4
	If no response, replace the solenoid (or relay).	3.1
	If the starter turns, but the engine doesn't, ensure that the flywheel ring gear is intact. If the gear is undamaged, replace the starter drive.	3.1
2.2—Determine whether ignition override switches are functioning properly (clutch start switch, neutral safety switch), by connecting a jumper across the switch(es), and turning the ignition switch to "start".	If starter operates, adjust or replace switch:	3.1
	If the starter doesn't operate:	2.3
2.3—Check the ignition switch "start" position: Connect a 12V test lamp or voltmeter between the starter post of the solenoid (or relay) and ground. Turn the ignition switch to the "start" position, and jiggle the key.	If the lamp doesn't light or the meter needle doesn't move when the switch is turned, check the ignition switch for loose connections, cracked insulation, or broken wires. Repair or replace as necessary:	3.1
	If the lamp flickers or needle moves when the key is jiggled, replace the ignition switch.	3.3

Checking the ignition switch "start" position

2.4—Remove and bench test the starter, according to specifications in the engine electrical section.	If the starter does not meet specifications, repair or replace as needed:	3.1
	If the starter is operating properly:	2.5
2.5—Determine whether the engine can turn freely: Remove the spark plugs, and check for water in the cylinders. Check for water on the dipstick, or oil in the radiator. Attempt to turn the engine using an 18" flex drive and socket on the crankshaft pulley nut or bolt.	If the engine will turn freely only with the spark plugs out, and hydrostatic lock (water in the cylinders) is ruled out, check valve timing:	9.2
	If engine will not turn freely, and it is known that the clutch and transmission are free, the engine must be disassembled for further evaluation:	Chapter 3

TROUBLESHOOTING

Section 3—Primary Electrical System

Test and Procedure	Results and Indications	Proceed to
3.1—Check the ignition switch "on" position: Connect a jumper wire between the distributor side of the coil and ground, and a 12V test lamp between the switch side of the coil and ground. Remove the high tension lead from the coil. Turn the ignition switch on and jiggle the key.	If the lamp lights:	3.2
	If the lamp flickers when the key is jiggled, replace the ignition switch:	3.3
	If the lamp doesn't light, check for loose or open connections. If none are found, remove the ignition switch and check for continuity. If the switch is faulty, replace it:	3.3

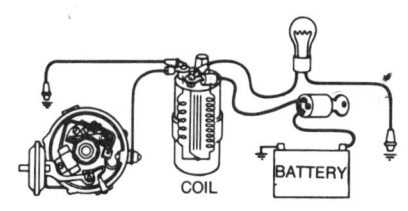

Checking the ignition switch "on" position

3.2—Check the ballast resistor or resistance wire for an open circuit, using an ohmmeter. See Chapter 3 for specific tests.	Replace the resistor or resistance wire if the resistance is zero. **NOTE:** *Some ignition systems have no ballast resistor.*	3.3

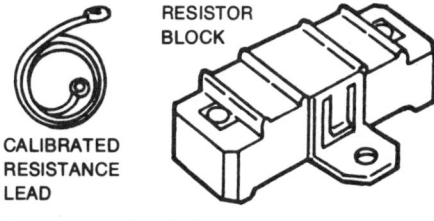

Two types of resistors

3.3—On point-type ignition systems, visually inspect the breaker points for burning, pitting or excessive wear. Gray coloring of the point contact surfaces is normal. Rotate the crankshaft until the contact heel rests on a high point of the distributor cam and adjust the point gap to specifications. On electronic ignition models, remove the distributor cap and visually inspect the armature. Ensure that the armature pin is in place, and that the armature is on tight and rotates when the engine is cranked. Make sure there are no cracks, chips or rounded edges on the armature.	If the breaker points are intact, clean the contact surfaces with fine emery cloth, and adjust the point gap to specifications. If the points are worn, replace them. On electronic systems, replace any parts which appear defective. If condition persists:	3.4

TROUBLESHOOTING

Test and Procedure	Results and Indications	Proceed to
3.4—On point-type ignition systems, connect a dwell-meter between the distributor primary lead and ground. Crank the engine and observe the point dwell angle. On electronic ignition systems, conduct a stator (magnetic pickup assembly) test. See Chapter 3.	On point-type systems, adjust the dwell angle if necessary. **NOTE:** *Increasing the point gap decreases the dwell angle and vice-versa.* If the dwell meter shows little or no reading; On electronic ignition systems, if the stator is bad, replace the stator. If the stator is good, proceed to the other tests in Chapter 3.	3.6 3.5

Dwell is a function of point gap

NORMAL DWELL (CLOSE / OPEN)	INSUFFICIENT DWELL (WIDE GAP / SMALL DWELL)	EXCESSIVE DWELL (NARROW GAP / LARGE DWELL)

Test and Procedure	Results and Indications	Proceed to
3.5—On the point-type ignition systems, check the condenser for short: connect an ohmmeter across the condenser body and the pigtail lead.	If any reading other than infinite is noted, replace the condenser	3.6

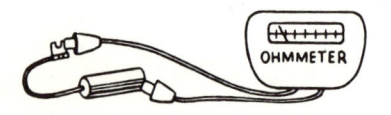

Checking the condenser for short

Test and Procedure	Results and Indications	Proceed to
3.6—Test the coil primary resistance: On point-type ignition systems, connect an ohmmeter across the coil primary terminals, and read the resistance on the low scale. Note whether an external ballast resistor or resistance wire is used. On electronic ignition systems, test the coil primary resistance as in Chapter 3.	Point-type ignition coils utilizing ballast resistors or resistance wires should have approximately 1.0 ohms resistance. Coils with internal resistors should have approximately 4.0 ohms resistance. If values far from the above are noted, replace the coil.	4.1

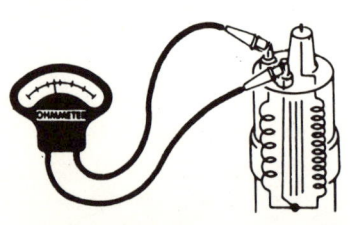

Check the coil primary resistance

TROUBLESHOOTING

Section 4—Secondary Electrical System
See Chapters 2–3 for service procedures

Test and Procedure	Results and Indications	Proceed to
4.1—Check for spark: Hold each spark plug wire approximately ¼" from ground with gloves or a heavy, dry rag. Crank the engine, and observe the spark.	If no spark is evident:	4.2
	If spark is good in some cylinders:	4.3
	If spark is good in all cylinders:	4.6

Check for spark at the plugs

4.2—Check for spark at the coil high tension lead: Remove the coil high tension lead from the distributor and position it approximately ¼" from ground. Crank the engine and observe spark. **CAUTION: This test should not be performed on engines equipped with electronic ignition.**	If the spark is good and consistent:	4.3
	If the spark is good but intermittent, test the primary electrical system starting at 3.3:	3.3
	If the spark is weak or non-existent, replace the coil high tension lead, clean and tighten all connections and retest. If no improvement is noted:	4.4
4.3—Visually inspect the distributor cap and rotor for burned or corroded contacts, cracks, carbon tracks, or moisture. Also check the fit of the rotor on the distributor shaft (where applicable).	If moisture is present, dry thoroughly, and retest per 4.1:	4.1
	If burned or excessively corroded contacts, cracks, or carbon tracks are noted, replace the defective part(s) and retest per 4.1:	4.1
	If the rotor and cap appear intact, or are only slightly corroded, clean the contacts thoroughly (including the cap towers and spark plug wire ends) and retest per 4.1:	
	If the spark is good in all cases:	4.6
	If the spark is poor in all cases:	4.5

Inspect the distributor cap and rotor

202 TROUBLESHOOTING

Test and Procedure	Results and Indications	Proceed to
4.4—Check the coil secondary resistance: On point-type systems connect an ohmmeter across the distributor side of the coil and the coil tower. Read the resistance on the high scale of the ohmmeter. On electronic ignition systems, see Chapter 3 for specific tests.	The resistance of a satisfactory coil should be between 4,000 and 10,000 ohms. If resistance is considerably higher (i.e., 40,000 ohms) replace the coil and retest per 4.1. **NOTE:** *This does not apply to high performance coils.*	

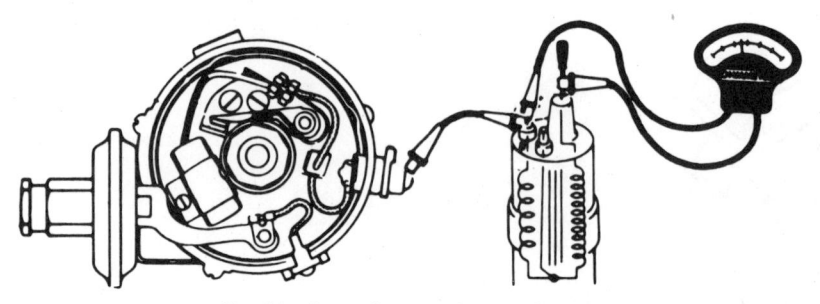

Testing the coil secondary resistance

4.5—Visually inspect the spark plug wires for cracking or brittleness. Ensure that no two wires are positioned so as to cause induction firing (adjacent and parallel). Remove each wire, one by one, and check resistance with an ohmmeter.	Replace any cracked or brittle wires. If any of the wires are defective, replace the entire set. Replace any wires with excessive resistance (over 8000 Ω per foot for suppression wire), and separate any wires that might cause induction firing.	4.6

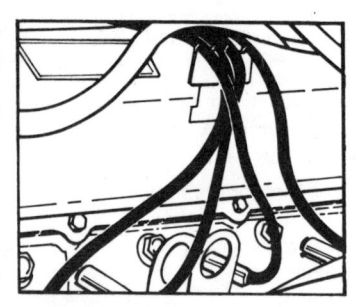

Misfiring can be the result of spark plug leads to adjacent, consecutively firing cylinders running parallel and too close together

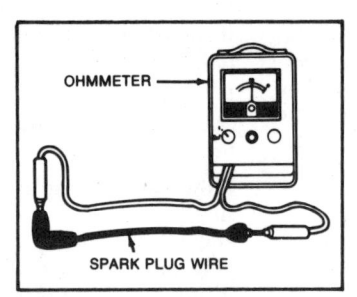

On point-type ignition systems, check the spark plug wires as shown. On electronic ignitions, do not remove the wire from the distributor cap terminal; instead, test through the cap

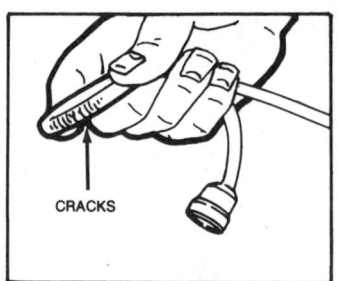

Spark plug wires can be checked visually by bending them in a loop over your finger. This will reveal any cracks, burned or broken insulation. Any wire with cracked insulation should be replaced

4.6—Remove the spark plugs, noting the cylinders from which they were removed, and evaluate according to the color photos in the middle of this book.	See following.	See following.

TROUBLESHOOTING

Test and Procedure	Results and Indications	Proceed to
4.7—Examine the location of all the plugs.	The following diagrams illustrate some of the conditions that the location of plugs will reveal.	4.8

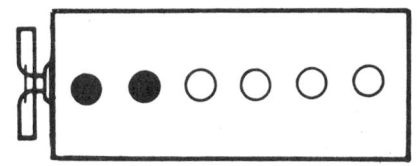

Two adjacent plugs are fouled in a 6-cylinder engine, 4-cylinder engine or either bank of a V-8. This is probably due to a blown head gasket between the two cylinders

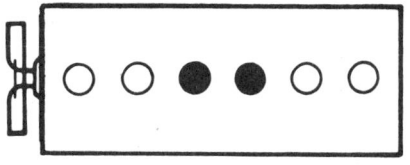

The two center plugs in a 6-cylinder engine are fouled. Raw fuel may be "boiled" out of the carburetor into the intake manifold after the engine is shut-off. Stop-start driving can also foul the center plugs, due to overly rich mixture. Proper float level, a new float needle and seat or use of an insulating spacer may help this problem

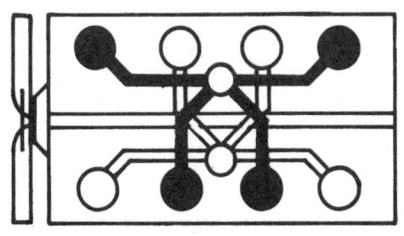

An unbalanced carburetor is indicated. Following the fuel flow on this particular design shows that the cylinders fed by the right-hand barrel are fouled from overly rich mixture, while the cylinders fed by the left-hand barrel are normal

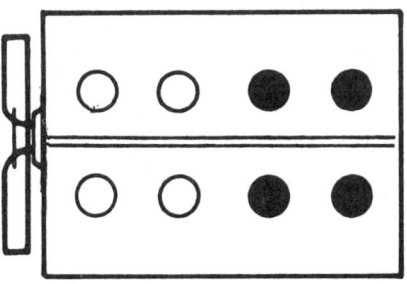

If the four rear plugs are overheated, a cooling system problem is suggested. A thorough cleaning of the cooling system may restore coolant circulation and cure the problem

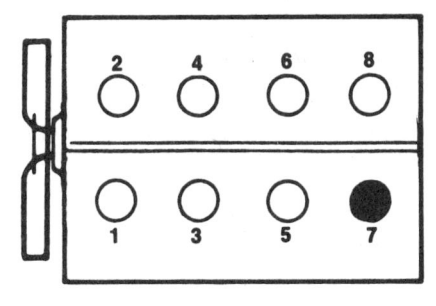

Finding one plug overheated may indicate an intake manifold leak near the affected cylinder. If the overheated plug is the second of two adjacent, consecutively firing plugs, it could be the result of ignition cross-firing. Separating the leads to these two plugs will eliminate cross-fire

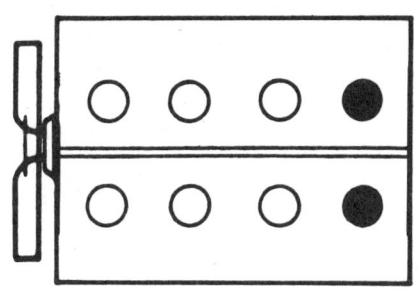

Occasionally, the two rear plugs in large, lightly used V-8's will become oil fouled. High oil consumption and smoky exhaust may also be noticed. It is probably due to plugged oil drain holes in the rear of the cylinder head, causing oil to be sucked in around the valve stems. This usually occurs in the rear cylinders first, because the engine slants that way

204 TROUBLESHOOTING

Test and Procedure	Results and Indications	Proceed to
4.8—Determine the static ignition timing. Using the crankshaft pulley timing marks as a guide, locate top dead center on the compression stroke of the number one cylinder.	The rotor should be pointing toward the No. 1 tower in the distributor cap, and, on electronic ignitions, the armature spoke for that cylinder should be lined up with the stator.	4.8
4.9—Check coil polarity: Connect a voltmeter negative lead to the coil high tension lead, and the positive lead to ground (**NOTE:** *Reverse the hook-up for positive ground systems*). Crank the engine momentarily.	If the voltmeter reads up-scale, the polarity is correct: If the voltmeter reads down-scale, reverse the coil polarity (switch the primary leads): **Checking coil polarity**	5.1 5.1

Section 5—Fuel System
See Chapter 4 for service procedures

Test and Procedure	Results and Indications	Proceed to
5.1—Determine that the air filter is functioning efficiently: Hold paper elements up to a strong light, and attempt to see light through the filter.	Clean permanent air filters in solvent (or manufacturer's recommendation), and allow to dry. Replace paper elements through which light cannot be seen:	5.2
5.2—Determine whether a flooding condition exists: Flooding is identified by a strong gasoline odor, and excessive gasoline present in the throttle bore(s) of the carburetor.	If flooding is not evident: If flooding is evident, permit the gasoline to dry for a few moments and restart. If flooding doesn't recur: If flooding is persistent: **If the engine floods repeatedly, check the choke butterfly flap**	5.3 5.7 5.5
5.3—Check that fuel is reaching the carburetor: Detach the fuel line at the carburetor inlet. Hold the end of the line in a cup (not styrofoam), and crank the engine.	If fuel flows smoothly: If fuel doesn't flow (**NOTE:** *Make sure that there is fuel in the tank*), or flows erratically: **Check the fuel pump by disconnecting the output line (fuel pump-to-carburetor) at the carburetor and operating the starter briefly**	5.7 5.4

TROUBLESHOOTING

Test and Procedure	Results and Indications	Proceed to
5.4—Test the fuel pump: Disconnect all fuel lines from the fuel pump. Hold a finger over the input fitting, crank the engine (with electric pump, turn the ignition or pump on); and feel for suction.	If suction is evident, blow out the fuel line to the tank with low pressure compressed air until bubbling is heard from the fuel filler neck. Also blow out the carburetor fuel line (both ends disconnected):	5.7
	If no suction is evident, replace or repair the fuel pump: NOTE: *Repeated oil fouling of the spark plugs, or a no-start condition, could be the result of a ruptured vacuum booster pump diaphragm, through which oil or gasoline is being drawn into the intake manifold (where applicable).*	5.7
5.5—Occasionally, small specks of dirt will clog the small jets and orifices in the carburetor. With the engine cold, hold a flat piece of wood or similar material over the carburetor, where possible, and crank the engine.	If the engine starts, but runs roughly the engine is probably not run enough. If the engine won't start:	5.9
5.6—Check the needle and seat: Tap the carburetor in the area of the needle and seat.	If flooding stops, a gasoline additive (e.g., Gumout) will often cure the problem:	5.7
	If flooding continues, check the fuel pump for excessive pressure at the carburetor (according to specifications). If the pressure is normal, the needle and seat must be removed and checked, and/or the float level adjusted:	5.7
5.7—Test the accelerator pump by looking into the throttle bores while operating the throttle.	If the accelerator pump appears to be operating normally:	5.8
	If the accelerator pump is not operating, the pump must be reconditioned. Where possible, service the pump with the carburetor(s) installed on the engine. If necessary, remove the carburetor. Prior to removal:	5.8

Check for gas at the carburetor by looking down the carburetor throat while someone moves the accelerator

5.8—Determine whether the carburetor main fuel system is functioning: Spray a commercial starting fluid into the carburetor while attempting to start the engine.	If the engine starts, runs for a few seconds, and dies:	5.9
	If the engine doesn't start:	6.1

206 TROUBLESHOOTING

Test and Procedure	Results and Indications	Proceed to
5.9—Uncommon fuel system malfunctions: See below:	If the problem is solved:	6.1
	If the problem remains, remove and recondition the carburetor.	

Condition	Indication	Test	Prevailing Weather Conditions	Remedy
Vapor lock	Engine will not restart shortly after running.	Cool the components of the fuel system until the engine starts. Vapor lock can be cured faster by draping a wet cloth over a mechanical fuel pump.	Hot to very hot	Ensure that the exhaust manifold heat control valve is operating. Check with the vehicle manufacturer for the recommended solution to vapor lock on the model in question.
Carburetor icing	Engine will not idle, stalls at low speeds.	Visually inspect the throttle plate area of the throttle bores for frost.	High humidity, 32–40° F.	Ensure that the exhaust manifold heat control valve is operating, and that the intake manifold heat riser is not blocked.
Water in the fuel	Engine sputters and stalls; may not start.	Pump a small amount of fuel into a glass jar. Allow to stand, and inspect for droplets or a layer of water.	High humidity, extreme temperature changes.	For droplets, use one or two cans of commercial gas line anti-freeze. For a layer of water, the tank must be drained, and the fuel lines blown out with compressed air.

Section 6—Engine Compression
See Chapter 3 for service procedures

6.1—Test engine compression: Remove all spark plugs. Block the throttle wide open. Insert a compression gauge into a spark plug port, crank the engine to obtain the maximum reading, and record.	If compression is within limits on all cylinders:	7.1
	If gauge reading is extremely low on all cylinders:	6.2
	If gauge reading is low on one or two cylinders: (If gauge readings are identical and low on two or more adjacent cylinders, the head gasket must be replaced.)	6.2
	Checking compression	
6.2—Test engine compression (wet): Squirt approximately 30 cc. of engine oil into each cylinder, and retest per 6.1.	If the readings improve, worn or cracked rings or broken pistons are indicated:	See Chapter 3
	If the readings do not improve, burned or excessively carboned valves or a jumped timing chain are indicated: NOTE: *A jumped timing chain is often indicated by difficult cranking.*	7.1

TROUBLESHOOTING

Section 7—Engine Vacuum
See Chapter 3 for service procedures

Test and Procedure	Results and Indications	Proceed to
7.1—Attach a vacuum gauge to the intake manifold beyond the throttle plate. Start the engine, and observe the action of the needle over the range of engine speeds.	See below.	See below

INDICATION: normal engine in good condition

Proceed to: 8.1

Normal engine
Gauge reading: steady, from 17–22 in./Hg.

INDICATION: sticking valves or ignition miss

Proceed to: 9.1, 8.3

Sticking valves
Gauge reading: intermittent fluctuation at idle

INDICATION: late ignition or valve timing, low compression, stuck throttle valve, leaking carburetor or manifold gasket

Proceed to: 6.1

Incorrect valve timing
Gauge reading: low (10–15 in./Hg) but steady

INDICATION: improper carburetor adjustment or minor intake leak.

Proceed to: 7.2

Carburetor requires adjustment
Gauge reading: drifting needle

INDICATION: ignition miss, blown cylinder head gasket, leaking valve or weak valve spring

Proceed to: 8.3, 6.1

Blown head gasket
Gauge reading: needle fluctuates as engine speed increases

INDICATION: burnt valve or faulty valve clearance. Needle will fall when defective valve operates

Proceed to: 9.1

Burnt or leaking valves
Gauge reading: steady needle, but drops regularly

INDICATION: choked muffler, excessive back pressure in system

Proceed to: 10.1

Clogged exhaust system
Gauge reading: gradual drop in reading at idle

INDICATION: worn valve guides

Proceed to: 9.1

Worn valve guides
Gauge reading: needle vibrates excessively at idle, but steadies as engine speed increases

White pointer = steady gauge hand

Black pointer = fluctuating gauge hand

TROUBLESHOOTING

Test and Procedure	Results and Indications	Proceed to
7.2—Attach a vacuum gauge per 7.1, and test for an intake manifold leak. Squirt a small amount of oil around the intake manifold gaskets, carburetor gaskets, plugs and fittings. Observe the action of the vacuum gauge.	If the reading improves, replace the indicated gasket, or seal the indicated fitting or plug: If the reading remains low:	8.1 7.3
7.3—Test all vacuum hoses and accessories for leaks as described in 7.2. Also check the carburetor body (dashpots, automatic choke mechanism, throttle shafts) for leaks in the same manner.	If the reading improves, service or replace the offending part(s): If the reading remains low:	8.1 6.1

Section 8—Secondary Electrical System
See Chapter 2 for service procedures

Test and Procedure	Results and Indications	Proceed to
8.1—Remove the distributor cap and check to make sure that the rotor turns when the engine is cranked. Visually inspect the distributor components.	Clean, tighten or replace any components which appear defective.	8.2
8.2—Connect a timing light (per manufacturer's recommendation) and check the dynamic ignition timing. Disconnect and plug the vacuum hose(s) to the distributor if specified, start the engine, and observe the timing marks at the specified engine speed.	If the timing is not correct, adjust to specifications by rotating the distributor in the engine: (Advance timing by rotating distributor opposite normal direction of rotor rotation, retard timing by rotating distributor in same direction as rotor rotation.)	8.3
8.3—Check the operation of the distributor advance mechanism(s): To test the mechanical advance, disconnect the vacuum lines from the distributor advance unit and observe the timing marks with a timing light as the engine speed is increased from idle. If the mark moves smoothly, without hesitation, it may be assumed that the mechanical advance is functioning properly. To test vacuum advance and/or retard systems, alternately crimp and release the vacuum line, and observe the timing mark for movement. If movement is noted, the system is operating.	If the systems are functioning: If the systems are not functioning, remove the distributor, and test on a distributor tester:	8.4 8.4
8.4—Locate an ignition miss: With the engine running, remove each spark plug wire, one at a time, until one is found that doesn't cause the engine to roughen and slow down.	When the missing cylinder is identified:	4.1

Section 9—Valve Train
See Chapter 3 for service procedures

Test and Procedure	Results and Indications	Proceed to
9.1—Evaluate the valve train: Remove the valve cover, and ensure that the valves are adjusted to specifications. A mechanic's stethoscope may be used to aid in the diagnosis of the valve train. By pushing the probe on or near push rods or rockers, valve noise often can be isolated. A timing light also may be used to diagnose valve problems. Connect the light according to manufacturer's recommendations, and start the engine. Vary the firing moment of the light by increasing the engine speed (and therefore the ignition advance), and moving the trigger from cylinder to cylinder. Observe the movement of each valve.	Sticking valves or erratic valve train motion can be observed with the timing light. The cylinder head must be disassembled for repairs.	**See Chapter 3**
9.2—Check the valve timing: Locate top dead center of the No. 1 piston, and install a degree wheel or tape on the crankshaft pulley or damper with zero corresponding to an index mark on the engine. Rotate the crankshaft in its direction of rotation, and observe the opening of the No. 1 cylinder intake valve. The opening should correspond with the correct mark on the degree wheel according to specifications.	If the timing is not correct, the timing cover must be removed for further investigation.	**See Chapter 3**

Section 10—Exhaust System

Test and Procedure	Results and Indications	Proceed to
10.1—Determine whether the exhaust manifold heat control valve is operating: Operate the valve by hand to determine whether it is free to move. If the valve is free, run the engine to operating temperature and observe the action of the valve, to ensure that it is opening.	If the valve sticks, spray it with a suitable solvent, open and close the valve to free it, and retest.	
	If the valve functions properly:	10.2
	If the valve does not free, or does not operate, replace the valve:	10.2
10.2—Ensure that there are no exhaust restrictions: Visually inspect the exhaust system for kinks, dents, or crushing. Also note that gases are flowing freely from the tailpipe at all engine speeds, indicating no restriction in the muffler or resonator.	Replace any damaged portion of the system:	11.1

Section 11—Cooling System
See Chapter 3 for service procedures

Test and Procedure	Results and Indications	Proceed to
11.1—Visually inspect the fan belt for glazing, cracks, and fraying, and replace if necessary. Tighten the belt so that the longest span has approximately ½" play at its midpoint under thumb pressure (see Chapter 1).	Replace or tighten the fan belt as necessary: *Checking belt tension*	**11.2**
11.2—Check the fluid level of the cooling system.	If full or slightly low, fill as necessary:	**11.5**
	If extremely low:	**11.3**
11.3—Visually inspect the external portions of the cooling system (radiator, radiator hoses, thermostat elbow, water pump seals, heater hoses, etc.) for leaks. If none are found, pressurize the cooling system to 14–15 psi.	If cooling system holds the pressure:	**11.5**
	If cooling system loses pressure rapidly, reinspect external parts of the system for leaks under pressure. If none are found, check dipstick for coolant in crankcase. If no coolant is present, but pressure loss continues:	**11.4**
	If coolant is evident in crankcase, remove cylinder head(s), and check gasket(s). If gaskets are intact, block and cylinder head(s) should be checked for cracks or holes. If the gasket(s) is blown, replace, and purge the crankcase of coolant: **NOTE:** *Occasionally, due to atmospheric and driving conditions, condensation of water can occur in the crankcase. This causes the oil to appear milky white. To remedy, run the engine until hot, and change the oil and oil filter.*	**12.6**
11.4—Check for combustion leaks into the cooling system: Pressurize the cooling system as above. Start the engine, and observe the pressure gauge. If the needle fluctuates, remove each spark plug wire, one at a time, noting which cylinder(s) reduce or eliminate the fluctuation.	Cylinders which reduce or eliminate the fluctuation, when the spark plug wire is removed, are leaking into the cooling system. Replace the head gasket on the affected cylinder bank(s). *Pressurizing the cooling system*	

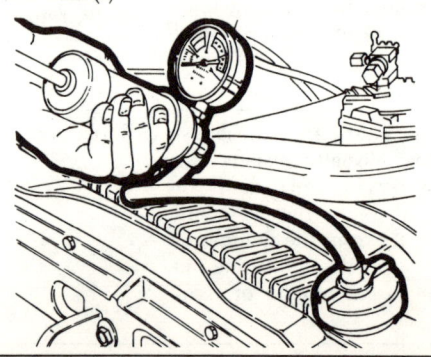

TROUBLESHOOTING

Test and Procedure	Results and Indications	Proceed to
11.5—Check the radiator pressure cap: Attach a radiator pressure tester to the radiator cap (wet the seal prior to installation). Quickly pump up the pressure, noting the point at which the cap releases.	If the cap releases within ± 1 psi of the specified rating, it is operating properly:	11.6
	If the cap releases at more than ± 1 psi of the specified rating, it should be replaced:	11.6

Checking radiator pressure cap

11.6—Test the thermostat: Start the engine cold, remove the radiator cap, and insert a thermometer into the radiator. Allow the engine to idle. After a short while, there will be a sudden, rapid increase in coolant temperature. The temperature at which this sharp rise stops is the thermostat opening temperature.	If the thermostat opens at or about the specified temperature:	11.7
	If the temperature doesn't increase: (If the temperature increases slowly and gradually, replace the thermostat.)	11.7
11.7—Check the water pump: Remove the thermostat elbow and the thermostat, disconnect the coil high tension lead (to prevent starting), and crank the engine momentarily.	If coolant flows, replace the thermostat and retest per 11.6:	11.6
	If coolant doesn't flow, reverse flush the cooling system to alleviate any blockage that might exist. If system is not blocked, and coolant will not flow, replace the water pump.	

Section 12—Lubrication
See Chapter 3 for service procedures

Test and Procedure	Results and Indications	Proceed to
12.1—Check the oil pressure gauge or warning light: If the gauge shows low pressure, or the light is on for no obvious reason, remove the oil pressure sender. Install an accurate oil pressure gauge and run the engine momentarily.	If oil pressure builds normally, run engine for a few moments to determine that it is functioning normally, and replace the sender.	—
	If the pressure remains low:	12.2
	If the pressure surges:	12.3
	If the oil pressure is zero:	12.3
12.2—Visually inspect the oil: If the oil is watery or very thin, milky, or foamy, replace the oil and oil filter.	If the oil is normal:	12.3
	If after replacing oil the pressure remains low:	12.3
	If after replacing oil the pressure becomes normal:	—

212 TROUBLESHOOTING

Test and Procedure	Results and Indications	Proceed to
12.3—Inspect the oil pressure relief valve and spring, to ensure that it is not sticking or stuck. Remove and thoroughly clean the valve, spring, and the valve body.	If the oil pressure improves: If no improvement is noted:	— 12.4
12.4—Check to ensure that the oil pump is not cavitating (sucking air instead of oil): See that the crankcase is neither over nor underfull, and that the pickup in the sump is in the proper position and free from sludge.	Fill or drain the crankcase to the proper capacity, and clean the pickup screen in solvent if necessary. If no improvement is noted:	12.5
12.5—Inspect the oil pump drive and the oil pump:	If the pump drive or the oil pump appear to be defective, service as necessary and retest per 12.1:	12.1
	If the pump drive and pump appear to be operating normally, the engine should be disassembled to determine where blockage exists:	See Chapter 3
12.6—Purge the engine of ethylene glycol coolant: Completely drain the crankcase and the oil filter. Obtain a commercial butyl cellosolve base solvent, designated for this purpose, and follow the instructions precisely. Following this, install a new oil filter and refill the crankcase with the proper weight oil. The next oil and filter change should follow shortly thereafter (1000 miles).		

TROUBLESHOOTING EMISSION CONTROL SYSTEMS

See Chapter 4 for procedures applicable to individual emission control systems used on specific combinations of engine/transmission/model.

TROUBLESHOOTING THE CARBURETOR
See Chapter 4 for service procedures

Carburetor problems cannot be effectively isolated unless all other engine systems (particularly ignition and emission) are functioning properly and the engine is properly tuned.

TROUBLESHOOTING

Condition	Possible Cause
Engine cranks, but does not start	1. Improper starting procedure 2. No fuel in tank 3. Clogged fuel line or filter 4. Defective fuel pump 5. Choke valve not closing properly 6. Engine flooded 7. Choke valve not unloading 8. Throttle linkage not making full travel 9. Stuck needle or float 10. Leaking float needle or seat 11. Improper float adjustment
Engine stalls	1. Improperly adjusted idle speed or mixture **Engine hot** 2. Improperly adjusted dashpot 3. Defective or improperly adjusted solenoid 4. Incorrect fuel level in fuel bowl 5. Fuel pump pressure too high 6. Leaking float needle seat 7. Secondary throttle valve stuck open 8. Air or fuel leaks 9. Idle air bleeds plugged or missing 10. Idle passages plugged **Engine Cold** 11. Incorrectly adjusted choke 12. Improperly adjusted fast idle speed 13. Air leaks 14. Plugged idle or idle air passages 15. Stuck choke valve or binding linkage 16. Stuck secondary throttle valves 17. Engine flooding—high fuel level 18. Leaking or misaligned float
Engine hesitates on acceleration	1. Clogged fuel filter 2. Leaking fuel pump diaphragm 3. Low fuel pump pressure 4. Secondary throttle valves stuck, bent or misadjusted 5. Sticking or binding air valve 6. Defective accelerator pump 7. Vacuum leaks 8. Clogged air filter 9. Incorrect choke adjustment (engine cold)
Engine feels sluggish or flat on acceleration	1. Improperly adjusted idle speed or mixture 2. Clogged fuel filter 3. Defective accelerator pump 4. Dirty, plugged or incorrect main metering jets 5. Bent or sticking main metering rods 6. Sticking throttle valves 7. Stuck heat riser 8. Binding or stuck air valve 9. Dirty, plugged or incorrect secondary jets 10. Bent or sticking secondary metering rods. 11. Throttle body or manifold heat passages plugged 12. Improperly adjusted choke or choke vacuum break.
Carburetor floods	1. Defective fuel pump. Pressure too high. 2. Stuck choke valve 3. Dirty, worn or damaged float or needle valve/seat 4. Incorrect float/fuel level 5. Leaking float bowl

TROUBLESHOOTING

Condition	Possible Cause
Engine idles roughly and stalls	1. Incorrect idle speed 2. Clogged fuel filter 3. Dirt in fuel system or carburetor 4. Loose carburetor screws or attaching bolts 5. Broken carburetor gaskets 6. Air leaks 7. Dirty carburetor 8. Worn idle mixture needles 9. Throttle valves stuck open 10. Incorrectly adjusted float or fuel level 11. Clogged air filter
Engine runs unevenly or surges	1. Defective fuel pump 2. Dirty or clogged fuel filter 3. Plugged, loose or incorrect main metering jets or rods 4. Air leaks 5. Bent or sticking main metering rods 6. Stuck power piston 7. Incorrect float adjustment 8. Incorrect idle speed or mixture 9. Dirty or plugged idle system passages 10. Hard, brittle or broken gaskets 11. Loose attaching or mounting screws 12. Stuck or misaligned secondary throttle valves
Poor fuel economy	1. Poor driving habits 2. Stuck choke valve 3. Binding choke linkage 4. Stuck heat riser 5. Incorrect idle mixture 6. Defective accelerator pump 7. Air leaks 8. Plugged, loose or incorrect main metering jets 9. Improperly adjusted float or fuel level 10. Bent, misaligned or fuel-clogged float 11. Leaking float needle seat 12. Fuel leak 13. Accelerator pump discharge ball not seating properly 14. Incorrect main jets
Engine lacks high speed performance or power	1. Incorrect throttle linkage adjustment 2. Stuck or binding power piston 3. Defective accelerator pump 4. Air leaks 5. Incorrect float setting or fuel level 6. Dirty, plugged, worn or incorrect main metering jets or rods 7. Binding or sticking air valve 8. Brittle or cracked gaskets 9. Bent, incorrect or improperly adjusted secondary metering rods 10. Clogged fuel filter 11. Clogged air filter 12. Defective fuel pump

TROUBLESHOOTING FUEL INJECTION PROBLEMS

Each fuel injection system has its own unique components and test procedures, for which it is impossible to generalize. Refer to Chapter 4 of this Repair & Tune-Up Guide for specific test and repair procedures, if the vehicle is equipped with fuel injection.

TROUBLESHOOTING ELECTRICAL PROBLEMS

See Chapter 5 for service procedures

For any electrical system to operate, it must make a complete circuit. This simply means that the power flow from the battery must make a complete circle. When an electrical component is operating, power flows from the battery to the component, passes through the component causing it to perform its function (lighting a light bulb), and then returns to the battery through the ground of the circuit. This ground is usually (but not always) the metal part of the car or truck on which the electrical component is mounted.

Perhaps the easiest way to visualize this is to think of connecting a light bulb with two wires attached to it to the battery. If one of the two wires attached to the light bulb were attached to the negative post of the battery and the other were attached to the positive post of the battery, you would have a complete circuit. Current from the battery would flow to the light bulb, causing it to light, and return to the negative post of the battery.

The normal automotive circuit differs from this simple example in two ways. First, instead of having a return wire from the bulb to the battery, the light bulb returns the current to the battery through the chassis of the vehicle. Since the negative battery cable is attached to the chassis and the chassis is made of electrically conductive metal, the chassis of the vehicle can serve as a ground wire to complete the circuit. Secondly, most automotive circuits contain switches to turn components on and off as required.

Every complete circuit from a power source must include a component which is using the power from the power source. If you were to disconnect the light bulb from the wires and touch the two wires together (don't do this) the power supply wire to the component would be grounded before the normal ground connection for the circuit.

Because grounding a wire from a power source makes a complete circuit—less the required component to use the power—this phenomenon is called a short circuit. Common causes are: broken insulation (exposing the metal wire to a metal part of the car or truck), or a shorted switch.

Some electrical components which require a large amount of current to operate also have a relay in their circuit. Since these circuits carry a large amount of current, the thickness of the wire in the circuit (gauge size) is also greater. If this large wire were connected from the component to the control switch on the instrument panel, and then back to the component, a voltage drop would occur in the circuit. To prevent this potential drop in voltage, an electromagnetic switch (relay) is used. The large wires in the circuit are connected from the battery to one side of the relay, and from the opposite side of the relay to the component. The relay is normally open, preventing current from passing through the circuit. An additional, smaller, wire is connected from the relay to the control switch for the circuit. When the control switch is turned on, it grounds the smaller wire from the relay and completes the circuit. This closes the relay and allows current to flow from the battery to the component. The horn, headlight, and starter circuits are three which use relays.

It is possible for larger surges of current to pass through the electrical system of your car or truck. If this surge of current were to reach an electrical component, it could burn it out. To prevent this, fuses, circuit breakers or fusible links are connected into the current supply wires of most of the major electrical systems. When an electrical current of excessive power passes through the component's fuse, the fuse blows out and breaks the circuit, saving the component from destruction.

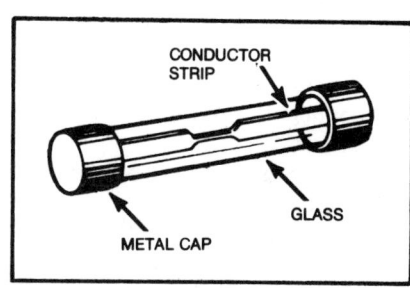

Typical automotive fuse

A circuit breaker is basically a self-repairing fuse. The circuit breaker opens the circuit the same way a fuse does. However, when either the short is removed from the circuit or the surge subsides, the circuit breaker resets itself and does not have to be replaced as a fuse does.

A fuse link is a wire that acts as a fuse. It is normally connected between the starter relay and the main wiring harness. This connection is usually under the hood. The fuse link (if installed) protects all the

216 TROUBLESHOOTING

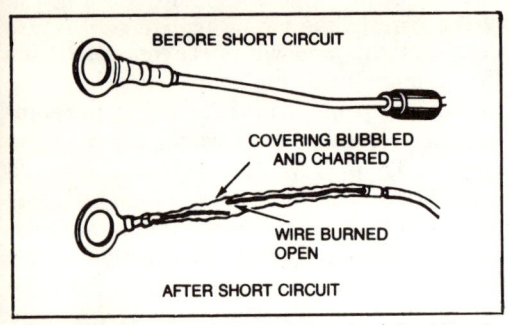

Most fusible links show a charred, melted insulation when they burn out

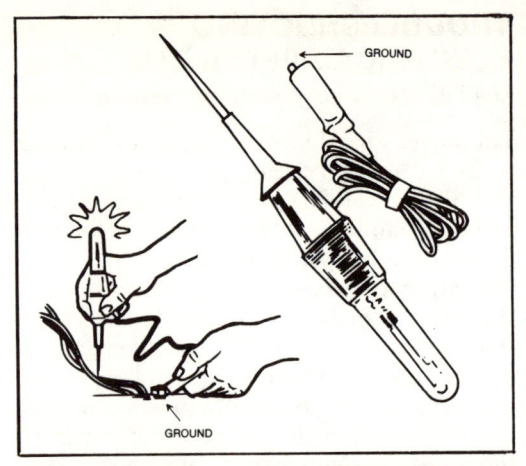

The test light will show the presence of current when touched to a hot wire and grounded at the other end

chassis electrical components, and is the probable cause of trouble when none of the electrical components function, unless the battery is disconnected or dead.

Electrical problems generally fall into one of three areas:

1. The component that is not functioning is not receiving current.
2. The component itself is not functioning.
3. The component is not properly grounded.

The electrical system can be checked with a test light and a jumper wire. A test light is a device that looks like a pointed screwdriver with a wire attached to it and has a light bulb in its handle. A jumper wire is a piece of insulated wire with an alligator clip attached to each end.

If a component is not working, you must follow a systematic plan to determine which of the three causes is the villain.

1. Turn on the switch that controls the inoperable component.
2. Disconnect the power supply wire from the component.
3. Attach the ground wire on the test light to a good metal ground.
4. Touch the probe end of the test light to the end of the power supply wire that was disconnected from the component. If the component is receiving current, the test light will go on.

NOTE: *Some components work only when the ignition switch is turned on.*

If the test light does not go on, then the problem is in the circuit between the battery and the component. This includes all the switches, fuses, and relays in the system. Follow the wire that runs back to the battery. The problem is an open circuit between the battery and the component. If the fuse is blown and, when replaced, immediately blows again, there is a short circuit in the system which must be located and repaired. If there is a switch in the system, bypass it with a jumper wire. This is done by connecting one end of the jumper wire to the power supply wire into the switch and the other end of the jumper wire to the wire coming out of the switch. If the test light lights with the jumper wire installed, the switch or whatever was bypassed is defective.

NOTE: *Never substitute the jumper wire for the component, since it is required to use the power from the power source.*

5. If the bulb in the test light goes on, then the current is getting to the component that is not working. This eliminates the first of the three possible causes. Connect the power supply wire and connect a jumper wire from the component to a good metal ground. Do this with the switch which controls the component turned on, and also the ignition switch turned on if it is required for the component to work. If the component works with the jumper wire installed, then it has a bad ground. This is usually caused by the metal area on which the component mounts to the chassis being coated with some type of foreign matter.

6. If neither test located the source of the trouble, then the component itself is defective. Remember that for any electrical system to work, all connections must be clean and tight.

TROUBLESHOOTING

Troubleshooting Basic Turn Signal and Flasher Problems
See Chapter 5 for service procedures

Most problems in the turn signals or flasher system can be reduced to defective flashers or bulbs, which are easily replaced. Occasionally, the turn signal switch will prove defective.

F = Front   R = Rear   ● = Lights off   ○ = Lights on

Condition		Possible Cause
Turn signals light, but do not flash	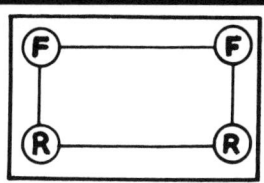	Defective flasher
No turn signals light on either side	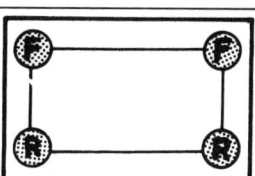	Blown fuse. Replace if defective. Defective flasher. Check by substitution. Open circuit, short circuit or poor ground.
Both turn signals on one side don't work	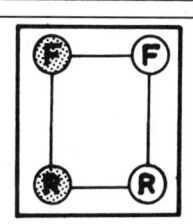	Bad bulbs. Bad ground in both (or either) housings.
One turn signal light on one side doesn't work	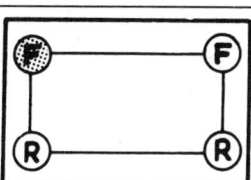	Defective bulb. Corrosion in socket. Clean contacts. Poor ground at socket.
Turn signal flashes too fast or too slowly	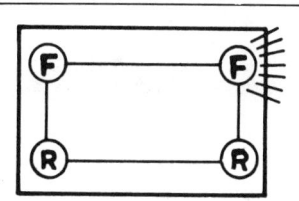	Check any bulb on the side flashing too fast. A heavy-duty bulb is probably installed in place of a regular bulb. Check the bulb flashing too slowly. A standard bulb was probably installed in place of a heavy-duty bulb. Loose connections or corrosion at the bulb socket.
Indicator lights don't work in either direction		Check if the turn signals are working. Check the dash indicator lights. Check the flasher by substitution.
One indicator light doesn't light		On systems with one dash indicator: See if the lights work on the same side. Often the filaments have been reversed in systems combining stoplights with taillights and turn signals. Check the flasher by substitution. On systems with two indicators: Check the bulbs on the same side. Check the indicator light bulb. Check the flasher by substitution.

Troubleshooting Lighting Problems
See Chapter 5 for service procedures

Condition	Possible Cause
One or more lights don't work, but others do	1. Defective bulb(s) 2. Blown fuse(s) 3. Dirty fuse clips or light sockets 4. Poor ground circuit
Lights burn out quickly	1. Incorrect voltage regulator setting or defective regulator 2. Poor battery/alternator connections
Lights go dim	1. Low/discharged battery 2. Alternator not charging 3. Corroded sockets or connections 4. Low voltage output
Lights flicker	1. Loose connection 2. Poor ground. (Run ground wire from light housing to frame) 3. Circuit breaker operating (short circuit)
Lights "flare"—Some flare is normal on acceleration—If excessive, see "Lights Burn Out Quickly"	High voltage setting
Lights glare—approaching drivers are blinded	1. Lights adjusted too high 2. Rear springs or shocks sagging 3. Rear tires soft

Troubleshooting Dash Gauge Problems

Most problems can be traced to a defective sending unit or faulty wiring. Occasionally, the gauge itself is at fault. See Chapter 5 for service procedures.

Condition	Possible Cause
COOLANT TEMPERATURE GAUGE	
Gauge reads erratically or not at all	1. Loose or dirty connections 2. Defective sending unit. 3. Defective gauge. To test a bi-metal gauge, remove the wire from the sending unit. Ground the wire for an instant. If the gauge registers, replace the sending unit. To test a magnetic gauge, disconnect the wire at the sending unit. With ignition ON gauge should register COLD. Ground the wire; gauge should register HOT.
AMMETER GAUGE—TURN HEADLIGHTS ON (DO NOT START ENGINE). NOTE REACTION	
Ammeter shows charge Ammeter shows discharge Ammeter does not move	1. Connections reversed on gauge 2. Ammeter is OK 3. Loose connections or faulty wiring 4. Defective gauge

TROUBLESHOOTING

Condition	Possible Cause

OIL PRESSURE GAUGE

Gauge does not register or is inaccurate	1. On mechanical gauge, Bourdon tube may be bent or kinked. 2. Low oil pressure. Remove sending unit. Idle the engine briefly. If no oil flows from sending unit hole, problem is in engine. 3. Defective gauge. Remove the wire from the sending unit and ground it for an instant with the ignition ON. A good gauge will go to the top of the scale. 4. Defective wiring. Check the wiring to the gauge. If it's OK and the gauge doesn't register when grounded, replace the gauge. 5. Defective sending unit.

ALL GAUGES

All gauges do not operate	1. Blown fuse
	2. Defective instrument regulator
All gauges read low or erratically	3. Defective or dirty instrument voltage regulator
All gauges pegged	4. Loss of ground between instrument voltage regulator and frame
	5. Defective instrument regulator

WARNING LIGHTS

Light(s) do not come on when ignition is ON, but engine is not started	1. Defective bulb 2. Defective wire 3. Defective sending unit. Disconnect the wire from the sending unit and ground it. Replace the sending unit if the light comes on with the ignition ON.
Light comes on with engine running	4. Problem in individual system 5. Defective sending unit

Troubleshooting Clutch Problems

It is false economy to replace individual clutch components. The pressure plate, clutch plate and throwout bearing should be replaced as a set, and the flywheel face inspected, whenever the clutch is overhauled. See Chapter 6 for service procedures.

Condition	Possible Cause
Clutch chatter	1. Grease on driven plate (disc) facing 2. Binding clutch linkage or cable 3. Loose, damaged facings on driven plate (disc) 4. Engine mounts loose 5. Incorrect height adjustment of pressure plate release levers 6. Clutch housing or housing to transmission adapter misalignment 7. Loose driven plate hub
Clutch grabbing	1. Oil, grease on driven plate (disc) facing 2. Broken pressure plate 3. Warped or binding driven plate. Driven plate binding on clutch shaft
Clutch slips	1. Lack of lubrication in clutch linkage or cable (linkage or cable binds, causes incomplete engagement) 2. Incorrect pedal, or linkage adjustment 3. Broken pressure plate springs 4. Weak pressure plate springs 5. Grease on driven plate facings (disc)

Troubleshooting Clutch Problems (cont.)

Condition	Possible Cause
Incomplete clutch release	1. Incorrect pedal or linkage adjustment or linkage or cable binding 2. Incorrect height adjustment on pressure plate release levers 3. Loose, broken facings on driven plate (disc) 4. Bent, dished, warped driven plate caused by overheating
Grinding, whirring grating noise when pedal is depressed	1. Worn or defective throwout bearing 2. Starter drive teeth contacting flywheel ring gear teeth. Look for milled or polished teeth on ring gear.
Squeal, howl, trumpeting noise when pedal is being released (occurs during first inch to inch and one-half of pedal travel)	Pilot bushing worn or lack of lubricant. If bushing appears OK, polish bushing with emery cloth, soak lube wick in oil, lube bushing with oil, apply film of chassis grease to clutch shaft pilot hub, reassemble. NOTE: Bushing wear may be due to misalignment of clutch housing or housing to transmission adapter
Vibration or clutch pedal pulsation with clutch disengaged (pedal fully depressed)	1. Worn or defective engine transmission mounts 2. Flywheel run out. (Flywheel run out at face not to exceed 0.005") 3. Damaged or defective clutch components

Troubleshooting Manual Transmission Problems
See Chapter 6 for service procedures

Condition	Possible Cause
Transmission jumps out of gear	1. Misalignment of transmission case or clutch housing. 2. Worn pilot bearing in crankshaft. 3. Bent transmission shaft. 4. Worn high speed sliding gear. 5. Worn teeth or end-play in clutch shaft. 6. Insufficient spring tension on shifter rail plunger. 7. Bent or loose shifter fork. 8. Gears not engaging completely. 9. Loose or worn bearings on clutch shaft or mainshaft. 10. Worn gear teeth. 11. Worn or damaged detent balls.
Transmission sticks in gear	1. Clutch not releasing fully. 2. Burred or battered teeth on clutch shaft, or sliding sleeve. 3. Burred or battered transmission mainshaft. 4. Frozen synchronizing clutch. 5. Stuck shifter rail plunger. 6. Gearshift lever twisting and binding shifter rail. 7. Battered teeth on high speed sliding gear or on sleeve. 8. Improper lubrication, or lack of lubrication. 9. Corroded transmission parts. 10. Defective mainshaft pilot bearing. 11. Locked gear bearings will give same effect as stuck in gear.
Transmission gears will not synchronize	1. Binding pilot bearing on mainshaft, will synchronize in high gear only. 2. Clutch not releasing fully. 3. Detent spring weak or broken. 4. Weak or broken springs under balls in sliding gear sleeve. 5. Binding bearing on clutch shaft, or binding countershaft. 6. Binding pilot bearing in crankshaft. 7. Badly worn gear teeth. 8. Improper lubrication. 9. Constant mesh gear not turning freely on transmission mainshaft. Will synchronize in that gear only.

TROUBLESHOOTING

Condition	Possible Cause
Gears spinning when shifting into gear from neutral	1. Clutch not releasing fully. 2. In some cases an extremely light lubricant in transmission will cause gears to continue to spin for a short time after clutch is released. 3. Binding pilot bearing in crankshaft.
Transmission noisy in all gears	1. Insufficient lubricant, or improper lubricant. 2. Worn countergear bearings. 3. Worn or damaged main drive gear or countergear. 4. Damaged main drive gear or mainshaft bearings. 5. Worn or damaged countergear anti-lash plate.
Transmission noisy in neutral only	1. Damaged main drive gear bearing. 2. Damaged or loose mainshaft pilot bearing. 3. Worn or damaged countergear anti-lash plate. 4. Worn countergear bearings.
Transmission noisy in one gear only	1. Damaged or worn constant mesh gears. 2. Worn or damaged countergear bearings. 3. Damaged or worn synchronizer.
Transmission noisy in reverse only	1. Worn or damaged reverse idler gear or idler bushing. 2. Worn or damaged mainshaft reverse gear. 3. Worn or damaged reverse countergear. 4. Damaged shift mechanism.

TROUBLESHOOTING AUTOMATIC TRANSMISSION PROBLEMS

Keeping alert to changes in the operating characteristics of the transmission (changing shift points, noises, etc.) can prevent small problems from becoming large ones. If the problem cannot be traced to loose bolts, fluid level, misadjusted linkage, clogged filters or similar problems, you should probably seek professional service.

Transmission Fluid Indications

The appearance and odor of the transmission fluid can give valuable clues to the overall condition of the transmission. Always note the appearance of the fluid when you check the fluid level or change the fluid. Rub a small amount of fluid between your fingers to feel for grit and smell the fluid on the dipstick.

If the fluid appears:	It indicates:
Clear and red colored	Normal operation
Discolored (extremely dark red or brownish) or smells burned	Band or clutch pack failure, usually caused by an overheated transmission. Hauling very heavy loads with insufficient power or failure to change the fluid often result in overheating. Do not confuse this appearance with newer fluids that have a darker red color and a strong odor (though not a burned odor).
Foamy or aerated (light in color and full of bubbles)	1. The level is too high (gear train is churning oil) 2. An internal air leak (air is mixing with the fluid). Have the transmission checked professionally.
Solid residue in the fluid	Defective bands, clutch pack or bearings. Bits of band material or metal abrasives are clinging to the dipstick. Have the transmission checked professionally.
Varnish coating on the dipstick	The transmission fluid is overheating

TROUBLESHOOTING DRIVE AXLE PROBLEMS

First, determine when the noise is most noticeable.

Drive Noise: Produced under vehicle acceleration.

Coast Noise: Produced while coasting with a closed throttle.

Float Noise: Occurs while maintaining constant speed (just enough to keep speed constant) on a level road.

External Noise Elimination

It is advisable to make a thorough road test to determine whether the noise originates in the rear axle or whether it originates from the tires, engine, transmission, wheel bearings or road surface. Noise originating from other places cannot be corrected by servicing the rear axle.

ROAD NOISE

Brick or rough surfaced concrete roads produce noises that seem to come from the rear axle. Road noise is usually identical in Drive or Coast and driving on a different type of road will tell whether the road is the problem.

TIRE NOISE

Tire noise can be mistaken as rear axle noise, even though the tires on the front are at fault. Snow tread and mud tread tires or tires worn unevenly will frequently cause vibrations which seem to originate elsewhere; *temporarily, and for test purposes only,* inflate the tires to 40–50 lbs. This will significantly alter the noise produced by the tires, but will not alter noise from the rear axle. Noises from the rear axle will normally cease at speeds below 30 mph on coast, while tire noise will continue at lower tone as speed is decreased. The rear axle noise will usually change from drive conditions to coast conditions, while tire noise will not. Do not forget to lower the tire pressure to normal after the test is complete.

ENGINE/TRANSMISSION NOISE

Determine at what speed the noise is most pronounced, then stop in a quiet place. With the transmission in Neutral, run the engine through speeds corresponding to road speeds where the noise was noticed. Noises produced with the vehicle standing still are coming from the engine or transmission.

FRONT WHEEL BEARINGS

Front wheel bearing noises, sometimes confused with rear axle noises, will not change when comparing drive and coast conditions. While holding the speed steady, lightly apply the footbrake. This will often cause wheel bearing noise to lessen, as some of the weight is taken off the bearing. Front wheel bearings are easily checked by jacking up the wheels and spinning the wheels. Shaking the wheels will also determine if the wheel bearings are excessively loose.

REAR AXLE NOISES

Eliminating other possible sources can narrow the cause to the rear axle, which normally produces noise from worn gears or bearings. Gear noises tend to peak in a narrow speed range, while bearing noises will usually vary in pitch with engine speeds.

Noise Diagnosis

The Noise Is:	Most Probably Produced By:
1. Identical under Drive or Coast	Road surface, tires or front wheel bearings
2. Different depending on road surface	Road surface or tires
3. Lower as speed is lowered	Tires
4. Similar when standing or moving	Engine or transmission
5. A vibration	Unbalanced tires, rear wheel bearing, unbalanced driveshaft or worn U-joint
6. A knock or click about every two tire revolutions	Rear wheel bearing
7. Most pronounced on turns	Damaged differential gears
8. A steady low-pitched whirring or scraping, starting at low speeds	Damaged or worn pinion bearing
9. A chattering vibration on turns	Wrong differential lubricant or worn clutch plates (limited slip rear axle)
10. Noticed only in Drive, Coast or Float conditions	Worn ring gear and/or pinion gear

TROUBLESHOOTING 223

Troubleshooting Steering & Suspension Problems

Condition	Possible Cause
Hard steering (wheel is hard to turn)	1. Improper tire pressure 2. Loose or glazed pump drive belt 3. Low or incorrect fluid 4. Loose, bent or poorly lubricated front end parts 5. Improper front end alignment (excessive caster) 6. Bind in steering column or linkage 7. Kinked hydraulic hose 8. Air in hydraulic system 9. Low pump output or leaks in system 10. Obstruction in lines 11. Pump valves sticking or out of adjustment 12. Incorrect wheel alignment
Loose steering (too much play in steering wheel)	1. Loose wheel bearings 2. Faulty shocks 3. Worn linkage or suspension components 4. Loose steering gear mounting or linkage points 5. Steering mechanism worn or improperly adjusted 6. Valve spool improperly adjusted 7. Worn ball joints, tie-rod ends, etc.
Veers or wanders (pulls to one side with hands off steering wheel)	1. Improper tire pressure 2. Improper front end alignment 3. Dragging or improperly adjusted brakes 4. Bent frame 5. Improper rear end alignment 6. Faulty shocks or springs 7. Loose or bent front end components 8. Play in Pitman arm 9. Steering gear mountings loose 10. Loose wheel bearings 11. Binding Pitman arm 12. Spool valve sticking or improperly adjusted 13. Worn ball joints
Wheel oscillation or vibration transmitted through steering wheel	1. Low or uneven tire pressure 2. Loose wheel bearings 3. Improper front end alignment 4. Bent spindle 5. Worn, bent or broken front end components 6. Tires out of round or out of balance 7. Excessive lateral runout in disc brake rotor 8. Loose or bent shock absorber or strut
Noises (see also "Troubleshooting Drive Axle Problems")	1. Loose belts 2. Low fluid, air in system 3. Foreign matter in system 4. Improper lubrication 5. Interference or chafing in linkage 6. Steering gear mountings loose 7. Incorrect adjustment or wear in gear box 8. Faulty valves or wear in pump 9. Kinked hydraulic lines 10. Worn wheel bearings
Poor return of steering	1. Over-inflated tires 2. Improperly aligned front end (excessive caster) 3. Binding in steering column 4. No lubrication in front end 5. Steering gear adjusted too tight
Uneven tire wear (see "How To Read Tire Wear")	1. Incorrect tire pressure 2. Improperly aligned front end 3. Tires out-of-balance 4. Bent or worn suspension parts

TROUBLESHOOTING

HOW TO READ TIRE WEAR

The way your tires wear is a good indicator of other parts of the suspension. Abnormal wear patterns are often caused by the need for simple tire maintenance, or for front end alignment.

Excessive wear at the center of the tread indicates that the air pressure in the tire is consistently too high. The tire is riding on the center of the tread and wearing it prematurely. Occasionally, this wear pattern can result from outrageously wide tires on narrow rims. The cure for this is to replace either the tires or the wheels.

Over-inflation

This type of wear usually results from consistent under-inflation. When a tire is under-inflated, there is too much contact with the road by the outer treads, which wear prematurely. When this type of wear occurs, and the tire pressure is known to be consistently correct, a bent or worn steering component or the need for wheel alignment could be indicated.

Under-inflation

Feathering is a condition when the edge of each tread rib develops a slightly rounded edge on one side and a sharp edge on the other. By running your hand over the tire, you can usually feel the sharper edges before you'll be able to see them. The most common causes of feathering are incorrect toe-in setting or deteriorated bushings in the front suspension.

Feathering

When an inner or outer rib wears faster than the rest of the tire, the need for wheel alignment is indicated. There is excessive camber in the front suspension, causing the wheel to lean too much putting excessive load on one side of the tire. Misalignment could also be due to sagging springs, worn ball joints, or worn control arm bushings. Be sure the vehicle is loaded the way it's normally driven when you have the wheels aligned.

One side wear

Cups or scalloped dips appearing around the edge of the tread almost always indicate worn (sometimes bent) suspension parts. Adjustment of wheel alignment alone will seldom cure the problem. Any worn component that connects the wheel to the suspension can cause this type of wear. Occasionally, wheels that are out of balance will wear like this, but wheel imbalance usually shows up as bald spots between the outside edges and center of the tread.

Cupping

Second-rib wear is usually found only in radial tires, and appears where the steel belts end in relation to the tread. It can be kept to a minimum by paying careful attention to tire pressure and frequently rotating the tires. This is often considered normal wear but excessive amounts indicate that the tires are too wide for the wheels.

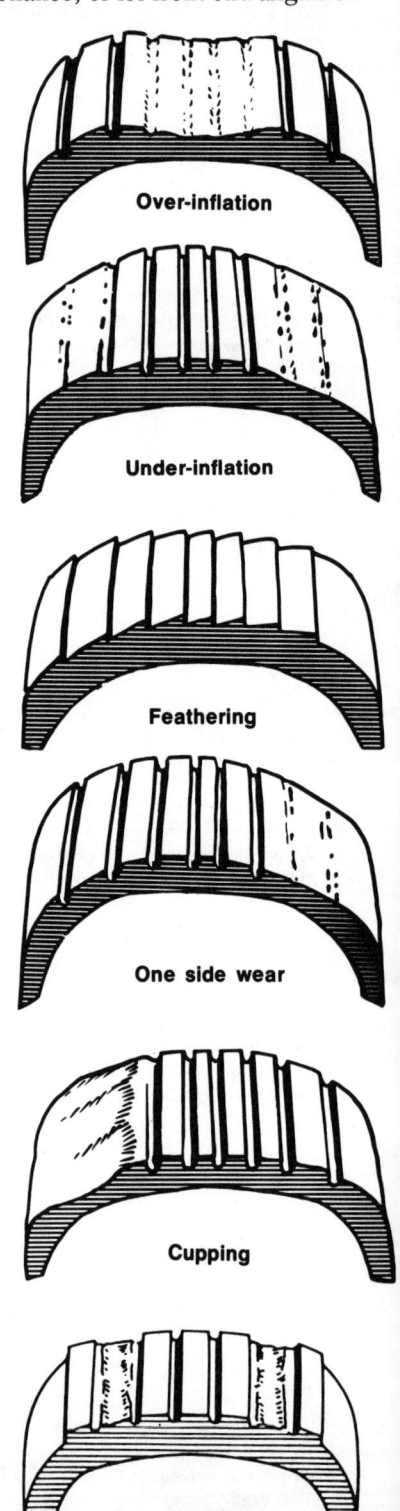

Second-rib wear

TROUBLESHOOTING

Troubleshooting Disc Brake Problems

Condition	Possible Cause
Noise—groan—brake noise emanating when slowly releasing brakes (creep-groan)	Not detrimental to function of disc brakes—no corrective action required. (This noise may be eliminated by slightly increasing or decreasing brake pedal efforts.)
Rattle—brake noise or rattle emanating at low speeds on rough roads, (front wheels only).	1. Shoe anti-rattle spring missing or not properly positioned. 2. Excessive clearance between shoe and caliper. 3. Soft or broken caliper seals. 4. Deformed or misaligned disc. 5. Loose caliper.
Scraping	1. Mounting bolts too long. 2. Loose wheel bearings. 3. Bent, loose, or misaligned splash shield.
Front brakes heat up during driving and fail to release	1. Operator riding brake pedal. 2. Stop light switch improperly adjusted. 3. Sticking pedal linkage. 4. Frozen or seized piston. 5. Residual pressure valve in master cylinder. 6. Power brake malfunction. 7. Proportioning valve malfunction.
Leaky brake caliper	1. Damaged or worn caliper piston seal. 2. Scores or corrosion on surface of cylinder bore.
Grabbing or uneven brake action—Brakes pull to one side	1. Causes listed under "Brakes Pull". 2. Power brake malfunction. 3. Low fluid level in master cylinder. 4. Air in hydraulic system. 5. Brake fluid, oil or grease on linings. 6. Unmatched linings. 7. Distorted brake pads. 8. Frozen or seized pistons. 9. Incorrect tire pressure. 10. Front end out of alignment. 11. Broken rear spring. 12. Brake caliper pistons sticking. 13. Restricted hose or line. 14. Caliper not in proper alignment to braking disc. 15. Stuck or malfunctioning metering valve. 16. Soft or broken caliper seals. 17. Loose caliper.
Brake pedal can be depressed without braking effect	1. Air in hydraulic system or improper bleeding procedure. 2. Leak past primary cup in master cylinder. 3. Leak in system. 4. Rear brakes out of adjustment. 5. Bleeder screw open.
Excessive pedal travel	1. Air, leak, or insufficient fluid in system or caliper. 2. Warped or excessively tapered shoe and lining assembly. 3. Excessive disc runout. 4. Rear brake adjustment required. 5. Loose wheel bearing adjustment. 6. Damaged caliper piston seal. 7. Improper brake fluid (boil). 8. Power brake malfunction. 9. Weak or soft hoses.

Troubleshooting Disc Brake Problems (cont.)

Condition	Possible Cause
Brake roughness or chatter (pedal pumping)	1. Excessive thickness variation of braking disc. 2. Excessive lateral runout of braking disc. 3. Rear brake drums out-of-round. 4. Excessive front bearing clearance.
Excessive pedal effort	1. Brake fluid, oil or grease on linings. 2. Incorrect lining. 3. Frozen or seized pistons. 4. Power brake malfunction. 5. Kinked or collapsed hose or line. 6. Stuck metering valve. 7. Scored caliper or master cylinder bore. 8. Seized caliper pistons.
Brake pedal fades (pedal travel increases with foot on brake)	1. Rough master cylinder or caliper bore. 2. Loose or broken hydraulic lines/connections. 3. Air in hydraulic system. 4. Fluid level low. 5. Weak or soft hoses. 6. Inferior quality brake shoes or fluid. 7. Worn master cylinder piston cups or seals.

Troubleshooting Drum Brakes

Condition	Possible Cause
Pedal goes to floor	1. Fluid low in reservoir. 2. Air in hydraulic system. 3. Improperly adjusted brake. 4. Leaking wheel cylinders. 5. Loose or broken brake lines. 6. Leaking or worn master cylinder. 7. Excessively worn brake lining.
Spongy brake pedal	1. Air in hydraulic system. 2. Improper brake fluid (low boiling point). 3. Excessively worn or cracked brake drums. 4. Broken pedal pivot bushing.
Brakes pulling	1. Contaminated lining. 2. Front end out of alignment. 3. Incorrect brake adjustment. 4. Unmatched brake lining. 5. Brake drums out of round. 6. Brake shoes distorted. 7. Restricted brake hose or line. 8. Broken rear spring. 9. Worn brake linings. 10. Uneven lining wear. 11. Glazed brake lining. 12. Excessive brake lining dust. 13. Heat spotted brake drums. 14. Weak brake return springs. 15. Faulty automatic adjusters. 16. Low or incorrect tire pressure.

TROUBLESHOOTING

Condition	Possible Cause
Squealing brakes	1. Glazed brake lining. 2. Saturated brake lining. 3. Weak or broken brake shoe retaining spring. 4. Broken or weak brake shoe return spring. 5. Incorrect brake lining. 6. Distorted brake shoes. 7. Bent support plate. 8. Dust in brakes or scored brake drums. 9. Linings worn below limit. 10. Uneven brake lining wear. 11. Heat spotted brake drums.
Chirping brakes	1. Out of round drum or eccentric axle flange pilot.
Dragging brakes	1. Incorrect wheel or parking brake adjustment. 2. Parking brakes engaged or improperly adjusted. 3. Weak or broken brake shoe return spring. 4. Brake pedal binding. 5. Master cylinder cup sticking. 6. Obstructed master cylinder relief port. 7. Saturated brake lining. 8. Bent or out of round brake drum. 9. Contaminated or improper brake fluid. 10. Sticking wheel cylinder pistons. 11. Driver riding brake pedal. 12. Defective proportioning valve. 13. Insufficient brake shoe lubricant.
Hard pedal	1. Brake booster inoperative. 2. Incorrect brake lining. 3. Restricted brake line or hose. 4. Frozen brake pedal linkage. 5. Stuck wheel cylinder. 6. Binding pedal linkage. 7. Faulty proportioning valve.
Wheel locks	1. Contaminated brake lining. 2. Loose or torn brake lining. 3. Wheel cylinder cups sticking. 4. Incorrect wheel bearing adjustment. 5. Faulty proportioning valve.
Brakes fade (high speed)	1. Incorrect lining. 2. Overheated brake drums. 3. Incorrect brake fluid (low boiling temperature). 4. Saturated brake lining. 5. Leak in hydraulic system. 6. Faulty automatic adjusters.
Pedal pulsates	1. Bent or out of round brake drum.
Brake chatter and shoe knock	1. Out of round brake drum. 2. Loose support plate. 3. Bent support plate. 4. Distorted brake shoes. 5. Machine grooves in contact face of brake drum (Shoe Knock). 6. Contaminated brake lining. 7. Missing or loose components. 8. Incorrect lining material. 9. Out-of-round brake drums. 10. Heat spotted or scored brake drums. 11. Out-of-balance wheels.

Troubleshooting Drum Brakes (cont.)

Condition	Possible Cause
Brakes do not self adjust	1. Adjuster screw frozen in thread. 2. Adjuster screw corroded at thrust washer. 3. Adjuster lever does not engage star wheel. 4. Adjuster installed on wrong wheel.
Brake light glows	1. Leak in the hydraulic system. 2. Air in the system. 3. Improperly adjusted master cylinder pushrod. 4. Uneven lining wear. 5. Failure to center combination valve or proportioning valve.

Appendix

General Conversion Table

Multiply by	To convert	To	
2.54	Inches	Centimeters	.3937
30.48	Feet	Centimeters	.0328
.914	Yards	Meters	1.094
1.609	Miles	Kilometers	.621
6.45	Square inches	Square cm.	.155
.836	Square yards	Square meters	1.196
16.39	Cubic inches	Cubic cm.	.061
28.3	Cubic feet	Liters	.0353
.4536	Pounds	Kilograms	2.2045
3.785	Gallons	Liters	.264
.068	Lbs./sq. in. (psi)	Atmospheres	14.7
.138	Foot pounds	Kg. m.	7.23
1.014	H.P. (DIN)	H.P. (SAE)	.9861
—	To obtain	From	Multiply by

Note: 1 cm. equals 10 mm.; 1 mm. equals .0394".

Conversion—Common Fractions to Decimals and Millimeters

Common Fractions	Decimal Fractions	Millimeters (approx.)	Common Fractions	Decimal Fractions	Millimeters (approx.)	Common Fractions	Decimal Fractions	Millimeters (approx.)
1/128	.008	0.20	11/32	.344	8.73	43/64	.672	17.07
1/64	.016	0.40	23/64	.359	9.13	11/16	.688	17.46
1/32	.031	0.79	3/8	.375	9.53	45/64	.703	17.86
3/64	.047	1.19	25/64	.391	9.92	23/32	.719	18.26
1/16	.063	1.59	13/32	.406	10.32	47/64	.734	18.65
5/64	.078	1.98	27/64	.422	10.72	3/4	.750	19.05
3/32	.094	2.38	7/16	.438	11.11	49/64	.766	19.45
7/64	.109	2.78	29/64	.453	11.51	25/32	.781	19.84
1/8	.125	3.18	15/32	.469	11.91	51/64	.797	20.24
9/64	.141	3.57	31/64	.484	12.30	13/16	.813	20.64
5/32	.156	3.97	1/2	.500	12.70	53/64	.828	21.03
11/64	.172	4.37	33/64	.516	13.10	27/32	.844	21.43
3/16	.188	4.76	17/32	.531	13.49	55/64	.859	21.83
13/64	.203	5.16	35/64	.547	13.89	7/8	.875	22.23
7/32	.219	5.56	9/16	.563	14.29	57/64	.891	22.62
15/64	.234	5.95	37/64	.578	14.68	29/32	.906	23.02
1/4	.250	6.35	19/32	.594	15.08	59/64	.922	23.42
17/64	.266	6.75	39/64	.609	15.48	15/16	.938	23.81
9/32	.281	7.14	5/8	.625	15.88	61/64	.953	24.21
19/64	.297	7.54	41/64	.641	16.27	31/32	.969	24.61
5/16	.313	7.94	21/32	.656	16.67	63/64	.984	25.00
21/64	.328	8.33						

Conversion—Millimeters to Decimal Inches

mm	inches	mm	inches	mm	inches	mm	inches	mm	inches
1	.039 370	31	1.220 470	61	2.401 570	91	3.582 670	210	8.267 700
2	.078 740	32	1.259 840	62	2.440 940	92	3.622 040	220	8.661 400
3	.118 110	33	1.299 210	63	2.480 310	93	3.661 410	230	9.055 100
4	.157 480	34	1.338 580	64	2.519 680	94	3.700 780	240	9.448 800
5	.196 850	35	1.377 949	65	2.559 050	95	3.740 150	250	9.842 500
6	.236 220	36	1.417 319	66	2.598 420	96	3.779 520	260	10.236 200
7	.275 590	37	1.456 689	67	2.637 790	97	3.818 890	270	10.629 900
8	.314 960	38	1.496 050	68	2.677 160	98	3.858 260	280	11.032 600
9	.354 330	39	1.535 430	69	2.716 530	99	3.897 630	290	11.417 300
10	.393 700	40	1.574 800	70	2.755 900	100	3.937 000	300	11.811 000
11	.433 070	41	1.614 170	71	2.795 270	105	4.133 848	310	12.204 700
12	.472 440	42	1.653 540	72	2.834 640	110	4.330 700	320	12.598 400
13	.511 810	43	1.692 910	73	2.874 010	115	4.527 550	330	12.992 100
14	.551 180	44	1.732 280	74	2.913 380	120	4.724 400	340	13.385 800
15	.590 550	45	1.771 650	75	2.952 750	125	4.921 250	350	13.779 500
16	.629 920	46	1.811 020	76	2.992 120	130	5.118 100	360	14.173 200
17	.669 290	47	1.850 390	77	3.031 490	135	5.314 950	370	14.566 900
18	.708 660	48	1.889 760	78	3.070 860	140	5.511 800	380	14.960 600
19	.748 030	49	1.929 130	79	3.110 230	145	5.708 650	390	15.354 300
20	.787 400	50	1.968 500	80	3.149 600	150	5.905 500	400	15.748 000
21	.826 770	51	2.007 870	81	3.188 970	155	6.102 350	500	19.685 000
22	.866 140	52	2.047 240	82	3.228 340	160	6.299 200	600	23.622 000
23	.905 510	53	2.086 610	83	3.267 710	165	6.496 050	700	27.559 000
24	.944 880	54	2.125 980	84	3.307 080	170	6.692 900	800	31.496 000
25	.984 250	55	2.165 350	85	3.346 450	175	6.889 750	900	35.433 000
26	1.023 620	56	2.204 720	86	3.385 820	180	7.086 600	1000	39.370 000
27	1.062 990	57	2.244 090	87	3.425 190	185	7.283 450	2000	78.740 000
28	1.102 360	58	2.283 460	88	3.464 560	190	7.480 300	3000	118.110 000
29	1.141 730	59	2.322 830	89	3.503 903	195	7.677 150	4000	157.480 000
30	1.181 100	60	2.362 200	90	3.543 300	200	7.874 000	5000	196.850 000

To change decimal millimeters to decimal inches, position the decimal point where desired on either side of the millimeter measurement shown and reset the inches decimal by the same number of digits in the same direction. For example, to convert 0.001 mm to decimal inches, reset the decimal behind the 1 mm (shown on the chart) to 0.001; change the decimal inch equivalent (0.039" shown) to 0.000039".

Tap Drill Sizes

National Fine or S.A.E.

Screw & Tap Size	Threads Per Inch	Use Drill Number
No. 5	44	37
No. 6	40	33
No. 8	36	29
No. 10	32	21
No. 12	28	15
1/4	28	3
5/16	24	1
3/8	24	Q
7/16	20	W
1/2	20	29/64
9/16	18	33/64
5/8	18	37/64
3/4	16	11/16
7/8	14	13/16
1 1/8	12	1 3/64
1 1/4	12	1 11/64
1 1/2	12	1 27/64

Tap Drill Sizes

National Coarse or U.S.S.

Screw & Tap Size	Threads Per Inch	Use Drill Number
No. 5	40	39
No. 6	32	36
No. 8	32	29
No. 10	24	25
No. 12	24	17
1/4	20	8
5/16	18	F
3/8	16	5/16
7/16	14	U
1/2	13	27/64
9/16	12	31/64
5/8	11	17/32
3/4	10	21/32
7/8	9	49/64
1	8	7/8
1 1/8	7	63/64
1 1/4	7	1 7/64
1 1/2	6	1 11/32

APPENDIX 231

Decimal Equivalent Size of the Number Drills

Drill No.	Decimal Equivalent	Drill No.	Decimal Equivalent	Drill No.	Decimal Equivalent
80	.0135	53	.0595	26	.1470
79	.0145	52	.0635	25	.1495
78	.0160	51	.0670	24	.1520
77	.0180	50	.0700	23	.1540
76	.0200	49	.0730	22	.1570
75	.0210	48	.0760	21	.1590
74	.0225	47	.0785	20	.1610
73	.0240	46	.0810	19	.1660
72	.0250	45	.0820	18	.1695
71	.0260	44	.0860	17	.1730
70	.0280	43	.0890	16	.1770
69	.0292	42	.0935	15	.1800
68	.0310	41	.0960	14	.1820
67	.0320	40	.0980	13	.1850
66	.0330	39	.0995	12	.1890
65	.0350	38	.1015	11	.1910
64	.0360	37	.1040	10	.1935
63	.0370	36	.1065	9	.1960
62	.0380	35	.1100	8	.1990
61	.0390	34	.1110	7	.2010
60	.0400	33	.1130	6	.2040
59	.0410	32	.1160	5	.2055
58	.0420	31	.1200	4	.2090
57	.0430	30	.1285	3	.2130
56	.0465	29	.1360	2	.2210
55	.0520	28	.1405	1	.2280
54	.0550	27	.1440		

Decimal Equivalent Size of the Letter Drills

Letter Drill	Decimal Equivalent	Letter Drill	Decimal Equivalent	Letter Drill	Decimal Equivalent
A	.234	J	.277	S	.348
B	.238	K	.281	T	.358
C	.242	L	.290	U	.368
D	.246	M	.295	V	.377
E	.250	N	.302	W	.386
F	.257	O	.316	X	.397
G	.261	P	.323	Y	.404
H	.266	Q	.332	Z	.413
I	.272	R	.339		

APPENDIX

Anti-Freeze Chart

Temperatures Shown in Degrees Fahrenheit +32 is Freezing

Quarts of ETHYLENE GLYCOL Needed for Protection to Temperatures Shown Below

Cooling System Capacity Quarts	1	2	3	4	5	6	7	8	9	10	11	12	13	14
10	+24°	+16°	+4°	−12°	−34°	−62°								
11	+25	+18	+8	−6	−23	−47								
12	+26	+19	+10	0	−15	−34	−57°							
13	+27	+21	+13	+3	−9	−25	−45							
14			+15	+6	−5	−18	−34							
15			+16	+8	0	−12	−26							
16			+17	+10	+2	−8	−19	−34	−52°					
17			+18	+12	+5	−4	−14	−27	−42					
18			+19	+14	+7	0	−10	−21	−34	−50°				
19			+20	+15	+9	+2	−7	−16	−28	−42				
20				+16	+10	+4	−3	−12	−22	−34	−48°			
21				+17	+12	+6	0	−9	−17	−28	−41			
22				+18	+13	+8	+2	−6	−14	−23	−34	−47°		
23				+19	+14	+9	+4	−3	−10	−19	−29	−40		
24				+19	+15	+10	+5	0	−8	−15	−23	−34	−46°	
25				+20	+16	+12	+7	+1	−5	−12	−20	−29	−40	−50°
26					+17	+13	+8	+3	−3	−9	−16	−25	−34	−44
27					+18	+14	+9	+5	−1	−7	−13	−21	−29	−39
28					+18	+15	+10	+6	+1	−5	−11	−18	−25	−34
29					+19	+16	+12	+7	+2	−3	−8	−15	−22	−29
30					+20	+17	+13	+8	+4	−1	−6	−12	−18	−25

For capacities over 30 quarts divide true capacity by 3. Find quarts Anti-Freeze for the 1/3 and multiply by 3 for quarts to add.

For capacities under 10 quarts multiply true capacity by 3. Find quarts Anti-Freeze for the tripled volume and divide by 3 for quarts to add.

To Increase the Freezing Protection of Anti-Freeze Solutions Already Installed

Number of Quarts of ETHYLENE GLYCOL Anti-Freeze Required to Increase Protection

Cooling System Capacity Quarts	From +20° F. to					From +10° F. to					From 0° F. to			
	0°	−10°	−20°	−30°	−40°	0°	−10°	−20°	−30°	−40°	−10°	−20°	−30°	−40°
10	1¾	2¼	3	3½	3¾	¾	1½	2¼	2¾	3¼	¾	1½	2	2½
12	2	2¾	3½	4	4½	1	1¾	2½	3¼	3¾	1	1¾	2½	3¼
14	2¼	3¼	4	4¾	5½	1¼	2	3	3¾	4½	1	2	3	3½
16	2½	3½	4½	5¼	6	1¼	2½	3½	4¼	5¼	1¼	2¼	3¼	4
18	3	4	5	6	7	1½	2¾	4	5	5¾	1½	2½	3¾	4¾
20	3¼	4½	5¾	6¾	7½	1¾	3	4¼	5½	6½	1½	2¾	4¼	5¼
22	3½	5	6¼	7¼	8¼	1¾	3¼	4¾	6	7¼	1¾	3¼	4½	5½
24	4	5½	7	8	9	2	3½	5	6½	7½	1¾	3½	5	6
26	4¼	6	7½	8¾	10	2	4	5½	7	8¼	2	3¾	5½	6¾
28	4½	6¼	8	9½	10½	2¼	4¼	6	7½	9	2	4	5¾	7¼
30	5	6¾	8½	10	11½	2½	4½	6½	8	9½	2¼	4¼	6¼	7¾

Test radiator solution with proper hydrometer. Determine from the table the number of quarts of solution to be drawn off from a full cooling system and replace with undiluted anti-freeze, to give the desired increased protection. For example, to increase protection of a 22-quart cooling system containing Ethylene Glycol (permanent type) anti-freeze, from +20° F. to −20° F. will require the replacement of 6¼ quarts of solution with undiluted anti-freeze.

Index

A
Air cleaner, 8, 98
Air conditioning, 16
    Sight glass inspection, 16
Alternator, 53
Antifreeze, 15
Automatic transmission
    Adjustment, 133
    Filter change, 131
    Pan removal, 131
Axle
    Fluid recommendations, 20
    Lubricant level, 20
Axle shaft
    Bearings and seals, 120

B
Ball joints, 140
Battery
    Jump starting, 28
    Maintenance, 9, 58
Belt tension adjustment, 11
Body, 178
Body work, 179
Brakes
    Adjustment, 157
    Bleeding, 162
    Caliper, 164
    Fluid level, 19
    Front brakes, 162
    Master cylinder, 158
    Parking brake, 176
    Rear brakes, 168
Bulbs, 117

C
Camber, 142
Camshaft, 70
Capacities, 21
Carburetor
    Adjustment, 44
    Overhaul, 102
    Replacement, 103
Caster, 142
Catalytic converter, 98
Charging system, 50
Chassis lubrication, 26
Clutch
    Adjustment, 128
    Replacement, 129
Coil (ignition), 44
Compression, 208
Connecting rod and bearings, 70
Control arm
    Lower, 140
Cooling system, 14
Crankcase ventilation (PCV), 9, 98
Crankshaft, 85
Cylinder head
    Removal and installation, 64
    Torque sequence, 65

D
Differential (transaxle)
    Fluid change, 20
    Ratios, 120
Distributor
    Removal and installation, 52
Door panels, 179
Drive axle, 120
Dwell angle, 39

E
Electrical
    Chassis, 108
    Engine, 49
Electronic ignition, 40
Emission controls, 95
Engine
    Camshaft, 70
    Cylinder head torque sequence, 65
    Exhaust manifold, 67
    Front cover, 67
    Identification, 8
    Intake manifold, 65
    Oil recommendations, 23
    Pistons and rings, 70
    Rebuilding, 76
    Removal and installation, 61
    Rocker arm (or shaft), 65
    Specifications, 60
    Timing belt, 67
    Tune-up, 34
Evaporative canister, 9, 98
Exhaust manifold, 67

F
Fan, 75
Fan belt adjustment, 11
Firing order, 53
Fluid level checks
    Battery, 20
    Coolant, 19
    Engine oil, 19
    Master cylinder, 19
    Power steering pump, 20
    Transaxle, 20
Front suspension, 137
    Ball joints, 138
    Lower control arm, 138
    Wheel alignment, 142
Front wheel bearing, 165
Fuel filter, 23
Fuel pump, 102
Fuel system, 102
Fuel tank, 107

INDEX

Fuses and flashers, 116
Fusible links, 56, 116

G

Gearshift linkage adjustment
    Automatic, 135
    Manual, 126
Generator (see Alternator)

H

Hand brake, 176
Headlights, 116
Heater, 108

I

Identification
    Vehicle, 7
    Engine, 8
    Transmission, 8
Idle speed and mixture, 45
Ignition switch, 149
Instrument cluster, 115
Intake manifold, 65

J

Jacking points, 28
Jump starting, 29

L

Light bulb specifications, 117
Lower control arm, 140
Lubrication
    Chassis, 26
    Differential, 20
    Engine, 23, 71
    Transmission, 20

M

Maintenance intervals, 24
Manifolds
    Intake, 65
    Exhaust, 67
Manual transmission, 124
Master cylinder, 158
Model identification, 7

N

Neutral safety switch, 136

O

Oil and fuel recommendations, 23
Oil change, 23
Oil filter (engine), 23
Oil pan, 71
Oil pump, 71

P

Parking brake, 176
Pistons and rings, 70
    Installation, 71
    Positioning, 71
PCV valve, 9
Power brakes, 157
Power steering, 154

R

Radiator, 73
Radio, 109
Rear axle, 170
Rear suspension, 142
Regulator, 54
Rear main oil seal, 73
Rings, 70
Rocker arm (or shaft), 65
Routine maintenance, 8
Rust spots, 180

S

Safety notice, ii
Scratches and dents, 182
Shock absorbers
    Front, 138
    Rear, 144
Spark plugs, 33
Specifications
    Alternator, 53
    Brakes, 168
    Capacities, 21
    Crankshaft and connecting rod, 60
    Fuses, 118
    General engine, 60
    Light bulb, 117
    Piston and ring, 61
    Starter, 57
    Torque, 60
    Tune-up, 34
    Valve, 60
    Wheel alignment, 142
Speedometer cable, 115
Springs
    Front, 138
    Rear, 142
Starter, 56
Steering
    Gear, 147, 154
    Linkage, 147, 154
    Wheel, 147
Stripped threads, 77

T

Thermostat, 75
Tie-rod, 143
Timing (ignition), 39
Tires, 21
Tools, 2

INDEX

Towing, 28
Transaxle, 120
Transmission
　Automatic, 131
　Manual, 124
　Fluid change, 131
Troubleshooting, 195
Tune-up
　Procedures, 33
　Specifications, 34
Turn signal switch, 149

U
U-joints, 120

V
Valves
　Adjustment, 45

　Service, 79
　Specifications, 60
Vehicle identification, 7

W
Water pump, 74
Wheel alignment, 142
Wheel bearings, 165, 170
Wheel cylinders, 175
Windshield wipers
　Arm, 17, 110
　Blade, 17, 110
　Linkage, 112
　Motor, 112

Chilton's Repair & Tune-Up Guides

The complete line covers domestic cars, imports, trucks, vans, RV's and 4-wheel drive vehicles.

BOOK CODE	TITLE	BOOK CODE	TITLE
# 7163	Aries 81-82	# 5821	GTX 68-73
# 7032	Arrow Pick-Up 79-81	# 6980	Honda 73-80
# 6637	Aspen 76-78	# 6845	Horizon 78-80
# 5902	Audi 70-73	# 5912	International Scout 67-73
# 7028	Audi 4000/5000 77-81	# 5998	Jaguar 69-74
# 6337	Audi Fox 73-75	# 7136	Jeep CJ 1945-81
# 5807	Barracuda 65-72	# 6739	Jeep Wagoneer, Commando, Cherokee 66-79
# 6931	Blazer 69-80	# 6962	Jetta 1980
# 5576	BMW 59-70	# 6931	Jimmy 69-81
# 6844	BMW 70-79	# 7059	J-2000 1982
# 5821	Belvedere 68-73	# 5905	Le Mans 68-73
# 7027	Bobcat	# 7055	Lynx 81-82 inc. EXP & LN-7
# 7045	Camaro 67-81	# 6634	Maverick 70-77
# 6695	Capri 70-77	# 6981	Mazda 71-80
# 6963	Capri 79-80	# 7031	Mazda RX-7 79-81
# 7059	Cavalier 1982	# 6065	Mercedes-Benz 59-70
# 5807	Challenger 65-72	# 5907	Mercedes-Benz 68-73
# 7037	Challenger (Import) 71-81	# 6809	Mercedes-Benz 74-79
# 7041	Champ 78-81	# 7128	Mercury 68-71 all full sized models
# 6316	Charger 71-75	# 6696	Mercury Mid-Size 71-78 inc. T-Bird, Montego & Cougar
# 7162	Chevette 76-82 inc. diesel	# 6780	MG 61-81
# 7135	Chevrolet 68-81 all full size models	# 6973	Monarch 75-80
# 6936	Chevrolet/GMC Pick-Ups 70-80	# 6542	Mustang 65-73
# 6930	Chevrolet/GMC Vans 67-80	# 6812	Mustang II 74-78
# 7051	Chevy Luv 72-81 inc. 4wd	# 6963	Mustang 79-80
# 7056	Chevy Mid-Size 64-82 inc. El Camino, Chevelle, Laguna, Malibu & Monte Carlo	# 6841	Nova 69-79
# 6841	Chevy II 62-68	# 7049	Omega 81-82
# 7059	Cimarron 1982	# 6845	Omni 78-80
# 7049	Citation 80-81	# 5792	Opel 64-70
# 7037	Colt 71-81	# 6575	Opel 71-75
# 6634	Comet 70-77	# 6473	Pacer 75-76
# 6316	Coronet 71-75	# 5982	Peugeot 70-74
# 6691	Corvair 60-69 inc. Turbo	# 7049	Phoenix 81-82
# 6576	Corvette 53-62	# 7027	Pinto 71-80
# 6843	Corvette 63-79	# 6552	Plymouth 68-76 all full sized models
# 6933	Cutlass 70-80	# 6934	Plymouth Vans 67-80
# 6324	Dart 68-76	# 5822	Porche 69-73
# 6962	Dasher 74-80	# 7048	Porche 924 & 928 76-81 inc. Turbo
# 5790	Datsun 61-72	# 6962	Rabbit 75-80
# 6960	Datsun 73-80	# 6331	Ramcharger/Trail Duster 74-75
# 6932	Datsun Z & ZX 70-80	# 7163	Reliant 81-82
# 7050	Datsun Pick-Ups 70-81 inc. 4wd	# 5821	Roadrunner 68-73
# 6324	Demon 68-76	# 5988	Saab 69-75
# 6554	Dodge 68-77 all full sized models	# 7041	Sapporo 78-81
# 6486	Dodge Charger 67-70	# 5821	Satellite 68-73
# 6934	Dodge Vans 67-80	# 6962	Scirocco 75-80
# 6326	Duster 68-76	# 7049	Skylark 80-81
# 7055	Escort 81-82 inc. EXP & LN-7	# 6982	Subaru 70-80
# 6320	Fairlane 62-75	# 5905	Tempest 68-73
# 6965	Fairmont 78-80	# 6320	Torino 62-75
# 6485	Fiat 64-70	# 5795	Toyota 66-70
# 7042	Fiat 69-81	# 7043	Toyota Celica & Supra 71-81
# 6846	Fiesta 78-80	# 7036	Toyota Corolla, Carina, Tercel, Starlet 70-81
# 7046	Firebird 67-81	# 7044	Toyota Corona, Cressida, Crown, Mark II 70-81
# 7128	Ford 68-81 all full sized models	# 7035	Toyota Pick-Ups 70-81
# 7140	Ford Bronco 66-81	# 5910	Triumph 69-73
# 6983	Ford Courier 72-80	# 7162	T-1000 1982
# 6696	Ford Mid-Size 71-78 inc. Torino, Gran Torino, Ranchero, Elite & LTD II	# 6326	Valiant 68-76
# 6913	Ford Pick-Ups 65-80 inc. 4wd	# 5796	Volkswagen 49-71
# 6849	Ford Vans 61-82	# 6837	Volkswagen 70-81
# 6935	GM Sub-compact 71-81 inc. Vega, Monza, Astre, Sunbird, Starfire & Skyhawk	# 6637	Volare 76-78
		# 6529	Volvo 56-69
# 6937	Granada 75-80	# 7040	Volvo 70-80
# 5905	GTO 68-73	# 6965	Zephyr 78-80

Chilton's Repair & Tune-Up Guides are available at your local retailer or by mailing a check or money order for **$9.95** plus **$1.00** to cover postage and handling to:

Chilton Book Company
Dept. DM
Radnor, PA 19089

NOTE: When ordering be sure to include your name & address, book code & title.